Grains of Sustenance

A Study of the Faith and Practice of Islam

www.grainsofsustenance.org

First published: 2012 CE (1433 AH)

ISBN: 978-0-615-54288-1

بِسْمِ اللهِ الرَّحْمَنِ الرَّحِيمِ

In the Name of God, the Compassionate, the Most Merciful

Preface

After the events which took place in the beginning of the new century and world media attention began to focus on Islam, truth and objectivity became casualties. As a result, Muslims have come under intense scrutiny from virtually all quarters, including governments, diverse organizations and individuals. There has also been an unrelenting, multifaceted barrage of unfair criticism and maligning, not only of Muslims, but also of Islam.

While web-based search engines provide numerous citations for topics related to Islam, erroneous information is intermingled with facts. Hence, a person seeking information about the pristine teachings and values of Islam and its views on contemporary issues is confronted with a plethora of commentaries and opinions from diverse sources. Incorrect or misleading information can easily contaminate the unsuspecting mind, limits its receptiveness, and may thus close the door to the truth.

The purpose of this book is to convey, in a concise manner, a basic understanding of the true message of Islam. It also seeks to provide an insight into the workings of the principles guiding Muslims, namely, the Islamic Shari'ah. It sheds light on how the Shari'ah addresses contemporary issues which impact today's society and provides the reader with the opportunity to contemplate.

All quotations from the Qur'an list the surah number, Arabic title and verse numbers. Arabic terms such as *ayat* (verse, plural *ayaat*) and *surah* (chapter) have been retained as it helps to distinguish from other scriptures. Additionally, other Arabic terms have also been used throughout the text in order to retain familiarity with the original.

Some topics, such as the spread of Islam, violence and holy war, are discussed in several chapters which may seem redundant. However, it was necessary to revisit those topics while exploring related issues because of their relevance to the subject matter under discussion. Each of these discussions offers additional insight.

Allah is the name God has given Himself. Therefore, throughout the text, Allah and God have been used interchangeably as having one and the same meaning.

Translations of the meaning of verses from the Qur'an were taken from several sources and included the following:

- The Meaning of the Glorious Qur'an, Text and Explanatory Translation by Muhammad Marmaduke Pickthall. Muslim World League-Rabita, New York.

- The Holy Qur'an with English Translation, Ilmi Nesriyat, Istanbul, Turkey, 2000.

- The Meaning of the Qur'an by S. Abul A'la Maududi. Islamic Publications Ltd., Lahore, Pakistan, 1976-1978.

- The Message of the Qur'an. Translated and Explained by Muhammad Asad. The Book Foundation, Bristol, England, 2003.

- The Holy Qur'an. Text, Translation and Commentary by A. Yusuf Ali, Amana Corp, Baltimore, Maryland, 1983.

- Translation of the meanings of The Noble Qur'an in English Language by Muhammad Taqi-ud-Din Al-Hilali and Muhammad Muhsin Khan. King Fahd Complex for the Printing of the Holy Qur'an, Madinah, S. Arabia.

- The Qur'an. The Noble Reading. Translation and Commentary by T.B. Irving. The Mother Mosque Foundation, Cedar Rapids, IA, 1991.

Arabic inscriptions that precede the verses from the Qur'an and those that follow the Name of God, His messengers and other pious individuals are follows:

Bismillah ir Rahman ir Raheem. In the Name of Allah, the Compassionate, the Most Merciful.

Subhanahu wa ta'la. Glory be to Him and all Praise. This is used when God's name is mentioned.

Sal-lallaho alaihi wa sal-lam. May Peace and Blessings of God be upon him. This is used whenever the name of Prophet Muhammad ﷺ is mentioned. The use of this invocation is in compliance with God's Commandment.

Alaihis salaam. May Peace be upon him. This is used whenever the name of a prophet of God is mentioned, other than Prophet Muhammad ﷺ.

Radi-allaho anhu. May Allah be pleased with him. This is used whenever the name of any of the virtuous companions of the Prophet ﷺ is mentioned.

Radi-allaho anha. May Allah be pleased with her. This is used whenever the name of one of the wives or virtuous women contemporaries of the Prophet ﷺ is mentioned.

Absolute knowledge is only with God. Despite a meticulous approach, errors are possible. This is also true for the translated meaning and the interpretation of verses from the Qur'an and translations of the Hadith. Therefore, if there are any errors, we pray to the Almighty for forgiveness as these were unintentional.

Finally, I wish to express my gratitude to Dr. Muzammil Siddiqi[1] for reviewing the manuscript and providing valuable comments and suggestions. I also wish to thank Mr. Muhammad Nur Abdullah[2] for his review and comments on the first four chapters and Dr. Hatem Bazian[3] for his review and comments on the section on Jerusalem in Chapter 5.

---

[1] Dr. Muzammil Siddiqi is the Director of the Islamic Society of Orange County, California and Chairperson of the Fiqh Council of North America. He served as President of the Islamic Society of North America from 1997-2001.

[2] Mr. Muhammad Nur Abdullah is a member of the Fiqh Council of North America and also served as President of the Islamic Society of North America from 2001-2005 and as Imam of the Dar us Salaam Mosque in Saint Louis, Missouri.

[3] Dr. Hatem Bazian is a Senior Lecturer in the Departments of Near Eastern and Ethnic Studies at the University of California, Berkeley and also an adjunct professor at the Boalt Hall School of Law at the University of California, Berkeley.

Introduction

And this your religion is one religion and I am your Lord, so keep your duty to Me. But they (mankind) have split their religion among them into sects, each sect rejoicing in what it has.

(Surah 23, Al Mu'minoon, ayaat 52-53)

Knowledge is light. Like light that displaces physical darkness, knowledge removes darkness from the mind. Like light permits the vision to recognize and shows the way, knowledge facilitates understanding. However, it comes only to those who seek it with an open mind. Furthermore, its usefulness depends upon the sources from which it is derived, its accuracy, whether pristine or manipulated to serve a particular purpose, to lead or mislead. Without knowledge, a person is unable to distinguish between right and wrong or good and bad, and is oblivious to the consequences of his/her actions or inactions. The absence or lack of knowledge also removes fear.

Knowledge forms the basis of Islam. It is knowledge of the Creator and the knowledge of His directives which guide every affair of the believer (*mu'min*). The source of this knowledge is God. The Divine approach was to provide knowledge about Himself and His Creation, the Criterion to distinguish between right and wrong, and the consequences of deviating from the guided path. It follows, that only those who acquire true knowledge, understand the implications and truly fear God, strive to obey Him and thus derive the benefits: *...the learned among His servants[1] fear God (alone)* (Surah 35, Al Fatir, ayat 28).

---

[1] *ibaadihil ulama: the learned among His servants. Ulama* (plural for *alim*) means the wise, literate, learned, knowing, erudite, ie., those with knowledge gained through learning.

Religious knowledge can have a peculiar effect upon people. While a little or superficial knowledge and understanding of Islam may be stimulating or even exhilarating, a deep and true understanding is immensely humbling and brings out the very best in human character. This attribute can serve as a means of differentiating between those with a genuine understanding and a shallow grasp. The loud voices do not belong to genuine scholars. On the other hand, superficial knowledge or a shallow understanding of Islam opens the door to misinterpretations and thus misrepresentation of the truth. Such individuals lack the necessary depth of information and understanding to arrive at balanced conclusions.

In Islam, knowledge is a double-edged sword. Those who seek, acquire and utilize it are exalted, while those who possess knowledge yet fail to utilize it beneficially, are accountable for not acting by it and/or for not disseminating it. In the Qur'an it is stated:

... God will raise to high ranks those of you who believe and those who have knowledge. And God is informed of what you do.
(Surah 58, Mujadila, ayat 11)

And the blind and the seeing are not equal, nor are those who believe and do good works equal to the evildoers ...
(Surah 40, Al Mu'min, ayat 58)

Islam is a complete *way of life*, a comprehensive *code of living*. The Islamic Shari'ah addresses every aspect of an individual's life. It provides guidance and requires adherence to the prescribed rules. Islam is peace, compassion, justice and equality. No other definition fits Islam. It encourages universal goodness and prohibits evil in every form. The Qur'an summarizes:

Is the reward of goodness anything but goodness?
(Surah 55, Ar Rahman, ayat 60)

The way of life prescribed by Islam fosters peace and contentment which leads to dissipation of the stresses induced by today's hectic lifestyles, occupational as well as personal. One does not have to embrace Islam to obtain that contentment. It already comes through accepting and following its principles while maintaining the faith in which a person was raised or had adopted. Islam is a choice and each person is free to believe or to not believe for nobody may be compelled.[2] At the same time, the onus is upon the individual to seek a change from stress to peace, for it is stated:

And that man has only that for which he makes effort.
(Surah 53, An Najm, ayat 39)

... God does not change the condition of a people until they first change that which is in their hearts ...   (Surah 13, Ar Ra'ad, ayat 11)

Ultimately, the message of Islam and its understanding are Divinely guided and assisted. The message is there for anyone who seeks it. Only those will benefit, who make the effort to seek it and strive to understand. Prophet Muhammad ﷺ summarized it as follows:[3]

The example of guidance and knowledge with which Allah has sent me is like abundant rain falling on the earth: some of which was fertile soil which absorbed rain water and brought forth vegetation and grass in abundance. Another portion of it was hard and held the rain water and Allah benefitted the people with it and they utilized it for drinking, making their animals drink from it and for irrigating the land for cultivation. And a portion of it was barren which could neither hold the water nor bring forth vegetation (that land provided no benefits).
The first is the example of the person who comprehends Allah's religion and gets benefit (from the knowledge) which Allah has revealed through me and learns and then teaches others. The last example is that of a person who does not care for it and does not take Allah's guidance revealed through me (he is like the barren land).

---

[2] Surah 2, Al Baqarah, ayat 256: *There is no compulsion in religion ...*

[3] The Translation of the Meanings of Sahih Al-Bukhari. MM Khan. Kazi Publications, Lahore, Pakistan, 1979. Volume I, Hadith 79, page 67.

Finally, whether exploring Islam through curiosity or for the purpose of contemplation, the reader must bear in mind that Islam is how and what Muslims should be, ie., the conduct of every individual professing to believe and follow Islam must conform to Islamic principles. If the conduct deviates from Islamic teachings, they as individuals, carry the burden of responsibility of being out of line. Islam, as a faith, cannot be made responsible for their actions.

Islam is a *middle course* that shuns extremes, both in personal and religious practices. Prophet Muhammad ﷺ said: *Those who go to extremes are doomed.*[4] He ﷺ also said:[5] *...do good deeds properly, sincerely and moderately, and worship Allah (God) in the forenoon and in the afternoon and during a part of the night, and "always adopt a middle, moderate, regular course" whereby you will reach your target (Paradise).*[6]

Today, the world is spinning into ever increasing chaos. In the West, there is disillusionment in the ability of the dominant persuasions (spiritual and otherwise) to provide means of comfort and answers that are meaningful and logical or sound guidance that could lead towards sustainable peace and harmonious coexistence. Even the illusions of comfort and security achieved through materialism appear to be fading as greed and personal enrichment strategies pull down world economies and destroy the well-being of hundreds of millions. As violence and chaos increase, so does the desire for peace, both outward and inner. In all this confusion and delusion, with an abundance of entertaining distractions, one beacon of hope remains and its light does not diminish despite all efforts to obscure it. This is a true beacon of hope, a philosophy without contradictions or covert motives, one that assures peace and tranquillity, and if exercised conscientiously, it guarantees contentment and harmony, both in the inner self and society at large. However, this peace and contentment may remain elusive for the vast majority of people because it will only be found by those who actively seek it.

---

[4] English Translation of Sahih Muslim. Darussalam, Riyadh, S Arabia, 2007. Volume 7, Hadith 6784, page 44.

[5] The Translation of the Meanings of Sahih Al-Bukhari. MM Khan, Kazi Publications, Lahore, Pakistan, 1979. Volume VIII, Hadith 470, page 313.

[6] emphasis added.

Contents

IV. Contemporary Issues

V. Glossary

I. The Fundamentals

Chapter One

Islam

Introduction

This day I have perfected your religion for you, and completed My favour upon you, and have chosen for you Islam as your deen.[1]

(Surah 5, Al Ma'idah, ayat 3)

The word Islam is derived from *silm* which means peace, to be safe, secure, protected from harm and to surrender or submit. In essence, Islam is *submission, purity and peace*. It is the complete submission to the Will of God. Peace, which is its ultimate goal, is attained by submitting to God and through purity of worship, ie., that there is nothing worthy of worship besides God (*La ilaaha illallah*). In addition to the inner peace and contentment through submission to God, there is peace with everything else, that is, with other people, all other living things, the environment, etc.

Islam is not just another religion in the traditional sense. It is a complete and comprehensive *code of living* providing answers to all questions, spiritual and secular, individual and social. Unlike the traditional concept of religion, ie., that of a private relationship between an individual and God, Islam encompasses all aspects of life for both the individual and society. This means that every moment in an individual's life, whether private or public, conduct and thought, are

---

[1] The Arabic word *deen* is commonly translated as religion. However, it has a much broader meaning than what is traditionally understood by the term religion. *Deen* is a way of life, a complete and comprehensive code of living.

subject to Islamic rules and guidelines. As stated in the verse quoted above, Islam is the name used by God to describe the way of life He has chosen for the believers.

While Islam provides a one-on-one communication between an individual and God, it is also a social institution with comprehensive rules guiding human behavior, individually and collectively. It is an all-inclusive system which addresses spiritual and worldly matters such as ethics, manners and morality, education, sciences, legal, social, political and economic issues. Through this code of living, peace and content-ment in this world and an appropriate preparation for the Hereafter can be achieved by any individual seeking to pursue such a goal.

The precursors of Islam are found in the Abrahamic Traditions. Abraham ﷺ was a true Muslim and the monotheistic religions stem from him through his sons Ishmael ﷺ (forefather of Muhammad ﷺ) and Issac ﷺ (forefather of Jesus ﷺ).[2] The message of Islam came to mankind through Prophet Muhammad ﷺ and was brought by the angel Gabriel ﷺ. The first revelations of the Qur'an were received in Makkah, Arabia. They continued after the Prophet ﷺ emigrated to Madinah. The period during which he received Divine revelations spanned twenty-three years.

> Say (O Muhammad): I am only a mortal the like of you. It is revealed to me that your Lord is only One God. So whoever hopes to meet his Lord, let him work righteousness, and let him not associate anyone with Him in the worship.   (Surah 18, Al Kahf, ayat 110)

The Meaning of God in Islam

God is One. The name Allah is identical to God. It is a name which God has given Himself: *Say, He is Allah, the One. Allah, the Eternal* (Surah 112, Al Ikhlas, ayaat 1-2). For an additional discussion, see Chapter 2, Allah ﷻ. To understand the implications of the Oneness or the Unity of

---

[2] Surah 2, Al Baqarah, ayat 131: *When his Lord said to him (Ibrahim): Submit yourself unto Me (aslim)! He said: I have submitted (aslamtu) to the Lord of the Worlds.*
Surah 3, 'Al Imraan, ayat 67: *Ibrahim was neither a Jew nor a Christian, but was an upright man who has surrendered to Allah and he was not of the polytheists.*
A Muslim is one who has willingly and by choice *submitted to the Will of God.* Also see under Muslims in this Chapter.

God in Islamic Belief, it is necessary to explore its broader meaning and Tauheed is the Arabic term which expresses this belief.

Tauheed

This includes the following:

- Belief in the Unity or Oneness of God (monotheism), ie., there is only One God of the entire creation
- Belief in the Oneness of worship, ie., there is nothing that has the right to be worshipped (or is worthy of being worshipped) besides God. Worship includes the *salat* (obligatory and non-obligatory prayers) and obedience and subordination to God's injunctions (to the Shari'ah) in all affairs, worldly and spiritual
- A third aspect of Tauheed is the belief in the Unity of God's Names/Attributes as described in the Qur'an and Sunnah

The opposite of Tauheed is *shirk* which means associating anyone or anything as a partner or equal to God, or to worship anything besides God. This includes praying to saints, icons, statues, etc., as represent-ations of God. *Shirk* is a major, unpardonable sin.[3] Similarly, assigning offspring to God is a major *shirk*. For an additional discussion on Tauheed see The Message of the Qur'an later in this chapter.

It does not befit the Majesty of Allah that He should beget a son. Glory be to Him! When He decrees a thing, He says to it only: Be! and it is.
(Surah 19, Maryam, ayat 35)

And the Jews said Ezra is the son of Allah and the Christians said the Messiah is the son of Allah. That is their saying with their mouths. They imitate the saying of those who disbelieved of old ...
(Surah 9, At Taubah, ayat 30)

And they say: The Beneficent has taken a son. Glory be to Him! Nay, they (whom they call His sons) are only His honoured servants. They do not speak until He has spoken, and they act by His command.
(Surah 21, Al Anbiya', ayaat 26-27)

---

[3] God has stated that He may forgive every sin except that of associating partners with Him.

And if any one of them were to say, "I am a god besides Him." We would reward him with Hell. Thus, We reward the wrongdoers.

(Surah 21, Al Anbiya', ayat 29)

Trinity from an Islamic Perspective

God is One and nothing can share in His Sovereignty. Therefore, Islam rejects the concept of trinity. The Qur'an quotes Jesus ﷺ who said to his disciples: *Allah is my Lord and your Lord; so worship Him. That is the straight path* (Surah 3, 'Al Imraan, ayat 51).

They surely disbelieve who say: Allah is the third of three, when there is no God save the One God.   (Surah 5, Al Ma'idah, ayat 73)

The Messiah, son of Mary, was no other than a messenger, messengers the like of whom have passed away before him. And his mother was a saintly woman. They both ate earthly food ...

(Surah 5, Al Ma'idah, ayat 75)

Jesus ﷺ is assigned the status of an esteemed messenger of God. Neither Jesus ﷺ nor any other prophet ever claimed to be God or the son of God.

... The Messiah himself said: O children of Israel, worship Allah, my Lord and your Lord. Whoever ascribes partners to Allah, for him Allah has forbidden Paradise. His abode is the Fire. For evildoers there will be no helpers.[4]   (Surah 5, Al Ma'idah, ayat 72)

Before you (Muhammad), the messengers We sent were only men whom We inspired. Ask those who have the Reminder,[5] if you do not know. And We did not give them (the prophets) bodies that could do without food, nor were they immortals.   (Surah 21, Al Anbiya', ayaat 7–8)

---

[4] Additional verses in which Jesus ﷺ denies ever having claimed to be the son of God are in Surah 5, Al Ma'idah, ayaat 116-118.

[5] *...who have the Reminder...* refers to scholars versed in sacred texts, ie., Torah and Bible.

The Miracles of Prophets

Miracles that were performed by prophets should not lead to the assumption that they possessed Divine powers. Well known are those that were performed by Jesus ﷺ. They were facilitated by God to impress upon the people the authenticity of the mission of Jesus ﷺ as a Prophet of God. The Qur'an quotes Jesus ﷺ:

> I come to you with a sign from your Lord, I fashion for you out of clay the likeness of a bird and I breathe into it and it is a bird, "by Allah's permission" (bi iznillah). I heal him who was born blind, and the leper, and I raise the dead, "by Allah's permission" (bi iznillah) ...[6]

> (Surah 3, 'Al Imraan, ayat 49)

Muslims

A Muslim is one who willingly and by choice *surrenders to the Will of God*. This means that anyone (person or creature) who obeys and lives by the laws of the Almighty is a Muslim. Every animal, insect and bird is a Muslim as they are obedient to the Laws of the Almighty. Every child is born a Muslim. As the child grows older, the external influences may lead him or her to adopt another faith by choice.

A believer (*mu'min*) is a person whose submission to God is conscientious, willful, wholehearted and complete, ie., complete subordination to the Will of God. This does not mean living in seclusion or in a sanctuary and devoting time only to worship. These are normal people who go about their daily lives while stringently abiding by Divine injunctions with respect to worship, personal as well as worldly affairs. While Muslims attain the status of believers, the terms believer and Muslim are not interchangeable. This distinction is found both in the Qur'an and the Sunnah.

By submitting him/herself to the Will of God, a Muslim is in peaceful coexistence with all of creation through Islam as *a way of life (deen)*. This includes the inanimate. Such peaceful coexistence with everything in nature is inherent to Islam. This, together with the pursuit of what is right and avoidance of what is wrong and evil, bestows upon the believers the status of being the best of creation.

---

[6] emphasis added.

You are the best community that has been raised up for mankind. You enjoin what is good and forbid what is evil, and you believe in Allah. And if the People of the Scriptures had believed, it would have been better for them. Some of them are believers, but most of them are evildoers.

(Surah 3, 'Al Imraan, ayat 110)

The foremost duty of a Muslim is to God. A Muslim loves God and obediently submits to Him. Furthermore, he/she accepts and reveres Muhammad ﷺ as the final Messenger of God and is also duty-bound to obey and follow him.

New Muslims

There are two occasions when a person can expect all past sins to be forgiven. After performing the Haj properly and when a non-Muslim person accepts Islam, ie., becomes a Muslim. On both occasions, the previous record of bad deeds and sins is wiped clean and the person starts out like a newborn, provided that he/she sincerely repents all sins. As an added bonus, God promises to replace those sins with *hasanaat*, ie., He will credit them as good deeds.

The Islamic Faith

There are five basic tenets of Islam, also called the Five Pillars. These are: Shahadah, Salat, Zakat, Sawm and Haj.

Shahadah

Literally, shahadah means to bear witness: *La ilaaha illallah, Muhammadur rasool ullah,* There is no god or deity besides Allah and Muhammad ﷺ is His messenger. Associating a partner with God is a major aberration, an unpardonable sin. A person may repent and seek forgiveness and thus reestablish his/her faith. A lesser aberration in this context of associating partners with God is giving worldly affairs preference over obligations prescribed by the Almighty.

Salat

Muslims are required to pray five obligatory prayers each day (in a twenty-four hour period): before dawn (*fajr*), mid-day (*zuhr*), mid-afternoon (*asr*), after sunset (*maghrib*), and at night (*isha*). These prayers are due at their prescribed times. There are concessions for those traveling and women are exempted from the obligatory prayers during their menses.

The word salat is derived from the root word *salw* and its meaning includes *supplication, honour, blessing, to contact or connect, to come close or near*. While salat is commonly translated as prayer, its meaning and implications are far-reaching. During the salat a person establishes a connection with God, and while in sajdah (prostration), he/she is closest to Him. The injunction in the Qur'an is *aqim-is salat,* meaning establish salat, ie., establish connection or contact with God. While praying a person is before God and the utmost concentration and appropriate etiquette are essential. Furthermore, by establishing this connection as required, five times a day, a person is less likely to veer off the prescribed course.

Zakat

Zakat or obligatory alms is payable upon the net worth of an individual's assets which exceed a minimum threshold (minimum wealth). This minimum threshold amount is called *nisab* and is equivalent to the value of three ounces of gold. Assets valued below the *nisab* are exempted. Zakat is payable on assets that reach or exceed the *nisab,* in the amount of 2.5 % of their value. Additionally, such assets must be in the individual's possession for twelve consecutive lunar months before zakat becomes due.

Zakat is collected by the Islamic State or other authorized Muslim organizations and is distributed to the poor and those in need. There are several categories of individuals who are eligible for Zakat. The purpose of this wonderful rule is, amongst others, to facilitate distribution of wealth in the society, provide for those in need and alleviate poverty. Above all, complying with this injunction, ie., paying the Zakat, is an act of worship and is appropriately rewarded. The same applies for other obligatory actions.

Sawm

Fasting during the month of Ramadan. The Muslim fast differs from most other types of fasting. The fast begins before dawn and ends immediately after sunset. During the fast, the person must abstain from food, drink, smoking and sexual activity. In addition, the fasting person must refrain from using hurtful or improper language, refrain from fighting or being provoked. Ramadan is month of immense blessings and Muslims are encouraged to maximize the benefits by doing everything that is good, including indulging in spiritual devotion and charitable activities.

The sick may abstain from fasting. Women are not permitted to fast during menstruation or immediately after childbirth. Fasting is not advised for the traveler and individuals who have attained fragile old age. The traveler must make up the missed fasts upon returning to the place of residence. Similarly, menstruating women must make up the missed days.

The term charitable activities requires some elaboration. In Islamic belief, any good deed done sincerely for the sake of pleasing God is considered an act of charity. Besides the common charitable acts such as generous giving, helping the poor and needy, etc., the definition includes such simple actions as removing a hindrance from the sidewalk to make it easy for the pedestrians, a smile when greeting another person, and a kind word spoken. During the month of Ramadan, the benefit for each charitable deed is multiplied.

Haj

This is the pilgrimage to the sacred places in and around Makkah. While this is an obligation, certain conditions must be met before one is permitted to travel for Haj. These include the ability to financially afford the travel, to be free from debt and other financial obligations and the travel must not be financed by borrowed money. While Haj is obligatory, certain other social matters may take precedence. For example, if a person has older parents who are in need of attention and care, tending to the parents takes precedence over going for Haj. This type of ruling is very typical for Islam where there is significant emphasis on moral and social obligations.

Additional Essential Beliefs

While the five basic tenets (the Five Pillars of Islam) constitute the core, Islamic Belief (*iman*) is far more comprehensive and also includes the following:[7,8]

- Belief in God
- Belief in the existence of angels
- Belief in the Revelations sent by God through all prophets
- Belief in all prophets and messengers sent by God
- Belief in the Day of Judgement (*youm ul Qiyamah*)
- Belief in Destiny/Fate (*al Qadar*)

Belief in God (*Iman bi Allah*)

The belief in the One God of everything that exists is at the heart of the Islamic Faith (see Tauheed and Chapter 2, Allah ﷻ). It is a part of the belief in the existence of certain things unseen. Included in this unseen are angels, predestination (*al Qadar*), Day of Resurrection and Judgement, Paradise and Hell.

Belief in the existence of angels

Angels were created from light. Unlike humans and the Jinn, angels do not possess an independent choice. They were created to worship God and follow exactly as He commands and also serve as messengers. The angel Gabriel ﷺ brought the Message of Islam to Prophet Muhammad ﷺ.

Belief in Revelations sent by God through all Prophets

Throughout history, numerous prophets brought the same basic message of Tauheed:[9] believe in One God who has no partner, no parent or offspring, do good and refrain from evil. Islam confirms all prophets. At the same time, it asserts the superiority of its final and comprehensive Message over all previous messages and scriptures. Believing in all Divine messages is a part of the Islamic Faith (*iman*).

And to you We have revealed the Book with the Truth, confirming whatever Book was before it, and a watcher over it. So judge between

---

[7] Iman means belief or faith.

[8] These are also known as the Six Pillars of Faith.

[9] Surah 21, Al Anbiya', ayat 25: *And we did not send any messenger before you but that We revealed to him: There is no god but Me, therefore worship Me alone.*

them by what Allah has revealed, and do not follow their desires away
from the Truth that has come to you ... (Surah 5, Al Ma'idah, ayat 48)

He it is Who has sent His messenger with guidance and the religion
(deen)[10] of Truth, that He may cause it to prevail over all religion. And
Allah is sufficient as a witness.   (Surah 48, Al Fath, ayat 28)

Of the previous Revelations mentioned in the Qur'an, the *Taurat*
(Torah) and *Injeel* (Gospel) refer to the original Commandments and
Injunctions given to Moses 🕮 and Jesus 🕮, respectively. The *Taurat*
mentioned in the Qur'an is not the Old Testament as we know it
today, nor is *Injeel* the Books of Gospel as we know them today, but
the original messages are contained in these texts.[11] Therefore, what
the Qur'an confirms is only those original messages that are contained
in these books and not the Torah, the Old Testament, Pentateuch or
Bible as we have today.

Belief in all prophets and messengers sent by God
Islam requires belief in the missions of all of God's prophets and
messengers and that they be respected without discrimination.[12] The
following are the names of some of the earlier prophets (peace be
upon them all) and the revelations mentioned in the Qur'an.

Idris (Enoch), Nur (Noah), Ibrahim (Abraham), Lut (Lot), Ismail
(Ishmael), Ishaq (Issac), Yaqoob (Jacob), Yusuf (Joseph), Daw'ud
(David), Sulaiman (Solomon), Musa (Moses), Haroon (Aaron), Ayyub
(Job), Yunus (Jonah), Zakariah (Zachariah), Yahya (John), Isa (Jesus)
Taurat (Torah), Zaboor (Psalms), Injeel (Gospel)

Prophets, messengers or guides were sent periodically to each and

---

[10] The Arabic word *deen* is commonly translated as religion. However, it has a much
broader meaning than what is traditionally understood by the term religion. *Deen* is
a way of life, a complete and comprehensive code of living. *Religion of Truth* refers to
Islam, the complete surrender to the Will of the One and Only God of all creation.

[11] Maududi SAA. The Meaning of the Qur'an. Islamic Publications Ltd, Lahore, Pakistan,
1976. Volume 2, pages 9-14.

[12] Surah 2, Al Baqarah, ayat 285: ...*We do not discriminate between any of His messengers..*

every nation on earth.[13] Such emissaries numbered over one hundred thousand. With the exception of the very last messenger, each one of them was sent to a particular nation, tribe or ethnic group.[14] All prophets were mission oriented pious individuals of very high moral and ethical standards and therefore any allegations of immoral behavior are totally rejected by Islam.[15] Some prophets were accorded a higher status than others but none ever claimed divinity or anything but a spiritual relationship with God.[16]

Birth and Ascension of Jesus ☸

The miraculous conception of Mary and birth of Jesus (peace be upon them both) are a part of Islamic belief. These are described in the Qur'an in a stirring narrative.[17] Additionally, in Islamic belief Jesus ☸ did not die nor was he ever even put on the cross.

> ... They slew him not, nor crucified him, but it appeared so to them; and those who disagree concerning it are in doubt thereof; they have no knowledge thereof except pursuit of a conjecture; they slew him not for certain. But Allah raised him up to Himself. Allah is Mighty, Wise.
>
> (Surah 4, An Nisa', ayaat 157-158)

> And remember when Allah said: O Jesus, I am gathering you and causing you to ascend to Me, and am cleansing you of those who disbelieve ...
>
> (Surah 3, 'Al Imraan, ayat 55)

---

[13] Surah 35, Al Fatir, ayat 24: *We have sent you (Muhammad) with the Truth, a bearer of glad tidings and a warner, and there is not a nation but a warner has passed among them.*

[14] As the last Messenger of God, Muhammad ☸ brought the final Message from God which was intended for all of mankind until the Day of Judgement.
Prophet Muhammad ☸ said: *Every prophet used to be sent to his nation exclusively but I have been sent to all mankind.* The Translation of the Meanings of Sahih Al-Bukhari. MM Khan, Kazi Publications, Lahore, Pakistan, 1979. Volume 1, Hadith 429, p 256.

[15] 2 Samuel 5:13 (King James Version): *And David took him more concubines and wives out of Jerusalem, after he was come from Hebron: ...*
2 Samuel 11-12 (New International Version): David and Bathsheba.
The Book of 1st Kings (King James Version), Chapter 11: verses 1-6: *But king Solomon loved many strange women,... And he had seven hundred wives, princesses, and three hundred concubines: and his wives turned away his heart.*

[16] Surah 2, Al Baqarah, ayat 253: *Of these Messengers (whom We sent for the guidance of mankind), We raised some in rank above the others...*

[17] Surah 3, 'Al Imraan, ayaat 42-50; Surah 19, Maryam, ayaat 16-35.

Was Jesus ﷺ different from any other mortal created by God? This question is also answered by God Almighty that Jesus ﷺ was created just like Adam: *The likeness of Jesus with Allah is as like the likeness of Adam. He created him of dust, then He said to him: Be! and he was* (Surah 3, 'Al Imraan, ayat 59).

The Final Message

All of God's prophets, including Moses ﷺ and Jesus ﷺ, are held in very high esteem and no difference in belief is assigned to them.[18] While the previous prophets and their messages focussed on certain regions and peoples, the final message from God through Prophet Muhammad ﷺ was destined for all of mankind and came in the most comprehensive form, incorporating those of all earlier prophets.[19] It is comprehensive because it provided a set of laws and rules (Shari'ah and Fiqh) and also established a code of living and conduct for all future generations of mankind through the real-life example in the person of the final messenger of God, Muhammad ﷺ.

And We have not sent you (O Muhammad) save as a bringer of good tidings and a warner to all mankind; but most of mankind know not.
(Surah 34, Saba, ayat 28)

In the Messenger of Allah you have a good example for him who hopes for Allah and the Last Day, and remembers Allah much.
(Surah 33, Al Ahzab, ayat 21)

Belief in the Day of Judgement

In the Qur'an and Hadith, many descriptions are used for the Day of Judgement (*youm ud deen*). Some of these are: *The Hour, The Final Day (youm ul 'akhir), Day of Accountability (youm ul hisaab), Day of Gathering (youm ul jammah), Day of Resurrection (youm ul qiyamah), Day of Mutual Disillusion (youm ut taghabun), Appointed Day (youm mim ma'loom)*. Each one of these descriptions emphasizes a particular aspect. The term

---

[18] Surah 2, Al Baqarah, ayat 285: *...We do not discriminate between any of His messengers.*

[19] Surah 42, Ash Shura, ayat 13: *He has ordained for you the same Religion which He enjoined on Noah and that which We enjoined on Abraham and Moses and Jesus saying - Establish the religion (deen) and be not divided therein...*

youm means *day*. This is not a day in the conventional sense since the duration of that day will be significantly longer.

Each and every person that ever lived will be assembled on that day and will have to account for each and every deed.[20] This will be the final process of accountability. Each person will be given his/her book of records which will contain minute details of the person's deeds. There will be no possibility for making excuses or denying since the record will be clear and complete. In addition, each body part will testify independently.

A simplified concept of the outcome is that good deeds will be weighed against the evil deeds. If the scale tips towards the good, Paradise is the reward, and if the evil deeds weigh more, Hell is the destination. In reality, it is much more complex, as many other things are factored into the final judgement. For example, if a person has wronged another, some of his/her good deeds will be taken away and given to the victim, which may change the balance significantly. However, the single most important and the determining factor is that of God's Mercy and Compassion. He may forgive anyone, at any time, at His discretion.

While the final reckoning with awarding of Paradise or punishment will be on the Day of Judgement, the actual process of accountability begins very shortly after a person dies and is buried. For the good, the grave is made spacious and a pleasant resting place. For the evil, punishment already begins in the grave. Thus, for every person, the grave/cemetery should serve as a reminder that life's end could be just around the corner, and that after death, the possibility to do good deeds or make amends also ceases.

When will the Day of Judgement come? No one except God has that knowledge. When asked about it, Prophet Muhammad ﷺ replied that he did not know. On many occasions, he would describe events that would occur prior to the Day of Judgement. These are recorded in the Hadith and are also discussed in Chapter 25, Qiyamah.

---

[20] Surah 60, Al Mumtahanah, ayat 3: *On the Day of Resurrection, neither your relatives nor your children shall avail you. He will part you (sort you out), and He is observing all your actions.*

Original Sin

The concept of the Original Sin does not exist in Islam. Each individual is solely responsible for his/her own actions. No person can or will bear responsibility for another's wrongdoing.[21] However, in the case where a person has initiated or encouraged a good or an evil act which is perpetuated, he/she will also get a share of the reward or responsibility each time that act is done. Thus, if someone has initiated a good deed and another person copies that good, the one who initiated it also gets a reward each time that deed is done, without it diminishing any party's reward. The same applies to an evil deed.[22] As life could end at any time, there may not be an opportunity to seek forgiveness or make amends for any wrongdoing. Therefore, Islam seeks to induce awareness of the consequences of one's actions, both short and long term.

And We have fastened every man's deeds to his neck and on the Day of Resurrection We shall bring out for him a book which he will find wide open. It will be said to him: Read your book (record of deeds); Your soul is sufficient this day as reckoner against you.

(Surah 17, Al Isra', ayaat 13-14)

On the Day when every soul will be confronted with all the good it has done, and all the evil it has done, it will wish that there were a great distance between it and its evil. Allah warns you to fear Him; and Allah is full of kindness to those that serve Him.

(Surah 3, 'Al Imraan, ayat 30)

And each one of them will come to Him on the Day of Resurrection, alone.   (Surah 19, Maryam, ayat 95)

---

[21] Surah 17, Al Isra', ayat 15: ... *No soul can bear another's burden. Nor do We punish until We have sent forth a messenger (to give warning).*

[22] This should encourage introspection. In this context, a Hadith states: *Whenever a person is killed unjustly, there is a share from the burden of the crime on the first son of Adam for he was the first to start the act of murdering (killing).* The Translation of the Meanings of Sahih Al-Bukhari. MM Khan, Kazi Publications, Lahore, Pakistan, 1979. Volume IV, Hadith 552, page 348.

Remember, one day you will appear before Allah and answer for your deeds. So beware, do not stray from the path of righteousness after I am gone. (Farewell Sermon of Prophet Muhammad ﷺ)

Belief in Destiny/Fate (*al Qadar*)

We have created all things according to a measure.
(Surah 54, Al Qamar, ayat 49)

The Arabic word *qadar* is translated as *destiny*. Its broader meaning includes: *the determination, dividing, judging,* and *a specified measure or amount (balance) including quantity, quality,* and *shape*. The meaning of the verb *yu qaddir* includes *to measure* or *decide upon quantity, quality, position, shape, etc.* Scholars define *al Qadar* as *Divine Measure* and *Judgement in the creation of all things in nature.*

The belief in Divinely directed destiny is an essential part of the Islamic faith. This a vast topic about which only little has been revealed. Hence, trying to determine the details is an exercise in futility. It is like trying to put together a large jigsaw puzzle with a handful of pieces. Moreover, learned individuals recommend neither to pursue this topic with any intensity nor give an opinion. What is known from the Qur'an and Hadith should be accepted. While we are permitted to seek knowledge about it, God's Wisdom must never be questioned. In the following is some very basic information.

Absolute knowledge and power belong to God. He had knowledge of whatever was to be created and He created according to His plan. Everything was created in a very determined fashion and was assigned a specific purpose.[23] He has written and placed all of this information in a well guarded record (*al lauh al mahfuz*). This is the record of every single thing that will ever come into existence. This knowledge God has not revealed to anybody. In addition, God maintains absolute control over all events preceding, during and after creation. Whatever happens in the universe is subservient to His Will and absolutely nothing can happen without His knowledge. Consequently, there is no

---

[23] Surah 87, Al A'la, ayaat 1-3: *Glorify the Name of your Lord, the Most High. Who created all things and well proportioned them. And Who has ordained their destinies and guided them.*

such thing as an accident or a coincidence.

And with Him are the keys of the unseen. None but He knows them.
And He knows whatever is in the land and in the sea. Not a leaf falls,
but He knows it, not a grain in the darkness (or depths) of the earth,
nor anything living or dead but (it is noted) in a clear Record.

(Surah 6, Al An'aam, ayat 59)

Each occurrence is purposeful though that purpose may not be
known to mankind. Every individual's destiny was decreed before the
beginning of creation.[24] Therefore, a believer will accept, no matter
what happens. If faced with something undesirable, a believer will say
God ordained it and He did what He willed. Similarly, if something
desirable happens, a believer will thank God for it was decreed by
Him.

No misfortune can befall in the earth or in yourselves, but it is recorded
in a book, before We bring it into being. That is easy for Allah. So that
you may not grieve for the good things you miss or be overjoyed at what
you gain ...   (Surah 57, Al Hadid, ayaat 22-23)

Thus, *al qadar* pertains to all of creation and includes when, where
and how its existence will unfold. For living creatures, this includes life
span, sustenance, time, place and mode of birth and death. For
mankind, this also includes personal qualities and the final destination,
ie., Paradise or Hell. Prophet Muhammad ﷺ said:

The happiness of the son of Adam (human beings) depends on his being
content with what Allah has decreed for him, and the misery of the son of
Adam results from his failure to seek Divine Guidance, and the misery of
the son of Adam results from in his being unhappy with what Allah has
decreed for him.[25]

---

[24] The destiny (*qadar*) of everything had been determined long before their creation:
Allah decreed the destinies fifty thousand years before He created the heavens and the
earth. English Translation of Jami' At-Tirmidhi, Darussalam, Riyadh, S Arabia, 2007.
Volume 4, Hadith 2156, page 217.

[25] English Translation of Jami' At-Tirmidhi, Darussalam, Riyadh, S Arabia, 2007. Volume
4, Hadith 2151, page 213.

Can destiny be changed?

Prophet Muhammad ﷺ said: *Nothing extends one's life span but righteousness (birr), nothing averts the Divine Decree but supplication, and nothing deprives a man of provision but the sin that he commits.*[26]

Supplication (*du'a*), which is a means of asking God for something, is also an important part of the Islamic faith. It is an act of worship and every person is encouraged to ask for all of his/her needs. This also puts into perspective the relationship between God, the One who provides from stores that never deplete, and the supplicant who seeks for his every need.

Faith in Practice

Issues pertaining to the practical aspects of Islam are discussed in Chapter 4, Islamic Law, Shari'ah and Fiqh. Some issues, particularly those pertinent to the foregoing, are discussed below.

Religion and State

There is no separation of religion and state. Traditionally, the Head of State was also the spiritual leader. This is the principle of the Caliphate. In the true Islamic system, the people are empowered. The affairs of the state are conducted by *shura'*. This is the principle of mutual consultation and involves both men and women. In an Islamic State virtually every issue is open to public debate and public input is expected.

Deed and Retribution

A crucial factor for judging the action of a person is the intention behind it. Deeds are recorded throughout life. On the Day of Judgement, this record of deeds will be presented and the person will be judged accordingly. It is of note, that issuing of credit for good or bad intentions and deeds occurs in a unique fashion. If a person intends to do a good act, a reward is given just for making that intention. If he/she carries through and does that good act, a multifold reward is given (ten to seven hundred times). If an individual intends

---

[26] English Translation of Sunan ibn Majah, Darussalam, Riyadh, S Arabia, 2007. Volume I, Hadith 90, page 139.

to do a bad or evil deed, note is made of that intention. If he/she does that bad deed, one such deed is written in his/her account or that person maybe forgiven. However, if that person should refrain from going through with that bad deed, a reward is given.[27]

Since there is accountability for every thought, action and spoken word, a person must remain cognizant of everything he or she does. This serves as a reminder and guides to what Islam requires, ie., to do what is good and avoid everything that is bad or evil.

We created man and We know the promptings of his soul, and We are nearer to him than his jugular vein. And besides this direct knowledge of Ours, two scribes (angels) sitting on his right and on his left, are recording everything. Each word he utters is recorded by a vigilant guardian.

(Surah 50, Qaf, ayaat 16-18)

On the Day of Judgement a person will not move until he is asked about five things: about his life and what he did with it; about his knowledge and what he did with it (ie., how he utilized it); about his wealth and how he (acquired) it and how he spent it; and about his youth and how he spent it.[28]

While there will be punishment for bad deeds, there is also always the hope for forgiveness (upon repentance) for Allah is Most Merciful, Loving and Forgiving.

(O Prophet) Say: O My servants who have transgressed against their souls! Do not despair of Allah's mercy! Surely, Allah forgives all sins; for He is Oft-Forgiving, the Most Merciful.

(Surah 39, Az Zumar, ayat 53)

And when those who believe in Our Revelations come to you, say: Peace be upon you. Your Lord has prescribed Mercy for Himself, so that if any of you does evil and repents afterwards and does good deeds, then

---

[27] The Translation of the Meanings of Sahih Al-Bukhari. MM Khan, Kazi Publications, Lahore, Pakistan, 1979. Volume VIII, Hadith 498, page 329.

[28] The English Translation of Jami' At-Tirmidhi, Darussalam, Riyadh, S Arabia, 2007. Volume 4, Hadith 2417, page 429.

assuredly He is Oft-Forgiving, Most Merciful.
(Surah 6, An An'aam, ayat 54)

Wrongdoing/Sin

There are two categories of sin: major and minor. The most significant sin is that of associating partners with God., ie., shirk. There is forgiveness for every sin if the individual sincerely repents and does not repeat it. All forgiveness is at the discretion of the Almighty.

Sins are further divided into those committed against another person, society or against oneself. Usually, sins against others, especially those considered detrimental to the well-being of society, are subject to more severe punishment. The fear of severe punishment for crimes such as theft, rape, fornication and adultery serves as a strong deterrent in an Islamic society. Before punishment is carried out, there must be verification by truthful witnesses or an uncoerced confession that the crime actually did occur. The judge's ruling must comply with the Shari'ah and judges are strictly accountable for their decisions. Even during the time of Prophet Muhammad ﷺ, harsh-appearing punishments were carried out very infrequently. For example, *ar rajam* (stoning for adultery) was used only a few times, and in those cases, the individuals themselves came forward to confess the crime and requested purification.[29] Homicide is subject to specific ruling under Shari'ah (see Chapter 4, Islamic Law, Shari'ah and Fiqh).

The biggest of the major sins are:[30]

- To join others as partners in worship with Allah
- To murder a human being
- To be undutiful towards one's parents
- And to make a false statement or to give a false witness

Prophet Muhammad ﷺ also warned: *Avoid the seven great destructive*

---

[29] By accepting the prescribed punishment in this life, the individuals are cleansed of the sin of adultery and are thus spared the severe punishment in the Hereafter. The Translation of the Meanings of Sahih Al-Bukhari. MM Khan, Kazi Publications, Lahore, Pakistan, 1979. Volume VIII, Hadith 806, page 528; Hadith 813-815, pages 534-536.

[30] The Translation of the Meanings of Sahih Al-Bukhari. MM Khan, Kazi Publications, Lahore, Pakistan, 1979. Volume IX, Hadith 10, page 5.

sins:[31]

- To join partners in worship with Allah
- To practice sorcery
- To kill the life which Allah has forbidden, except for a just cause
- To use or deal in *riba* (usury/interest)
- To devour the property of an orphan
- To turn one's back to the enemy and flee the battlefield
- To slander chaste women who guard their chastity and are good believers

Islam teaches that there are three categories of deeds: those that are permitted, those that are clearly prohibited and those that are unclear or doubtful. The Muslim is told to avoid the prohibited and steer clear of the doubtful because of the uncertainty.

The opposite of sin is piety (*taqwa*). The essentials of piety are adherence to obligatory religious duties and refraining from sin. God describes those with piety as:

Those who believe and do righteous deeds, their Lord guides them by their faith ...   (Surah 10, Yunus, ayat 9)

... And those who refrain from gross sins and shameful deeds and, when they are angry, forgive.   (Surah 42, Ash Shura, ayat 37)

The Qur'an

Had it been possible for a Qur'an to cause the mountains to move, or the earth to be torn asunder, or the dead to speak, (this Qur'an would have done so) ...   (Surah 13, Ar Ra'ad, ayat 31)

Literally, Qur'an means lecture, the reading. It is the Final Message from God for all of mankind and it incorporates all previous Divine messages. It is a compilation of Divine Revelations which were brought to Prophet Muhammad ﷺ by the angel Gabriel ﷿ over a

---

[31] The Translation of the Meanings of Sahih Al-Bukhari. MM Khan, Kazi Publications, Lahore, Pakistan, 1979. Volume VIII, Hadith 840, pages 560-561.

period of twenty-three years. The Qur'an was transmitted in the Arabic language. It has 114 *surahs* (chapters) of variable length. In each *surah*, there are a variable number of *ayaat* (verses). Some verses were revealed while the Prophet ﷺ was in Makkah and others were revealed during his time in Madinah.

The source of the Qur'an is *al lauh al mahfuz* (The Guarded Tablet). This is the Record of all information and was written before creation began. The Qur'an is the only Divine Revelation which has been preserved in its original form. God has made that His responsibility: *We have, without doubt, sent down the Reminder (the Qur'an) and We preserve it* (Surah 15, Al Hijr, ayat 9).

Soon after they were revealed, the verses of the Qur'an were recorded by scribes and committed to memory by many. Each year, during the month of Ramadan, the angel Gabriel ؑ would visit Prophet Muhammad ﷺ and rehearse the verses that had been revealed up to that time. During the last Ramadan before the Prophet ﷺ died, Gabriel ؑ rehearsed the entire Qur'an twice. The printed book we have today is preserved in that form and in the same sequence as the Prophet ﷺ left it for all Muslims.

Revelation of verses of the Qur'an came at different times and for different occasions. After receiving a revelation, the Prophet ﷺ would be exhausted and sweating and remarked that each occasion left him with heaviness on the chest. He also said that after each revelation it were as if *the words were imprinted in my mind*.

Each word and each sentence in the Qur'an is purposeful. Most meanings are clear even in translations of the text. Some meanings may be difficult to grasp, and here learned scholars play an important role in helping with the interpretation.

The Living Language of the Qur'an

Arabic, the language in which the Qur'an was revealed, is a uniquely expressive language. In order to understand the meanings of some of the verses, it may require an explanatory text called a *tafseer*.[32] The latter also puts into perspective the events that may have been associated with the revelation of those particular verses. The *tafseer* is

---

[32] *Tafseer* is the explanation and commentary on the meanings of the Qur'an (exegesis).

usually the result of a lifelong study by dedicated scholars who are masters in the Arabic language.

Even in the best of translations, the command and appeal of the original Arabic text may be lost. It is not always easy to convey the precise meaning and vernacular of the source language. Different translators may choose different words and phrases, using the vocabulary of the language into which the Qur'an is being translated, as they attempt to express their understanding of the original text. Importantly, the language of the Qur'an cannot be meaningfully translated and interpreted by just anyone who speaks Arabic, equipped with a dictionary. The Prophet ﷺ stated: *If anyone interprets the Book of Allah in the light of his opinion, even if he is right, he has erred.*[33]

The Message of the Qur'an

Surely, this your religion is one religion, and I am your Lord, so worship Me.   (Surah 21, Al Anbiya', ayat 92)

And it (this Qur'an) is a guidance and a mercy for believers.
                                        (Surah 27, An Naml, ayat 77)

And We send down in the Qur'an that which is a healing and a mercy for believers, though to the evildoers it adds nothing but ruin.
                                        (Surah 17, Al Isra', ayat 82)

Thus We have revealed it to be a judgement of authority in Arabic ...
                                        (Surah 13, Ar Ra'ad, ayat 37)

The message of the Qur'an is that of Tauheed, the prophethood and the Hereafter.

Tauheed [34]

God is One, without partner, parent, or offspring and He Alone is worthy of worship. In the Qur'an, God addresses people in different

---

[33] Sunan Abu Dawud. English Translation with Explanatory Notes. A Hasan. Kitab Bhavan, New Delhi, 1997. Volume 3, Hadith 3644, page 1036.

[34] Also see the discussion on Tauheed on pages 3-4 of this chapter.

ways: O mankind, O children of Adam, O children of Israel,[35] O people of the Book,[36] O Muslims, O you who believe. A clear distinction is made between persons who simply accept that *God is One, with no partner (ie., Muslims)* and those who are *believers* (ie., *mu'minoon*). The latter are those whose submission to God is wholehearted and complete: *...we hear and we obey...* (Surah 2, Al Baqarah, ayat 285); *Truly, my worship and my sacrifices and my living and my dying are for Allah, Lord of the Worlds* (Surah 6, Al An'aam, ayat 162).

Since God created mankind for the purpose of worshiping Him alone, a believer's life is an expression of the complete and unconditional submission to God by strictly following the Qur'an and Sunnah. *Worship* is the translation of the Arabic word *ibadah*. The meaning of *ibadah* is much broader. It includes worship and prayer in the conventional sense, but importantly, it is the state of constant awareness of one's responsibility towards God and that of consciously avoiding everything that is prohibited and might incur His displeasure.

Prophethood (*risala*)

Messengers and warners were sent to admonish and guide all nations that ever existed and ended with the last Prophet of God, Muhammad ﷺ. In past generations, those who heeded the warnings were saved from calamity while those who rejected it were destroyed. History is full of examples where nations and empires corrupted with power and wealth turned to disbelief and were subsequently destroyed. Disbelief here does not mean only denying that God is One, it also includes moral and social decadence.

Hereafter (*'akhira*)

Life on earth ends at the time of death only to resume in the Hereafter and that second life is perpetual. That life will be spent either in Paradise (*Jannah*) or in Hell (*Jahannam*). Every person will be held accountable for his/her deeds. Each person will be assigned a final destination on the Day of Judgement. The life in Paradise will be blissful while Hell will be tormentful. To provide a measure, Prophet Muhammad ﷺ said: *This fire of yours, which the sons of Adam*

---

[35] This refers to the descendants of the Prophet Jacob ﷺ.

[36] Those who received the earlier Revelations, primarily the Jews and Christians.

(humankind) kindle, is one part from seventy parts of the heat of Hell.[37]

Reading the Qur'an

This (the Qur'an) is insight from your Lord and a guidance and a mercy for a people that believe. And when the Qur'an is recited, listen to it and pay heed, that you may obtain mercy.

(Surah 7, Al A'raaf, ayaat 203-204)

The Qur'an is unlike any other book. It has a unique style, and therefore, the reader must discard the idea that he/she is reading a conventional book. The topics are not grouped in chapters and verses pertaining to a particular subject may be followed by those which address a different subject. Furthermore, the subject is repeated in other ways. In order to understand this style, the reader must bear in mind that the Qur'an was revealed over a period of twenty-three years. Accordingly, the verses addressed the ongoing needs of the Islamic community during the different phases of establishment.[38]

The Qur'an is meant to be read frequently, if not daily. It contains advice, guidance, warnings and accounts of previous peoples and prophets. It describes scientific and natural phenomena and counsels the reader to reflect upon the meanings and to take heed and prepare for the meeting with the Creator. Everything in the Qur'an has a purpose and every story carries a message.

While most sections are easily understood, some are more difficult to understand and must be interpreted using both the historical and textual context. Yet, there are verses that remain unexplained. The reader must read and understand that which is easy and seek help and guidance from scholars (ie., *tafseer*) for the rest. Failing to put the information into proper context invariably leads to misunderstanding and deprives the reader of its true meaning and message.

Even though the text was revealed gradually and over a twenty-three year period, there is no contradiction in the Qur'an. The Arabic

---

[37] English Translation of Jami' At-Tirmidhi, Darussalam, Riyadh, S Arabia, 2007. Volume 4, Hadith 2589, page 568.

[38] Maududi SAA. The Meaning of the Qur'an. Islamic Publications Limited, Lahore, Pakistan, 1978. Volume I, pages 7-36.

language can be difficult to translate. Thus, the translation may not convey the same as the original text. The scholars dedicated to the pursuit of understanding the message and meaning of the Qur'an, ie., *tafseer*, use specific rules and guidelines for this task. Through the *tafseer*, there can be an understanding of many of the verses whose meaning is otherwise not readily apparent to the reader.

The Qur'an is the Word of God and should be handled with appropriate respect. No one should touch it unless in a state of purity (*tahara*) (Surah 56, Al Waqi'ah, ayat 79). In practical terms, this means performing the *wudu* (ablution required of Muslims before obligatory prayers and reading the Qur'an) or taking a bath if there has been sexual activity, and wearing clean clothes. Non-Muslims seeking knowledge about Islam are permitted to handle the translations of the Qur'an.

Hadith and Sunnah (Prophetic Traditions)

There are three components of the Prophetic Traditions: statements made by Prophet Muhammad ﷺ, his actions and approvals, and his descriptions (sifaat/shama'il). The Arabic word *Hadith* is translated as meaning speech, conversation, talk, interview, narrative, account or report.[39] Strictly, this definition covers only his statements. However, its broader meaning is generally used and refers to all the acts, words, and rulings of Prophet Muhammad ﷺ, ie., his Traditions. This includes whatever is known to us about him by virtue of the notes, records and recollections of his wives, family members and other companions (may God be pleased with them all). A *Hadith Qudsi* is a narrative in which Prophet Muhammad ﷺ reported what was said by God. Unlike the Qur'an, those are not God's words.

The word *Sunnah* also means tradition. It is used in reference to the actions of the Prophet ﷺ, such as his habits and mannerism. Both *Hadith* and *Sunnah* carry the same authority since both his speech and actions were Divinely inspired and guided.

Nor does he speak of his own desire. This is no other than an inspired

---

[39] The plural for Hadith in *Ahadith*. For purposes of simplicity, only the singular form, Hadith, is used also when referring to the plural.

Revelation. Which one of mighty powers has taught him.

(Surah 53, An Najm, ayat 3-5)

... Say, I follow only that which is inspired in me from my Lord ...

(Surah 7, Al A'raaf, ayat 203)

Prophet Muhammad ﷺ lived his life in accordance with the guidance he received from God. Therefore, there is absolutely no discrepancy between what is revealed in the Qur'an and his Sunnah. The latter has been the source of guidance for all Muslims in every sphere of life and he is the role model for those who faithfully submit to Islam.[40] He ﷺ said: *I have left two things with you. As long as you hold fast to them, you will not go astray. They are the Book of Allah and the Sunnah of His Prophet.*[41]

After the Qur'an, the Sunnah is the second source for the Shari'ah. The importance of the Sunnah is emphasized in the Qur'an.

Say (O Muhammad to mankind), If you love Allah, follow me; Allah will love you and forgive you your sins. Allah is Forgiving, Merciful.

(Surah 3, 'Al Imraan, ayat 31)

O you who believe! Obey Allah and obey the Messenger and render not your actions vain. (Surah 47, Muhammad, ayat 33)

Whoever obeys the Messenger, obeys Allah and whoever turns away, We have not sent you as a warder over them.

(Surah 4, An Nisa', ayat 80)

The Sunnah is recorded in books of Hadith. During the Prophet's ﷺ lifetime, Hadith were put into writing by notable contemporaries such as Abdullah ibn Amr ؓ and later by Abdullah ibn Abbas ؓ, Abu Huraira ؓ and others. The first systematic compilation arranged by subject was undertaken by Al Zuhri at the end of the first century AH upon the

---

[40] Surah 33, Al Ahzab, ayat 21: *Verily in the Messenger of Allah you have a good example for him who hopes for Allah and the Last Day, and remembers Allah much.*

[41] Al-Muwatta of Imam Malik ibn Anas. Madinah Press, Inverness, Scotland, 2004. The Decree, 46.3, page 380.

directive of Khalifah Umar ibn Abdul Aziz (99-101 AH). The first compilation in book form was by Imam Malik (93-179 AH). Hadith were collected and compiled through a very rigorous system of authentication and corroboration which often necessitated traveling far and wide. These comprehensive books are a tremendous source of information. Some of the prominent Hadith scholars and their works are listed below:

Muhammad bin Ismail bin   Sahih Al-Bukhari
Al-Mughirah Al-Bukhari
(194-256 AH / 808-870 CE)

Abu'l Hussain Muslim bin Hajjaj   Sahih Muslim
al Qushayri an-Nishapuri
(206-261 AH / 821-875 CE)

Sulaiman bin al-Ash'ath bin Ishaq   Sunan Abu Dawud
bin Bashir bin Shaddad bin Amr
bin Imran Abu Dawud (202-275 AH)

Abu Isa bin Sawrah bin Musa bin   Jami' At-Tirmidhi
ad-Dahhak as-Sulami ad-Darir
Al-Bughi at-Tirmidhi (200-279 AH)[42]

Abu Abdur-Rahman Nasa'i   Sunan Nasa'i
(died 303 AH)

Abu Abdullah Muhammad bin   Sunan ibn Majah
Yazeed bin Abdullah Rab'i
al-Qazvini (ibn Majah)
(209-273 AH/ 824-888 CE)

Abu Abdullah Malik bin Anas   Muwatta' of Imam Malik
(93-179 AH)

---

[42] The exact date of birth is uncertain. Different accounts place it between 200 and 209 AH.

Over the years, attempts were made to forge Hadith in order to push a point of view, please a ruler, or in the pursuit of some other motive. Sources of such Hadith were identified by the learned scholars as these Hadith were uncorroborated. The Prophet ﷺ may have been aware of this possibility and had said: *Whoever lies upon me, then let him take his seat in the Fire (of Hell).*[43]

Violence and Islam

There is a misconception that Islam is violent. This is not fortuitous. It appears to be part of an unfortunate disinformation campaign against Islam and Muslims. It is unfortunate, not only because it is totally incorrect, but because prejudice closes the mind to rationality and essentially robs the person of the opportunity to learn about a way of life that guarantees peace. That is, peace within oneself and peace with everything around, and peace in eternity. Today, a large number of people in affluent societies are turning away from religion, frequently towards atheism, disenchanted with the traditional Western religions. It would be truly unfortunate if erroneous information about Islam would succeed in closing the minds of people and deprive them of an opportunity to achieve contentment and peace. (For an additional discussion on this topic see Chapter 21, Creative Terminology for Islam and Muslims)

Islam is the religion of peace through submission to God. Peace (*As Salaam*) is also one of the Attributes of God. It is also the name for Paradise (*Dar as Salaam*, abode of peace). Peace is also the word used by Muslims all over the world as a greeting, namely, *as salaam o alaikum*, may peace be upon you.

While the ultimate goal of Islam is peace, it cannot always be achieved by words or by turning the other cheek. History, including recent events, shows that the humble and peace loving, perceived as weak, are frequently subjected to aggression and oppression. God, in His infinite wisdom, remedied this potential predicament for the followers of Islam. In no uncertain terms, He has made it clear in the Qur'an that injustice, oppression and killing of the innocent are strictly

---

[43] English Translation of Jami' At-Tirmidhi, Darussalam, Riyadh, S Arabia, 2007. Volume 5, Hadith 2659, page 59.

prohibited. However, the aggressor who uses force may understand only the language of force. Consequently, the use of force is permitted the when it becomes the only remaining means to stop oppression and injustice, and establish peace.

War and aggression were disliked by Prophet Muhammad ﷺ. Unlike today's professional killer robots in uniform, the Muslims were urged to seek peace and security through prayer rather than engage in military combat. Consequently, Divine Revelations prepared the Muslims for the unavoidable.

Warfare is ordained for you, though it is hateful to you; but it may happen that you hate a thing which is good for you and it may happen that you love a thing that is bad for you. Allah knows, you do not know.
(Surah 2, Al Baqarah, ayat 216)

... persecution is worse than killing. (Surah 2, Al Baqarah, ayat 217)

Misrepresentation of Islamic Texts

Occasionally, phrases from verses of the Qur'an and Hadith are quoted out of context and the meanings misrepresented in order to justify the vilification of Islam and Muslims and to portray them as being violent. Examples of such misrepresentation are discussed below.

Verse 5 of Surah 9, At Taubah states:
Then, when the sacred months have passed, slay the idolators wherever you may come upon them, and take them captive, and besiege them, and lie in wait for them at every conceivable place.[44] But if they repent and establish worship and pay the poor due, then leave their way free (let them go their way). Allah is Forgiving, Merciful.

Phrases from this verse have been misused to propagate the opinion that Islam teaches violence (*...slay the idolators wherever you may come upon them...*) and that there is forced conversion in Islam (*But if they repent and establish worship and pay the poor due,...*). Both allegations

---

[44] That is, *do everything that may be necessary and advisable in warfare*. The Message of the Qur'an. Translated and Explained by Muhammad Asad. The Book Foundation, Bristol, England, 2003. Page 289.

are unfounded. To understand their meanings, these and other similar verses must be viewed in both their textual and historical contexts.

For textual context, any one phrase or sentence cannot simply be quoted as having an independent meaning. This is illogical, and if deliberate, it is misrepresentation of facts. Every verse of the Qur'an must be interpreted against the background of the Qur'an as a whole.[45] The importance of the historical context is knowing when and for what reason the verse was revealed. The latter provides key information and facilitates an understanding of the meaning and purpose.

Interpretation of Verses in Historical and Textual Context

The first twenty-nine verses of Surah 9, At Taubah, address issues pertaining to some specific events.[46] These verses were revealed in the month of Shawwal (tenth month of the Islamic Calendar) in the ninth year after Hijrah. Pagan Arab tribes living in adjacent territories had made treaties with the new Muslim State in Madinah. While the Muslims strictly abided by the terms of those treaties, as did some of the tribes, others violated them repeatedly with ceaseless hostile acts (Surah At Taubah, ayaat 7-10,13). The treaty violators were given four months *notice of termination* for the treaties and a choice of coming to terms by accepting and living in peace with the Muslims, or war.[47] As was customary with public announcements, this treaty termination was announced during the Haj in the same year. *Sacred months* in Verse 5 of Surah At Taubah refers to the months in which warfare is prohibited for Muslims.[48] Three of these are consecutive months and occurred during that four month notice period.

The tribes who were put on notice had violated the terms of a peace treaty (Treaty of Hudaibiya') by murdering innocent people belonging to a pagan tribe allied with the Muslim State. This verse

---

[45] The Message of the Qur'an. Translated and Explained by Muhammad Asad. The Book Foundation, Bristol, England, 2003. Page 289.

[46] Maududi SAA. The Meaning of the Qur'an. Islamic Publications Ltd., Lahore, Pakistan, 1978. Volume IV, pages 158-169.

[47] For rules governing treaties see Islamic Rules of Warfare in Chapter 24, Suicide, Killing and War.

[48] These are the seventh (Rajab), eleventh (Dhul Qa'dah), twelfth (Dhul Hijjah) and first (Muharram) months in the Islamic calendar.

relates to warfare that was *already in progress* with people who had violated their treaty obligations and were guilty of aggression.[49] Thus, by going against the treaty violators, the Muslims were honouring their pledge and coming to the aid of non-Muslims who they were obliged to help, pursuant to the terms of a treaty.

The second sentence: *But if they repent and establish worship and pay the poor due, then leave their way free (let them go their way)...* cannot be construed as compelling anyone to accept Islam. It gives those who refrain from aggression, the option to accept Islam or continue in their ways of life. This is further explained in the subsequent verse (see below).

The next verse (ayat 6 of Surah 9, At Taubah) states: *And if anyone of the idolators seeks your protection, then protect him so that he may hear the word of Allah and afterward convey him to his place of safety. That is because they are a folk that know not.* Clearly, the injunctions *...protect him...* and *...convey him to his place of safety...* do not permit forced conversion but re-affirm that there is no coercion in matters of faith.

Thus, it requires some imagination to deduce that Islam preaches forceful conversion. No one may be compelled to accept Islam, because in Islam a person has to *willingly* submit to God. Compulsion does not make a person a Muslim. There is no inquisition in Islam and the Qur'an clearly prohibits forceful conversion: *There is no compulsion in religion* (Surah 2, Al Baqarah, ayat 256).

Historically, the relationship between Muslims and non-Muslim citizens of a Muslim state has been that of mutually beneficial peaceful coexistence. The rules of interaction with non-Muslims (individuals, communities or states) are explicit and dictate that those in peaceful coexistence with Muslims are entitled to just and kind treatment.[50] Islam assures the freedom of religion and the Islamic State is obliged to protect its minorities who live peacefully. Additional information on this topic may be found in Chapter 11, Minorities under Muslim Rule.

---

[49] The Message of the Qur'an. Translated and Explained by Muhammad Asad. The Book Foundation, Bristol, England, 2003. Pages 289 and 290.

[50] Surah 60, Al Mumtahanah, ayaat 8-9: *Allah does not forbid you to be kind and equitable to those who have neither made war on your religion nor have driven you from your homes. Allah loves the equitable. Allah only forbids you to make friends with those who fought against you on account of your religion and driven you from your homes or abetted others to do so. Those who make friends with them are wrongdoers.*

Verse 123 of Surah 9, At Taubah states: *O you who believe! Fight those of the disbelievers who are near to you, and let them find firmness in you, and know that God is with those who keep their duty to Him.* This too must be understood in the appropriate historical context. The Byzantine Christians in Syria to the north, in collusion with the pre-Islamic Persians who were occupying the territories that constitute the present day Iraq, had started an insurgency against the new Muslim State and also incited the non-Muslim Arab tribes living in bordering areas. This Divine directive has to be understood in that light, meaning that it applied to those people and under those existing circumstances and refers to the Tabuk Expedition (9 AH).

Surah 2, Al Baqarah, ayat 191 states: *Kill them wherever you find them...* This is just one part of the verse. It refers to *...those who fight against you...* and the verse continues: *...and drive them out of the places from which they drove you, for tumult and persecution are worse than killing.*

While Islam permits warfare, it is not encouraged. Prophet Muhammad ﷺ did not like war. He called it deceit and urged Muslims to seek peace and security through prayer rather than engaging in war.[51] His mission was that of guidance and mercy and not that of war and destruction: *(O Muhammad!) We have only sent you as a Mercy for all worlds* (Surah 21, Al Anbiya', ayat 107).

For additional information, the reader is referred to a paper by Dr. Jamal Badawi: Muslim and non-Muslim Relations. Reflections on Some Quranic Texts.[52]

Concluding Commentary

O you who believe! Bow down and prostrate yourselves, and worship your Lord, and do good, that perhaps you may prosper. And strive for Allah with the endeavour which is His right. He has chosen you and has not laid upon you in religion any hardship; the faith of your father Abraham.

---

[51] The Translation of the Meanings of Sahih Al-Bukhari. MM Khan, Kazi Publications, Lahore, Pakistan, 1979. Volume IV, Hadith 268, page 167.

[52] http://www.islamawareness.net/MusChristRelations/reflections.html
Last accessed April 2011.

*He named you Muslims previously and in this Scripture, that the
Messenger may be a witness against you, and that you may be witnesses
against mankind. So establish the prayers, pay the zakat, and hold fast to
Allah. He is your protecting Friend. An excellent Protector and an
excellent Helper!*   (Surah 22, Al Haj, ayaat 77-78)

Islam is a perfectly balanced, well-organized and beautiful way of life,
providing both contentment in the present life and the keys to eternal
happiness. It is what the Creator intended for all of us. It is by no
means a complicated faith or difficult to follow.

A man once came to Prophet Muhammad ﷺ and inquired about
Islam. The Prophet ﷺ said:[53]

*You have to offer prayers perfectly five times in a day and night
(twenty-four hours).* The man asked: Is there any more (praying)?
The Prophet ﷺ replied: *No, but if you want to offer the nawafil (non-
obligatory) prayers (you can).*

The Prophet ﷺ then said: *You have to observe fasts during the month
of Ramadan.* The man asked: Is there any more fasting? The Prophet
ﷺ replied: *No, but if you want to observe the nawafil (non-obligatory)
fasts (you can).*

Then the Prophet ﷺ said to him: *You have to pay the Zakat (obligatory
charity).* The man asked: Is there anything other than the Zakat for
me to pay? The Prophet ﷺ replied: *No, unless you want to give alms of
your own.* And then that man went away saying: By Allah! I will
neither do less nor more than this. The Prophet ﷺ said: *If what he
said is true, then he will be successful (i.e., he will be granted Paradise).*

Reflecting upon the following verses from the Qur'an will provide
additional glimpses of the message of Islam.

O you who believe! Fulfill your undertakings!
                    (Surah 5, Al Ma'idah, ayat 1)

*... Establish worship and enjoin kindness and forbid iniquity, and
persevere whatever may befall you ...* (Surah 31, Luqman, ayat 17)

---

[53] The Translation of the Meanings of Sahih Al-Bukhari. MM Khan, Kazi Publications,
Lahore, Pakistan, 1979. Volume I, Hadith 44, page 39.

Give to the near of kin their due, and the needy and the wayfarer and do not squander your wealth wastefully.

(Surah 17, Al Isra', ayat 26)

Surely, this Qur'an guides to that which is most right, and gives good tidings to the believers who do good works that theirs will be a great reward.   (Surah 17, Al Isra', ayat 9)

It is reported from Abu Dawud that there are four authentic Hadith from the Messenger of God, Muhammad ﷺ that are sufficient for a Muslim to follow his religion. These are:[54]

- The reward of the deeds depends upon the intentions [55]
- Indeed among the excellence of a person's Islam is that he leaves what does not concern him [56]
- None of you will have faith till he wishes for his (Muslim) brother what he likes for himself [57]
- That which is lawful is clear and that which is unlawful is clear, and between them are matters which are unclear which many people do not understand. Whoever guards against the unclear matters, he will protect his religion and his honour, but whoever falls into that which is unclear, he will soon fall into that which is unlawful [58]

---

[54] Sunan Abu Dawud. English Translation with Explanatory Notes. Kitab Bhavan, New Delhi, 1997. Volume 1, pages iii-x. Introduction.

[55] The Translation of the Meanings of Sahih Al-Bukhari. MM Khan, Kazi Publications, Lahore, Pakistan, 1979. Volume 1, Hadith 1, page 1

[56] English Translation of Jami At-Tirmidhi, Darussalam, Riyadh, S Arabia, 2007. Volume 4, Hadith 2317, page 352.

[57] The Translation of the Meanings of Sahih Al-Bukhari. MM Khan, Kazi Publications, Lahore, Pakistan, 1979. Volume 1, Hadith 12, page 19.

[58] English Translation of Sahih Muslim. Darussalam, Riyadh, S Arabia, 2007. Volume 4, Hadith 4094, page 320.

Chapter Two

ALLAH سبحانه وتعالى

Allah is the light of the heavens and the earth. The similitude of His Light is as a niche wherein is a lamp. The lamp is in a glass. The glass is as it were a shining star. This lamp is kindled from a blessed tree, an olive neither of the East nor of the West, whose oil would almost glow forth (of itself) though no fire touched it. Light upon light, Allah guides to His Light whom He will. And Allah speaks to mankind in allegories, and Allah is Knower of all things.   (Surah 24, An Nur, ayat 35)

The Concept of God

Throughout ages, out of admiration or fear, man has needed a deity for worship. The deity was assigned different forms because it was, and often still remains, difficult to imagine the existence of an All-Powerful yet unseen Being. The idols, figurines and icons used as representations are creations of the human mind and products of human hands. An All-Powerful God, the Creator of everything that exists, the Object of worship, can hardly be represented by human imagination and artisanship.

Islam provokes logical reasoning by challenging the mind to think and contemplate. Something as magnificent and awe-inspiring as the universe and all the wonders of creation that are known to man can only be the creation of One more magnificent and more powerful than the creation itself. This most powerful Creator simply cannot be conceptualized in human terms.

This All-Powerful, All-Capable Source of all creation is Allah, the One and only God. Allah is not only *the Muslim God* or *God of the Muslims*. This is the Name of the One God of all of mankind, the God of Adam, Noah, Abraham, Ishmael, Issac, Moses, Jesus, and Muhammad (peace be upon them all) and of all of creation, without exception, from the very beginning to the end of time.[1]

The Name

The name Allah predates the Islamic period. Arab Christians and Jews also used this name for God. Allah is the name God has given Himself: *Say, He is Allah, the One. Allah, the Eternal.* (Surah 112, Al Ikhlas, ayaat 1-2).

Over the course of time, pursuant to the quest for a physical form to which man could relate, this name was assigned to various deities, including a moon deity. The assignment of a physical form to Allah is solely the figment of human imagination. The desire for God to be or be represented by a physically identifiable deity may indicate a particular form or level of spirituality. Fundamental to Islam is the belief in the unseen and God is a part of that unseen.

The name Allah is synonymous with God. Therefore, in the following and elsewhere in this book, these are used interchangeably to mean one and the same.

The Being

We may not speculate about the Divine form and nature based upon our own reasoning because we are unable to comprehend any aspect of it, other than what God has already disclosed. Similarly, we may not form a mental image of God as it is no different from a painting, wood or stone carving, etc., which simply represents human imagination.

In Muslim belief, God is unique and nothing in the entire creation can be compared with Him. Only He knows Himself and only He can

---

[1] *rabbal alameen* - Lord of the worlds, of the universe, Surah 1, Al Fateha, ayat 1.

describe Himself. His Being is not visible in this world, yet we know Him through His creations, through the descriptions and *attributes* found throughout the Qur'an. While no one will see God in this life, the believers will be able to see Him in the Hereafter. In the following are a few verses from the Qur'an in which God describes Himself.

Say, He is Allah, the One! Allah the Eternal, He was not born, nor does He have offspring and there is none comparable to Him.

(Surah 112, Al Ikhlas, ayaat 1-4)

Allah, there is no God besides Him, the Living, the Self-Existing. Neither slumber nor sleep overtakes Him. His are all things in the heavens and on earth. Who can intercede with Him except by His permission? He knows what is before them (His creatures) and what lies behind them, while they can grasp only that part of His knowledge which He will. His authority extends over the heavens and earth, and it does not tire Him to guard and preserve them both. For He is the Most High, the Tremendous.   (Surah 2, Al Baqarah, ayat 255)[2]

Allah, There is no God but Him, the Living, the Self-Existing. He has sent down to you (Muhammad) the Book (the Qur'an) which has brought the Truth, confirming that which preceded it, and He sent down the Taurat (Torah) and the Injeel (Gospel)[3] before this, as a guidance to mankind; and He sent down the Criterion (of distinguishing between right and wrong, ie., the Qur'an). Those who disbelieve in the signs of Allah shall receive a severe punishment; and Allah is Mighty, Able to Requite.

(Surah 3, 'Al Imraan, ayaat 2-4)

---

[2] This verse is also known as *ayat ul Kursi*. The Arabic word *kursi*, which means chair, is used figuratively to express authority. Maududi SAA, The Meaning of the Qur'an. Islamic Publications Ltd., Lahore, Pakistan, 1978. Volume 1, page 185.

[3] The *Taurat* mentioned in the Qur'an refers to the original Commandments and Injunctions given to Moses ﷺ. The last remaining copy was lost with the destruction of Jerusalem and the Temple of Solomon ﷺ. Thus, *Taurat* in the Qur'an is not the Pentateuch of the Old Testament as we know it today, but the original commandments are contained in the latter. Similarly, *Injeel* (Gospel) does not refer to the Books of Gospel as we know them today. The *Injeel* mentioned in the Qur'an is contained therein. Maududi SAA. The Meaning of the Qur'an. Islamic Publications Ltd., Lahore, Pakistan, 1976. Volume 2, pages 9-14.

And to Allah belongs all that is in the heavens and all that is in the earth. And Allah is ever encompassing all things.

(Surah 4, An Nisa', ayat 126)

He is Allah, besides whom there is no other god, the Knower of the invisible and the visible. He is the Compassionate, the Merciful.
He is Allah, besides whom there is no other god, the Sovereign Lord, the Holy One, the Source of Security, the Keeper of Faith, the Guardian, the All-Mighty, the Compeller, the Superb. Glorified be Allah above the partners they ascribe to Him. He is Allah, the Creator, the Originator, the Fashioner. His are the most beautiful Names. All that is in the heavens and the earth glorifies Him, and He is the Mighty, the Wise.

(Surah 59, Al Hashr, ayaat 22-24)

Was man created in the Image of God?

According to Christian and Jewish belief *God created man in his own image.*[4] It follows that God would resemble a human being. According to Muslim belief, mankind has absolutely no clue of God's image. It is stated in the Qur'an: *...There is nothing like Him...*[5] and *Vision cannot comprehend Him, but He comprehends all vision...*[6]

In a Hadith, Prophet Muhammad ﷺ said: *God created Adam in his own image...*[7] The emphasis is on *his own image,* meaning that Adam and all subsequent generations of humans were endowed with an identifying image of their own. Occasionally, the Arabic text is erroneously translated as stating *His* image, implying God's image. If understood metaphorically, it could mean that man was endowed with some qualities which resemble the Divine, but not the physical image of God.

---

[4] Genesis 1:27 (King James Version): *So God created man in his own image, in the image of God created he him; male and female created he them.*

[5] This is how God describes Himself in Surah 42, Ash Shura, ayat 11.

[6] Surah 6, Al An'aam, ayat 103.

[7] Reported by Muslim. Al-Ahadith Al-Qudsiyyah. Translated by AK Kazi and AB Day. Dar al-Iman, Tripoli, Lebanon, 1996. Hadith 31, page 61.

Will anyone be able to see God?

No human has ever seen God and no one will see Him before the Day of Judgment. A Hadith Qudsi states: ...*no living person can see Me without dying...*,[8] meaning that nothing will survive the impact of seeing God. The only persons who will be able to see God are those who are granted Paradise by virtue of their conduct on earth.[9] The Hadith Qudsi further states: ...*the people of Paradise will see Me. These are the ones whose eyes do not die and whose bodies do not wither.*

God revealed a token of His Being to Moses ﷺ. That impact made Moses ﷺ unconscious (Surah 7, Al A'raaf, ayat 143). God also spoke to Moses ﷺ without revealing His Image. Similarly, God communicated with His other Messengers without revealing His Image.[10] Prophet Muhammad ﷺ was privileged to be in the presence of God during the Night Journey (Isra' and Miraj) but he never saw Him. When asked, the Prophet ﷺ replied that he saw light.[11] In this context, light can have several meanings. The physical phenomenon of light representing the *veil of God,* or as an attribute of God, meaning the One by whom everything is made visible or illuminated, ie., the One who brings the believer out of the darkness of ignorance and disbelief and into the light of knowledge and truth.[12]

Use of the pronoun We

In many verses of the Qur'an, God has used the pronoun *We.* This may give rise to confusion in some minds as to why God uses the plural form when He is only One. The Arabic of the Qur'an is a regularly spoken language and the use of *We* instead of *I* is simply a

---

[8] Reported by Al Hakim. Al-Ahadith Al-Qudsiyyah. Translated by AK Kazi and AB Day. Dar al-Iman, Tripoli, Lebanon, 1996. Hadith 157, page 272.

[9] Sahih Muslim. M Matraji. Darul-Isha'at, Karachi, Pakistan, 1998. Volume I-A, Hadith 181 and 181R1, page 255.

[10] Surah 42, Ash Shura, ayat 51: *And it is not given to any mortal that Allah should speak to him unless it be by revelation or from behind a veil, or that He sends a messenger (an angel) who, by His Command, reveals whatever He wills. He is Exalted, Wise.*

[11] Sahih Muslim. M Matraji. Darul-Isha'at, Karachi, Pakistan, 1998. Volume I-A, Hadith 177, page 247-248 and Hadith 178, page 251.

[12] Surah 2, Al Baqarah: ayat 257: ...*He brings them out from darkness into light. As for those who disbelieve, their supporters (and helpers) are false deities. They bring them out of light into darkness...*

linguistic peculiarity.[13] It is a form of speaking that is not only common in Arabic but also in English and most other languages. There is nothing in the Qur'an or the Hadith which contradicts that there is only One God. While some verses use the plural form, others unequivocally state that God is One: *Say, He is Allah, the One!* (Surah 112, Al Ikhlas, ayat 1), *Truly, your Lord is One...* (Surah 37, As Saffat, ayat 4).

Where is Allah ?

It is a common notion shared by many religions that God is in heaven. The definition of heaven is vague. Is it a physical space in the skies above the earth or is it Paradise whose location we do not know? How can God be contained in something He has created, ie., the universe, physical space and time and also controls everything that exists in it?

In Islamic belief God is Omnipresent, and by His very nature, He cannot be confined to any physical space or dimension. He is with us wherever we are, by virtue of His Knowledge, and knows of every thought that occurs in our minds and every action we take though we may not appreciate His Divine presence. The heavens and endless outer space are dwarfed by the magnificence of the Almighty.

And they have not esteemed Allah as He has the right to be esteemed; when the whole earth is His handful on the Day of Resurrection and the heavens are rolled in His right hand. Glory to Him! And High is He above all that they ascribe to Him as partners. (Surah 39, Az-Zumar, ayat 67)

Purpose of Creation

Mankind was created for the sole purpose of worshipping the Creator: *I created the jinn and humans only that they should worship Me* (Surah 51, Ad Dhariyat, ayat 56). Everything in nature is subservient to God. With the exception of humans and Jinns, everything follows, without choice and unquestioningly, the laws of nature which were

---

[13] Surah 26, Ash Shu'ara, ayat 192-195: *And verily it is a revelation of the Lord of the Worlds, which the True Spirit (Angel Gabriel) has brought down upon your heart, that you may be one of the warners, in plain Arabic speech.*

put into place by God. Since humans and Jinns were given a choice, they are also subject to accountability. Each person is accountable only for his/her own actions: ...*No soul will bear the burden of another*... (Surah 39, Az Zumar, ayat 7).

Attributes of God

Knowledge about God comes from the Qur'an and the Hadith of Prophet Muhammad ﷺ. In many verses of the Qur'an, God disclosed some aspects of His Being and His Attributes. Also commonly known as the *Names of Allah*, these attributes define for mankind some of the Divine characteristics. Some of these attributes are listed below together with the English translations. The translation, consisting of one or more words, does not do justice to the actual meaning and implication of the attribute. Therefore, the interested reader is referred to other texts to gain a better understanding.[14]

In addition to providing these attributes, God encourages the use of the senses and reasoning to enhance our knowledge of Him. Muslims are encouraged to learn these attributes. For the individual, they serve several purposes. Firstly, God has commanded that the suppliant call Him by these Names when seeking help. Secondly, Muslims are encouraged to behave in a fashion that would resemble these attributes, eg., by showing compassion, generosity and kindness, by being forgiving and loving, helping others, being truthful, honest, just and fair in all dealings, showing patience, etc. This was precisely what Prophet Muhammad ﷺ did. Practicing his example guides to the middle path, which is the true spirit of Islam.

Attribute	**Translation and Meaning**
Ar Rahman	The Beneficent, The Compassionate, The Infinitely Good
Ar Raheem	The Most Merciful
Al Salaam	The Source of Peace, The Flawless, free from all defects

---

[14] Al-Ghazali. The Ninety-nine Beautiful Names of God. Translated with Notes by DB Burrell and N Daher. The Islamic Texts Society, Cambridge, UK, 1999.

Al Azeez	The Mighty, The Eminent
Al Khaliq	The Creator
Al Musawwir	The Fashioner, arranges in finest detail the form of things created
Al Ghaffar	The Continually Forgiving, He who is full of forgiveness
Al 'Alim	The All-Knowing, comprehends every thing by knowing every aspect of it
Al Hakam	The Indisputable Judge, The Arbitrator, no one corrects or overturns His ruling or decree
Al Adl	The Just, just action emanates from Him
Al Lateef	The Subtle, The Benevolent, The Most Gracious
Al Khabir	The Totally Aware, aware of everything, no secret is hidden from Him
Ash Shakoor	The Appreciative, The Grateful, One who gives manifold reward for good deeds
Al Kareem	The Generous
Al Mujeeb	The Responsive, Answerer of prayers
Al Hakeem	The Wise
Al Wadood	The Loving, who wishes well for all creatures
Ash Shaheed	The Witness, Knower of the visible and invisible
Al Wakeel	The Trustee,
Al Waliyy	The Protecting Friend, Patron
Al Hayy	The Living
Al Qayyum	The Self-Subsisting, Self-Existing
Al Wahid	The One, The Unique, One who can neither be divided or duplicated
Al Samad	The Eternal, to whom one turns in need, The One who depends on none and all others depend upon Him
Al Awwal	The First
Al Akhir	The Last
At Tawwab	The Ever-Relenting, Acceptor of repentance
Ar Ra'oof	The Full of pity
Maalik ul Mulk	King of absolute Sovereignty

Zul Jalaali wal Ikram	Lord of Majesty and Bounty (Generosity)
An Nur (Noor)	The Light, One by whom everything is made visible
Al Baqi	The Everlasting, Forever
As Saboor	The Patient, One who has patience
	The Most Forbearing

Concluding Commentary

Your God is One God. There is no god besides Him, He is the Compassionate, the Merciful. (Surah 2, Al Baqarah, ayat 163)

And your Lord has decreed that you worship none but Him... (Surah 17, Al Isra', ayat 23)

Allah! There is no God save Him. He will gather you all to a Day of Resurrection about which there is no doubt. (Surah 4, An Nisa', ayat 87)

In Islam, love, respect and obedience to God take precedence over all other matters. Prophet Muhammad ﷺ said: *Worship Allah as if you see Him. Although you do not see Him, indeed He sees you...*[15] This advice also applies to every other deed of a person who has accepted Islam as the way of life. Since nothing is ever hidden from God, the believer takes precaution to avoid everything (from thoughts, speech to actions) that could incur God's displeasure.

Fundamental to Islam is the belief in the *ghaib* (the invisible or unseen).[16] God cannot be understood in terms of human knowledge or logic, and in this respect, it is often the cardinal shortcoming of human intelligence that a recognizable form must be available in order

---

[15] Recorded by Tabarani. Muntakhab Ahadith. Kandhlavi MY, Annayyar, Karachi, Pakistan. Hadith 226, page 219.

[16] While *ghaib* is frequently translated as meaning "the unseen", its meaning and implications are far greater when applying this term to God and His Creations. God is a part of this unseen and He alone knows its details: *...the Knower of the invisible and the visible...* (Surah 59, Al Hashr, ayat 22); *He (alone) knows the unseen, and does not reveal to anyone His secret...* (Surah 72, Al Jinn, ayat 26).

for man to be able to relate. Such an object then represents God's image or His Power and Ability. In Islamic Belief, the assignment of any kind of image, partner, associate, offspring or co-authority, is equivalent to belittling the Majesty of God and is strictly forbidden.

The All-Powerful and All-Mighty God, is directly accessible to all, irrespective of their religious affiliation. While humans make the distinction, Allah listens to and provides for all His creatures, including those who do not believe in Him: ...*I answer the prayer of the suppliant when he calls to Me...* (Surah 2, Al Baqarah, ayat 186). However, a person gets only that which he/she seeks: *I am as My servant thinks of Me...*[17]

Allah is the Protector of those who believe. He brings them out from
darkness into light. As for those who disbelieve, their supporters
(and helpers) are false deities. They bring them out of light into
darkness. Such are the dwellers of the Fire. They will abide therein
forever. (Surah 2, Al Baqarah, ayat 257)

Say (O Muhammad): Call on those whom you assume to be deities
besides Him. They have no power to rid you of misfortune nor to
change it. Those to whom they call seek (for themselves) means of
access to their Lord, as to which of them shall be the nearest; and
they hope for His mercy and fear His wrath. For the wrath of your
Lord is something to be dreaded!
(Surah 17, Al Isra', ayaat 56-57)

---

[17] Recorded by At Tabarani. Al-Ahadith Al-Qudsiyyah. Translated by AK Kazi and AB Day. Dar al-Iman, Tripoli, Lebanon, 1996. Hadith 61, page 230.

Chapter Three

Muhammad ﷺ

Introduction

God is the Light which brings the believer out of darkness and Prophet Muhammad ﷺ is the guide to that Source of Light. Muhammad ﷺ was the last of the prophets sent by God. He was a man of unreproachable character, of exemplary compassion, integrity, sincerity, humbleness, honesty and patience. These and other noble qualities earned him the title of *the truthful and the trustworthy* (*as sadiq al amin*) long before the prophethood.

The Prayer of Abraham ﷺ

Prophet Abraham ﷺ brought his wife Hagar (Hajar) and their infant son Ishmael to the uninhabited desert valley of Makkah in Arabia, in compliance with the instruction he had received from God. Before he returned home, Abraham ﷺ made a prayer:

> ﷺ ... *My Lord make this a region of peace and bestow fruits upon those of its people who believe in Allah and the Last Day. He answered: As for those who disbelieve, I shall leave them in contentment for a while, then I shall compel them to the punishment of the fire, and that is the worst abode.* (Surah 2, Al Baqarah, ayat 126)

Many years later, Abraham ﷺ returned to the place where he had left them, and together with his son Ishmael (peace be upon them), they rebuilt the Ka'ba.

> And when Abraham and Ishmael were raising the foundations of the House, they prayed: Our Lord, Accept from us this act. You are indeed the All-Hearing, the All-Knowing.
> Our Lord! and make us submissive to You and of our seed a nation submissive to You, and show us our ways of worship, and relent towards us. You are indeed the Forgiving, the Merciful.
> Our Lord, And "raise up from among them a messenger" who shall recite Your revelations to them and shall teach them the Scriptures and the wisdom, and shall purify them. You are the Powerful, the Wise.[1]
>> (Surah 2, Al Baqarah, ayaat 127-129)

Prophet Muhammad ﷺ was the answer to that prayer of Prophet Abraham ﷺ. He said:

> I was the seal of the prophets, in Allah's knowledge, even when Adam was being kneaded from his clay. I can inform you of its preludes:
> The prayer of Abraham, the glad tidings Jesus gave of me and the vision which my mother had of me. Likewise, all mothers of prophets had visions of them.[2]

His ﷺ Name

Muhammad means *highly praised*. In pre-Islamic Arabia, it was an uncommon name. This name was chosen by his grandfather, Abd al-Muttalib. When asked why he had chosen such an unusual name for his orphaned grandson, Abd al-Muttalib answered: *Because I wanted God to praise him in heaven and His creatures to praise him on earth.*[3] He was named Ahmad (*the praised one*) by his mother Amina.

---

[1] emphasis added.
[2] Tafsir Ibn Kathir. Al-Firdous Ltd, London, England, 1998. Part I, page 252.
[3] Ibn Kathir, Al Sira al Nabawiyya. The Life of the Prophet Muhammad ﷺ. Garnet Publishing, Reading, UK, 1998. Volume I, page 150.

The Biblical Prophesies

The coming of Prophet Muhammad ﷺ was foretold in previous Scriptures. Below are a few verses from the Qur'an and passages from the Old and New Testaments which contain these prophesies. The correct interpretation of the prophesies and the recognition of their fulfillment will benefit those who sincerely and open-mindedly seek the truth.

From the Qur'an

And when Jesus, son of Mary said: O Children of Israel , I am the Messenger of Allah to you, confirming that which was revealed before me in the Torah, and bringing good tidings of a messenger who will come after me, whose name is Ahmad.[4] Yet when he has come to them with clear proofs, they say: This is mere magic.

(Surah 61, As Saff, ayat 6)

Those who follow the messenger, the Prophet who can neither read nor write, whom they find described in the Torah and the Gospel which are with them. He will enjoin on them that which is right and forbid them that which is wrong. He will make lawful for them all good things and prohibit for them only the foul; and he will relieve them of their burden and the fetters that they used to wear. Then those who believe in him, and honour him, and help him, and follow the light which is sent down with him; they are the successful.   (Surah 7, Al A'raaf, ayat 157)

O people of the Scripture! Now Our messenger has come to you making things plain, after an interval (between) messengers, lest you should say: There came not to us a messenger of glad tidings nor any warner. Now has a bringer of glad tidings and a warner come to you. And Allah is Able to do all things.   (Surah 5, Al Ma'idah, ayat 19)

From the Old Testament

The LORD thy God will raise up unto thee a Prophet from the midst of thee, of thy brethren, like unto me; unto him ye shall hearken;

(Deutronomy 18, verse 15, KJV 2000)[5]

---

[4] The praised one.

[5] KJV: King James Version.

I will raise them up a Prophet from among their brethren, like unto thee, and will put my words in his mouth; and he shall speak unto them all that I shall command him.   (Deutronomy 18, verse 18, KJV 2000)

And this is the blessing, wherewith Moses the man of God blessed the children of Israel before his death.
And he said, The LORD came from Sinai, and rose up from Se'ir unto them; He shined forth from mount Paran, and He came with ten thousands of saints: from his right hand went a fiery law for them.
          (Deutronomy 33, verse 1-2, KJV 2000)

And there arose not a prophet since in Israel like unto Moses, whom the LORD knew face to face.   (Deutronomy 34, verse 10, KJV 2000)[6]

The sceptre shall not depart from Judah, nor a lawgiver from between his feet, until Shiloh come; and unto him shall the gathering of the people be.
          (Genesis 49, verse 10, KJV)

The stone which the builders refused is become the head stone of the corner. This is the LORD's doing; it is marvelous in our eyes.
          (Psalm 118, verses 22-23, KJV)

From the New Testament
And I will pray the Father, and he shall give you another Comforter that he may be with you for ever.   (John 14, verse 16)[7]

When the Counselor has come, whom I will send to you from the Father, the Spirit of truth, who proceeds from the Father, he will testify about me.
          (John 15, verse 26, World English Bible)

... for if I don't go away, the Counselor won't come to you. But if I go, I will send him to you. When he has come, he will convict the world

---

[6] New American Bible, 1991: *Since then no prophet has arisen in Israel like Moses, whom the LORD knew face to face.*
New American Standard Bible: *Since that time no prophet has risen in Israel like Moses, whom the LORD knew face to face.*

[7] English Revised Version. The Douay-Rheims Bible reads *...another Paraclete.*
http://bible.cc/john/14-16.htm Last accessed May 2011.

about sin, about righteousness and about judgement;
(John 16, verses 7-8)

However, when he, the Spirit of truth, has come, he will guide you into all truth, for he will not speak from himself; but whatever he hears, he will speak. He will declare to you things that are coming. He will glorify me, for he will take from what is mine, and will declare it to you.
(John 16, verses 13-14)

I indeed baptize you with water unto repentance, but He who is coming after me is mightier than I, whose sandals I am not worthy to carry. He will baptize you with the Holy spirit and fire.
(Matthew 3, verse 11, NKJV)[8]

Jesus saith unto them, Did ye never read in the scriptures, The stone which the builders rejected, the same is become the head of the corner: this is the Lord's doing, and it is marvelous in our eyes? Therefore say I unto you, The kingdom of God shall be taken from you, and given to a nation bringing forth the fruits thereof. And whosoever shall fall on this stone shall be broken: but on whomsoever it shall fall, it will grind him to powder.
(Matthew 21, verses 42-44)

Analysis and Comments on Biblical Prophesies in Light of the Qur'anic Verses and Hadith

Although there may be arguments to the contrary, a logical interpretation of these Biblical prophesies leaves little doubt that both Moses and Jesus (peace be upon them) foretold the coming of Prophet Muhammad ﷺ. Since this is intended only as a brief discussion, other prophesies found in the Bible will not be addressed. The interested reader is referred to the book *Prophesies of the Prophets*.[9]

For an explanation of the terms *Paran, Spirit of truth, Shiloh* and *Paraclete*, we may have no alternative but to rely upon the translations and explanations provided in the present editions of the Judeo-

---

[8] NKJV: New King James Version.

[9] Prophesies of the Prophets. English Translation of *Bashaa i run Nabiyeen* by Hafiz MI Kandhlavi. Maktaba Yaqeen, Darut Tasnif Ltd., Karachi, Pakistan.

Christian Scriptures. The original words spoken by Moses and Jesus (peace be upon them) may never be known to us. The language spoken by Jesus ﷺ and his followers was Aramaic. His words may have been written down but no authentic records exist. The first writings of his sayings were in Greek and Hebrew and were later translated from Greek into other languages. In contrast, the Qur'an, the actual Words of God, and the Hadith, the words spoken by the last Messenger of God, were preserved in their Arabic original. To extract the exact meanings and understand the context in which the Qur'anic verses were revealed or what Prophet Muhammad ﷺ said, one can refer to the original text in Arabic. That is not possible for the Biblical passages as one can only refer back to non-Aramaic texts.

From the Qur'an, there is ample awareness that some of the meanings or the emphasis of the original may be lost in translation. Additionally, a translation often includes some bias of the translator, ie., his/her understanding of the meaning of the original text as well as use of the vernacular of the language into which the original is being translated. The latter is frequently unavoidable, if an understanding of the text is to be communicated. A second translation from the first increases the unintended biases.

For discussion of Biblical prophesies and the understanding of their implications, the following need some elaboration: the geographic location of *Paran,* the place where Ishmael ﷺ grew up, and the identity of the *Spirit of truth, Comfortor, Paraclete, Shiloh,* or *Counselor.*

Background

Prophet Abraham ﷺ is considered the father of the Monotheistic Faiths, ie., of those who believe in One God (Jews, Christians and Muslims). Abraham ﷺ had two sons, the brothers Ishmael ﷺ (from his second wife Hagar) and Isaac ﷺ (from his first wife Sarah). Moses and Jesus (peace be upon them) were from the offspring of his second son, Isaac ﷺ. There was only one known prophet from the offspring of Ishmael ﷺ, the older son of Abraham ﷺ, and that was Prophet Muhammad ﷺ.

Paran

The true location of *Paran* is not known from the Biblical sources, although it is referred to as being in the region of the Sinai peninsula of the present day Egypt. The Biblical texts refer to it as *The Wilderness of Paran, Desert of Paran* and *Mount Paran.* All three descriptions, taken separately or together, fit the geography of Makkah (Arabia) and its immediate surroundings. Additionally, Prophet Abraham's ﷺ second wife Hagar and their son Ishmael ﷺ were relocated to the *wilderness of Paran,* and that is where Ishmael ﷺ grew up: *And he dwelt in the wilderness of Paran;* (Genesis 21, verse 21).

From the Hadith, it is known that Ishmael ﷺ and Hagar were brought to the valley of Makkah.[10] Thus, both sources seem to suggest that *Paran* refers to the present day location of Makkah. In addition, the Bible and Hadith describe the spring from which Hagar and Ishmael (peace be upon them) got water. To this date, that spring remains a source of water for pilgrims. It is called *zamzam* and is located near the Ka'ba, in Makkah. The hillocks *Safa* and *Marwa,* from where Hagar searched the surroundings for help, are also located close to the *zamzam* spring. Although it was remote from other human habitation (*wilderness of Paran*), this place was on a well established caravan route.

Paraclete, Comfortor, Counselor

There is debate about the term *paraclete* (or its translated meanings) which is said to have been used by Jesus ﷺ. One must bear in mind that Jesus ﷺ spoke Palestinian Aramaic and not Greek, and the English translations of today's Bibles refer back to the Greek *original.* We will never know whether Jesus ﷺ used the Aramaic word with the meaning *periklutos or parakletos* and it is also immaterial.

Periklutos is translated as meaning *praised one, one who praises most, praiseworthy, admired one* or *glorified one. Parakletos* is translated as meaning *one who intercedes on someone's behalf, an advocate, counselor, one called to help alongside, helper, one who consoles, or comfortor.* In the various versions of the Bible it is translated as comfortor (comforter), counselor, helper, monitor, encourager, instructor and advocate. Paraclete is used in the Douay-Rheims Bible.

---

[10] This is detailed in a lengthy Hadith. The Translation of the Meanings of Sahih Al-Bukhari. MM Khan. Kazi Publications, Lahore, Pakistan, 1979. Volume IV, Hadith 583, pages 372-379.

Spirit of truth

When the Counselor has come, whom I will send to you from the Father, the Spirit of truth, who proceeds from the Father, he will testify about me.

(John 15, verse 26, World English Bible)

However, when he, the Spirit of truth, has come, he will guide you into all truth, for he will not speak from himself; but whatever he hears, he will speak. He will declare to you things that are coming.

(John 16, verse 13)

From these verses, it is evident that the *Counselor* refers to the same as the *Spirit of truth,* and by that Jesus ﷺ was clearly referring to *a person* other than himself, someone who was to come after he left.[11,12]

Understanding the Meaning of what Jesus ﷺ said

Arguments over whether Jesus ﷺ said *periklutos* or *parakletos* are essentially futile since these are over the meanings of a translated word (from Palestinian Aramaic into Greek) written down many decades after it was spoken. What is more important, and also more relevant, is the message he wanted to convey to his listeners. Interestingly, the message comes out to be identical for both these words and points squarely in the direction of Prophet Muhammad ﷺ.

If indeed Jesus ﷺ used the word *periklutos*, it is identical to the meanings of the Arabic names of Prophet Muhammad ﷺ, namely, Ahmad and Muhammad (praiseworthy, highly praised). In addition, it is reflective of his status as the Final Messenger of God, his character and life style (*admired one* or *glorified one*). He was constantly engaged in the remembrance of God and was thankful for all His blessings (*one who praises most*). When asked why he was engaged in such exceptionally intensive voluntary devotion, Prophet Muhammad ﷺ replied: *When Allah ﷻ has blessed me so much, should I not be a grateful*

---

[11] http://bible.cc/john/14-16.htm Matthew Henry's Concise Commentary 14:12-17. Last accessed May 2011.

[12] English Revised Version: *And I will pray the Father, and he shall give you another Comforter, that he may be with you for ever.*
http://erv.scripturetext.com/john/14.htm Last accessed May 2011.
Weymouth New Testament: *And I will ask the Father, and He will give you another Advocate to be for ever with you—the Spirit of truth.*
http://weymouthbible.com/john/14.htm Last accessed May 2011.

servant?[13]

However, if Jesus ﷺ used the word *parakletos,* as asserted in some Christian literature, the qualities conveyed hereby are some of the very attributes which describe Prophet Muhammad ﷺ. Briefly, he is the only prophet who has been granted the right to intercession for the believers on the Day of Judgement (*one who intercedes on someone's behalf*).[14] He championed the rights of the poor, women, children, animals and environment (*an advocate*). (Also see Chapter 12, Human, Environmental, Animal and Other's Rights) He was a counselor for perfection in the worship of God, for doing good deeds and eliminating evil. A helper, comfortor and consoler for all of humanity: *...is grievous, full of concern for you, for the believers full of compassion, merciful* (Surah 9, At Taubah, ayat 128); *And We have only sent you as a mercy for all worlds* (Surah 21, Al Anbiya', ayat 107).

Analysis of the Biblical Prophesies

Deutronomy 18, verse 15 states: *...will raise up unto **thee** a Prophet from the midst of **thee**, of **thy** brethren, like unto me;...* and Deutronomy 18, verse 18 states: *I will raise **them** up a Prophet from among **their** brethren, like unto thee,...*[15] These verses clearly refer to two distinct nations, ie., from the two sons of Abraham, Ishmael and Isaac (peace be upon them all). Verse 15 refers to a prophet from the descendants of Moses ﷺ, an Israelite, while verse 18 clearly refers to a prophet from a nation other than that of Moses ﷺ. After Abraham ﷺ, all prophets were from his descendants. Since the prophet mentioned in Deutronomy 18, verse 18 excludes the descendants of Moses ﷺ, it can only be referring to the descendants of Ishmael ﷺ, ie., Prophet Muhammad ﷺ. The Qur'an confirms the fulfillment of that promise in Deutronomy 18, verse 18: *We have sent to you a messenger as witness against you, as We did send a messenger to Pharaoh* (Surah 73, Al Muzzammil, ayat 15).

Additionally, the last part of verse 18 carries a very specific message that can apply only to Prophet Muhammad ﷺ: *...and will put my words in*

---

[13] Shamaa-il Tirmidhi. Darul Ishaat, Karachi, Pakistan, 2001. Worship and Devotions of Sayyidina Rasulullah ﷺ. (248) Hadith 1, pages 269-270.

[14] The Translation of the Meanings of Sahih Al-Bukhari. MM Khan. Kazi Publications, Lahore, Pakistan. 1979. Volume VI, Hadith 3, pages 3-5.

[15] emphasis added.

his mouth; and he shall speak unto them all that I shall command him. In the Qur'an, God says about Prophet Muhammad ﷺ: *Nor does he speak of his own desire. It is no other than an inspired Revelation. Which one of mighty powers has taught him* (Surah 53, An Najm, ayaat 3-5); *...Say, I follow only that which is inspired in me from my Lord...* (Surah 7, Al A'raaf, ayat 203).

Deutronomy 33, verse 2 refers to three different prophets: *...The LORD came from Sinai,...* refers to where Moses ﷻ received the Ten Commandments; *...and rose up from Se'ir unto them;...* refers to Jesus ﷻ; *...he shined forth from mount Paran,...* refers to the prophet who came after Jesus ﷻ and received his inspiration on Mount Paran.[16] The only Prophet who came after Jesus ﷻ was Muhammad ﷺ. In addition, this verse states *...and he came with ten thousands of saints...*[17] This refers to the numerous virtuous companions of Prophet Muhammad ﷺ. He is the only prophet known to have had a large contemporaneous following of virtuous individuals (*sahabah ikram*, esteemed companions), a large number of whom undoubtedly qualify as being saintly persons.

The last part of Deutronomy 33, verse 2 states: *...from his right hand went a fiery law for them.* Only one law fits that description and that is the Islamic Shari'ah which was established by Prophet Muhammad ﷺ. The description *fiery law* aptly describes the strict Shar'iah Laws. The last word in that verse (*them*) again identifies the people who received that *fiery law* as being other than the followers of Moses and Jesus (peace be upon them).

Deutronomy 34, verse 10 states: *And there arose not a prophet since in Israel like unto Moses, whom the LORD knew face to face.* In the Monotheistic Traditions (Judaism, Christianity and Islam), there were only two prophets who are known to have been physically in the presence of God. Moses ﷻ asked to see God and was shown a token

---

[16] Prophet Muhammad ﷺ received the first Divine Revelation on *Jabal an Noor* (Mountain of Light), a small mountain outside the city of Makkah.

[17] When he returned to liberate Makkah from the pagans and rid the Ka'ba of its idols in 8 AH, Prophet Muhammad ﷺ was accompanied by ten thousand Muslims, all of whom were observing a fast. The Translation of the Meanings of Sahih Al-Bukhari. MM Khan. Kazi Publications, Lahore, Pakistan, 1979. Volume V, Hadith 574, page 400.

of His Being, ie., he came *face to face* with God.[18] The other prophet who came *face to face* with God was Prophet Muhammad ﷺ during the Isra' and Miraj. Also see Chapter 5, Isra', Miraj and Jerusalem.

Genesis 49, verse 10 states: *The sceptre shall not depart from Judah, nor a lawgiver from between his feet, until Shiloh come; and unto him shall the gathering of the people be.* This verse indicates that the prophethood (*sceptre*) was to transfer to a non-Israelite but not until the arrival of Shiloh.[19] This does not refer to Jesus ﷺ as he was an Israelite. Additionally, the *gathering of the people* would be to Shiloh. This prophesy finds confirmation in a Hadith. Prophet Muhammad ﷺ said: *I have five names. I am Muhammad. I am Ahmad. I am al-Mahi (the effacer) by whom Allah effaces disbelief. I am al-Hashir (the gatherer) before whom people are gathered. I am al-'Aqib (the last).*[20]

Psalm 118, verses 22-23 (KJV) and Matthew 21, verses 42-44 (KJV). Christian writers maintain that the *stone which the builders refused,* ie., the Jews rejected and it *become the head stone of the corner* or *become the head of the corner* refers to Jesus ﷺ. When put into context with Matthew 21, verses 43-44, it seems to be referring to a different person: *The kingdom of God shall be taken from you, and given to a nation bringing forth the fruits thereof.* The *kingdom of God* was taken away from the Israelites and given to a nation from Ishmael ﷺ.

Additionally, Matthew 21, verse 44 states: *whosoever shall fall on this stone shall be broken; but on whomsoever it shall fall, it will grind him to powder.* It cannot be referring to Jesus ﷺ because of his known gentle personality. This verse describes the fate of those who sought violent confrontation with Prophet Muhammad ﷺ and his esteemed companions. In the Qur'an, it is stated: *...and those who are with him are stern against the disbelievers and merciful among themselves* (Surah 58, Al Fath, ayat 29). At Badr (2 AH), a well equipped enemy with significant numerical advantage (three times as many soldiers) was defeated when they attacked the believers (*...whosoever shall fall on this stone shall be*

---

[18] Surah 7, Al A'raaf, ayat 143.

[19] *Shiloh* means: *he who is to be sent, the person who grants and bestows peace.*

[20] Al-Muwatta of Imam Malik ibn Anas. Madinah Press Inverness, Scotland, 2004. The Names of the Prophet ﷺ, 61.1, page 424.

broken...). Those against whom he ✹ campaigned were also destroyed (*...on whomsoever it shall fall, it will grind him to powder*). The latter includes the Makkan and other idol worshipping tribes, the Jewish tribes in and around Madinah, and the defeat of the pre-Islamic Persians, and the Byzantines in Syria and Palestine by the Prophet's ✹ successors.

Matthew 21, verse 43 states: *...The kingdom of God shall be taken from you, and given to a nation bringing forth the fruits thereof (KJB).* The following is a commentary from People's New Testament: *The kingdom was taken from the Jews and given to the chosen nation; not any particular nation, but those chosen out of the nations to be a peculiar people.*[21]

Prophesies in the Gospel of John

John 14, verse 16: *And I will pray the Father, and he will give you another Counselor,...* Instead of the term *Counselor,* some versions of the Bible use other translated meanings of the Greek original (*parakletos*), namely, comforter (*one who consoles*), advocate (*one who intercedes on our behalf*), helper (*one called to help alongside*), monitor, encourager, and instructor. Paraclete is used in the Douay-Rheims Bible. Jesus ﷺ himself may have been a counselor, comforter or paraclete, but in this verse he clearly announces the coming of *another* such person besides himself. Being concerned, kind, compassionate, gentle, merciful, etc., are qualities expected of a comforter. That is also the description in the Qur'an of the final Prophet of God: *...is grievous, full of concern for you, for the believers full of compassion, merciful* (Surah 9, At Taubah, ayat 128). *And We have only sent you as a mercy for all worlds* (Surah 21, Al Anbiya', ayat 107).

John 14, verse 16: *...to be with you for ever.* The Counselor who was to come would be with the believers forever. Additionally, he would come only after Jesus ﷺ is gone *...for if I don't go away, the Counselor won't come to you. But if I go, I will send him to you* (John 16, verse 7). The phrase *...to be with you for ever* can only refer to everlasting spiritual presence since the counselor who Jesus ﷺ was to send would be a

---

[21] http://bible.cc/matthew/21-43.htm Last accessed May 2011.

person and no human possesses immortality in this life.[22] In other words, his message and guidance would influence the conduct of the believers forever, ie., to the Day of Judgement. This applies to the teachings of Prophet Muhammad ﷺ which were meant, by design, to prepare the believers for the next life (Hereafter) by inducing consciousness of the truth and righteousness of conduct. In the Qur'an, it is stated: *Then those who believe in him, and honour him, and help him, and follow the light which is sent down with him; they are the successful* (Surah 7, Al A'raaf, ayat 157).

John 15, verse 26: *...the Counselor, ...Spirit of truth, ...he will testify about me.* The Qur'an and Prophet Muhammad ﷺ testify about the prophethood and virtues of Jesus and his mother Mary (peace be upon them). In the Qur'an it is stated: *He (Jesus) said: Verily I am a slave of Allah. He has given me the Scripture and appointed me a Prophet. And He has made me blessed wheresoever I be... Such was Jesus, son of Mary. It is a statement of the truth about which they dispute* (Surah 19, Maryam, ayaat 30-31 and 34).

Another such testimony in the Qur'an is the refutation of the crucifixion of Jesus ﷺ (*... he will testify about me*): *They slew him not, nor crucified, but it appeared so to them; and those who disagree concerning it are in doubt thereof; they have no knowledge thereof except pursuit of a conjecture; they slew him not for certain. But Allah raised him up to Himself. Allah is Mighty, Wise* (Surah 4, An Nisa', ayaat 157-158).

John 16, verse 14: *He will glorify me, for he will take from what is mine, and will declare it to you.* Jesus ﷺ is a revered and respected prophet of Islam and his message to the people of his time was unambiguous and also identical to that of Prophet Muhammad ﷺ (*...he will take from what is mine, and will declare it to you*). He ﷺ said: *Both in this world and in the Hereafter, I am the nearest of all the people to Jesus, the son of Mary. The prophets are paternal brothers; their mothers are different, but their religion is one.*[23] *And if the person believes in Jesus and then believes in me, he will*

---

[22] Matthew Henry's Concise Commentary 14:12-17: *The expressions used here and elsewhere, plainly denote **a person**, and the office itself includes all the Divine perfections.* Emphasis added. http://bible.cc/john/14-16.htm Last accessed May 2011.

[23] The Translation of the Meanings of Sahih Al-Bukhari. MM Khan. Kazi Publications, Lahore, Pakistan, 1979. Volume IV. Hadith 652, page 434.

get a double reward.[24]

> *The Messiah himself said: O Children of Israel, worship Allah, my Lord
> and your Lord.* (Surah 5, Al Ma'idah, ayat 72)

> *And when Jesus came with clear proofs of Allah's sovereignty, he said:
> I have come to you with wisdom, and to make plain some of that
> concerning which you differ. So keep your duty to Allah, and obey me.
> Lo Allah, He is my Lord and your Lord. So worship Him. This is the
> right path.* (Surah 43, Az Zukhruf, ayaat 63-64)

Prophet Muhammad ﷺ conveyed the same message: *Say (O
Muhammad): I am commanded to worship Allah, making religion pure for
Him only* (Surah 39, Az Zumar, ayat 11); *And whosoever obeys God and His
messenger will achieve a splendid Triumph* (Surah 33, Al Ahzaab, ayat 71).

John 16, verse 13: *However, when he, the Spirit of truth, has come, he
will guide you into all truth...* As sadiq al amin means the truthful and the
trustworthy. This was how Muhammad ﷺ was referred to long before
he received the Divine Revelations (*wahi*). This designation fits the
Biblical description, *Spirit of truth*. In addition, Islam, to which Prophet
Muhammad ﷺ guided mankind, is the Truth: *Verily, this is the absolute
truth with certainty* (Surah 56, Al Waqi'ah, ayat 95). Thus, the biblical
description is in perfect harmony, ie., *the Spirit of truth*, guiding *into all
truth*. Furthermore, God says: *He it is Who has sent His Messenger with
the guidance and the religion of Truth, that He may cause it prevail over all
religions, and Allah suffices as a witness* (Surah 48, Al Fath, ayat 28).

John 16, verse 13: *...for he will not speak from himself; but whatever he
hears, he will speak.* Verses in the Qur'an say the same about Prophet
Muhammad ﷺ: *Nor does he speak of his own desire. It is no other than an
inspired Revelation* (Surah 53, An Najm, ayaat 3-4); *Say (O Muhammad, to
mankind): I warn you only by the Inspiration* (Surah 21, Al Anbiya', ayat 45);
and *...Say, I follow only that which is inspired in me from my Lord...* (Surah 7,
Al A'raaf, ayat 203).

---

[24] The Translation of the Meanings of Sahih Al-Bukhari. MM Khan. Kazi Publications,
Lahore, Pakistan, 1979. Volume IV. Hadith 655, page 435.

When asked how Divine revelation came to him, Prophet Muhammad ﷺ said: *...the Angel sometimes comes to me with a voice which is like the sound of a ringing bell and when this state is over, I remember what the Angel has said...; and sometimes the Angel comes to me in the shape of a man and talks to me...*[25]

John 16, verse 8: *...he will convict the world about sin, about righteousness and about judgement.* Verses from the Qur'an convey the same message.

... He will enjoin on them that which is right and forbid them that which is wrong. He will make lawful for them all good things and prohibit for them only the foul;... Then those who believe in him, and honour him, and help him, and follow the light which is sent down with him; they are the successful.   (Surah 7, Al A'raaf, ayat 157)

... a messenger of their own who recites to them His revelations, and purifies them, and instructs them in the scripture and in wisdom...
                                        (Surah 3, 'Al Imraan, ayat 164)

And We have written in the Zaboor,[26] *after the Reminder,*[27] *that My righteous servants shall inherit the earth. Surely, in this (Qur'an) is a message for people who truly worship God.*
                                   (Surah 21, Al Anbiya', ayaat 105-106)

The Qur'an is also known as *Al Furqan*, The Criterion (for judging between right and wrong). (Also see the section on the Qur'an in Chapter 1, Islam) On the Day of Judgement, each prophet will serve as a witness for or against the people/nation to which he was sent. This is the Day that was promised by all prophets and it will be the Day when the decision is made for each individual's permanent abode, Paradise or the Fire of Hell. Jesus ﷺ will be give testimony about the people to whom he delivered God's message.

---

[25] The Translation of the Meanings of Sahih Al-Bukhari. MM Khan. Kazi Publications, Lahore, Pakistan, 1979. Volume IV. Hadith 438, page 293.

[26] *Zaboor* here refers to all the books revealed by God, namely all Scriptures.

[27] *Reminder* here refers to *Al Lauh al Mahfuz*, ie., the Guarded Tablet or Book of Decrees that is with God.

*And when Allah says: O Jesus, son of Mary ! Did you ever say to the
people: Make me and my mother deities beside Allah?
He (Jesus) will say: Be Glorified! It was not mine to say that to which I had
no right. If I used to say it, then You knew it. You know what is in my
mind, and I do not know what is in Your mind. Indeed, You, only you, are
the Knower of things hidden.
I spoke to them only that which You commanded me, (saying): Worship
Allah, my Lord and your Lord. I was a witness to their conduct as long as I
remained among them, and when You took me You watched over them;
You are Witness over all things.* (Surah 5, Al Ma'idah, ayaat 116-117)

In Islamic belief, Jesus ﷺ will return to earth and will be a just ruler.[28]
As a Prophet of God, he will follow Islam, the religion that God has
chosen for all of mankind. In the Qur'an, it is stated: *There is not one of
the People of the Scripture (Jews and Christians) but will believe in him (in
Jesus as Prophet of God) before his death (of Jesus), and on the Day of
Resurrection he (Jesus) will be a witness against them* (Surah 4, An Nisa', ayat
159).

John 16, verse 13: *...He will declare to you things that are coming.* In the
Hadith, there are numerous prophesies of Prophet Muhammad ﷺ
about events that were to occur during his lifetime, in the years after
his death, and about events that are unfolding today. There are also
numerous Hadith describing events that will precede the end of the
World. For additional information on this subject see Chapter 25,
Qiyamah.

The Biblical prophesies discussed in the foregoing are words which
the Bible ascribes to Moses and Jesus (peace be upon them).
Unmistakably, these were prophesies about the coming of another
great person, a messenger of God. This person would confirm the
prophethood of Jesus ﷺ, reiterate his message and teachings and guide
to the truth that there is only One God. He would receive inspiration
to speak what God wanted him to convey to mankind. The message
and teachings of this prophet would stay with mankind forever

---

[28] Sunan Abu Dawud. English Translation with Explanatory Notes. A Hasan. Kitab
Bhavan, New Delhi, 1997. Volume 3, Hadith 4310, page 1203.

because it was to be the last messenger of God with His Final Message. He would establish rules of conduct and establish criteria for distinguishing right and good from wrong and sinful and he would inform mankind of things to come. After Jesus ﷺ, there was only one person who fits this description in its entirety and that was Prophet Muhammad ﷺ.

Muhammad's ﷺ Family, Birth, Early Life

His family belonged to the noble and influential Makkan tribe, the Quraish. They were the custodians of the shrine of the Ka'ba. Muhammad ﷺ was born in Makkah on Monday, 12 Rabi Al Awwal 570 CE. His father, *Abd Allah,* died a short time before his birth while on a business trip to Yathrib (Madinah). He was named Muhammad ﷺ by his grandfather and Ahmad (meaning *the praised one*) by his mother Amina. His early childhood was spent in the countryside, away from Makkah, in the foster care of Haleema.[29] At that time, it was customary for city children to be given for nursing to women from desert tribes where the climatic conditions were healthier. His mother died when he was five years old and his care was transferred to his grandfather Abd al-Muttalib. His grandfather died two years later and Muhammad ﷺ came under the guardianship of his uncle Abu Talib.

He ﷺ did not get any formal education and was not taught to read or write. As an older child, he tended to flocks of sheep and herded camels in the hills around Makkah. At the age of twelve, he took the opportunity to accompany his uncle Abu Talib on a business trip to Syria. Many years later, he joined the business of a wealthy Makkan noblewoman, Khadeeja bint Khuwaylid ﷺ. The business flourished tremendously under his management and Khadeeja ﷺ sent him a proposal for marriage, which he accepted. He was twenty-five years old. She was fifteen years older than him and had been widowed twice.

---

[29] Ibn Kathir. Al Sira al Nabawiyya. The Life of the Prophet Muhammad. Garnet Publishing, Reading, UK, 1998. Volume I, page 161-162.

First Divine Revelation and Prophethood

The first revelation came to Muhammad ﷺ when he was forty years old. He had a habit of secluding himself for meditation and soul searching in a cave on the top of *Jabal an Noor*, a mountain outside Makkah. On one such occasion, he described the appearance of the angel Gabriel ﷺ who asked him to read. He responded by saying: *I do not know how to read.* Gabriel ﷺ asked three times and each time he replied: *I do not know how to read.* Then, Gabriel ﷺ recited:

Read! In the Name of your Lord who created (all that exists).
Who created man from a clot. Read! Your Lord is the Most Bountiful.
Who taught by the pen. Taught man what he did not know.[30]

He ﷺ was shaken by this unexpected experience and hurried back to his house and described it to his wife Khadeeja ﷺ. She comforted and reassured him. Later, she took him to a cousin, Waraqa bin Naufal.[31] Waraqa was a very literate individual who had knowledge of the teachings of the Gospel and had earlier converted to Christianity. Upon hearing the events, Waraqa remarked:[32] *This is the same angel (Gabriel ﷺ) who was sent to Moses ﷺ. I wish I were young.* He also said: *...for nobody brought the like of what you have brought, but was treated with hostility. If I were to remain alive till your day (when you start preaching), then I would support you strongly.*

For the first three years, Prophet Muhammad ﷺ preached only to his family and close friends. The first Muslims were his wife Khadeeja, Ali ibn Abu Talib (his first cousin), Abu Bakr and Zaid (may Allah be pleased with them). He conveyed the message to the Makkans after he received the Divine Command: *Arise and warn! And magnify your Lord!* (Surah 74, Al Muddassir, ayaat 2-3).

The Hijrah

Hijrah means emigration. The Hijrah took place in the month of Rabi al-Awwal and marks the beginning of the Islamic Calendar. After

---

[30] These are the first five verses of Surah 96, Al 'Alaq.

[31] He was a man of advanced age. He died a short while after he spoke with Prophet Muhammad ﷺ.

[32] The Translation of the Meanings of Sahih Al-Bukhari. MM Khan. Kazi Publications, Lahore, Pakistan, 1979. Volume VI, Hadith 478, pp 450-453.

almost thirteen years of uninterrupted persecution, Prophet Muhammad ﷺ accepted the invitation of the people of Yathrib (Madinah) to move to their city. The Prophet ﷺ entered Madinah on 12 Rabi al Awwal (2 July 622 CE). The Hijrah was the turning point in the history of Muslims. The original name of the city was Yathrib. After the Prophet ﷺ moved there, the city was renamed *Madinat un Nabi,* City of the Prophet. It is also called *Madinah Munawara.*[33] Many Muslims had already emigrated to Madinah in the preceding years and were known as the *muhajireen.* These and the local Muslims (*ansar* or helpers) welcomed the Prophet ﷺ to Madinah.

The Madinah Years

With the arrival of the Prophet ﷺ, the first Islamic State was established in Madinah. The initial tasks were building a place of worship, establishing an Islamic social order and framing an Islamic constitution. The place of worship that was built came to be known as the *Masjid al Nabwi* or the *Prophet's Mosque.* The Islamic social order included fostering bonds of brotherhood between the emigrant (*muhajireen*) and local (*ansar*) Muslims. The Constitution (*The Madinah Constitution*) was the first ever written State Constitution.[34] It defined the rights and obligations of the citizens of Madinah, including the different resident Jewish tribes. It guaranteed non-Muslims the freedom to practice their faiths, protection of their places of worship and properties. Treaties that were mutually agreed upon and signed with the Jewish tribes stipulated, that collectively, each party carried the responsibility of upholding the terms of the treaty. This placed the liability on the entire party for any violation of the treaty by an individual or group.

There were continuous efforts by the Quraish of Makkah to destabilize the new Islamic State. These resulted in several military encounters. Most notable amongst these were the Battles of Badr (16 Ramadan 2 AH; December 623 CE), Uhud (11 Shawwal 3 AH; December 624 CE) and the Siege of Madinah. The latter began in the month of Shawwal 5 AH (January 627 CE) and is known as the Battle

---

[33] *Munawara* means enlightened.

[34] Hamidullah M: The First Written Constitution in the World. 1986.

of the Trench (*Ghazwa al Khandaq*) or *Ghazwa al Ahzaab*. An all out military engagement did not occur at the last mentioned. The Muslims had prepared a massive trench to protect Madinah from the large force comprising of Makkans, Abyssinian mercenaries and other Arab tribes (known as *al Ahzaab*, the Confederates) who besieged the city for about two weeks. The enemy withdrew, frustrated by the physical barrier of the trench and after being exposed to an unprecedented, severe, easterly windstorm that lasted for three days.[35] A peace treaty was signed in the month of Dhul Qa'dah 6 AH (January 628 CE) at Hudaibiya'.[36]

Conflicts provoked by Jewish Tribes

A formal treaty with Jewish tribes of Madinah (Banu Nadir, Banu Quraizah, Banu Qainuqa) assured them equal rights of citizenship and freedom to practice their faith. Their initial perception of the new Prophet ﷺ was that he inclined towards Judaism. This perception may have been reinforced by the fact that during prayer the Muslims faced in the direction of Jerusalem for the first sixteen or seventeen months after the Prophet's ﷺ move to Madinah. This changed rather abruptly when Muslims were ordered to face in the direction of the Ka'ba in Makkah (Surah 2, Al Baqarah, ayat 144).

The Banu Nadir violated terms of the peace treaty which had been signed upon the arrival of the Prophet ﷺ in Madinah. When he sought to peacefully mend the treaty violations, they treacherously prepared to assassinate him. They were besieged in their forts (4 AH, 625 CE), and after their surrender, they were exiled but were permitted to take their movable property.[37]

During the Battle of the Trench, the Banu Quraizah tribe violated the terms of their treaty with the Muslims and sided with the enemy. In addition, they attacked the unarmed civilian Muslim population consisting mainly of women and children who had been moved to a

---

[35] Ibn Kathir. Al Sira al Nabawiyya. The Life of the Prophet Muhammad. Garnet Publishing, Reading, UK, 2000. Volume III, pages 125-137.

[36] Ibn Kathir. Al Sira al Nabawiyya. The Life of the Prophet Muhammad. Garnet Publishing, Reading, UK, 2000. Volume III, pages 235-238.

[37] Ibn Kathir. Al Sira al Nabawiyya. The Life of the Prophet Muhammad. Garnet Publishing, Reading, UK, 2000. Volume III, pages 100-101.

safe location in Madinah, for protection from the invading Quraish.[38] The Banu Quraizah surrendered after a brief siege (5 AH, 627 CE).

The final and decisive confrontation between the Jewish tribes and Muslims occurred at Khaibar (7 AH, 628 CE). After their defeat, their plea for mercy were accepted by Prophet Muhammad ﷺ and a new peace agreement was signed.

Liberation of Makkah

This marked the beginning of the end of the pagan era in Arabia. Makkah's defenders, overwhelmed by the large number of Muslims, surrendered without a fight in the month of Ramadan 8 AH (630 CE). Prophet Muhammad ﷺ declared general amnesty, excepting those convicted for criminal offenses. This amnesty included those who had bitterly persecuted and physically tormented Muslims while the latter resided in Makkah. There was no retribution or vengeance. This magnanimous act of forgiveness for even the most hostile of enemies exemplifies the character of Prophet Muhammad ﷺ, something that cannot be found elsewhere in the annals of history. It is conduct that all believing Muslims strive to emulate.

In Makkah, clearing the Ka'ba of the 360 idols was a moment of significance. It restored the Sanctuary to its original status, for the Worship of the One and only God of the universe. While the idols were being destroyed, the Prophet ﷺ recited the following verse from the Qur'an: ...*Truth has come and falsehood has vanished away. For falsehood is ever bound to vanish* (Surah 17, Al Isra', ayat 81).

His ﷺ Death

Prophet Muhammad ﷺ performed the last Haj in 10 AH (632 CE). This is also known as the *Farewell Pilgrimage*. He had sensed the approaching end of his life. At the Haj, he addressed the multitude of pilgrims that were gathered. Excerpts from that sermon are reproduced below.

---

[38] Ibn Kathir. Al Sira al Nabawiyya. The Life of the Prophet Muhammad. Garnet Publishing, Reading, UK, 2000. Volume III, page 140.

- *O People, just as you regard this month, this day, this city as sacred, so regard the life and property of every Muslim as a sacred trust*
- *Return the goods entrusted to you to their rightful owners*
- *Remember that you will indeed meet your Lord, and that He will indeed reckon your deeds*
- *Allah has forbidden you to take usury, therefore all interest obligation shall henceforth be waived. Your capital, however, is yours to keep. You will neither inflict nor suffer inequity*
- *All the bloodletting of the Days of Ignorance is waived*
- *Hurt no one so that no one may hurt you*
- *Beware of Satan, for the safety of your religion. He has lost all hope that he will ever be able to lead you astray in big things. If you obey him in other than major sins, he will be pleased with that*
- *O People, it is true that you have certain rights with regard to your women, but they also have rights over you. Remember that you have taken them as your wives only under Allah's trust and with His permission. If they abide by your right, then to them belongs the right to be fed and clothed in kindness*
- *Treat your women well and be kind to them for they are your partners and committed helpers*
- *And it is your right that they do not allow anyone into your homes without your approval*
- *O People, listen to me in earnest, worship Allah, say your five daily prayers, fast during the month of Ramadan, and give your wealth in Zakat. Perform Haj if you can afford to*
- *All mankind is from Adam and Eve, an Arab has no superiority over a non-Arab nor a non-Arab has any superiority over an Arab; also a white has no superiority over black nor a black has any superiority over white - except by piety and good action*
- *Know that every Muslim is a brother to another Muslim and that the Muslims constitute one brotherhood. Nothing shall be legitimate to a Muslim which belongs to a fellow Muslim unless it was given freely and willingly. Do not, therefore, do injustice to yourselves*
- *Remember, one day you will appear before Allah and answer your deeds. So beware, do not stray from the path of righteousness after I am gone*

- *O People understand the words which I convey to you*
- *I leave behind me two things, the Qur'an and my example, the Sunnah, and if you follow these you will never go astray*
- *All those who listen to me shall pass on my words to others and those to others again; and may the last ones understand my words better than those who listen to me directly*
- *Be my witness, O Allah, that I have conveyed your message to your people*

After addressing the pilgrims, he 🌸 recited the following verse from the Qur'an:

... This day are those who disbelieve in despair of ever harming your religion; so do not fear them, fear Me! This day have I perfected your religion for you and completed My favour to you, and have chosen for you as deen (religion) al Islam... (Surah 5, Al Ma'idah, ayat 3)

Prophet Muhammad 🌸 fell ill shortly after returning from Makkah and died on 12 Rabi al-Awwal 11 AH (Monday, 8 June 632 CE) and is buried in Madinah, Arabia. He was sixty-three years old.[39]

His 🌸 Character and Conduct [40,41]

Virtually everything is known about the life and personality of Prophet Muhammad 🌸 by virtue of the authentically recorded observations of the multitude of individuals around him (also known as the esteemed companions, *sahabah ikram*) and information provided by his wives and other family members. There are accurate records of his physique, manners, conduct, speech, life style and teachings, etc. There is possibly no other individual in history who was the subject of such intense scrutiny.

Prophet Muhammad 🌸 was of perfectly balanced temperament, truthful to a fault, patient, humble, polite, kind, gentle and forgiving by

---

[39] The Translation of the Meanings of Sahih Al-Bukhari. MM Khan. Kazi Publications, Lahore, Pakistan, 1979. Volume IV, Hadith 736, pages 483.

[40] Shamaa-il Tirmidhi. Darul Ishaat, Karachi, Pakistan, 2001, (215) Hadith 3, pages 210-211; (318) Hadith 6, page 345; (325) Hadith 13, page 352; (330) Hadith 5, page 364; (334) Hadith 9, pages 369-370.

[41] Hai MA, Uswai Rasool-e-Akram 🌸, Darul Ishaat, Karachi, Pakistan, 1987.

nature. He never took revenge for any personal matter. He disliked war and sought to avoid it. Calling it deceit, he urged Muslims to seek peace and security through prayer rather than engaging in military conflict.[42] If injured by the enemy, instead of getting angry, he would pray for them: *My Lord, forgive them,* or *O Lord, show my people the right path for they know not what they do.*[43] He smiled a lot, never quarreled, never used foul or abusive language. Criticism never provoked or angered him and no praise would ever make him proud. His manner captivated those around him.

He ﷺ desired no privilege and lived as an equal although he was Head of State. He avoided placing himself in prominent places in gatherings, so much so, that it was frequently difficult to locate him. His speech was clear and concise and easily understood, never offensive or belittling of anybody, nor loose talk or gossip. He led a very simple life and had no inclination for material wealth. His meals were simple and frequently a meal or two had to be skipped because of the lack of food in the house. He helped with the household chores. He loved children and the poor.

A lot of his time was spent in devotion. When asked why he spent so much time in devotion, Prophet Muhammad ﷺ remarked:[44] *When Allah ﷻ has blessed me so much should I not be a grateful servant?* That he was the servant of God, was displayed by his actions. In essence, his life was filled with devotion, reverence and fear of the Almighty.[45]

Prophet Muhammad ﷺ placed great emphasis on fulfilling obligations and observing the rights of others. He advised: *Pay the labourer his wages before his sweat dries*[46] and that *He is not a believer who eats his fill while his neighbour goes hungry.*[47] Importantly, he practiced what he advised. His exemplary character and conduct are a role model that all

---

[42] For an additional discussion on this subject, see Islamic View of Warfare in Chapter 24, Suicide, Killing and War.

[43] Sahl ibn Sa'd, At-Tabarani, Volume 6, Hadith 5862, page 162.

[44] Shamaa-il Tirmidhi. Darul Ishaat, Karachi, Pakistan, 2001. Worship and Devotions of Sayyidina Rasulullah ﷺ. (248) Hadith 1, pages 269-270.

[45] The Arabic term describing this state is: *taqwa*. This is translated as piety, consciousness and fear of the One Almighty God.

[46] Reported by Ibn Majah. Muntakhab Ahadith. Kandhlavi MY, Annayyar, Karachi, Pakistan. Hadith 252, page 479.

[47] Reported by Tabarani. Muntakhab Ahadith. Kandhlavi MY, Annayyar, Karachi, Pakistan. Hadith 229, page 472.

believing men and women seek to emulate. This is also the advice from the Almighty: *Indeed in the messenger of Allah you have a good example for him who looks towards Allah and the Last Day and remembers Allah much* (Surah 33, Al Ahzaab, ayat 21).

His Family Life

Prophet Muhammad had all together twelve wives. Ten of them were alive at the time of his death. They all lived very simple lives in simple dwellings without luxuries, frequently subsisting on dates and water for lengthy periods of time as that was the only food in the house. They were a source of comfort and support, providing advice when needed, accompanied him on journeys, provided support for the troops and nursed the wounded. They are respected and revered by all Muslims as the *Mothers of the Believers* (may God be pleased with them all). The names of his wives are:[48]

Khadeeja bint Khuwaylid, Saudah bint Zam'ah,
A'isha Siddiqa bint Abu Bakr, Hafsah bint Umar ibn al Khattab,
Zaynab bint Khuzaymah, Umm Salama Hind bint Abi Umayya,
Zaynab bint Jah'sh, Juwayriah bint al Harith,
Umm Habiba Ramla bint Abu Sufyan, Safiyya bint Huyay ibn Akhtab,
Maymuna bint al Harith, Mariyah al Qibtiyah

He had altogether seven children, four girls and three boys. Their names were: Qasim, Abdullah, Zaynab, Ruqayyah, Umm Kulthum, Fatima' and Ibrahim. With the exception of his youngest son Ibrahim who died in infancy (10 AH), all children were from his first wife Khadeeja bint Khuwaylid .

There has been criticism about his multiple marriages. This is ill-advised and based upon poor, incorrect or absent background information. In some cases, this criticism may attempt to malign the character of one of the most noble and respectable individuals that ever lived. The issues at the basis of the criticisms are polygamy and marriage to A'isha . Both of these are discussed below. For additional discussion on polygamy, see Chapter 7, Marriage.

---

[48] May God be pleased with them all.

Polygamy in Historical Context

Polygamy was not an Islamic or Muslim innovation as may be perceived today as a result of the widespread disinformation. In times past, even long before the proclamation of Islam, polygamy was very common. Many earlier prophets, including Abraham, Jacob, David, and Solomon (peace be upon them), had multiple wives. Solomon ≉ is reported to have had seven hundred wives (The Book of 1st Kings, Chapter 11, verse 3). The Bible also states that David ≉ had several wives (King James Version: 2 Samuel 5, 13; 2 Samuel 11, 2-5).

Historically, multiple marriages were not infrequent amongst rulers and nobles and often served a political purpose. That practice also existed in Arabia and such marriages were considered tokens of friendship and for sealing relationships and treaties. In such cases, the women were often considered mere commodities. Thus, polygamy was practiced for political, social, and not only physical reasons. The Islamic perspective on polygamy is different and it is noteworthy that Islam restored dignity and rights to women. This is discussed in Chapter 7, Marriage and Chapter 9, Women's Issues.

The Prophet's ≉ Marriages

It is necessary to examine the circumstances and associated wisdom for his multiple marriages before drawing any conclusions. Polygamy is practiced worldwide. Although only a few faiths officially permit polygamy, it is more prevalent today and exists in the form of extramarital and adulterous affairs and other perverted practices. By allowing polygamy (ie., polygyny) and regulating relationships through specific rules, Islam provided dignity and equality to women, converting their status from chattel to that of an equal partner.

Although he was Head of the Muslim State, Prophet Muhammad ≉ led a very simple life, devoid of personal riches or luxuries. The lives of his wives were not easy: effort and sacrifice and not luxurious homes with servants. The Prophet's ≉ obligations kept him busy and frequently away from home. In addition, he spent a significant amount of time in prayer and devotion. Most of his marriages were later in life when physical needs no longer play a major role in a man's life. Besides, even a cursory look at his character should dispel any notion of lust. With the exception of A'isha ≉, most of his wives were older and many had been married previously.[49] He treated all his wives with kindness and equality.

The first marriage to Khadeeja ﷺ, at the age of twenty-five years, was monogamous. She was fifteen years older than him, had been widowed twice and also had children from her previous marriages. Khadeeja ﷺ died when he was about fifty years old. He was a devoted husband and did not remarry for three years after her death. All other marriages took place between the ages of fifty-three and sixty years. Prophet Muhammad ﷺ died at the age of sixty-three years.

Reasons for the Prophet's ﷺ multiple Marriages

One important point, which is often overlooked when the issue of the Prophet's ﷺ multiple marriages is discussed, is that he was no ordinary mortal like the rest but the Messenger of God. Not only was he sent to teach religion to mankind but also to serve as a living example on how to conduct the affairs of everyday life. Therefore, everything he did had a very specific purpose, often outside the grasp of our speculative minds. With hundreds of pairs of eyes watching every move and hundreds of ears listening to every word he spoke, his mission was to set the ultimate example of morality.

The reasons for his multiple marriages fall into two categories: personal and those related to his mission.

Personal

As a man seeking to fulfill his physical and social needs, the desire for a family and home. His first marriage to Khadeeja ﷺ falls in this category.

Mission Related

As a Prophet of God who married several women for reasons related to his mission. His wives were carefully selected and were an indispensable source of information that was gathered by living with him. This information would have been unavailable otherwise. Their contribution has served to educate generations of Muslims.

---

[49] Seven were widows and three were divorcees.

The Transmission of Prophetic Traditions

During those times, the main mode for the transmission of information was by word of mouth. Consequently, people would commit to memory the Prophet's ﷺ sayings and actions. To accurately convey such information to future generations, it was necessary to have corroborating narrations from several sources. For additional information on this topic, see Hadith and Sunnah (Prophetic Traditions) in Chapter 1, Islam.

Prophet Muhammad ﷺ was perhaps the only prophet who did not have much privacy. Details, including spoken words and actions, of his public and private life are meticulously preserved in the Hadith. His life's example is a manual for the conduct of all affairs, public and personal, for all Muslims. Much of this information had to be preserved by the keen and observant wives and other companions. The contributions to the Hadith pertaining to his personal life could not have come from any other source but his wives. Over 3,000 Hadith are attributed to his wives alone.[50]

For Sealing Relationships

Four of the Prophet's ﷺ closest companions (the first four Khalifahs) were related to him through marriage: Abu Bakr ؓ was the father of his wife A'isha ؓ, Umar ibn al Khattab ؓ was the father of his wife Hafsah ؓ, Uthman bin Affan ؓ was married to two of his daughters, Ruqayyah ؓ and Umm Kulthum ؓ (in succession), and Ali ibn Abu Talib ؓ was married to his youngest daughter Fatima' ؓ. His marriage to Juwayriah bint al Harith brought an end to the hostile relationship with the Banu Mustaliq. Safiyya bint Huyay ibn Akhtab was the daughter of the chief of the Banu Nadir.

Practical Role Model

Prophet Muhammad ﷺ was a practical role model for all times with respect to behavior towards spouses and women in general. Hence, his private life is of great importance to women. His conduct towards his wives sets the best example that can be found for how men should treat their spouses. This applies to all men, not only Muslim men. He

---

[50] Azami MM. Studies in Early Hadith Literature. American Trust Publications, Indianapolis, IN, 2001.

said: *The most perfect Muslim in the matter of faith is one who has excellent behavior; and the best among you are those who behave best towards their wives.*[51]

Marriage to A'isha ﷺ

Prophet Muhammad's ﷺ marriage to A'isha ﷺ has been criticized on the ill-informed assumption that she was a minor at the time of the marriage. This opinion is partly based on a narration from Urwah.[52] Not only is it mathematically incorrect, but it is also refuted by statements made by A'isha ﷺ herself (see below). Others place her age at seventeen years at the time of *nikah* and nineteen years at the time of the marriage.[53] Needless to say, birth records are not available and the only information which provides a means for calculating A'isha's ﷺ chronological age are narrations and historical events.

There is historical evidence, that in the prevailing social traditions, girls were considered women as soon as they began to menstruate and were given in marriage at that age. That was customary for all the dwellers of Arabia: pagans, Christians, Jews, and others alike. Well before her *nikah* (betrothal) to Prophet Muhammad ﷺ, A'isha ﷺ had been engaged to a non-Muslim man, indicating that she had already reached puberty, and by local customs, she was considered a woman and of marriageable age. This is also supported by other recorded historical events which are described below. Additionally, the marriage was by consent.

Determination of A'isha's ﷺ Chronological Age

A sequence of events must be taken into account when attempting to determine A'isha's ﷺ chronological age at the time of her marriage. Dates of some early (before the Hijrah) important events were based on the pagan calendar. The latter had several problems as the pre-Islamic Arabs often switched around the months and used intercalation. Therefore, it is difficult to synchronize the months/years

---

[51] Reported by Tirmidhi. Riyad us Saleheen, Kitab Bhavan, New Delhi, 1987. Hadith 278, page 180.

[52] The Translation of the Meanings of Sahih Al-Bukhari. MM Khan. Kazi Publications, Lahore, Pakistan, 1979. Volume VII. Hadith 88, page 65.

[53] Shaikh FR. Chronology of Prophetic Events. Ta Ha Publishers, London, England, 2001. Pages 90-92.

with those of the Julian calendar (CE). In order to avoid confusion from overlapping years, the earlier date calculations shown below are primarily according to the *Am al-Fil* (AF).[54] That pre-Islamic pagan system was abolished following an injunction from God (Surah 9, At Taubah, ayaat 36-37) and a declaration by Prophet Muhammad ﷺ during the Last Pilgrimage in 10 AH.

- Of Abu Bakr's ؓ four children, all of whom were born before Islam, A'isha ؓ was the youngest. Her older sister Asma' ؓ was ten years her senior and was born in 26 AF. Accordingly, A'isha ؓ was born in 36 AF
- Khadeeja ؓ, the Prophet's ﷺ first wife, died in 49 AF
- A'isha's ؓ *nikah* took place three years after Khadeeja's ؓ death,[55] in the month of Shawwal, 52 AF. That was in Makkah, between six and seven months before the emigration (Hijrah) in 622 CE

Impressions from her early life provide corroboration that A'isha ؓ was born well before Muhammad ﷺ received the First Revelation in 40 AF (610 CE). She said: *I have seen my parents following Islam since I reached the age of understanding ('aqil).*[56] She also said: *This revelation, ie., ayat 45 of Surah 54, Al Qamar, was revealed to Muhammad ﷺ at Makkah while I was a playful little girl.*[57] This is an early Makkan Surah.

From the foregoing, at the time of *nikah,* she was at the very least sixteen years of age. The marriage was first consummated around eighteen months after the Hijrah in the month of Shawwal 2 AH when she was around eighteen years old. But, God knows best.

---

[54] *Am al-Fil* or the Year of the Elephant. The event of significance from which this name is derived was the attach on Makkah by Abraha with his elephant borne troops.

[55] The Translation of the Meanings of Sahih Al-Bukhari. MM Khan. Kazi Publications Lahore, Pakistan, 1979. Volume VIII. Hadith 33, page 22.

[56] The Translation of the Meanings of Sahih Al-Bukhari. MM Khan. Kazi Publications, Lahore, Pakistan, 1979. Volume I. Hadith 465, page 276.
The Arabic expression *reached the age of understanding* indicates a stage of maturation that is reached when the child is around five or six years of age.

[57] The Translation of the Meanings of Sahih Al-Bukhari. MM Khan. Kazi Publications, Lahore, Pakistan, 1979. Volume VI. Hadith 399, pp 369-370.

The Wisdom of Marriage to A'isha 鑾

A'isha 鑾 came from a family known for learning and possessing vast amounts of knowledge. Her father, Abu Bakr 鑾, was a source of encyclopedic information on tribal ancestries and poetry. She inherited his abilities and during the nine years she lived with the Prophet 鑾, she imbibed and preserved a vast amount of precious knowledge about Islam which would have otherwise been unavailable. It has been stated that she was the most knowledgeable person about Islamic Jurisprudence and a significant number of legal rulings were transmitted through her. She is also one of the very few persons responsible for the transmission of over two thousand Hadith.

She lived for forty-seven years after the death of Prophet Muhammad 鑾.[58] During these latter years, she taught Islam to an innumerable number of individuals eager to learn from the one who had been taught by the teacher himself, ie., the Prophet 鑾. She is considered one of the most eminent Islamic scholars and is held in extremely high esteem by all Muslims.

Marriage to Zaynab bint Jah'sh 鑾

The Marriage to Zaynab bint Jah'sh 鑾 is discussed in Chapter 8, Family and Social Issues.

Marriage to Mariyah al Qibtiyah 鑾

Was she a slave, concubine, or wife? Mariyah 鑾 is also used by some who attempt to malign the character of Prophet Muhammad 鑾 by suggesting that she was a concubine. It is not surprising for such accusations to surface because they originate from the same sources that believe and accept that Prophets David and Solomon (peace be upon them) had concubines, ie., were adulterous. Islam rejects those accusations outright. They were pious individuals and prophets of God. Similarly, the allegations against the character of the noble Prophet Muhammad 鑾, are both ill conceived and baseless.

Mariyah al Qibtiyah (Maria) 鑾 was a Coptic Christian slave owned by Egypt's Governor who was also a Christian. He gave Mariyah as a gift to the Prophet 鑾 in response to an invitation to Islam. During the course of her journey to Madinah, with the returning companions

---

[58] A'isha 鑾 died in 58 AH.

(sahabah), Mariyah ؓ learned about Islam and the Prophet ﷺ. She accepted Islam before arriving in Madinah and the Prophet ﷺ married her.

His ﷺ Mission

In the Qur'an, Prophet Muhammad ﷺ is described as a mercy for the *worlds,* not just for Muslims or mankind: *(O Muhammad)! We have only sent you as a mercy for the worlds (rahmatal lil alameen).*[59] His mission was that of delivering and disseminating the Message of Almighty God. It is summarized in what he said during the Farewell Sermon. The salient points are discussed below:

- Belief in One God and adherence to the tenets of Islam
- Shari'ah: laws, social and moral codes for individuals and society
- Rules of justice, honesty, fairness and equality

Belief in One God and adherence to the tenets of Islam

The belief in One God is known as *Tauheed.* There is only One God and He is the only One worthy of worship and nothing (spiritual or material) should be worshipped besides Him. God is Almighty and All Capable. He is unseen and there can be no material representation of His Image because nothing known to mankind has the likeness of God. However, His Attributes provide an insight about His Being. For an additional discussion on this topic see Tauheed in Chapter 1, Islam and Chapter 2, Allah سبحانه وتعالى.

The believer should adhere to the tenets of Islam and be mindful of God's omnipresence. He/she should be of firm and unshakable faith, full of sincerity and conviction. He/she should pray the five daily prayers, fast during the month of Ramadan, give the Zakat and perform Haj (if it can be afforded). Furthermore, the believer should strive to seek God's pleasure through acts of worship and good deeds and steer clear of the prohibited and everything else that could incur His displeasure.

---

[59] Surah 21, Al Anbiya', ayat 107.

Shari'ah: laws, social and moral codes for individuals and society

Prophet Muhammad ﷺ said: *I leave behind me two things, the Qur'an and my example, the Sunnah, and if you follow these you will never go astray.*[60]

The Shari'ah is derived from four sources: the *Qur'an*, the *Sunnah* of the Prophet ﷺ (his Traditions), *Ijma* (consensus of the Companions of the Prophet ﷺ and Muslim scholars), and *Ijtihaad* which is the personal judgement of Muslim scholars derived in conformity with the Qur'an and Sunnah. Shari'ah is discussed in more detail in Chapter 4, Islamic Law, Shari'ah and Fiqh.

Shari'ah guides every aspect of a Muslim's life, provides moral codes and a system of social justice. It disallows racial or ethnic profiling and acts of vengeance and establishes equality for all. Superiority of one individual over another is only by virtue of piety and excellence of character.

It instills the consciousness of God (taqwa): *Remember, one day you will appear before Allah and answer your deeds. So beware, do not stray from the path of righteousness after I am gone.* This consciousness of accountability before God keeps the believer from acting unjustly or immorally and from usurping the rights of others.

The Islamic Shari'ah requires the removal of social barriers (*Know that every Muslim is a brother to another Muslim and that the Muslims constitute one brotherhood*) and inspires domestic harmony (*Treat your women well and be kind to them for they are your partners and committed helpers. Remember that you have taken them as your wives only under Allah's trust and with His permission. If they abide by your right, then to them belongs the right to be fed and clothed in kindness*).

With respect to spousal relationships, there is a threefold message: *taken them as your wives*, *under Allah's trust* and *in kindness*. The first phrase clearly defines the only allowable physical-sexual relationship between man and woman, ie., through marriage. The second point emphasizes that the marriage contract is a solemn pledge, a trust.[61]

---

[60] From the Farewell Sermon of the Prophet ﷺ. Quotes from the sermon in this and the next section appear in italics.

[61] For additional information and details, see Chapter 7, Marriage. Homosexual relationships are strictly prohibited by Islam.

The Islamic view of a trust is that of a significant obligation which must be honored and with it come all the obligations of responsibility, fairness, kindness, respect, etc. At first glance, *in kindness*, may seem self explanatory. However, kindness also refers to everything else that is not covered under *feeding and clothing*. The believers look towards the role model of the Prophet ﷺ in shaping their conduct towards women.

Rules of justice, honesty, fairness and equality

Establishment of basic human rights and economic justice, including the fundamental rights of each individual with respect to his/her person, property and honour (*so regard the life and property of every Muslim as a sacred trust. Return the goods entrusted to you to their rightful owners*).[62] Also established were laws providing basic rights to women and orphans. Previously, both were considered property and were inherited. Islam abolished that practice and established women's rights over fourteen hundred years ago. Some of those basic rights were granted to European and American women in the nineteenth and twentieth centuries. For an additional discussion on this subject see Chapter 9, Women's Issues.

Usury and interest were prohibited (also see Chapter 4, Islamic Law, Shari'ah and Fiqh and Chapter 10, Business Ethics and Financial Dealings). Usury is the unfair system of exploitation of the financially underprivileged that existed at that time and continues to scourge society today. There was prohibition of the usurpation of the property of others. Laws facilitating the circulation of personal wealth through payment of *zakat* and rules of inheritance and distribution of personal property were introduced. Bequeathing of personal property through Wills was limited to one third of the total estate while the remainder remained subject to the Islamic laws of inheritance, thus safeguarding the rights of heirs. Also established were women's right to inherit from deceased relatives and the right to own property in sole ownership.

---

[62] For the safeguarding of the rights of non-Muslims and minorities, see Chapter 11, Minorities under Muslim Rule.

Living Islam

When asked about the Prophet's ﷺ character, his wife A'isha ﷺ stated: *It was the Qur'an.* Anas ﷺ said:[63] *I served the Prophet ﷺ for ten years in Madinah. I was an adolescent, therefore all my services were not according to the desire of my master. However, he never said a word of displeasure to me; neither "why did you do this" nor "why did you not do that".* He lived by the rules he preached. His every action was guided by the consciousness of God and by the fear of displeasing Him. By and large, his life was an open book for all to follow. If there ever was a man of flawless character, it was Muhammad ﷺ. This is not just the impression of believers, but what God Almighty said about him: *And surely you (O Muhammad) are of a magnificent character* (Surah 68, Al Qalam, ayat 4).

Miracles of Prophet Muhammad ﷺ

The demand for miracles originated from those of weak faith needing reassurance or those who wanted proof of the authenticity of prophethood. The miracles he ﷺ performed were of two kinds. To provide a sign of prophethood, and more often, to fulfill a need of the people around him.

In the first instance, there was the occasion of the splitting of the moon which is documented in several Hadith.[64] In the latter, there are numerous instances in which water, food, or both were provided to fulfill an immediate need. One of these occurred during a journey. Some of the accompanying persons had gone out in search of water and came across a woman carrying water (in skins) for her family. These were brought to the Prophet ﷺ. He rubbed the openings of the water skins where after enough water came out of them to quench the thirst of forty men and also enough to fill their water containers, with no diminution of the original. Upon returning to her village, that woman remarked: *I have met either the greatest magician or a prophet as*

---

[63] Reported by Abu Dawud. Muntakhab Ahadith. Kandhlavi MY. Annayyar, Karachi, Pakistan. Hadith 66, page 418. Emphasis added.

[64] The Translation of the Meanings of Sahih Al-Bukhari. MM Khan. Kazi Publications, Lahore Pakistan, 1979. Volume IV. Hadith 830 and 831, page 533; and Volume V. Hadith 208-211, pages 132-133.

the people claim.[65]

In another miracle, one bowl provided water for *wudu* for several hundred persons.[66] Similar to what Jesus ﷵ said when performing his miracles (*bi iznillah*, ie., with Allah's permission), Prophet Muhammad ﷺ said: *Come to the blessed water, and the Blessing is from Allah.* Some of the other miracles involved meals,[67] dates,[68] and rain.[69]

Concluding Commentary

O Prophet! We have sent you as a witness and a bringer of good tidings and a warner. And as one who invites to Allah by His permission, and as a lamp spreading light. (Surah 33, Al Ahzaab, ayaat 45-46)

Conventional human wisdom would dictate that an educated and literary person would be required to convince a civilized society to believe in One God, toss away their 360 idols, and refrain from acts that were destructive for the social and moral fabric of their society. The One with Knowledge of the unseen knew otherwise. He says: *God knows, you (people) do not know* (Surah 2, Al Baqarah, ayat 216). Thus, for the task of conveying His final message to mankind, God Almighty chose a man who possessed neither eloquence nor a formal education, a man who could neither read nor write and possessed no knowledge of previous Scriptures, ie., the Torah and Gospel. However, this messenger excelled in many other qualities, many of which are difficult, if not impossible, to retain in a position of power

---

[65] The Translation of the Meanings of Sahih Al-Bukhari. MM Khan. Kazi Publications, Lahore, Pakistan, 1979. Volume IV, Hadith 771, pages 496-497.

[66] *Wudu* (ablution) is the required ablution in preparation for prayer or for reading the Qur'an. The Translation of the Meanings of Sahih Al-Bukhari. MM Khan. Kazi Publications, Lahore, Pakistan, 1979. Volume IV. Hadith 772, pages 497- 498; Hadith 773-776, pages 498-500;
At Hudaibiya', Hadith 777, page 500; and Hadith 779, page 502.

[67] The Translation of the Meanings of Sahih Al-Bukhari. MM Khan. Kazi Publications, Lahore, Pakistan, 1979. Volume IV. Hadith 778, pages 500-502; and Hadith 781, pages 503-504.

[68] The Translation of the Meanings of Sahih Al-Bukhari. MM Khan. Kazi Publications, Lahore, Pakistan, 1979. Volume IV. Hadith 780, pages 502-503.

[69] The Translation of the Meanings of Sahih Al-Bukhari. MM Khan. Kazi Publications, Lahore, Pakistan, 1979. Volume IV. Hadith 782, pages 504-505.

with unchallenged authority. He ﷺ was a man of unreproachable character and integrity, inherently honest, humble, soft-spoken, unassuming, gentle and kind.

While there is magic in eloquence, with time and realization, the magical effects fade even though it is artificially illuminated. Truth does not change, undergo revision or reinterpretation. It simply stands out. Like a shining lamp, it is all the more striking, the greater the darkness around it.

The message of Islam is likened to a light: *O people of the Scripture! Now has Our messenger come to you... Now there has come to you a light from Allah and a plain Scripture (Qur'an)* (Surah 5, Al Ma'idah, ayat 15). That *light* came with the Messenger of God, Muhammad ﷺ, to illuminate the world with the knowledge and beauty of God.

It is of importance to note, that neither is the message of Islam anything novel, nor was it ever claimed to be as such. It is a message that had already been conveyed to mankind through previous prophets: *Nothing is said to you (Muhammad) that has not already been said to the Messengers before you* (Surah 41, Fussilat, ayat 43). Additionally, the coming of the Final Messenger was prophesied by Moses and Jesus (peace be upon them) and these prophesies were known to the Jewish and Christian scholars, but were concealed, as the *sceptre* (prophethood) was to pass on to a different nation: *Those to whom We gave the Scriptures recognize this Revelation as they recognize their own sons. But some of them knowingly conceal the Truth* (Surah 2, Al Baqarah, ayat 146).

Even as the prophethood of Muhammad ﷺ was, and still continues to be denied by some, so were most of the other prophets. Needless to say, that closing the eyes to the truth cannot make it go away. The illusion of security is constructed upon a tenuous belief as the individual's accountability of deeds on the Day of Judgement also cannot be made to go away. It is stated in the Qur'an:

O believers! Observe your duty to Allah. And let every soul look to that which it sends forward for the morrow. And observe your duty to Allah, for He is cognizant of all your actions. And be not like those who forgot Allah, therefore He caused them to forget their souls.

(Surah 59, Al Hashr, ayaat 18-19)

Prophet Muhammad ﷺ provided the perfect example for the conduct of life's affairs. He demonstrated how to achieve the balance between worldly and spiritual matters without compromising the one or the other. Key aspects of his message were the *Tauheed* (that there is only One God), consciousness of God's omnipresence and the importance of staying on a middle course by avoiding extremes in all matters, including spiritual. Consciousness of God means avoiding His displeasure by staying away from everything that is evil, immoral, or harmful for oneself or for others, and striving to seek His closeness by doing and encouraging actions that are good, of kindness and fairness.

O you who believe! Remember Allah with much remembrance. And glorify Him early and late. He it is who blesses you, and His angels bless you, that He may bring you forth from darkness into light; and He is Merciful to the believers.   (Surah 33, Al Ahzaab, ayaat 41-43)

He ﷺ brought the realization that even when a person is by him/herself, with no other soul in sight, he or she is not alone since every action is witnessed and recorded. Every individual will be held accountable for all actions and nobody will bear the burden of another. Therefore, the individual must live a life that maximizes the good and minimizes, if not eliminates, all the not so good deeds.

No other person in history has had his/her life observed and recorded in such meticulous detail. There is no other person whose exemplary conduct is so closely emulated in the daily life of millions of people in virtually every region of the globe. He ﷺ lived Islam which does not separate religion and state. Prophet Muhammad ﷺ is *the only man in history who was supremely successful on both the religious and secular levels.*[70] Despite the innumerable good he brought and the good he taught, Prophet Muhammad ﷺ and the Message of Islam are often poorly understood.[71]

---

[70] Hart MH. The 100. A Ranking of the Most Influential Persons in History. Revised and Updated, 1992. Citadel Press. www.kensingtonbooks.com

[71] Abualrab J, 50 Righteous and Humane Concepts Brought by Muhammad ﷺ The Prophet of Mercy. Madinah Publishers and Distributors, 2007. www.IslamLife.com. Also see Chapter 23, Crusades and Holy War; Chapter 12, Human, Environmental, Animal and Other's Rights; and Chapter 24, Suicide, Killing and War.

Those who reject the Message (the Qur'an) when it comes to them (are guilty). And indeed it is a Book of exalted power. No falsehood can approach it from before or behind it. It is sent down by One Full of Wisdom, Worthy of all Praise.

(Surah 41, Fussilat, ayaat 41-42)

Whoever obeys Allah and His messenger, they are with those to whom Allah has shown favour, of the Prophets and the sincere, and the martyrs, and the righteous. The best of company are they!

(Surah 4, An Nisa', ayat 69)

Then those who believe in him (Muhammad ﷺ), and honour him, and help him, and follow the light which is sent down with him; they are the successful. (Surah 7, Al A'raaf, ayat 157)

Chapter Four

Islamic Law
Shari'ah and Fiqh

Introduction

Allah commands justice and kindness, and giving to kinsfolk, and forbids all shameful deeds, wickedness and oppression. He admonishes you so that you may take heed.

(Surah 16, An Nahl, ayat 90)

For each of you, We have prescribed a law and a clear way.[1]

(Surah 5, Al Ma'idah, ayat 48)

These verses summarize some of the basic principles that govern every action of Muslims, as individuals and collectively. The salient points being justice (*adl*), compassion (*ihsan*), goodness (*maroof*) and shunning all evil (*munkar*).

Islam guides mankind to an unambiguously defined path, clearly distinguishing between what is good and desirable and that which is not good or evil and must be avoided. This guidance comes through the Shari'ah which establishes the rules and regulations for the way of life that was prescribed by God.

Shari'ah is a path or road leading to an intended destination or a specific goal. The literal meaning of the word is a tributary leading to

---

[1] This refers to previous nations/peoples to whom prophets were sent with laws. The basic message was identical for all of them. Tafsir ibn Kathir, Al-Firdous, Ltd, London, England, 2000. Part 6, pages 182-183.

the main stream, the right path or road. Frequently, it is incorrectly translated as meaning *Islamic Law*. While the Shari'ah does incorporate rules and regulations that every Muslim must follow in daily life, its implications are quite far-reaching. It is a guide for virtually all aspects of living and includes both spiritual and worldly matters. As indicated by its meaning, it is *the road* Muslims must travel to achieve the ultimate goal, ie., the complete submission to God.

Secular Laws and the Shari'ah

Secular laws are a system of rules, regulations and ordinances enacted and enforced by governmental authorities and address mainly the external aspects of human behavior. With some exceptions, these are devoid of guidelines for ethical or moral responsibility. In Western societies, laws that addressed moral behavior are increasingly being ignored or overturned by judicial bodies. Furthermore, being a law-abiding citizen in compliance with secular laws is not necessarily synonymous with being ethical or of good moral standing.[2]

Shari'ah, on the other hand, is the law of God and has as its basis high moral and ethical standards. It addresses both the inner and external aspects of a person's behavior, individually and collectively as a society. Its objective is to promote general goodness in people and society by establishing that which is good and ethical and shunning everything bad, evil and immoral. Shari'ah requires that the individual and society eliminate inequality, injustice, immorality and all other sources of evil. Only goodness (individual and collective, as a society or nation) is compatible with Shari'ah. Any form of behavior that does not qualify as being "good", ie., being unjust, unfair, unfaithful, dishonest, immoral, etc., is incompatible with Shari'ah.

Enforceability of the Shari'ah

The term *law*, as used and understood in Western society, has a different meaning in its implication and usage when referring to Shari'ah. These are religion-based laws and rules, and with a few

---

[2] In the context of this discussion, morality is understood as defined by religious texts and teachings, in particular those of Islam.

exceptions such as criminal justice (*hudood* laws),[3] they are not enforceable by any governmental or judicial authority as there may not be any compulsion in the matter of religion.

Since Islam is a comprehensive way of life, the secular and religious aspects are inseparable and the Shari'ah covers every aspect of human behavior. That includes the conscience and intentions, unspoken thoughts and even contemplated but uncommitted actions. Only actual deeds that transgress the limits set by God are subject to punishment, not merely thoughts that may have contemplated an immorality or other evil, since a thought or intention may never be carried through.

Compliance with the Shari'ah is voluntary and is guided by an individual's relationship with God: reverence, love, fear of His displeasure, and consciousness of the accountability both in this life and after death. God requires that His rules be followed and that the individual seek His pleasure by obeying His Commandments and through acts of goodness, and to be fearful of His displeasure and wrath which may be incurred by deviating from the prescribed path. The consequences for all deeds (reward, punishment or forgiveness) is determined and dispensed by God alone. The authority for retribution of misdeeds against fellow humans have been relegated, in part, to those with administrative authority.

Compliance requires that the intended Shari'ah objectives be established. This is achieved by following the Sunnah of Prophet Muhammad ﷺ and by striving to emulate his noble qualities such as honesty, integrity, sincerity, politeness, truthfulness, compassion, fairness, kindness, generosity, etc.

Indeed in the messenger of Allah you have a good example for him who looks towards Allah and the Last Day and remembers Allah much.

(Surah 33, Al Ahzaab, ayat 21)

Fiqh and Shari'ah

The literal meaning of Fiqh is *understanding* or *discernment*. By

---

[3] *hudood* refers to the limits of the permissible and prohibited which have been set by God.

another definition, it is *the science of deducing Islamic laws from evidence found in the Qur'an and Sunnah,* ie., *the true understanding of the Religion.* Thus, Fiqh is the knowledge of the Law.

Since the understanding of the Qur'an and Sunnah forms the basis of Fiqh, it is also subject to some interpretational differences amongst learned scholars (*fuqaha*). Imam Abu Hanifa ﷺ, a respected Muslim scholar [80-150 AH (689-759 CE)] defined it as *a person's knowledge of his rights and duties.* Other jurists define it as *legal rules pertaining to conduct* (*shari ahkaam*). The difference between Shari'ah and Fiqh is that the former constitutes the law, while the latter is the knowledge of that law, the jurisprudence. Shari'ah and Fiqh provide rulings in matters which guide the individual to the straight path, ie., to distinguish between right and wrong in every aspect of life.

The Purpose of Shari'ah

The purpose of the Shari'ah is to protect and preserve the five essentials listed below. Each one of these is intimately linked with the others.

- Faith/religion (*deen*)
- Life (*nafs*)
- The family (*nasl*)
- The intellect (*'aql*)
- Property (*maal*)

Protection of faith/religion (*deen*)

Faith/religion secures the well-being of the individual with focus on the Hereafter, ie., protection from torment of Hell (*Jahannam*). In addition, it secures the well-being of the society by following the Divine instructions pertaining to conduct, moral, social and otherwise. The remaining four elements [life (*nafs*), family (*nasl*), intellect (*'aql*), property (*maal*)] serve to preserve the interests of the *deen* insofar as they promote ethical and moral behavior in the individual, in the community and society at large.

The protection of *deen* extends to all persons and includes their places of worship, namely, mosques, churches, temples, etc. Its broader implication is a guaranty for the freedom to practice the faith of one's choice.

Protection of human life (*nafs*)

The sanctity of human life is established by Shari'ah, and in this respect, no distinction is made between a Muslim and non-Muslim. Furthermore, the Shari'ah's protection includes all other living creatures. Also see Chapter 11, Minorities under Muslim Rule and Chapter 12, Human, Environmental, Animal and Other's Rights.

Protection of family (*nasl*)

This includes the general concepts of human rights, justice and fairness in dealing with others, maintaining the integrity of the family and respecting the rights accorded to spouses and children.

Protection of intellect (*'aql*)

Intellect may be understood as being the ability to reason and understand. Unlike other creations, humans and Jinn possess higher intellectual ability. They can choose what they wish to do and are therefore held responsible for their actions. Consequently, things that alter the ability of the mind to rational thinking and reasoning are prohibited, ie., mind-altering substances such as alcohol and other recreational drugs. This is not simply a ritualistic prohibition. In the Qur'an, it is acknowledged that there are some potential benefits in alcohol but its vices outweigh the good, therefore, it is prohibited.[4]

They ask you (Muhammad) about khamr (intoxicating drink) and gambling, say: In both is great harm and some benefit for mankind; but their sin is greater than their benefit. ...

(Surah 2, Al Baqarah, ayat 219)

Protection of property (*maal*)

Wealth is a major cause of conflict (interpersonal, societal and geopolitical). Shari'ah formulates strict rules to protect wealth and property. It also establishes guidelines for its expenditure.

---

[4] Also see Chapter 8, Family and Social Issues.

The Goals of Shari'ah

The goals of Shari'ah are to establish the following:
- Justice and equality in the community/society (*adl* and *qist*)
- Rights and obligations for individuals and society (*huqooq*)
- The practice of consultation (*shura*)
- Focus on general public interest (*masalih*)
- Achievement of success and salvation in this life and the Hereafter (*falah*)

Shari'ah is a course set by God. In order to live by the rules of Islam, one has to live in accordance with the Shari'ah. Compliance with the rules of Shari'ah requires that the intended goals be established. In other words, it is a complete and comprehensive package encompassing all aspects of conduct and includes inner thoughts and intentions. Those who accept and comply, follow this path to success, both in this life and the Hereafter.[5]

The verse quoted at the beginning of this chapter prescribes *adl* (justice) and *ihsan* (compassion). These must be, without exception, towards all of creation. The litmus test is one's actions. If either of these two elements is missing in the consequence of one's actions, the behavior cannot be in accordance with Shari'ah and a reassessment of that action is necessary, with readjustment of course.

Development of the Shari'ah

During the lifetime of Prophet Muhammad ﷺ, guidance was provided by the revelation of verses of the Qur'an, often pertaining to a particular subject matter. On numerous occasions, inspiration from God was relayed through the words and actions of the Prophet ﷺ.[6] On a number of other occasions, Prophet Muhammad ﷺ made decisions based upon his own reasoning and he also allowed his companions to do the same. These sources and proceedings form the basis of Shari'ah as understood and implemented.

---

[5] For a definition of *success* see the Concluding Commentary.

[6] Surah 53, An Najm, ayaat 3-5 : *Nor does he speak of his own desire. It is no other than an inspired Revelation. Which one of mighty powers has taught him.*

Sources for the Shari'ah

There are four sources from which the Shari'ah is derived:

- The Qur'an (the Words of God)
- The Sunnah of Prophet Muhammad ﷺ
- *Ijma'* of the companions *(sahabah)* of the Prophet ﷺ and also the *consensus* of Muslim Scholars
- *Ijtihaad,* personal judgement of Muslim scholars derived in conformity with the Qur'an and Sunnah

The Qur'an

The Qur'an, as the primary and most important source for the Shari'ah, provides both general and specific guidelines and directives. Its main emphasis is on faith and moral conduct, both for the individual and society as a whole. It provides the general principles, rules and regulations that are essential for a community based on Islam. In addition, there is specific prohibition of certain actions such as gambling, alcohol consumption, murder, and extramarital relationships. There are also succinct rules of inheritance, of reciprocity, conflict resolution and those governing prisoners, oaths and treaties, etc.

The Sunnah

Prophet Muhammad ﷺ delivered the message of Islam under Divine guidance. He spent every moment of his inspired life in guiding, directing, and leading those who believed and followed his message. Importantly, he taught by example, living by God's guidance in whatever he did or said. His life, teachings and actions constitute the Sunnah, the second source for the Shari'ah.

The authority of the Sunnah is unequivocally established in the Qur'an. It elaborates upon the rulings in the Qur'an, providing necessary explanations and details, eg., on how to pray, fast, etc. It also provides guidance on matters not explicit in the Qur'an. The Sunnah is recorded in books of Hadith. For additional information on Sunnah and Hadith see Chapter I, Islam.

In the following are a few verses from the Qur'an which emphasize the importance of the Sunnah.

O you who believe! Obey Allah and obey the messenger ...

and if you have a dispute concerning any matter, refer it to Allah and the messenger, ...   (Surah 4, An Nisa', ayat 59)

And whatever the messenger gives you, take it. And whatever he forbids, abstain from it.   (Surah 59, Al Hashr, ayat 7)

... He will enjoin on them that which is right and forbid them that which is wrong. He will make lawful for them all good things and prohibit for them only the foul ...   (Surah 7, Al A'raaf, ayat 157)

He who obeys the messenger, obeys Allah ...
                           (Surah 4, An Nisa', ayat 80)

Ijma' (Opinion by Consensus)

The *unanimous* opinion of the companions (*sahabah*) of Prophet Muhammad ﷺ and Muslim scholars, in understanding, interpreting, and applying any point of law not specified in the Qur'an and Sunnah, forms the third source for the Shari'ah. The Ijma' is bound by the limits set by the Qur'an and Sunnah. It provides an important mechanism for the Muslim society to adapt to changing world situations by permitting consensus rulings on contemporary issues and problems. It also permits reevaluation of earlier interpretations in light of the existing world and societal situations.

Ijtihaad (Personal Reasoning)

This method is used by scholars for rendering a binding legal opinion (a new ruling) in matters (new issues faced by the Muslim society) for which there is no clear cut directive in the Qur'an or Sunnah. It is an opinion of scholars that uses analytical deduction and is based upon a study of existing evidence from the Qur'an, Sunnah and Ijma'. It involves several levels of effort which include: opinion (*ra'y*), analogy (*qiyas*), equity (*istihsan*), public good (*istislah*), etc.

The use of deduction from the Qur'an and Sunnah was established by the Prophet ﷺ himself. After his death, the Khalifahs and other *sahabah* established the principles of *ijma'* and *ijtihaad* and also relied upon mutual consultation (*shura*) to make rulings that became necessary in response to specific situations and problems (*al fiqh al waqi*). The latter started with the expansion of the Muslim Commonwealth which brought with it issues that were not directly addressed by existing laws. The use of local customs of the new territories was approved provided these did not stand in contradiction with the Shari'ah.

Punishments prescribed by Shari'ah

Much has been confabulated about the punishments prescribed under Shari'ah. Each criminal action and its prescribed punishment must be viewed in the context of the severity of the offense and its effects upon the victim, the victim's family, and the society. Of fundamental importance is the proof of guilt. Eyewitnesses are required for conviction unless the offender admits to the crime voluntarily, without duress or torture. The latter is strictly prohibited. Also unacceptable are methods that extrapolate guilt by association or any other method of legalistic deduction.

Other points of consideration are the nature of the crime: was it material or moral, against an individual or society. Deviation from the path of faith and denial of Tauheed (that there is only One God) is a very serious offense, but it is considered a crime against oneself. It has no prescribed punishment under Shari'ah, unless the individual seeks to undermine the Muslim State or society. Crimes against other people are punishable by physical punishment which serves a twofold purpose: punishment for the criminal offense and to serve as a deterrent for other would-be perpetrators.

Sentencing must be fair and without racial or religious prejudice. While penalties have been fixed, there is room for discretion and adjustment based upon ijtihaad (personal reasoning), for reasons that may be compelling in nature.[7]

Thus, when assessing the prescribed punishments, it must be borne in mind that the very purpose of Shari'ah is to protect, amongst others, life, family and property. The wisdom and justice behind these laws may not be apparent to the casual observer, especially in those

---

[7] If the administrative authority rules with partiality resulting in injustice to the plaintiff or defendant, the person making the unjust ruling remains answerable to God. An unfair or unjust ruling by law enforcers (eg., judges) is considered a very serious offense.

societies where many ethical and moral crimes go unpunished or receive only insignificant punishment.

If a criminal escapes punishment in this life, because of social or political influence or flaws in the judicial system, that punishment surely awaits him/her on the Day of Reckoning, unless forgiven by God. No one will escape the final accountability for his/her actions and the punishment in this worldly life may be only a fraction of what may await the criminal in the next, the eternal life.

For the victim of a crime, forgiveness, mercy and compassion are encouraged. Yet, retribution or compensation is permitted for those who are not able to forgive. The following example illustrates this point. For a person convicted for murder after a fair trial (or the accused admits, without coercion, to having committed the crime), the heirs of the victim are afforded three options under Shari'ah:

- Ask for the death penalty
- Receive compensation for the loss, usually financial
- Forgive the murderer, ie., no punishment. However, in this case, the judge retains the right to sentence the accused for that particular crime *in the public interest,* ie., enforcing *community rights*

There is wisdom behind these choices. If the victim's heirs are able to forgive, their reward is with God.[8] The second option provides compensation, eg., to make up for the loss of the bread earner, but seeking the death penalty is an act of vengeance and provides no material benefit.

The punishment for theft is another example. The prescribed punishment for admitted theft is the cutting of a hand. This may seem very harsh in today's environment where theft at all levels seems to be tolerated with little repercussion. However, stealing is wrong and causes hardship for the victims and may even lead to other, more serious crimes, by the perpetrator. While the punishment seems harsh, it is also a deterrence for other would-be thieves. There are strict preconditions which must be fulfilled before a thief is committed

---

[8] Numerous verses in the Qur'an encourage forgiveness. Additionally, a Hadith states: *No one suffers any bodily injury and forgives this, except that Allah raises his rank by a degree and removes a sin from him.* English Translation of Jami' At-Tirmidhi, Darussalam, Riyadh, S Arabia, 2007. Volume 3, Hadith 1398, p182.

to losing a hand, and in practice, very few individuals meet this fate. In societies where such laws are implemented, there is virtually no theft or robbery.

In a Muslim society, adultery is considered a serious crime. In Western society, it has become socially accepted behavior. Adultery destroys the lives of many individuals and corrupts the moral fabric of society. Consequently, the punishment for adultery is also severe.

Adaptation of the Shari'ah to changing situations

Islam, being the final message from God, is good for all times and all geographic locations. Thus, to be able to guide all generations, the Shari'ah has to be applicable in every place and at all times. Unlike the uninformed representations of some individuals, the Shari'ah is not *a collection of antiquated laws*. It is a living law which has the inherent ability to adapt to every given situation.

Of the four sources that constitute the Shari'ah, the first two (the Qur'an and the Sunnah) are unalterable. The remaining two, Ijma' and Ijtihaad, provide the vehicle for the adaptability of Shari'ah to all times and places. Its rulings are universally applicable and are not influenced by emotional, economic, ethnic, social or political issues. Further insight into the workings of the Shari'ah and its ability to adapt may be found in the section on Science and Bioethical Issues.

Concluding Commentary

For each of you, We have prescribed a law and a clear way.
(Surah 5, Al Ma'idah, ayat 48)

Shari'ah has a central role in Islamic practice. It provides the guidance to mankind for the fulfillment of the purpose of their creation, which is the worship of the Creator, through complete submission to Him. As the definition of the word Shari'ah indicates, it is a path leading to the obedience of the Creator, providing success both in this world and the Hereafter. The ultimate measure for success is the achievement of Divine acceptance and good pleasure: *...the greatest bliss of all is the pleasure of Allah. That is the supreme success* (Surah 9, At Taubah, ayat 72).

Success in this worldly life may be gauged differently. By some standards, particularly those of affluent societies, this may mean financial and professional accomplishment, notoriety, acceptance in societal circles, etc. While the believing Muslim is encouraged to strive, he/she will often find contentment in accepting a simpler, low-key life style and absence of extravagance.

Spiritually, Shari'ah promotes God-consciousness and sense of accountability. Since mistakes can be expected despite the best endeavour, Islam provides the vehicle for ongoing course-correction and redemption through seeking forgiveness, regular prayer and remembrance of God, charity and fasting. The individual who is conscious of his/her faith is also committed to the sanctity of life, the integrity of the family, and respects the honour and property of others. Furthermore, such a person will neither place him/herself in a situation which could lead to undesirable or prohibited acts, nor resort to the use of substances which provide freedom from inhibition.

Shari'ah provides guidance for every aspect of a Muslim's life, for issues related to worship and general conduct, family and inheritance, individual rights, morals, political, social and economic matters. Just like water sustains life, Shari'ah sustains the integrity of the Muslim soul. Muslims must accept and follow the Shari'ah throughout their lives.

Shari'ah applies equally to everyone and at all times and no one is above it. There are no concessions for rank, social or political status. Although the initial rules were formulated at the time of Prophet Muhammad ﷺ, it has remained remarkably adaptable to all changes, including socioeconomic, political and geographic. The Shari'ah remains as valid in its applicability today as it was in times past. This is possible because of the incorporation of ingenious mechanisms into the sources from which the rulings are derived which allow it to address all contemporary issues.

Chapter Five

Isra' and Miraj, Jerusalem

Introduction

Glory be to Him Who carried His servant by night from the Inviolable Place of Worship[1] to the Far Distant Place of Worship[2] whose surroundings We have blessed, that We might show him some of our signs! He is the Hearer, the Seer.
(Surah 17, Al Isra', ayat 1)

His sight never swerved, nor did it go wrong! For truly he did see of the greater Signs of his Lord. (Surah 53, An Najm, ayaat 17-18)

Isra' and Miraj refer to the Night Journey and Heavenly Visitation of Prophet Muhammad ﷺ which occurred about eighteen months before the Hijrah (emigration) to Madinah. Upon the order from God, he was taken from the *Masjid al Haram* in Makkah to the *Masjid al Aqsa* in Jerusalem. From there, he ascended to the heavens and met Adam ﷺ and other earlier Prophets. It was during the Miraj that the five daily prayers were prescribed for Muslims.

---

[1] *Masjid al Haram:* The Inviolable Place of Worship (or The Sacred Mosque) is the mosque in Makkah, Arabia which is built around the Ka'ba.

[2] *Masjid al Aqsa:* The Far Distant Place of Worship (The Farthest Place of Worship or The Far Distant Mosque) refers to the Noble Sanctuary (al Har'am al Sharif) in Jerusalem (Al Quds).

This event was concluded within the course of several hours. Prophet Muhammad ﷺ had never been to Jerusalem prior to this Night Journey. As expected, those doubting the event quizzed him about the city. His succinct answers were silencing. The Prophet ﷺ said: *When the people of Quraish did not believe me, I stood up in Al Hijr and Allah displayed Jerusalem in front of me and I began describing it to them while I was looking at it.*[3]

Some writers suggest that the Isra' and Miraj were not a physical experience.[4] For those who believe that Moses ؑ parted the sea for his followers to escape pursuit by the Pharaoh and that Jesus ؑ raised the dead and healed the blind and the leper, there is little choice but to believe that the Night Journey and Heavenly Visitation of Prophet Muhammad ﷺ were physical experiences since they were facilitated by the exact same Almighty God.

Neither is this event a "story" nor did Prophet Muhammad ﷺ "seek" the advice of Moses and other Prophets.[5,6] It is evident from the Hadith (see the next section), that Prophet Moses ؑ volunteered some important advice based upon the experience with his own followers.

---

[3] The Translation of the Meanings of Sahih Al-Bukhari. MM Khan. Kazi Publications, Lahore, Pakistan, 1979. Volume V, Hadith 226, page 142.

[4] Armstrong K: Islam's Stake. Why Jerusalem Was Central to Muhammad. ... *Muslim texts make it clear that this was not a physical experience but a visionary one (not dissimilar to the heavenly visions of the Jewish Throne Mystics at this time).* http://www.time.com/time/2001/jerusalem/islam.html Last accessed May 2011. Comment: It is unclear to which *Muslim texts* the author was referring.

[5] The meanings of the word *story* include: *narrative, fiction, falsehood.* This author had also suggested that the *Isra' and Miraj* was only a *visionary* event. The meanings of the latter term include *imaginary* and *fantastic.* See footnote 4 and 6.

[6] Armstrong K: Islam's Stake. Why Jerusalem Was Central to Muhammad. *The centrality of Jerusalem in Muslim spirituality is apparent in the "story" of Muhammad's mystical Night Journey to Jerusalem... On his way up he "sought the advice" of Moses, Aaron, Enoch, Jesus, John the Baptist and Abraham before entering the presence of God. The "story" shows the "yearning" of the Muslims to come from far-off Arabia right into the heart of the monotheistic family, symbolized by Jerusalem.* Emphasis added. http://www.time.com/time/2001/jerusalem/islam.html Last accessed May 2011.

The Isra' and Miraj

In the following is a description of the Isra' and Miraj, abbreviated from several Hadith.[7,8]

- Al Buraq[9] was brought to Prophet Muhammad ﷺ and he set out with the angel Gabriel ☽. The first leg of the journey took them from Makkah to the *Masjid al Aqsa* in Jerusalem. Here, he led an assembly of earlier prophets in a congregational prayer. Subsequently, accompanied by Gabriel ☽, he ascended to the different levels of heaven

- In the nearest heaven, he met Adam ☽. In the second heaven, he met Isa ☽ (Jesus) and Yahya ☽ (John). In the third heaven, he met Yusuf (Joseph), in the fourth he met Idris (Enoch), in the fifth he met Haroon (Aaron), in the sixth he met Musa (Moses) and in the seventh heaven he met Ibrahim (Abraham) (may peace be upon them all)

- He was shown *Al Bait al Ma'mur* (The Sacred House of God) where each day prayers are performed by a fresh batch of seventy thousand angels. Then, he was shown *Sidrat ul Muntaha*. This is a tree in the seventh heaven (*the Lote Tree of the utmost boundary*) and at its root originated four rivers: two were hidden, while the other two were apparent. Gabriel ☽ informed him that the two hidden rivers were in Paradise and the visible rivers were the Nile and Euphrates

- A container full of wine, another with milk and a third with honey were presented to him. Prophet Muhammad ﷺ took the container with milk. Thereupon, Gabriel ☽ told him that his choice represented the true faith (*al fitrah, ie., Islam*) which he and his Ummah (ie., Muslims) were following[10]

- It was here that he received the injunction for fifty prayers (*salat*) every day and night. While returning he met Moses ☽

---

[7] The Translation of the Meanings of Sahih Al-Bukhari. MM Khan. Kazi Publications, Lahore, Pakistan, 1979. Volume IV, Hadith 429, pages 287-290.

[8] The Translation of the Meanings of Sahih Al-Bukhari. MM Khan. Kazi Publications, Lahore, Pakistan, 1979. Volume V, Hadith 227, pages 143-148.

[9] *Buraq* was the name of the heavenly steed which transported the Prophet ﷺ during Isra' and Miraj. He described it as being a white animal, smaller than a mule and larger than a donkey.

[10] The Translation of the Meanings of Sahih Al-Bukhari. MM Khan. Kazi Publications, Lahore, Pakistan, 1979. Volume V, Hadith 227, pages 143-148.

who inquired: *What have you been ordered to do?* On learning about the fifty prayers, Moses ﷺ advised Prophet Muhammad ﷺ *...return to your Lord and request Him (to reduce the number of prayers)...* as it would be too difficult for his followers to comply. Prophet ﷺ returned and ultimately the number of daily prayers was reduced to five and each good deed would be credited *as if it were ten good deeds.*

The Significance of Isra' and Miraj

This event took place at a time of great difficulty for the Prophet ﷺ and the Muslims as persecution by the Makkan pagans was intense. It served to reassure him of the importance of his mission as a Prophet of God and bestow courage and dignity upon the Muslims. In addition, it put to test the faith of the early Muslims. This event is mentioned in two surahs of the Qur'an, Al Isra' (Surah 17) and An Najm (Surah 53).

Each stage of this event has a particular significance:
- Journey from Makkah to Jerusalem (Al Quds)
- The congregational prayer of all prophets in Al Quds, at *al Masjid al Aqsa*
- Ascent to the celestial regions, meeting earlier prophets and receiving the injunction for the daily prayers (*salat*)
- Disclosure of some of the signs of God (see verses quoted at the beginning of this chapter)
- Choice between wine, milk, and honey

Journey from Makkah to Jerusalem (Al Quds)

The journey from the *Masjid al Haram* in Makkah to the *Masjid al Aqsa* in Jerusalem, a region which hosted numerous previous prophets, symbolizes the spiritual singularity of both regions and the respective religions. It also symbolizes the universality of Prophet Muhammad's ﷺ message, in distinction to the ethnic, regional or temporally limited messages of the earlier prophets.

The congregational prayer of all prophets at *al Masjid al Aqsa*

In Jerusalem, Prophet Muhammad ﷺ prayed at *al Masjid al Aqsa*, leading a congregation of earlier prophets. It is immaterial whether this event was physical or spiritual, because in either case, it represents his role as the leader of all Prophets (*Imam al Anbiya'*). The role assigned to him was that of unification of all prior messages under Islam, as the surrender to the Will of the One Almighty God. It confirms that his Message was a guidance for all people.

It also emphasizes the importance to Muslims of the Al Aqsa Sanctuary, which includes the Al Aqsa Mosque and the Dome of the Rock Mosque. Besides being the place for his ascension to the heavens (Miraj), it was also the first *qibla* (the direction in which Muslims face to pray) for about three years before the Hijrah to Madinah and for about sixteen months thereafter. The Al Aqsa Mosque is as sacred as the Sacred Mosque in Makkah and the Prophet's Mosque in Madinah.

Ascent to the celestial regions and the injunction for prayers (*salat*)

During the Heavenly Visitation (Miraj), the daily prayers (*salat*) were prescribed. All other directives (fasting, Zakat, Haj, etc) were prescribed on earth. That the prayers were prescribed in heaven serves to underline their immense importance in Islam. The prescribed daily prayers are recognized as a Divine gift to all Muslims which enables them to connect with and worship Almighty God in a regular fashion. It also symbolizes spiritual ascension to heaven for every Muslim while engaged in prayer.

Disclosure of some signs and choice between wine and milk

Prophet Muhammad ﷺ was shown *Al Bait al Ma'mur* (The Sacred House of God) and *Sidrat ul Muntaha*: *...that We might show him some of our signs!* (Surah 17, Al Isra', ayat 1). These were glimpses of Paradise. The significance of the choice between wine and milk which were offered to the Prophet ﷺ is explained in the Hadith. Milk symbolized true faith (*al fitrah*). His selection of milk indicated that his guidance would lead his followers (Ummah) to the true faith.[11] The selection of wine would have meant that his followers would have been misled.

Physical or Spiritual Journey

The Isra' and Miraj were a miracle, like the miracles of previous prophets. A dream or spiritual journey cannot be construed as being a miracle. This event is very extraordinary and it is mentioned in two

---

[11] Literally, *ummah* means *nation/community*.

surahs, Al Isra' and An Najm.

Each word in the Qur'an is purposeful. Surah 17, Al Isra', ayat 1 states: *Glory be to Him Who carried His servant by night...* There are two words which indicate the physical nature of this event: *carried* and *servant.* Here, the meaning and implication of *carried* (or transported) as being a physical phenomenon does not need further elaboration. The Arabic word for *servant* is *'abd* (also translated as slave) refers to a whole person and includes both body and soul.

Verse 60 of the same surah (Al Isra'), states: *...And We made what We have shown you now (ru'yal-latee) and also the cursed tree[12] mentioned in the Qur'an as a trial for mankind...* The Arabic word *ru'ya* is indicative of physically seeing with the eyes and does not refer to a vision or a dream.[13] That this was a physical event and not a dream or spiritual journey, is reiterated in the commentary on this verse by Ibn Abbas ﷺ: *The sights which God's Prophet ﷺ was shown on the Night Journey when he was taken to Bait al Maqdis (Jerusalem) were actual sights, (not dreams). And the cursed tree mentioned in the Qur'an is the tree of Zaqqum itself.*[14]

In the Presence of God سبحانه وتعالى

Prophet Muhammad ﷺ was shown *Al Bait ul Ma'mur* (The Sacred House) but he did not see God. When asked what he saw, his answer was: Light. The question, whether the Prophet ﷺ saw God, was also put to his wife A'isha ﷺ. Her reply was:[15] *...Whoever tells you that Muhammad ﷺ saw his Lord, is a liar.* She recited the following verses: *Vision cannot comprehend Him, but He comprehends all vision. He is the Subtle, the Aware* (Surah 6, An An'aam, ayat 103); *And it is not granted to any mortal that Allah should speak to him unless it be by revelation or from behind a veil, or that He sends a messenger...* (Surah 42, Ash Shura, ayat 51).

Another Hadith quotes A'isha ﷺ:[16] *Whoever claimed that (the Prophet)*

---

[12] The tree of *Zaqqum* is at the bottom of Hell. The bitter fruit of this tree will be the food of those cast into Hell. Surah 56, Al Waqi'ah, ayaat 52-53.

[13] The Meaning of the Qur'an. Maududi SAA, Islamic Publications Ltd., Lahore, Pakistan. Volume VI, pages 149-154.

[14] The Translation of the Meanings of Sahih Al-Bukhari. MM Khan. Kazi Publications, Lahore, Pakistan, 1979. Volume V, Hadith 228, pages 148-149.

[15] The Translation of the Meanings of Sahih Al-Bukhari. MM Khan. Kazi Publications, Lahore, Pakistan, 1979. Volume VI, Hadith 378, page 359.

[16] The Translation of the Meanings of Sahih Al-Bukhari. MM Khan. Kazi Publications, Lahore, Pakistan, 1979. Volume IV, Hadith 457, page 301.

Muhammad ﷺ *saw his Lord, is committing a great fault, for he only saw Gabriel in his genuine shape in which he was created, covering the whole horizon.* While he did not see God, Prophet Muhammad ﷺ was shown several remarkable sights, including glimpses of Paradise and Hell: *For truly he did see of the greater Signs of his Lord* (Surah 53, An Najm, ayat 18).

Jerusalem (Al Quds)[17]

A portion of the old city of Jerusalem is one of the three most sacred places for Muslims. The other two localities that were blessed by God are Makkah and Madinah. Jerusalem is important to Muslims for several reasons. Firstly, it was blessed and designated a *masjid* by God [*al Masjid al Aqsa* or *The Far Distant Place of Worship whose surroundings We have blessed,* (Surah 17, Al Isra', ayat 1)]. Secondly, this was the first *qibla* for Muslims. Thirdly, it was the site for the Miraj, ie., the ascension to the heavens during the Night Journey. Additionally, it was the place where Prophet Muhammad ﷺ prayed, leading the congregation of previous prophets.

The Sacred Mosque in Makkah (*al Masjid al Haram*) was first place on earth to be designated a *masjid,* ie., a place of worship, and a Sacred Sanctuary. This occurred before the creation of Adam ﷺ. Forty years later, a small area in ancient Jerusalem became the second place to be designated a *masjid,* namely, the *Masjid al Aqsa.*[18] Madinah is the third of the three places to receive Divine Blessings. Madinah is one place where the Dajjal (Antichrist) will not be able to enter.[19] See Chapter 25, Qiyamah, for a discussion on the Dajjal.

Each of these sanctuaries is very dear to all Muslims. A prayer (*salat*) made in any one of these sanctuaries carries a several hundred-fold greater benefit than in any other place. Prophet Muhammad ﷺ said: *Do not set out on a journey except for three mosques, ie., al Masjid al Haram (the Sacred Mosque in Makkah), al Masjid al Nabwi (the Prophet's* ﷺ

---

[17] Also see Chapter 23, Crusades and Holy War.

[18] English Translation of Sahih Muslim. Darussalam, Riyadh, S Arabia, 2007. Volume 2, Hadith 1161, page 15.

[19] English Translation of Jami At-Tirmidhi. Darussalam, Riyadh, S Arabia, 2007. Volume 4, Hadith 2242, page 291.

mosque in Madinah), and al Masjid al Aqsa (in Jerusalem).[20]

The Name *Al Quds*

Al Quds is the most commonly used Islamic name for Jerusalem and means *purified, blessed, sacred, holy*.[21] This designation, ie., *al Quds*, was bestowed centuries before Prophet Abraham ﷺ came to this region. Other names are *al Bayt al Maqdis* which means *Sacred or Holy House* and *al Bayt al Muqaddas* which means a *purified, sacred place, free from polytheism*.[22] These latter name refers to Jerusalem and the adjacent areas, namely, the region that is Palestine. It is also known as *al Ard al Muqaddasa*, meaning *The Sacred or Holy Land* and refers to Palestine and other adjacent regions, possibly the region that lies between the rivers Nile and Euphrates.

The First Qibla

The *qibla* is the direction towards which Muslims face during prayer (*salat*). Initially, Muslims faced towards Jerusalem. Some writers suggested that by turning towards Jerusalem during prayer, Muslims were *symbolically reaching out toward the Jewish and Christian God, whom they were committed to worshipping, and turning their back on the paganism of Arabia*.[23] This opinion is incorrect. In Islamic belief, there no "Jewish", "Christian", or "Muslim" God. There is just One God of all that exists, *Rabbal Alameen*, the Lord of the worlds. The Muslims were simply obeying the Commandment of that One and Only God, ie., to face in the direction of Jerusalem, when praying. Here, the only symbolism was that all Muslims turned towards one specific direction while worshipping the One and Only God, and that represents unity of the Islamic faith.

The switch in the direction of prayer, to face Makkah instead of Jerusalem, took place while Prophet Muhammad ﷺ was in Madinah.

[20] The Translation of the Meanings of Sahih Al-Bukhari. MM Khan. Kazi Publications, Lahore, Pakistan, 1979. Volume II, Hadith 281, page 157.

[21] Other historical names of the city were Urrusalim (Canaanite), Elia or Ilia (Roman), Jebus and Salem.

[22] H Bazian: Jerusalem in Islamic Consciousness. A textual survey of the Muslim claims and rights to the Sacred City. University of California Berkeley, 2006, pages 17-21. ISBN 1-4276-0619-6

[23] Armstrong K: Islam's Stake. Why Jerusalem Was Central to Muhammad. http://www.time.com/time/2001/jerusalem/islam.html Last accessed May 2011.

The sole reason for it was a Commandment from God:

... And We appointed the qibla which you formerly observed only that We might know him who follows the messenger, from him who turns on his heels. In truth, it was a hard test except for those whom Allah guided ..

... Surely, We shall make you turn (in prayer) toward a qibla which is dear to you. So turn your face toward the Masjid al Haram (Ka'ba in Makkah), and you O' Muslims, wherever you may be, turn your faces (when you pray) toward it. Those who have received the Scripture know that (this Revelation) is the Truth from their Lord. And Allah is not unaware of what they do. (Surah 2, Al Baqarah, ayaat 143-144)

There was a sizable Jewish population in Madinah. The scholarly amongst them recognized that Muhammad ﷺ was the promised messenger [*Those who have received the Scripture know that (this Revelation) is the Truth from their Lord*]. The directive to change the direction of worship from Jerusalem to Makkah weeded out those whose pretended to be following Islam.

The foolish amongst the people will say: What has turned them from the qibla which they formerly observed? Say: To Allah belong the East and the West. He guides whom He will onto a straight path.
(Surah 2, Al Baqarah, ayat 142)

Brief Overview of the Pertinent History of Jerusalem

- After the Great Flood, the region was inhabited by the descendants of Noah ﷺ who are also known as Canaanites. Those living in Jebus (Jerusalem) were called Jebusites
- 1800 BC or thereabouts, Prophet Abraham ﷺ migrated to this region: *And We rescued him and (his nephew) Lot (and brought them) to the land which We have blessed for all peoples*[24] (Surah 21, Al Anbiya', ayat 71)
- Around 1184 BC, the Israelites invaded the Land of Canaan
- 1000 BC or thereabouts, (800 years after Prophet Abraham ﷺ migrated to the region), King David (Prophet Dawud ﷺ)

---

[24] "All" includes everyone, not just one particular nation or religious group.

captured Jerusalem

- 960–927 BC, the reign of Solomon (Sulaiman ﷺ). David and Solomon (peace be upon them) ruled for a total of 73 years after which their kingdom disintegrated.[25] Following a Revelation from God,[26] Solomon ﷺ had a place built for the worship of God (a masjid, also known as the Temple of Solomon or the First Temple)
- 587/586 BC, the place of worship (masjid, temple) built by Solomon ﷺ was destroyed
- 516/515 BC, the place of worship (masjid, temple) was rebuilt
- 63 CE, it was destroyed by the Romans and was never rebuilt
- 620 CE, Isra' and Miraj of Prophet Muhammad ﷺ
- 631 CE (9 AH), a delegation of Christian Arabs, consisting of members of several different tribes from Jerusalem and adjacent regions, visited the Prophet ﷺ in Madinah and embraced Islam. They returned home to Palestine to establish the first Muslim community
- 637 CE (16 AH), Jerusalem came under Muslim rule after the signing of the Surrender Treaty (al 'Uhda al Umaria)
- 637 CE (16 AH), Umar ibn Khattab ﷺ had a mosque constructed at the south side of the Sanctuary. This is the *Al Aqsa Mosque*. The original building was a wooden structure. Construction of a stone/mortar building was started by the Khalifah Abd al Malik ibn Marwan and was completed in 705 CE (86 AH)
- 685 CE (66 AH), construction of the Dome of the Rock Mosque was commissioned by Khalifah Abd al Malik ibn Marwan. It was completed around 691 CE (72 AH). The *Dome of the Rock Mosque* is situated in the middle of the Al Aqsa Sanctuary

Of note is that the exact location of the Temple of Solomon, which was completely destroyed over 1900 years ago, has not been found

---

[25] Seventy-three year rule over Jerusalem. I Chronicles 29:27 and II Chronicles 9:30.

[26] Siddiqi M : Status of Al-aqsa Mosque.
http://infad.usim.edu.my/modules.php?op=modload&name=News&file=article&sid=9006&mode=thread&order=0&thold=0   Last accessed May 2011.

despite extensive search and excavation. In 637 CE (16 AH), upon acceptance of the conditions of the Surrender Treaty (al 'Uhda al Umaria), the inhabitants of Jerusalem formally transferred all political rights to the Muslim rulers.[27] From that time onward, with relatively brief periods of control by the Crusaders, Muslims had ruled Jerusalem and surrounding regions for over thirteen centuries.

The Muslim Sanctuaries of Jerusalem (Al Quds)

In the following is a brief description and discussion of the significance of each of the main structures. For additional information, the reader is referred to: Jerusalem in Islamic Consciousness. A textual survey of the Muslim claims and rights to the Sacred City by Dr. Hatem Bazian (see footnote 27).

Al Masjid al Aqsa (The Far Distant Place of Worship)

Al Masjid al Aqsa refers to the entire Sanctuary, inclusive of all its buildings and other structures. This is an approximately 35.5 acre, rectangular plateau in the heart of old Jerusalem (Al Quds). It is also know as al Har'am al Sharif which means The Noble Sanctuary. Al Aqsa means far distant. The literal meaning of masjid is a place of worship, a place for sajdah (prostration during prayer). The term masjid is generic for a place of worship and does not specify a particular structure but is commonly used for a mosque.

This place was given the designation of a place for worship, al Masjid al Aqsa, by God.[28] After the Sacred Mosque in Makkah, this was the second place on earth to be designated a masjid, for the worship of the One God of the universe. At that time, there was no man-constructed structure known to be in existence.[29] The Sacred Mosque in Makkah had been designated a place of worship forty years earlier.[30]

---

[27] Bazian H: Jerusalem in Islamic Consciousness. A textual survey of the Muslim claims and rights to the Sacred City. University of California Berkeley, 2006, pages 107-139. ISBN 1-4276-0619-6

[28] Surah 17, Al Isra', ayat 1.

[29] English Translation of Sahih Muslim. Darussalam, Riyadh, S Arabia, 2007. Volume 2, Hadith 1161, page 15.

[30] English Translation of Sahih Muslim. Darussalam, Riyadh, S Arabia, 2007. Volume 2, Hadith 1161, page 15.

Thus, Makkah and Al Quds (Jerusalem) were *places of worship* and Sacred Sanctuaries, well before the arrival of Prophet Abraham ﷺ to that region. The designation *al Masjid al Aqsa* (*The Far Distant Place of Worship*) distinguishes it from the first and the most important House of Worship built on earth, namely, the Ka'ba in Makkah.

Together with *al Masjid al Aqsa*, the entire region has a special religious status (*...whose surroundings We have blessed,...*).[31] It is called *al Bayt al Maqdis* (The Sacred or Holy House) and *al Ard al Muqaddasa* (The Sacred or Holy Land) and its sanctity was reconfirmed by the events of the Isra', the Night Journey, during which Prophet Muhammad ﷺ was brought from Makkah to this spot in Al Quds. This is the place where he led the previous prophets in prayer, a congregation which must have filled the entire 35.5 acre plateau. Additionally, in the middle of the Sanctuary is the rock from where he ﷺ ascended to the heavens (Miraj).

Al Aqsa Mosque

This mosque is located at the southern part of the plateau. The original wooden mosque was built by the second Khalifah, Umar ibn al Khattab ﷺ, around 637 CE. *Al Aqsa Mosque* should not be confused with the *Mosque of Umar* which is located next to the Church of the Holy Sepulchre.

Dome of the Rock (Qubbat as Sakhrah)

This mosque is located in the middle of the plateau. The building covers the rock from where Prophet Muhammad ﷺ ascended to the heavens during his Night Journey. It is an unmistakable building which adorns the city's skyline with its gold colored dome.

Al Buraq Wall

This is a part of the western wall of the al Aqsa Mosque (also known as the Wailing Wall). It is named after the heavenly steed (al Buraq) which transported Prophet Muhammad ﷺ on the Night Journey. Prophet Muhammad ﷺ had tied al Buraq at this wall.

---

[31] Surah 17, Al Isra', ayat 1.

Al Aqsa Islamic Endowment (*waqf*)

The buildings and structures in the Noble Sanctuary (*al Har'am al Sharif*), including the two mosques and the western wall of the *al Aqsa Mosque*, ie., *al Buraq Wall*, are included in an Islamic *waqf* (endowment).[32] All included structures enjoy the same legal and spiritual status as the al Aqsa Mosque itself. Currently, the buildings house a museum, schools and center for higher learning. This endowment trust is inviolable and the responsibility for its preservation falls upon all Muslims, all over the world.

Jerusalem and Multiple Facets of the Same Faith

Muslims revere all Prophets of God. Islam, which is the *submission to God*, is the same religion that was preached by all previous prophets. Their basic message was that of *Tauheed*, that is, God is One. Each nation received a messenger from God and for each nation there was a specific law (a Shari'ah). The succession of prophets was concluded with the Last Messenger of God who reiterated the teachings of all previous prophets and brought a comprehensive law (a Shari'ah) that was good for all times.

A part of the old city of Jerusalem was assigned the privileged status of *masjid*, ie., *place of worship*. This is the *Masjid al Aqsa*. It is also called as *al Bayt al Maqdis* (The Sacred or Holy House) or *al Har'am al Sharif* (The Noble Sanctuary) and the entire region is known as *al Ard al Muqaddasa* (The Sacred or Holy Land). This designation came forty years after that of the first earthly House of Worship in Makkah. Neither of these places of worship received this extraordinary privilege in conjunction with any particular faith or people and the sole purpose of such designation was for the worship of the One God of the universe.

By virtue of its being a blessed region (*al Ard al Muqaddasa*), it has

---

[32] Sheikh M. S. Al-Munajjid: Confusion About Al-Aqsa Mosque.
http://infad.usim.edu.my/modules.php?op=modload&name=News&file=article&sid=9
250&mode=thread&order=0&thold=0 Last accessed May 2011.
Ikrimah Sabri: Buildings Surrounding Al-Aqsa Mosque.
http://www.islamonline.net/servlet/Satellite?pagename=IslamOnlineEnglishAsk_Schol
ar/FatwaE/FatwaE&cid=1119503543550 Last accessed March 2009.

witnessed many prophets. A few of the names are familiar: Abraham, Lot, David, Solomon, Jesus (peace be upon them all). The last of the great prophets to stay in that region was Jesus ﷺ. About 620 years later, the region was blessed by a brief visit from the Final Messenger of God, Muhammad ﷺ, during the Isra' and Miraj.

The region was designated *al Ard al Muqaddasa* (The Sacred or Holy Land) millennia before the times of Prophets David and Solomon (peace be upon them). History also shows that entire region was inhabited by others, long before the influx of Israelites. Those people also witnessed prophets who preached the exact same message from God. Thus, *al Ard al Muqaddasa* (The Sacred or Holy Land) served as the amalgamation point for all those messengers and their singular message, namely, God is One.[33]

After the destruction of the second Temple, there was no significant Jewish presence in the region. For many centuries, Jerusalem and the surrounding areas have been home to millions of Palestinians. In the turbulent times that grip the region today, the concern of Muslims worldwide is that the traditional multi-ethnic composition of the city and surrounding areas is being drastically and illegally altered. Ironically, Muslim protection and tolerance of Jews is being repaid by intolerance and eviction.

Concluding Commentary

Prophets went through distress and times of uncertainty. Although their belief in God remained unshakable, they may have desired some Divine reassurance. While not much is known about actual words of most earlier prophets, we do know from the Qur'an, that Abraham and Moses (peace be upon them) sought some *signs* from God.

The period preceding the Isra' and Miraj was very difficult for Prophet Muhammad ﷺ and the Muslims because of the intense persecution by the pagans and the death of the Prophet's ﷺ wife Khadeeja ﷺ and his uncle Abu Talib. The latter's influence in the affairs of the Quraish protected the Prophet ﷺ from physical harm at the hands of the Makkan pagans. We have no way of knowing his inner

---

[33] There were over a hundred thousand prophets sent to mankind. A prophet or messenger came to every nation.

thoughts in that hostile environment, but we do know with certainty, that God is aware of what every person thinks or wishes.

While the pagans may not have believed him when he related the events of Isra' and Miraj the following day, Prophet Muhammad ﷺ was reassured. This miraculous event also gave the small Muslim community courage and strength to stand up to the hostilities.

God is infinite and is certainly not restricted by time or place. Humans function at a vastly different level and are quite restricted by their limitations. Thus, to communicate with man, God uses that mode of communication which man is able to understand. Since the revelation of the Qur'an was intended through Muhammad ﷺ, it was brought in the only language he was able to understand. The same applied to all earlier prophets. Visual communication is based on the same principle. Having seen the things God wanted him to see (*that We might show him of our signs!*), Prophet Muhammad ﷺ was able to describe them to his companions, who also transmitted that information to latter generations (through the Hadith). Seeing took it from the abstract to the actual.

God says about Al Quds (Jerusalem): ...*whose surroundings We have blessed...* (Surah 17, Al Isra', ayat 1). Jerusalem and surrounding areas have seen a large number of prophets, but that region has also witnessed, and continues to witness, some of the greatest turmoil and possibly the most gruesome human behavior. From the Muslim standpoint, *Al Quds* (Jerusalem) does not belong only to the followers of one particular faith. It belongs to all who believe in the One God of the universe, to share and cherish its sanctity in peaceful coexistence.

Chapter Six

Jihad
The Struggle to Self-Discipline

Introduction

Indeed, among the greatest types of Jihad is a just statement (kalimat al-'adl) before a tyrannical ruler.[1]

Shari'ah and Jihad are two of the most misunderstood and also most misrepresented Islamic terms in the Western media vocabulary. Jihad is a uniquely noble undertaking with the purpose of striving for overall goodness, rectitude and justice, to benefit both Muslims and non-Muslims alike.

First and foremost, Jihad is the inner struggle of the individual to change oneself (thoughts and actions) in such a fashion so as to make God's acceptance of all actions the sole objective. This means abiding by the principles of Islam, ie., honesty, integrity, fairness, morality, compassion for others, and doing overall general goodness. This is achieved through purification of the self so that every action seeks to please God. It pursues the true meaning of *submission to God,* ie., Islam, which is the ultimate goal of every believer. It is the passport to contentment and lasting inner peace. It is simply doing good for seeking Divine mercy and acceptance before the inevitable Day of Accountability.

---

[1] *... a just statement before a tyrannical ruler* means admonishing a tyrannical ruler to do good and refrain from doing wrong. English Translation of Jami' At-Tirmidhi, Darussalam, Riyadh, S Arabia, 2007. Volume 4, Hadith 2174, page 233.

On the day when every soul will come pleading for itself, and every soul shall be paid in full for what it did, and they shall not be wronged.

(Surah 16, An Nahl, ayat 111)

Collectively, Jihad is the struggle to oppose social and other evils such as those that cause injustices, inequality, suppression of freedom, aggression, exploitation and oppression of innocent people. The ultimate goal is to remove injustices. With justice comes peace and harmony and it is the duty of every Muslim to uphold justice under all circumstances.

O you who believe! Stand out firmly for God as witnesses to fair dealings, and let not the hatred of others make you to swerve to wrong and depart from justice. Be just; that is next to piety. And fear God. For God is informed of what you do. (Surah 5, Al Ma'idah, ayat 8)

Jihad to bring about justice and peace may necessitate fighting (warfare) as well as other sacrifices. The permission to fight is conditional: *And fight in the cause of Allah those who fight against you but do not commit aggression because Allah does not like aggressors* (Surah 2, Al Baqarah, ayat 190). Islamic rules of military engagement prohibit harming non-combatants, the elderly, women and children, or the wanton destruction of property and crops. The Shari'ah also explicitly prohibits the extradition of prisoners to a party that may subject them to torture.

Understanding Jihad

To be able to understand the Islamic practice of Jihad, the meanings of two terms need to be understood. These are *nafs* and *jihad*. In addition, it is necessary to know that every action is judged by the underlying intention, and in the final analysis, it is the individual's accountability on the Day of Judgement that matters. The sincerity with which a task is pursued and the intensity of the individual's desire for a good relationship with God determine the final results. Since the ultimate goal is God's acceptance of all actions, the onus is upon the individual to endeavour towards that goal. One cannot plead ignorance because the rules have been laid out very clearly.

Nafs is commonly translated as meaning the *soul*. Other meanings of this word include mind, psyche, person, self, and individual. In the context of this discussion, it is the voice within which prompts an individual for or against a certain course of action, ie., the conscience. The nafs is endowed with the ability to discern between the good and the evil. Further, it is under the individual's control to choose a course or action which leads to good or one that lead to the prohibited.

> *And by the nafs and Him who perfected it. And inspired it with conscience of what is wrong for it and what is right for it. He has indeed prospered who purifies it. And he is indeed a failure who corrupts it.*
> (Surah 91, Ash Shams, ayaat 7-10)

Jihad in the literal sense means to *struggle* or *strive*. It is a generic term which implies an all-round struggle against evil in every form. In the context of religion, it means making the utmost effort to adhere to the teachings of Islam. This struggle can be broken down into two broad categories: inner or personal (individual) and external (collective) struggle.

The Inner Struggle

The major and most significant component of Jihad is the inner struggle which covers a wide range of thoughts and activities. It is through this process that a person fights off wishes and desires for things and actions that are prohibited in Islam. It is a continuing process of internal course correction which keeps the believer on the prescribed path of honesty, integrity, fairness, etc., that constitute the *siraatal mustaqeem* (the straight path). This most important aspect of an individual's Jihad is called *tazkiyah*, the process of continuous self-regulation and purification. If done to seek God's pleasure and approval, it constitutes the *inner Jihad*.

This inner struggle is the means by which an individual stays afloat and does not drown in the flood waters that are sweeping away the moral and ethical norms of society. It is the struggle to adhere to the Islamic religious rules and expectations such as safeguarding the integrity and respecting sanctity of the family; being fair and honest in all dealings; being polite even towards rude people; controlling anger; refraining from acts of revenge, gossip and the use of undesirable language; and in general, withstanding the temptations created by the culture of selfishness and greed, deceit and dishonesty, consumerism and waste. This inner struggle of striving to continuously and actively maintain a course and conduct which fits the mold provided by the Shari'ah is the ongoing *Jihad* within the person. If successful, it assures a good outcome for all actions as stated in the verse cited above (Surah 91, Ash Shams, ayaat 7-10). Indeed, this may be the biggest form of Jihad faced by individuals today.

The External Struggle

The struggle against external factors is a relatively small component, but nevertheless a very important aspect of Jihad. It is important because the individual participating in the Jihad is answering God's call to facilitate justice and help the weak and oppressed. Additionally, in the course of this endeavour, the individual risks the most valuable of possessions, ie., life and well-being. Whether a person lives or is killed, it is a win-win situation:

To him who fights in the cause of God, whether he is slain or gets victory, on him We shall bestow a great reward.

(Surah 4, An Nisa', ayat 74)

Conditions for External Struggle

Shari'ah mandates high ethical and moral standards. Since Jihad is a struggle with the goal of seeking God's acceptance, anything that is contrary to Shari'ah is simply unacceptable. Therefore, by its very definition, Jihad subscribes to upholding the highest ethical and moral standards. The rules of Shari'ah may never be violated and a Muslim is never permitted to go against the Commandments of God. The discussion that follows must be understood in the light of these facts.

The primary goal of this type of Jihad is to bring peace and harmony through establishment of justice. If these goals can be achieved by peaceful means, then that is the preferred route: *And if they incline to peace, you also incline to it, and trust in Allah. He is the Hearer, the Knower* (Surah 8, Al Anfaal, ayat 61). If peaceful means do not bring about a resolution, the use of force is permitted. During the course of any conflict, the Islamic rules for war must be stringently observed. These detail the permitted and the prohibited and war as a part of Jihad is no different. Rules of warfare are discussed in Chapter 24, Suicide, Killing and War.

Jihad is permitted for the following reasons:
- Protecting Muslims and/or a Muslim State and its citizens, including non-Muslim citizens
- Securing the rights of those prevented freedom of religious expression
- Securing freedom for the weak, persecuted and oppressed

Through the institution of Jihad, Islam makes it a moral obligation for Muslims to defend and protect their own collective rights and also those of others who seek their assistance. The ultimate aim is that of achieving peace and harmony and removing inequity. Protection of Muslims from oppression and persecution and the defense of a Muslim State and its citizens against external aggression are legitimate and just reasons for warfare and also fall under Jihad.

And fight in the cause of Allah those who fight against you but do not commit aggression because Allah does not like aggressors ...
Though killing is bad, persecution is worse than killing ...

(Surah 2, Al Baqarah, ayat 190-191)

This verse was the first injunction for Jihad. It highlights the narrow focus for Jihad, ie., the sole purpose of war was to stop aggression. The injunction *do not commit aggression* clearly restricts the aim of the Jihad to stopping the aggressor and prohibits other potential motivations such as material gain (acquisition of territories or goods) and revenge. There cannot be Jihad against those who neither forcibly oppose nor oppress. Additionally, no harm should come to non-combatants, children, women, elderly and the wounded, and there should be no wanton destruction of property, orchards, crops, or animals, nor mutilation of the slain enemy.[2]

---

[2] Maududi SAA. The Meaning of the Qur'an. Islamic Publications Ltd., Lahore, Pakistan, 1978. Volume·1, pages 146-147.

To those against whom war is made, permission is given to fight, because they have been wronged, and Allah is indeed able to give them victory. They are those who have been expelled from their homes unjustly, only because the said, Our Lord is Allah. Allah will surely help those people who help Him. Truly, Allah is Strong, Almighty.

(Surah 22, Al Haj, 39-40)

Helping the weak and oppressed to secure their freedom also falls under Jihad. It also applies to helping non-Muslims who are oppressed or enslaved by a tyrant or foreign occupation and seek the help of Muslims. It is a moral obligation in such situations. Examples are the liberation of Coptic Christians of Egypt and North African Berbers from Byzantine occupation, enslavement and exploitation.

And why should you not fight for the cause of Allah and of the weak among men and of the women and the children who are crying: Our Lord, rescue us from this town whose people are oppressors! Give us from Your presence one who will protect; and give us from Your presence one who will help.   (Surah 4, An Nisa', ayat 75)

Jihad fi Sabeelillah

Jihad means to strive or struggle and *jihad fi sabeelillah* means *striving in the cause (or way) of God.* It is also translated as *striving for the sake of God.* Since every Jihad is *in the cause of* or *for the sake of God (fi sabeelillah),* there can be nothing sinister about it. On the contrary, it is something desirable as it represents a means of self-purification in the form of the inner Jihad. If more individuals would practice it, perhaps the world would become a better place to live.

The expression, *jihad fi sabeelillah,* is often misrepresented by the media and some writers (Western as well as others) who portray this as meaning *fighting* or *war in the name* of God. The Arabic word for name is *ism,* like in *Bismillah* which means *in the Name of God.* The Arabic word for fighting is *qital.* Simple mistranslation or misrepresentation? Since these individuals profess to know so well everything else about Islam, it could hardly be an innocent translation error. On the other hand, if they have such poor knowledge of these simple matters, it raises questions about the accuracy of the remainder of their writings and reporting.

When fighting (warfare) is involved, the expression is *qital fi sabeelillah (fighting in the cause of God)*. The distinction is necessary, since only a small aspect of Jihad involves participation in a war effort. In either case, there is absolutely nothing ignoble about Jihad because it is always for a just cause with sincere intentions. Since God is just and demands justice, He requires the believers to follow and obey all His rules which are incorporated into the Shari'ah. Therefore, nothing can be considered *jihad fi sabeelillah* unless it conforms to the Shari'ah. Anything done in compliance with Shari'ah cannot, by definition, have even a trace of evil. Shari'ah, which is God's Law and evil are complete opposites.

Since the main focus for Jihad is to please God, it cannot be for an evil or illicit purpose such as territorial gain, subjugation of a people or the control of their natural resources. Furthermore, every Muslim knows that there is a *Day of Reckoning*, therefore, every action of a believer is with God-consciousness, ie., anything that might displease God is avoided because:

On the Day when every soul will be confronted with all the good it has done, and all the evil it has done, it will wish that there were a great distance between it and its evil. Allah warns you to fear Him; and Allah is full of kindness to those that serve Him (ibaad).[3]

(Surah 3, 'Al Imraan, ayat 30)

Qital fi sabeelillah (fighting in the cause of God) remains the ultimate and highest form of Jihad. This is done only for clear cut reasons and a determined purpose. It is not up to anyone in the general populace to determine which cause demands a Jihad. The learned must make that determination after studying the circumstances. It is important to be clear about the purpose and circumstances as misjudgment can lead to harming innocent persons, and injustice is clearly prohibited.

And slay not the life which Allah has forbidden save with right ...
(Surah 17, Al Isra', ayat 33)

---

[3] *ibaad* refers to individuals who are obedient and conscientiously follow God's Commandments.

Establish worship and enjoin kindness and forbid iniquity, and persevere whatever may befall you ...   (Surah 31, Luqman, ayat 17)

The *Holy War* Concept

The term *holy war* was coined by the Latin Crusaders. They not only coined this term but also enacted its meaning by carrying out genocidal killings in the name of religion. Jihad has nothing in common with those *holy wars*. Warfare under the aegis of Jihad is for a noble cause, for freedom, justice and peace, and embodies compassion towards innocents. There is no authentic record of killings by Muslims purely for the sake of eliminating those of a different faith. On the contrary, Muslim history is replete with evidence of tolerance and respect for individuals of other faiths. Muslim Spain and Muslim India are two examples. Had the Muslims carried out a *holy war* similar to that of the Crusaders or the Spaniards, there would not have been any non-Muslim left in those countries.

During the Spanish *reconquista*, the conquered territories were subjected to ethnic cleansing. Muslims and Jews were killed or expelled from Spain. Those who remained were forced to convert to Christianity or face the sword. In order to enforce the "orthodoxy" of the converts, the Inquisition was instituted (1478 CE) and was under direct control of the Spanish monarchy. The purpose of the Inquisition was to maintain Catholic orthodoxy of Spain. It was abolished in 1834 CE. There is no such event in Muslim history.

In contrast, when the Muslims established themselves in the Iberian Peninsula, the locals were allowed to keep their faith, property and social status. There was no forced conversion to Islam because it is prohibited.[4] Similarly, in greater Syria and Palestine, after the first one hundred years of Muslim rule, only about six percent of the population was Muslim.[5]

For additional discussion on Holy War see Chapter 21, Creative Terminology for Islam and Muslims and Chapter 23, Crusades and Holy War.

---

[4] *There is no compulsion in religion* (Surah 2, Al Baqarah, ayat 256).

[5] Courbage Y, Fargues P. Christian and Jews under Islam. Translated by Judy Mabro. IB Tauris Publishers, London, 1997. Page 11.

Jihad, the Freedom of Belief and the Spread of Islam

As noted above, Jihad is always for a noble cause. It cannot be used for wrongful purposes and it is for this reason that no authority ever calls out Jihad without due consideration of the necessity.[6]

Forced conversion to Islam is a myth and the idea is also illogical. Force may enable occupation of a country and subjugation of its people but does not lead to their acceptance of the faith of the conqueror or occupiers. There is no place for coercion or compulsion in religion because it is prohibited in Islam. In addition, accepting Islam and becoming a Muslim must be a sincere *choice*. God requires that entering into Islam be wholehearted and complete. No person can be *forced* to believe. The responsibility of Muslims is only that of conveying the message of Islam. People are free to believe as they choose:

Invite (all) to the Way of your Lord with wisdom and beautiful preaching; and reason with them in ways that are best and most gracious. For your Lord knows best, who have strayed from His Path, and who receive guidance.   (Surah 16, An Nahl, ayat 125)

But if they turn away, your duty is only to convey the clear message.
                    (Surah 16, An Nahl, ayat 82)

Was Islam Spread by the sword?

There is a baseless, yet widespread, notion that Islam was *spread by the sword*. This notion has been propagated by some historians and Orientalists. One of the reasons for this belief may have been the rapid expansion of the Muslim Commonwealth which started during the Caliphate of Umar ibn al Khattab . Most of the territories acquired during that and subsequent periods still have a majority Muslim population or a sizable Muslim minority, with the exception of Latin regions of Europe and others subjected to ethnic cleansing and inquisitions. With the Muslim armies came Muslim governance. In those countries, Islam was spread by example, living a life guided by

---

[6] The erroneous designation of a campaign as a Jihad by Western news media or by some individuals does not make it a Jihad. Essentially, this is a misrepresentation. Such sources may posses neither the knowledge nor the authority to designate a campaign as being Jihad.

the virtuous Islamic principles and not by force.

A testimonial to the peaceful spread of Islam is that the regions with the largest Muslim populations, ie., Southeast Asia and the East Indies, in particular Indonesia, never saw a single Muslim soldier. Muslim travelers and seafaring merchants traded in those lands. Their high morals and ethical standards attracted the local populations to Islam. The only wars these nations ever witnessed were those waged by the European colonialists.

For additional information on this subject see Chapter 21, Creative Terminology for Islam and Islamic View of Warfare in Chapter 24, Suicide, Killing and War.

Jihad and Muslim Wars in Perspective

In the context of the foregoing, the following is a brief review of three early conflicts faced by the Muslim Commonwealth shortly after it was established. For additional information see Chapter 22, Islamic History.

Byzantine Wars

The Byzantines (also known as the Eastern Roman Empire), after defeating the Persians (622-626 CE), directed their military activities against the new Muslim State in Madinah. They were in the process of amassing a large army at the northern frontier (in Syria) with the intention of crushing the Muslims (8 AH, 629 CE). The attack was averted by a skillful strategy employed by Prophet Muhammad ﷺ. He sent a small force against the Byzantines who had not yet completed preparations for the invasion. Although beaten at the ensuing *Battle of Mutah*, the Muslim forces were able to foil the Byzantine invasion.

Byzantine hostilities resumed in the eastern parts of Arabia and were occasionally coordinated with and supported by the pre-Islamic Persians. A repeat encounter saw Byzantine defeat at *Ajnadain* (13 AH, 634 CE).[7] Their hostilities continued and they were finally expelled from Syria and Palestine after their defeat at the *Battle of Yarmuk* (15 AH, 636 CE) and subsequently from Egypt (20 AH, 640 CE). Although

---

[7] Dates are accurate for the Islamic calendar (AH) and approximate for the Current Era (CE) as these calendars use different methods of calculation.

territories were acquired as a result of the retreat, and the subsequent departure of the Byzantines from those lands, each one of these wars was strictly a military campaign against hostile elements.

Persian Wars

The pre-Islamic Persian empire included much of the region that constitutes the present day Iraq. The Persians made raids into Muslim territories, instigated rebellion, supported hostile tribes, threatened the security and the very existence of the new Muslim State. Several battles were fought against them with their final defeat in circa 642 CE. Each one of these was strictly a defensive or preemptive military campaign.

North African Wars

After their defeat in Egypt, the Byzantines pulled back to their North African territories where they continued the practice of oppression and exploitation of the native Berber population. In an attempt to free themselves of the Byzantine occupiers, the Berbers requested help from Amr ibn 'Aas, the Muslim Governor of Egypt. Their request was granted and the Byzantines were expelled by Muslim troops under Uqba bin Nafey. The new territories were called Al Maghrib (the West).

Concluding Commentary

And fight them until there is no more persecution[8] and Allah's way is established instead.[9] But if they desist, then let there be no hostility except against the evildoers (those guilty of cruelty and brutality).

(Surah 2, Al Baqarah, ayat 193)

---

[8] *...until there is no more fitnah*, meaning there is no more persecution, oppression, or a state of tribulation.

[9] *... Allah's way is established instead (and religion is for Allah)...*, ie., until God can be worshipped without fear of persecution, and none is compelled to bow down in *awe* before another human being. The Message of the Qur'an. Translated and Explained by Muhammad Asad. The Book Foundation, Bristol, England, 2003. Page 52.

Fight for the sake of Allah those who fight against you, but do not begin
hostilities. Allah does not love the aggressors.

(Surah 2, Al Baqarah, ayat 190)

This Qur'an guides to that which is straightest, and gives glad tidings to
the believers who do good works that theirs will be a great reward.

(Surah 17, Al Isra', ayat 9)

Islam is a religion of peace. The root word for Islam is *silm*. Its
meanings include peace (*salaam*), to be safe, secure, and protected
from harm. Prophet Muhammad ﷺ said: *Spread Salaam (peace), so you*
may be raised higher.[10] Allah encourages peace and reconciliation, not
war. Nevertheless, fighting is prescribed if becomes the only remaining
option for overcoming oppression and/or aggression.

Jihad is the striving towards the ideal within oneself and in society.
The inner Jihad attempts to bring about a change in oneself by
suppressing the morally and socially undesirable inclinations of the
nafs. The external Jihad strives to bring relief for the oppressed and
persecuted, and those subjected to aggression and exploitation, and
may involve fighting (warfare). In every Jihad, the sole purpose is to
seek God's acceptance. The benefits from a Jihad are inner peace, the
satisfaction of having contributed constructively to the alleviation of
suffering, and the anticipation of a reward in the Hereafter.

Neither is every Jihad a war nor does every war entail Jihad. Wars
are either for justifiable and legitimate reasons, such as Jihad, or they
are motivated by greed, prejudice and evilness (taghoot).[11]

Those who believe fight in the cause of Allah and those who reject faith
fight in the cause of evil. So fight against the friends of Satan. Indeed ever
feeble is the plot of Satan.   (Surah 4, An Nisa', ayat 76)

---

[10] *raised higher* means a rank that is closer to God. Muntakhab Ahadith. Kandhlavi MY.
Annayyar, Karachi, Pakistan. Hadith 90, page 427.

[11] *Taghoot* is derived from *tagha* which means to exceed or overstep proper bounds
or limits. *Taghoot* is one who rebels against God and exerts to make His (God's)
subjects subservient to himself. *Taghoot* maybe Satan, a priest, religious or political
leader, king or state. Maududi SAA. The Meaning of the Qur'an. Islamic Publications
Ltd., Lahore, Pakistan, 1978. Volume 1, page 186.

Those who *fight in the cause of evil* spread unnecessary turmoil and destruction, harm innocent people, destroy farms, crops and orchards, brutally occupy, oppress and exploit the weak, and steal their natural resources. All these are manifestations of the evil inclinations of the *nafs*. These are the evil forces which the Jihad aims to counter and bring about justice and peace. This is the struggle *in the cause of Allah*.

Islam prohibits oppression. Today, as in times past, oppression remains the most frequent reason for the external struggle. Historically, in all cases where a Jihad was sanctioned by learned Muslim scholars, there was evidence for gross injustices, oppression, persecution and unjustified bloodshed. Here, Jihad was only in response to those injustices and the associated violence. There has never been a cavalier approach towards Jihad as there is no room for collateral damage. The decision for Jihad always balances the responsibility to strive for justice and peace with the possibility of avoiding conflict by seeking peaceful solutions. Therefore, the door to a peaceful solution always remains open.

II. Family and Society

Chapter Seven

Marriage

Introduction

✿ And among His signs is that He created for you spouses (azwaaj)[1] from among yourselves, that you may dwell in tranquillity with them and He has put love and mercy between you. Verily, in these are signs for those who reflect.   (Surah 30, Ar Rum, ayat 21)

The freedom of sexual expression championed by elements in affluent societies can be linked to some of the moral and social ills of today's society. Annually, over 800,000 "legalized" abortions are performed in the United States.[2] In American women, it is estimated that about half of the pregnancies are unintended.[3,4] The incidence of sexually transmitted diseases [Chlamydia, gonorrhea, syphilis, HIV (Human Immunodeficiency Virus), Human Papilloma Virus, Herpes, genital warts, etc] is on the rise. Chlamydia infections, which are the most common, infect over four percent of the adolescent US

---

[1] *azwaaj* (plural of *zauj*) is derived from *zawaj* which means both *a pair* and *one of a pair*, a couple, or double.

[2] Pazol K, Zane SB, Parker WY, et al. Abortion Surveillance - United States, 2007. Morbidity and Mortality Weekly Report (*MMWR*). Last accessed May 2011. http://www.cdc.gov/mmwr/preview/mmwrhtml/ss6001a1.htm?s_cid=ss6001a1_w

[3] Finer LB and Henshaw SK, Disparities in rates of unintended pregnancy in the United States, 1994 and 2001. Perspectives on Sexual and Reproductive Health, 2006, 38:90–96.

[4] Also see Chapter 14, Reproductive Issues: Abortion, Contraception and Sterilization

population with one million new cases reported in 2006[5] and over 1.2 million cases reported in 2009.[6] Chlamydial infections also increase the risk of uterine cervical cancer and are associated with a host of other illnesses such as pelvic inflammatory disease, ectopic pregnancy, infertility, pneumonia, eye and vascular diseases.

Since Islam embodies the highest of virtues and moral standards, it encourages a lifestyle that fulfills those goals. Sexual contact of any nature is prohibited outside of marriage and the only form of marriage that is recognized is the union of a man and a woman. Islam encourages marriage as it protects the integrity of the society. Prophet Muhammad ﷺ said: *O young people, whoever among you can marry, should marry, because it helps him lower his gaze and guard his modesty.*[7]

Islam seeks to build a morally pure and socially responsible human society. Thus, from the Islamic perspective, it is not possible to singularly discuss marriage without considering other factors such as family, parents, and social responsibilities. The following discussion must be viewed in that overall context.

Purpose and Philosophy

Islam recognizes human nature and regulates societal structure so as to fulfill the needs of both the individual and community. Marriage fosters social responsibility and also establishes a bond between families. While friends and relatives can provide significant social support, a spouse provides an enduring and mutually strengthening lifelong partnership.

In the Qur'an, one of the qualities of believers is defined as follows: *their affairs are a matter of mutual consultation.* The Shari'ah makes the spouse an equal partner and should therefore be consulted for all

---

[5] Miller WC, Ford CA, Morris M, et al. Prevalence of Chlamydial and Gonococcal Infections Among Young Adults in the United States. JAMA 2004;291:2229-2236. Chlamydia - STD Surveillance 2006.

[6] Since there is significant underreporting, it is estimated that the actual incidence of chlamydial infections in the United States is about 2.8 million cases per year. Sexually Transmitted Diseases (STDs). Chlamydia - CDC Fact Sheet. http://www.cdc.gov/std/chlamydia/stdfact-chlamydia.htm Last accessed May 2011

[7] The Translation of the Meanings of Sahih Al-Bukhari. MM Khan, Kazi Publications, Lahore, Pakistan, 1979. Volume VII, Hadith 4, page 4.

important decisions. The latter also advances spousal relations and establishes mutual trust.

Biological factors start to manifest around puberty. Recognizing their importance, Islam encourages early marriage for both young men and women. Marriage brings with it responsibility, mutual respect and protection from immoral practices, thus playing an important role in maintaining the moral integrity of society. Societies that condone "sexual freedom" suffer the burden of its consequences which include high divorce rates, broken families with psychological trauma to the neglected spouse and children, unwanted pregnancies, abortions, child abuse and abandonment, sexually transmitted diseases and the fallout from other forms of promiscuous behavior.

Choice of Spouse

In the Qur'an, the word used for spouse is *zauj*. Its meanings include one of a pair, a mate, a partner, or couple.[8] The implication being that it is more than a just a traditional husband or wife. Thus, it is necessary to make the right choice and Islam provides that guidance. While a man or woman must be able to see and know the other person, courtship/dating is not permitted.

The most important criterion directing choice of spouse is the faith of the individual and not external appearance, social status, position, power, or wealth. The Prophet ﷺ said: *A woman is married for four things, ie., her wealth, her family status, her beauty and her religion. So you should marry the religious woman (otherwise) you will be a loser.*[9] With respect to wealth, God says: *If they be poor, Allah will enrich them of His Bounty. Allah is of ample means, Aware* (Surah 24, An Nur, ayat 32).

Marriage with certain relatives is not permitted.[10] In addition to the immediate and some other close family members, this prohibition includes foster siblings.[11] There are also several temporary prohibitions

---

[8] Also see footnote 1.

[9] The Translation of the Meanings of Sahih Al-Bukhari. MM Khan, Kazi Publications, Lahore, Pakistan, 1979. Volume VII, Hadith 27, pages 18-19.

[10] Surah 4, An Nisa', ayaat 22-24.

[11] Foster siblings, ie., infants who were nursed by the same woman. This means suckling at the breast more than five times or having been fed with her pumped breast milk. Also seen under Adoption in Chapter 8, Family and Social Issues.

which include the following:[12,13]

- Two sisters may not be married to one man at the same time
- A girl and her aunt may not be married to one man at the same time
- A man may not be married to more than four women at one time
- Marriage is prohibited during the *iddah*, ie., the waiting period after divorce or death of the husband
- A woman may not take a second husband while she is married to the first one, ie., polyandry is prohibited

Interfaith Marriage

A Muslim man may marry a Christian or Jewish woman and she may not be pressured to convert to Islam but should remain free to practice her faith.[14] Although such a marriage is permissible, it is not encouraged.[15] A Muslim woman is not permitted to marry a non-Muslim man. One of the reasons being that she may not be provided the tolerance and freedom to practice her faith with a non-Muslim husband. In addition, the Islamic upbringing of the children may not be guaranteed. In order for a non-Muslim man to marry a Muslim woman, he must first become a Muslim through a conscientious and genuine conversion to Islam and not only to satisfy the requirement. It is not permissible for a Muslim man or woman to marry the followers of non-monotheistic faiths such as Hinduism or Buddhism.[16]

---

[12] Surah 4, An Nisa', ayat 23.

[13] The Translation of the Meanings of Sahih Al-Bukhari. MM Khan, Kazi Publications, Lahore, Pakistan, 1979. Volume VII, Hadith 45, page 34.

[14] Christians and Jews are also known as *ahl al Kitaab* or *People of the Book,* ie., those who were recipients of earlier Divine Revelations and profess to follow a mono-theistic faith. By requirement, the children have to be brought up as Muslims.

[15] There are several reasons. It may deprive a Muslim woman of a husband and also the children may grow up as non-Muslims. Depending upon the societal environment (Muslim or non-Muslim) and the strength of the individual's conviction, weaknesses may develop in his faith which may also lead him away from Islam.

[16] Marriage to those considered *mushrik* is prohibited, Surah 2, Al Baqarah, ayat 221. One of the reasons for prohibiting such a marriage is that the influence of the *mushrik* spouse (including the family and environment) may eventually lead the individual away from Islam and to *shirk* (associating partners with God).

Marriage Requirements and Ceremony

The Arabic term for marriage is *nikah*. In addition to the four basic requirements listed below, it includes a short sermon which emphasizes the virtues of this sunnah and also serves to remind the couple of their respective responsibilities. Marriage is a contract between a man and a woman and the Qur'an refers to it as a *solemn pledge (misaqan ghaleeza)*.[17] Like any other mutually agreed upon contract, it brings with it certain responsibilities. These are discussed later in this chapter under Spousal Relationship and Responsibilities.

The marriage ceremony may be conducted anywhere with the exception of a non-Muslim place of worship. The place recommended by the Prophet ﷺ is a mosque. A civil marriage in a City Hall, Municipal Office, Borgerlig Vielse or Standesamt is also valid with no requirement for an additional Islamic marriage contract.

The basic requirements for marriage are:
- Proposal and uncoerced acceptance
- Mahr
- Witnesses
- Written contract

Proposal and uncoerced acceptance

In Islamic tradition, it is the custom for the bride's father (or other close male relative in the event the father is not alive) to act as her representative (*wakeel*) at the marriage ceremony. Marriage without consent of the girl is invalid.[18] A girl is considered to be of marriageable age when she reaches puberty. Cultural traditions and family pressures, both running contrary to Islamic teachings, may result in deviation from these principles. Therefore, there are specific guidelines to protect the girl's right to accept or reject any proposal. Marriage of children, of pre-pubertal girls, by coercion or force, is prohibited.

Mahr

This is a gift from the groom to the bride. It is often incorrectly

---

[17] Surah 4, An Nisa', ayat 21.

[18] The Translation of the Meanings of Sahih Al-Bukhari. MM Khan, Kazi Publications, Lahore, Pakistan, 1979. Volume VII, Hadith 69, page 52.

translated as meaning dowry. Its purpose is to serve as a security should the marriage be terminated. Upon consummation of the marriage, it becomes the wife's personal property and she may dispose of it as she pleases. Its value is fixed by agreement between the two parties, before or at the time of the marriage. It can be money or other goods which must be of benefit. The wife may forego a part or all of it or defer receiving it at a date mutually agreed upon. It is considered a debt owed by the husband to the wife and even after the husband's death, it is payable from his estate.

Thus, the Islamic practice of *mahr* differs fundamentally from the traditional dowry, e.g., in the European or Hindu practice. In European practice, the possession of dowry passed on to the husband. In South Asia, following the Hindu tradition, dowry is the price paid by the groom (and his family) to the bride's family.

Witnesses

A minimum of two adult witnesses of sound mind (must be able to understand the marriage terms) are required to be present at the time of the agreement. The marriage must be a publicized affair and secrecy is prohibited. If otherwise unavailable, publicity requirement may be satisfied by the presence of the two required witnesses. In addition, the Prophet Muhammad ﷺ recommended a wedding banquet (*walima*).

Written contract

According to Islamic practice, the marriage contract is a written document signed by the bride (or guardian on her behalf), the groom and two witnesses. The marriage contract is without term limits. Any contractual arrangement that involves marriage for a specified period is prohibited although it may fulfill all other criteria. Consequently, a temporary marriage (*muta'*) is not permissible.

Spousal Relationship and Responsibilities

... They are a garment (libaas) for you and you are a garment (libaas) for them ...[19]

This is a succinct description of the expected relationship between the spouses. A garment covers and it conceals what is intended to be private and not for display. It comforts, protects from the elements, and it is also an item of beautification and show. The spousal relationship is similar: mutual support and protection, insuring privacy with concealment of shortcomings and faults, providing comfort and adornment.

Interpersonal differences and conflicts in spousal relationships can be anticipated in almost every marriage. Consequently, guidance and solutions are provided in the Qur'an and Sunnah. To avoid or minimize the effects of marital discord, responsibilities and rights are assigned to each spouse. In order to understand these spousal responsibilities and rights, it is necessary to be familiar with what is expected of believers.[20]

As a basic principle, every group of individuals, irrespective of size, is advised to elect a leader (*ameer*). This person assumes the responsibility of spokesperson, and to an extent, for guiding the affairs of the group. The same principle applies to the family. The only difference is that the family members do not choose that person as God has already made that decision. This responsibility of leadership, caring and providing for the family is assigned to the husband.[21]

Marriage is a contract between husband and wife, a trust and a *solemn pledge* to live by the rules and guidelines provided by Shari'ah. Trust is a part of faith (*iman*), and as believers (*mu'minoon*), both

---

[19] Surah 2, Al Baqarah, ayat 187. The Arabic term *libaas* means garment, body cover, dress, mantle, something that covers, or to clothe.

[20] A believer or *mu'min* (plural *mu'minoon*) is a person whose submission to God is conscientious, willful, wholehearted and complete. Also see Glossary.

[21] Surah 4, An Nisa', ayat 34: *Men shall take full care of women (qawwamoona alanisa'), because Allah has given the one more than the other and because they support them (women) from their means.* The word used to describe these obligations assigned to men is *qawwamoon* which is derived from *qa'im*. Its meanings include: *protector, to be responsible for, to be watching over, maintainer, manager of affairs, one who takes full care.*

spouses are expected to adhere to their commitments and fulfill their obligations. It is stated in the Qur'an: *O you who believe, fulfill your obligations (uqood)*[22] (Surah 5, Al Ma'idah, ayat 1); and believers are defined as: *And those who keep their trusts*[23] *and their pledges* (Surah 23, Al Mu'minoon, ayat 8).

Responsibilities and Rights

Men (husbands) must provide for their families according to their means. The position of "head of household" is only that of responsibility and not of superiority. The wife is to be treated with honour, respect and dignity. Her needs must be satisfied and neglect is not permissible. She is entitled to her rights but must also fulfill her obligations.

Prophet Muhammad ﷺ said: *...give them food from what you have for yourself, and clothe them by which you clothe yourself and do not beat them, and do not scold them.*[24] Additionally, in his Farewell Sermon, he ﷺ said: *...I enjoin good treatment of women, for they are under your care and you have no right to treat them otherwise, unless they commit clear indecency.*[25] Men's rights over women include: *...that they do not allow anyone whom you dislike to enter your houses.*[26]

The life and conduct of Prophet Muhammad ﷺ serve as an example for all Muslims. His wives were companions, not servants. He helped with household chores and he never hit or abuse anyone of them. His wife A'isha ؓ said: *The Messenger of God ﷺ never beat any of his servants, or wives, and his hand never hit anything.*[27]

---

[22] *Uqood* has a broad meaning and implications. It includes any promise, pledge, oath (verbal or written), obligation, contract, etc. Honesty, with living-up to all commitments, is a fundamental principle of the Islamic social order.

[23] Fulfill all duties, obligations and responsibilities that have been prescribed, including those of morality, truthfulness and honesty.

[24] This Hadith lays out the husband's responsibility to provide for and share with his wife from his resources and also clearly prohibits spousal abuse.
Sunan Abu Dawud. English translation with Explanatory Notes. A Hasan. Kitab Bhavan, New Delhi, 1997. Volume 2, Hadith 2139, page 575.

[25] English Translation of Sunan Ibn Majah. Darussalam, Riyadh, S Arabia, 2007. Volume 3, Hadith 1851, pages 61-62.

[26] English Translation of Sunan Ibn Majah. Darussalam, Riyadh, S Arabia, 2007. Volume 3, Hadith 1851, pages 61-62.

[27] English Translation of Sunan Ibn Majah. Darussalam, Riyadh, S Arabia, 2007. Volume 3, Hadith 1984, page 134.

For her part, the wife must be mindful of her husband's needs and those of their family, provided that his wishes and instructions do not run contrary to any Islamic injunctions. In the Qur'an, believing women are described as follows: ...*So virtuous women are the obedient, and guard in (the husband's) absence what Allah would have them guard...*[28] (Surah 4, An Nisa', ayat 34). A Hadith of Prophet Muhammad ﷺ states: ...*there is no provision better than a virtuous wife.*[29]

Resolution of Marital problems

If marital problems are caused by the husband's actions, the recommended course of action is a dialogue with the use of reasoning. If this fails, arbitration is recommended. For arbitration, individuals from both the husband's and wife's family should be used. If the situation cannot be resolved through arbitration, the wife may appeal to a judge (court) for a ruling.

Similarly, if the problem is due to the wife's actions, a dialogue between the spouses is recommended with the use of reasoning. If this fails, arbitration is recommended to resolve the issue. If discord is due to a serious matter, such as indifference to the husband or the family's needs or unacceptable conduct, and dialogue and reasoning have failed, physical separation and admonition may be used: ... *As for those from whom you fear rebellion (disloyalty and ill conduct), admonish them (first) and (next) banish them to beds apart: and wadribu hunna. Then, if they obey you, seek not a way against them. Allah is ever High Exalted, Great.* (Surah 4, An Nisa', ayat 34)

The arabic term *wadribu hunna* is often translated as meaning *to scold* or *to beat*. The accurate translation of its meaning is *to strike without leaving a mark or without causing pain or injury (ghayr mubarrih)*. This symbolic measure is permitted only if the wife *has become guilty of immoral conduct in an obvious manner.*[30] Prophet Muhammad ﷺ detested the idea of someone beating his wife[31] and unequivocally prohibited

---

[28] Guard the husband's interests (property and reputation) and her own virtue (chastity) as ordained by God.

[29] English Translation of Sunan Ibn Majah. Darussalam, Riyadh, S Arabia, 2007. Volume 3, Hadith 1855, page 64.

[30] see footnote 31.

[31] The Message of the Qur'an. Translated and Explained by Muhammad Asad. The Book Foundation, Bristol, England, 2003. Page 127.

spousal abuse: *...and do not beat them, and do not scold them.*[32]

Of the remedial actions outlined in this verse, the final step constitutes the last resort prior to divorce. It gives qualified permission for symbolic physical warning to be used only in the face of a specific, serious problem and may not be construed as generally permitting harsh treatment of wives.[33] The premise being that this symbolic physical warning may impress upon the wife the seriousness of the issue and bring about reconciliation and thus avoid divorce.

If the matter is resolved through the steps outlined, no additional action may be taken out of vengeance or to ostracize: *Then, if they obey you, seek not a way against them* (Surah 4, An Nisa', ayat 34). Since the ultimate goal is reconciliation, a genuine attempt must be made to avoid divorce. Any form of abrasive behavior by the husband, physical or emotional abuse, or insult, is counterproductive. The use of profanities and abusive language run contrary to accepted Islamic behavior.[34] The use of symbolic physical warning is considered a lesser evil than divorce and may impress upon the wife the seriousness of the matter. The two Hadith that follow, emphasize the essentials of spousal relationships.

The most perfect Muslim in the matter of faith is one who has excellent behavior; and the best among you are those who behave best towards their wives.[35]

Any woman dies while her husband is pleased with her, then she enters paradise.[36]

---

[32] Sunan Abu Dawud. English translation with Explanatory Notes. A Hasan. Kitab Bhavan, New Delhi, 1997. Volume 2, Hadith 2139, page 575. Also see footnote 24.

[33] *fahishatin mubayyana:* manifest indecent behavior. English Translation of Jami At-Tirmidhi, Darussalam, Riyadh, S Arabia, 2007. Volume 2, Hadith 1163, pp 531-532.

[34] *The believer does not insult the honour of others, nor curse, nor commit fahisha' (obscene or indecent act/behavior), nor is he foul (ie., uses foul language).* English Translation of Jami At-Tirmidhi, Darussalam, Riyadh. S Arabia, 2007. Volume 4, Hadith 1977, p 76.

[35] Reported by Tirmidhi. Riyad us Saleheen, Kitab Bhavan, New Delhi, 1987. Hadith 278, page 180.

[36] English Translation of Jami At-Tirmidhi, Darussalam, Riyadh, S Arabia, 2007. Volume 2, Hadith 1161, page 530.

Polygamy

Should He not know what He created? And He is the Subtle (Al Lateef),[37]
the totally Aware.   (Surah 67, Al Mulk, ayat 14)

Polygamy is defined as having multiple spouses. While its implied meaning is multiple wives (polygyny), its definition also includes polyandry (multiple husbands). Islam permits polygyny and prohibits polyandry. Under Islamic law, a man may be married to a maximum of four women at one time. This is a permission and not an encouragement. In the discussion that follows, polygamy will be used as meaning polygyny (multiple wives).

Polygamy has been practiced since the earliest of times. Many of the earlier prophets were polygamous [eg., Abraham, Jacob, David, Solomon (peace be upon them all)] and Judaism and Christianity, in their original scriptures, did not forbid polygamy. Similarly, Islam does not prohibit polygamy but regulates the practice to protect the interests of women.

While the strictly regulated practice of polygamy in Islam is bemoaned by Westerners and often portrayed as being an aberrant custom, much of Western society accepts the widespread polygamous practice of adulterous and non-matrimonial cohabitation. To regulate the polygamous nature of men, Islam permits polygamy with responsibility, in contrast to the practice of illicit polygamy without responsibility. In the Islamic alternative, the woman is not only provided a home and security, but also respect, dignity and fulfillment of all her needs.

God, the Creator, is best aware of human needs and has therefore provided an option, under Shari'ah, for the individual who is thus inclined. The permission to marry several women serves to protect the individual from straying off the prescribed moral course, and by the same token, it protects society from moral decadence. Societies that shun or outlaw polygamy but permit adultery and multiple extramarital relationships, suffer the consequences such as trauma of abandonment, high rates of abortion, illegitimate children, and sexually

---

[37] *Al Lateef:* This attribute of God has the following meanings: *The Subtle One, Knower of the innermost secrets, The Benevolent, The Most Affectionate.*

transmitted diseases, etc.

From the social aspect, polygamy plays an important role by fulfilling a need. It permits widows and divorcees to remarry, providing them the opportunity to fulfill the quest for companionship and support, and also provides a home for orphaned children. However, polygamy is permitted only conditionally. Therefore, it must have a justifiable reason: to fulfill a social responsibility, in case of sickness of the first wife, infertility, etc. Whether those conditions are heeded or not, depends solely upon those who take on the responsibility and with every responsibility also comes accountability.

> ... *marry women of your choice, two or three or four; but if you fear that you cannot deal justly (with so many), then only one or (the captives) that your right hands possess. Thus, it is more likely that you will not do injustice.*[38]   (Surah 4, An Nisa', ayat 3)

The expression *that your right hands possess (ma malakat aimanukum)* is frequently misunderstood and also misrepresented. This expression refers to women who were captured during war and enslaved, before the abolition of slavery by Islam. These enslaved women prisoners were often used as sex objects by their captors. Therefore, women who taken captive and later released, were no longer accepted in their respective communities because of the stigma, often based solely upon suspicion of having been used by their captors, and would end up on the streets. Islam provided an acceptable alternative for them, ie., freedom from captivity without ransom and marriage. Islam prohibits concubines and temporary marriages.

The practice of slavery was deeply rooted in society and Islam sought its gradually eradication.[39] By suggesting marriage to women slaves (*that your right hands possess*), Islam initiated the process of emancipation. This meritorious act was thus characterized by Prophet Muhammad ﷺ: *Anyone who sets his slave girl free and then marries her,*

---

[38] The verses of Surah An Nisa' dealing with multiple marriages were revealed after the Battle of Uhud where many Muslim men were martyred leaving behind widows and orphans. Similar situations have developed in Iraq, Palestine, Afghanistan, Libya and Somalia as a result of conflicts.

[39] Similarly, alcohol consumption which was also a deeply rooted custom, was abolished in a gradual fashion.

will have a double reward.[40]

Subsequently, Islam abolished slavery altogether and it remains prohibited. It is of importance to note, that slavery which was being practiced during that early period of Islam (early seventh century CE), was fundamentally different from the practice of slavery in North America or in other parts of the world. Unlike the treatment rendered to slaves in North America, if a female slave was impregnated by her master, she became free and her child was born free. The following Hadith highlights some of the responsibilities that came with ownership of slaves.

Your slaves are your brethren upon whom Allah has given you authority. So, whoever has his brother under his control, should him feed them with the like of what he eats and clothe them with the like of what he wears. You should not overburden them with what they cannot bear, and if you do so, help them in their hard job with their work.[41]

Responsibilities in multiple marriages

Multiple marriages are subject to certain rules. Each one of the wives must be treated with equality, compassion and kindness and all must be provided equivalent accommodation and amenities, food, clothing and financial support, etc. There are clear directives to not mistreat physically or emotionally, neglect one or openly favor one over another. This may seem easy, while in reality, it is a very difficult task even for the most conscientious man.

You will never be able to deal equally between your wives, however much you desire (to do so). But do not turn away altogether (from one wife), leaving her, as in suspense.[42] *If you do good and keep from evil, surely Allah is ever Forgiving, Merciful.* (Surah 4, An Nisa', ayat 129)

---

[40] Sunan Abu Dawud. English Translation with Explanatory Notes. A Hasan. Kitab Bhavan, New Delhi, 1997. Volume 2, Hadith 2048, page 547.

[41] The Translation of the Meanings of Sahih Al-Bukhari. MM Khan. Kazi Publications, Lahore, Pakistan, 1979. Volume III, Hadith 721, page 434.

[42] *as in suspense* means *as if hanging in the air, in neglect.*

Divorce and Khula

In cases of marital discord, means of reconciliation must be exhausted for the preservation of the marriage and for safeguarding the interests of the family. Prophet Muhammad ﷺ said: *Of all the lawful acts, the most detestable to Allah is divorce.*[43]

The Arabic word for divorce is *talaq* which means to set free (from the contract/bond of marriage). Once divorced, a couple may not remarry unless the woman marries another man and consummates the marriage. This serves as a deterrent against impulsive or frivolous pronouncement of divorce. *Khula* is termination of the marriage at the request of a wife.[44]

Iddah

The *iddah* is a period of waiting which is prescribed for women after divorce or death of the husband. After a divorce, the *iddah* is three menstrual periods.[45] This also allows for manifestation of a pregnancy. A woman is not allowed to remarry during the *iddah* or pregnancy.

Concluding Summary

O Children of Adam! Let not Satan seduce you in the same manner as he got your (first) parents out of the Garden, stripping them their raiment (of innocence) to expose their shame, for he and his tribe watch you from a position where you cannot see them. We have made the devils protecting friends of those who do not believe. (Surah 7, Al A'raaf, ayat 27)

Recent times have witnessed a radical change in the world order of morality with domination of vocal liberal attitudes that promote, condone or simply tolerate extramarital relationships, aberrant sexual practices (including homosexuality and homosexual "marriage"),

---

[43] Sunan Abu Dawud. English translation with Explanatory Notes. A Hasan. Kitab Bhavan, New Delhi, 1997. Volume 2, Hadith 2173, page 586.

[44] The wife may request annulment of the marriage for any reason. In such cases, she has to return the *mahr* and the *iddah* (waiting period) is the course of one menstrual period.

[45] Surah 2, Al Baqarah, ayat 228.

homosexual clergy, etc. Acceptance or tolerance of immoral practices blunts the affect, leading to acceptance or tolerance of other unbecoming acts. Immorality is recognized as having been a major contributing factor in the decline and destruction of many past civilizations.

Marriage serves multiple purposes for both the individual and community. In addition to fulfilling the individual's need for licit companionship, it contributes to better emotional and physical health. As a lifetime partnership, marriage teaches responsibility and respect, and protects from immoral practices that ruin societies.

Beautified is the life of the world for those who disbelieve; they make a jest of the believers. But those who keep their duty to God will be above them on the Day of Resurrection. God gives without restriction to whom He will.   (Surah 2, Al Baqarah, ayat 212)

Chapter Eight

Family and Social Issues

Introduction

And your Lord has decreed, that you worship none but Him, and that you be dutiful to your parents. If either or both of them attain old age in your life, (show no sign of disrespect/impatience) and do not even say 'uff' to them, nor rebuke them, but speak kind words to them (address them with honour).[1] And lower unto them the wing of humility and tenderness, and say: My Lord! Have mercy on them both as they did care for me when I was small. (Surah 17, Al Isra', ayaat 23-24)

And We have enjoined upon man concerning his parents: his mother bears him in weakness upon weakness, and his weaning is in two years. Give thanks to Me and to your parents. To Me is (your final) journey. (Surah 31, Luqman, ayat 14)

In some segments of Western society, older parents are perceived as an impediment to freedom and a burden that is best placed in someone else's care, such as a nursing home, senior or assisted living communities. In the United States of America, of the over thirty-three million persons above the age of sixty-five years, about 1.4 million find themselves in nursing homes at the mercy of strangers.[2] Each year,

---

[1] *uff*, similar to *ugh* is an expression of displeasure or dissatisfaction.

[2] Statistics on Nursing Homes and Their Residents (2008 data).
http://www.therubins.com/homes/stathome.htm
209. Nursing home residents 65 years old and over.
http://www.allcountries.org/uscensus Last Accessed May 2011.

abuse or neglect by someone on whom they depend for care or protection, is estimated to affect between one to two million Americans aged sixty-five or older.[3] The alleged perpetrator is a relative of the victim in over 54 % the cases: an adult child in 32.6%, some other family member in 21.5% and a spouse or intimate partner in 11.3 % of cases.[4]

Some children may be emotionally detached or indifferent towards their aging parents. The latter, together with society at large, share the responsibility for instilling such attitudes. Neglect during childhood produces a weaker bond between parent and child. In addition, encouraging "independence" and living away from home may have unintentionally contributed to alienation.

Parents in Muslim Society

In the Qur'an, many verses that direct Muslims to obedience and kindness[5] towards parents follow the Commandment to worship One God. This sequence stresses the exalted status assigned to parents. Muslims are forbidden to display even the slightest displeasure towards parents, including verbal or physical show of disrespect, rebuke or impatience. This applies to all parents, also those who are not Muslim. Parents must be obeyed unless their request runs contrary to the Commandments of God and those of His Messenger, Prophet Muhammad ﷺ. It is an obligation that is not only highly meritorious but also an expression of faith. When asked which deeds were most loved by God, the Prophet ﷺ replied: *To offer prayers at their earliest stated times. To be good and dutiful to one's parents. To*

---

[3] As few as one in fourteen cases of elder abuse may ever be reported. Forms of abuse include neglect, physical, emotional, sexual, abandonment and financial or material exploitation. Elder Mistreatment: Abuse, Neglect, and Exploitation in an Aging America (2003) Committee on National Statistics (CNSTAT). http://www.nap.edu/openbook.php?record_id=10406&page=1 http://www.ncea.aoa.gov/ncearoot/main_site/pdf/publication/FinalStatistics050331pdf Last accessed May 2011.

[4] The 2004 Survey of State Adult Protective Services: Abuse of Adults 60 Years of Age and Older. Last accessed May 2011. http://www.ncea.aoa.gov/NCEAroot/Main_Site/pdf/021406_60PLUS_REPORT.pdf

[5] Usually translated as kindness or goodness, *birr* has a broader meaning which includes: overall virtuous conduct, respectfulness, obedience, honour, compassion, and patience.

participate in Jihad (to strive/struggle) for Allah's Cause.[6]

Responsibility towards Parents

Islam recognizes and rewards the sacrifices of dutiful parents. God has linked gratitude towards parents to the Commandment to be thankful to Him. The affection, tolerance and care provided to their children by devoted parents (particularly mothers) can never be repaid by a child. Thus, regardless of what a person does for them, the gratitude owed to parents can never be deemed as being *paid in full.* This is elucidated by the narrative about a young man who carried his mother for Haj (pilgrimage to Makkah) all the way from Yemen, a journey of several hundred miles through mountains and desert. He asked the Prophet ﷺ whether, through that service, he had repaid his mother for all that she had done for him. The Prophet ﷺ replied in the negative.

For adult Muslim children, it is not only a moral obligation, but also a legal responsibility under the Shari'ah, to provide for the needs of aging parents, especially if the latter do not have the financial means. In a Muslim society, living close to elderly parents or having them live in their children's home (if necessary) assures their protection, comfort and care.

Caring for parents and providing them company are considered equivalent to a superior form of Jihad and being dutiful to parents even takes priority over voluntary devotional activity.[7] Prophet Muhammad ﷺ said: *May his nose be rubbed in the dust. The one whose parents, one or both of them, reach old age during his lifetime and he does not enter paradise (through serving and obeying them).*[8]

The obligations towards parents do not cease upon their death.

---

[6] The Translation and Meanings of Sahih Al-Bukhari. MM Khan, Kazi Publications, Lahore, Pakistan, 1979. Volume VIII, Hadith 1, page 1.
For the definition and an explanation of the meaning of Jihad, see Chapter 6, Jihad, The Struggle to Self-Discipline.

[7] The English Translation of Sahih Muslim. Darussalam, Riyadh, S Arabia, 2007. Volume 6, Hadith 6504 and 6507, pages 414-417.

[8] The English Translation of Sahih Muslim. Darussalam, Riyadh, S Arabia, 2007. Volume 6, Hadith 6510, page 420. The expression *...may his nose be rubbed in the dust...* is the equivalent of *shame on him.*
...and he does not enter paradise... means that person does not obtain the Divine Blessings provided by serving and obeying parents.

Prayers and virtuous deeds of children benefit their deceased parents.[9] A person once asked Prophet Muhammad ﷺ whether there was any act of kindness he could do towards his parents after their death. The Prophet ﷺ replied:[10]

> You can invoke blessings on them, seek forgiveness for them, carry out their final instructions after their death, join ties of relationship which are dependent on them and honour their friends.

Non-Muslim Parents

Islam does not make any distinction whether the parents are Muslim or not. Non-Muslim parents must also be treated kindly and obeyed except if they demand something that is not permitted by Islamic rules, as the duty towards God comes first:

> But if they strive to make you join in worship with Me (as partner) things of which you have no knowledge, then do not obey them. Yet bear them company in this world with justice (and consideration), and follow the way of those who turn to Me. In the end the return of you all is to Me, and I shall tell you what you used to do. (Surah 31, Luqman, ayat 15)

Parents hold the Keys

> He who wishes that his life span be prolonged and his provisions increased should treat his parents well and maintain his bonds of kinship.[11]

Through the status awarded them by God, parents hold the keys to their children's ultimate success (material as well as spiritual) or failure. Parent's pleasure brought on by their children brings God's

---

[9] Among the actions and good deeds for which a believer will continue to receive rewards even after his death are: knowledge which he taught and spread, virtuous children which he left behind, Qur'an which he left as an inheritance, a mosque that he built, a rest house which he built for travelers, a stream (a well) which he caused to flow, a charity which he gave from his wealth while he was alive and healthy. For all these he will continue to receive rewards after his death. Reported by Ibn Majah. Muntakhab Ahadith, Kandhlavi MY. Annayyar, Karachi, Pakistan. Hadith 38, page 259.

[10] Sunan Abu Dawud. English Translation by A Hasan, Kitab Bhawan, New Delhi, 1997. Volume 3, Hadith 5123, page 1423. ...join ties of relationship which are dependent on them... means maintaining ties with relatives.

[11] Musnad Ahmad. Muntakhab Ahadith. Kandhlavi MY. Annayyar, Karachi, Pakistan. Hadith 257, page 482.

pleasure while the parent's displeasure may incur His wrath.[12] Alone obedience to parents fulfills a religious obligation with its inherent benefits and Divine Blessings while insult or disobedience are considered major sins. A parent's supplication for their children is a great source of God's blessing as such a prayer is always accepted.

The status of the mother is significantly higher than that of the father. While an explanation may be the hardships of pregnancy and childbirth and effort associated with caring for the infant and continuing with other duties, the precise reasons are known only to God.[13]

And We have enjoined on man kindness to his parents. In pain did his mother bear him, and in pain did she give birth to him, and the carrying of the child to his weaning is thirty months ...
                                      (Surah 46, Al Ahqaf, ayat 15)

O mankind: Reverence your Guardian Lord Who created you from a single soul, and from it created its mate... Reverence God in Whose Name you demand your mutual rights, and reverence the wombs (that bore you):[14] for God ever watches over you.
                                      (Surah 4, An Nisa', ayat 1)

The father is the middle gate to Paradise; so if you wish, either neglect that gate (by disobeying him), or protect it (by obeying him).[15]

---

[12] English Translation of Jami' At-Tirmidhi. Darussalam, Riyadh, S Arabia, 2007. Volume 4, Hadith 1899, page 23. *The Lord's pleasure is in the parent's pleasure, and the Lord's displeasure is in the parent's displeasure.* Parent's displeasure which is justified and for a legitimate reason.

[13] When asked who was most deserving of good treatment, Prophet Muhammad ﷺ said: *Your mother, (again) your mother, (again) your mother, then your father, then your nearest relatives according to the order (of nearness).* Sahih Muslim, Al-Jami'-us-Sahih by Imam Muslim. M Matraji. Darul-Isha'at, Karachi, Pakistan, 1998. Volume IV-A, Hadith 2548R1, page 164.

[14] *...and (reverence) the wombs (that bore you)* also means: *be dutiful toward your parents* (MM Picthall, The Glorious Qur'an) also *refrain from violating relations between kinsfolk.* Maududi SAA, The Meaning of the Qur'an. Islamic Publications Ltd., Lahore, Pakistan, 1976. Volume II, page 93.

[15] English Translation of Jami' At-Tirmidhi. Darussalam, Riyadh, S Arabia, 2007. Volume 4, Hadith 1900, page 24.

Children and Family

*To Allah belongs the Sovereignty of the heavens and the earth. He creates
what He wills. He gives daughters to whom He wills, and sons to whom
He wills. Or He gives both sons and daughters to whom He will and
leaves barren whom He will. Indeed He is Knower, Powerful.*

(Surah 42, Ash Shura', ayaat 49-50)

The family is at the center of Islamic society. Therefore, Islam
teaches strong family relationships which lead to a cohesive society.
The wife (mother) is not obliged to work as providing for the family's
material needs is the responsibility of the husband (father).
Consequently, the mother can devote her efforts to the well-being of
the family. Such a setup prevents childhood neglect with its attendant
adverse effects on health, behavioral and cognitive development which
become apparent in adolescence and adulthood.

Children

Data released by the Centers for Disease Control and Prevention
indicate that each year, hundreds of thousands of children are abused
and neglected in the United States of America: over 900,000 children
younger than eighteen years of age, of which over 91,000 were less
than twelve months old, and of these, 33 % were less than one week
old.[16]

Such statistics indicate a break down of the societal structure.
Furthermore, children who suffer maltreatment are not only at higher
risk for unbecoming conduct during adolescence and adulthood
(violence, alcohol, drug abuse) but are also at greater risk for chronic
health problems (obesity, diabetes, cancer, and cardiovascular
disease). Frequently, they are also abusive towards their own offspring
and relatives, repeating the cycle. Additionally, neglect and abuse are a
major cause of child mortality in the industrialized nations.

---

[16] Thousands Of Infants Abused, Neglected. Morbidity and Mortality Weekly Report,
2008, April 4;57(13):336-339. MorningRounds@ama.custombriefings.com
Nonfatal Maltreatment of Infants-United States, October 2005--September 2006.
http://www.cdc.gov/mmwr/preview/mmwrhtml/mm5713a2.htm Last accessed May
2011.

A Child is a Gift from God

Islam considers a child a gift from God. A child is conceived and a pregnancy is completed at the sole discretion of God. While the vast majority of people take this blessing for granted, a significant percentage struggle to fulfill the desire of having their own offspring. Muslim parents must choose good names for their children and are obligated to provide all necessities, both social and material: love and affection, compassion, a home, food, clothing, security/protection (from physical and emotional harm), and education (religious and secular). Child abuse, neglect or abandonment are strictly prohibited. Even in war situations, the Shari'ah explicitly prohibits harming non-combatant women, children and the elderly. Prophet Muhammad ﷺ serves as the role model on how to treat children.

Rights of children

Mothers shall suckle their children for two whole years: (that is) for those who wish to complete the suckling ... (Surah 2, Al Baqarah, ayat 233)

Breast-feeding is recommended, but if the mother is either unable or unwilling, a wet-nurse may be employed and compensated appropriately. Breast-fed infants are healthier, with fewer gastro-intestinal problems, show better development and may even have a higher IQ than those fed with formula.[17] Additional benefits include mother-child bonding, security, and passage of health protective secretions (immunity) to the child through the breast milk. In a study published in the Annals of Rheumatic Diseases, the authors found that women who were breast-feeding for thirteen months or longer had a reduction in the risk of Rheumatoid Arthritis by about half.[18] A shorter duration of breast-feeding was associated with a lesser reduction of the risk.

For some time, breast feeding had been abandoned in some segments of Western society for reasons that including the stated

---

[17] Monterrosa, EC, et al: Predominant Breast-Feeding from birth to six months is associated with fewer gastrointestinal infections and increased risk for iron deficiency among infants. J Nutr 138:1499-1504, 2008.

[18] Pikwer M, et al: Breast-Feeding, but not oral contraceptives, is associated with a reduced risk of rheumatoid arthritis. Ann Rheum Dis. Online publication, 13 May 2008.

belief that lactation could increase the risk of cancer, for cosmetic, and social reasons, eg., freedom from the perceived inconvenience of carrying the baby around and feeding it every few hours. These societies now appear to have rediscovered breast-feeding as science has shown its numerous benefits and Western physicians have begun to encourage this practice.

Education

Prophet Muhammad ﷺ said: *No father gives his child any better gift than good education.*[19] The acquisition of knowledge is a must for every Muslim male and female. Education includes subjects taught in secular educational institutions and also moral and religious education.

Equal Treatment of all Children

Parents are obliged to treat all their children equally. No distinction may be made between males and females. If one child is given a gift, the others must be given an equivalent gift. Prophet Muhammad ﷺ warned: *Be afraid of Allah, and be just to your children.*[20] Furthermore, a child may not be excluded from inheriting from his/her biological family.

Family

Indeed the most perfect believer in faith is one who has the best manners and is the kindest to his family.[21]

One of the many wonderful benefits of Islam is that all good intentions are rewarded and all good actions taken with the intention of pleasing God are considered acts of charity. Providing for one's family is an obligation. If it is done with the intention of pleasing God, it also becomes an act of charity.

Rules guiding family relationships assign rights and responsibilities to each member, thereby assuring harmony. Since they are a religious

[19] Reported by Tirmidhi. Muntakhab Ahadith. Kandhlavi MY. Annayyar, Karachi, Pakistan. Hadith 220, page 469.

[20] The Translation of the Meanings of Sahih Al-Bukhari. MM Khan, Kazi Publications, Lahore, Pakistan, 1979. Volume III, Hadith 760, page 459.

[21] Reported by Tirmidhi. Muntakhab Ahadith. Kandhlavi MY. Annayyar, Karachi, Pakistan. Hadith 43, page 412.

obligation, the Islamic values endure and survive adverse Western influences such as those affecting other aspects of Muslim society, economy and culture.

There is considerable emphasis on maintaining family ties: regular communication, friendly relationships, fulfilling obligations owed to others, providing emotional and material support, etc. As a general principle from the Sunnah of the Prophet ﷺ which guides interaction with others, Muslims are encouraged to overlook the faults and undesirable actions of others and avoid vengeance.

The broader Islamic concept of family extends far beyond the traditional definition, ie., that of husband, wife, children and near relatives. All Muslims constitute a global sisterhood and brotherhood, meaning that every Muslim is obliged to be concerned about the well-being of other Muslims, no matter where they reside and what language they speak, and should be prepared to provide for their needs. Prophet Muhammad ﷺ: *He who is engaged in fulfilling his brother's need, Allah will fulfill his needs.*[22] In keeping with the universal nature of the Message of Islam, it includes all of humanity.

Adoption

... nor has He (God) made those who you claim (to be your sons) your sons.[23] *Such is only your (manner of) speech by your mouths. But God tells you the truth and He shows the right way. Proclaim their real parentage.*[24] *That is more equitable in the sight of God. But if you do not know their fathers' names, then they are your brethren in the faith and mawalikum (under your care). And there is no blame on you in the mistakes that you make unintentionally: what counts is the intention of your hearts. And God is Forgiving, Most Merciful.*

(Surah 33, Al Ahzab, ayaat 4-5)

---

[22] Brother here means a fellow Muslim. Reported by Abu Dawud. Muntakhab Ahadith, Kandhlavi MY. Annayyar, Karachi, Pakistan. Hadith 159, page 449.

[23] The declaration (or going through the legal proceedings) of "adoption" does not and cannot make the "adopted" individual a person's real child. This refers to the pre-Islamic practice of adoption, which was in many ways, similar to the present day practice of adoption in Western society.

[24] Call them by the names of their real (biological) fathers.

In this section, the term *adoption* is used in the generic sense, ie., taking a child into the family and caring for his/her needs. There are fundamental differences between the Western practice of adoption and that which is permissible under Shari'ah. These differences are explained below.

Adoption in the Pre-Islamic period

In pre-Islamic Arabia, adopted children were given the adopting family's name, became heirs and also assumed the adopting father's lineage.[25] Islam abolished that practice. Events that were a prelude to the abolishment of that practice are discussed below. Given the sacredness of such deep rooted cultural practices, Islam brought home the realization that the pre-Islamic adoption practices were none other than make-believe and also deceitful, ie., that of taking in a stranger and assigning him/her the status of a biological offspring.

Adoption in Contemporary Western society

In European-American societies, adoption is defined as *The official transfer through the court system of all of the parental rights that a biological parent has to a child, along with an assumption by the adopting parent of all of the parental rights of the biological parents that are being terminated and are assumed in their entirety by the adoptive parents.* With the transfer of all parental rights and responsibilities to the adoptive parent(s) there is *no legal difference between the adoptive parents' biological and adopted children.*[26]

Children that are given up for adoption may be orphaned, unwanted by their biological parent(s) or abandoned by them. Increasingly, there is also an element of child trafficking.[27] Frequently, the adoptive parent(s) must pay substantial sums of money to acquire the child.

---

[25] This is similar to today's practice of adoption in Western and other societies.

[26] http://glossary.adoption.com/adoption.html http://en.wikipedia.org/wiki/Adoption
Last accessed May 2011.

[27] Kidnap or salvation? Debate rages on Chad children. November 2, 2007.
http://www.reuters.com/article/worldNews/idUSL0260632620071102
Ordeal of Chad children in 'kidnap' row. http://news.bbc.co.uk/2/hi/africa/7067659.stm
Chad case children 'not orphans'. http://news.bbc.co.uk/2/hi/africa/7072714.stm
In this particular case, a French adoption agency was involved in kidnaping Chadian children with the intention of flying them to Europe on a chartered aircraft and then selling them to Europeans seeking to adopt children.

After the adoption process, the adopted child assumes a new identity by taking the adoptive family's name and many or all ties with the biological parents are severed. Such an adoption can be viewed as a falsification of reality and blurring of the natural order of society. Since many of these children are born out of wedlock, adoption may seek to hide the illegitimacy and/or the paternity.

Adoption and Shari'ah

Islam prohibits the Western or pre-Islamic type of adoption. This prohibition serves to protect the rights of the child, parents (adoptive and biological), and others who may be affected by it, as well as society at large. What the Shari'ah permits is a form of adoption which preserves the child's independent identity and lineage. It encourages Muslims to raise children who are not their own offspring, including orphaned, abandoned and destitute children.[28] This type of adoption is called *kafalah,* which is essentially a legal guardianship, custodianship or fostering.[29] In the guardian's family, the child is accorded all of the benefits of the biological offspring, ie., the guardian treats the child as though it was his own but without ascribing the child to himself. In addition, the guardian may not give this child certain rights which are reserved (through Shari'ah) for his biological children.

The Shari'ah prohibits adoption which permanently severs all rights of biological parents.[30] It also forbids depriving a child of his/her biological parent's name or falsification of identity and lineage by assuming the adoptive parent's name. The Shari'ah requires that the biological identity and heritage of the child be maintained. By prohibiting Western type adoption practices which obscure a child's biological identity and heritage, it seeks only to eliminate the act of assigning offspring status to the "adopted" child while retaining all other benefits, ie., the adopting parents would *treat the child in exactly the same manner as they would their own biological offspring.*

---

[28] This is a highly rewarded act of charity.

[29] *Kafalah* (from *kafeel)* means answerable and responsible for, protector, guardian. Under Shari'ah, such a relationship is that of a legal guardian. This incorporates a promise to provide a home, food, clothing, education, protection, etc., for a minor, in the same fashion as for one's own biological offspring.

[30] The Arabic term for Western type adoption is *at tabanni.*

Shari'ah accorded Rights of Adopted Children

- The child retains his/her biological identity. The lineage may not be altered nor the paternal identity obscured. Therefore, the child must retain the biological father's family name and may not assume the guardian's name. This enables identification of the biological family (for medical and genetic purposes) and to prevent unintended marriage to a sibling or to others prohibited by Shari'ah
- The guardian family does not replace the biological family and only serves as a caregiver for someone else's child. Additionally, the child does not assume the status of a sibling or *mahram*,[31] ie., marriage between such a child and members of the guardian's family (including biological offspring) would be permissible. If the mother (the guardian's wife) breast feeds the child, a different relationship is established, ie., one closer to that of a biological sibling, and therefore, intermarriage is prohibited
- The child remains an heir of his/her biological parents. Under Shari'ah, a father may not deprive his biological children of inheritance. The child cannot inherit from the guardian in the same manner as the guardian's biological children.[32] If the child were to receive inheritance from the guardian (as would be the case after Western type adoption), this would deprive the rightful heirs (biological children and family of the guardian) of their share of inheritance. It may be perceived as usurpation of the rights to their full inheritance and is not conducive to peace and harmony in the family
- If the child is endowed with property/wealth, the guardian is required to manage it honestly and diligently, as a trustee. The guardian may use some of the child's wealth to defray the cost of the child's care

---

[31] Mahram is a person to whom marriage is not permitted.

[32] Islamic inheritance laws have explicit rules. Two thirds of the deceased's property is subject to these rules. One third may be bequeathed through a Will during the lifetime of the individual. The adopted child may be given through the latter process.

As with most Shari'ah rulings, enforcement is left up to the conscience and integrity of the individual, respect for the Divine and the fear of retribution:

> *Come not near the wealth of the orphan save with that which is better till he come to strength; and keep the covenant. Lo! of the covenant it will be asked.* (Surah 17, Al Isra', ayat 34)

> *Those who devour the wealth of orphans wrongfully, they do but swallow the fire into their bellies, and they will be exposed to the burning flame.* (Surah 4, An Nisa', ayat 10)

Pre-Islamic Adoption of Zaid bin Haritha

In keeping with the prevailing Arab traditions and before the prophethood, Muhammad ﷺ adopted a young boy by the name of Zaid. As a young child, Zaid had been kidnapped and sold into slavery. He was bought by Hakim ibn Huzam who gave the boy to his aunt Khadeeja ؈. After their marriage, Khadeeja ؈ gifted Zaid to Muhammad ﷺ. While Zaid was in their household in Makkah, his family was able to locate him and came to claim him. Instead of returning with them, Zaid opted to remain with Muhammad ﷺ who set him free and adopted him. This adoption was done in accordance with the pre-Islamic customs, and thus, he came to be known as Zaid ibn Muhammad (Zaid, son of Muhammad). However, subsequent to revelation of verses of the Qur'an that required declaration of the adopted person's real parentage (Surah 33, Al Ahzab, ayaat 4-5), Zaid was called by his biological father's name, Zaid bin Haritha.

As an "adopted" son, the local pre-Islamic customs made him eligible to inherit and also assume Muhammad's ﷺ lineage. Muhammad ﷺ arranged for Zaid to be married to his cousin, Zaynab bint Jah'sh. The marriage did not last because of incompatibility of the spouses and Zaid sought permission to divorce his wife. Initially, he was discouraged, but after several appeals, he was granted permission.

This divorce took place several years after the Message of Islam had been proclaimed. Prophet Muhammad ﷺ found Zaid a new wife (Umm Kulthum bint Uqbah) and he ﷺ married Zaynab. According to Islamic rules, a child that is "adopted" does not acquire the status of a biological offspring. Therefore, there was nothing prohibiting Prophet

Muhammad's ﷺ marriage to Zaynab:

Muhammad is not the father of any man among you, but he is the Messenger of Allah and the Seal of the Prophets; and Allah is Aware of all things. (Surah 33, Al Ahzab, ayat 40)

While the pre-Islamic Arab customs prohibited marriage to the divorcee of an "adopted" son,[33] Islam was to expose the fallacy of such adoption and abolished that practice forever. It is clear from verses of the Qur'an (Surah 33, Al Ahzab, ayaat 37-39) that Prophet Muhammad ﷺ was apprehensive of marrying Zaynab after she had been divorced by Zaid. That was because of the concerns for going against prevailing cultural traditions and anticipated slanderous reaction of the non-Muslim populace. On the other hand, Muslims had been reassured of the legality of this union through Divine Revelation. It is also necessary to understand, that the Prophet ﷺ was obliged to follow the Divine Commandments. This marriage eliminated, for all times, the fallacious practice of "adoption" which conferred biological offspring status to the "adopted" child.

O Prophet ! Keep your duty to God and do not obey the disbelievers and the hypocrites. God is Knower, Wise. And follow that which is inspired in you from your Lord. God is aware of what you do. (Surah 33, Al Ahzab, ayaat 1-2)

Islam unequivocally prohibits a person marrying the divorcee of a biological offspring. Islam does not prohibit marriage to the divorcee of an unrelated person brought up (fostered) under guardianship, after due consideration of the Shar'iah rules of marriage, ie., the *mahram* status (persons to whom marriage is prohibited).

General Social Issues

Is the reward for goodness anything but goodness? (Surah 55, Ar Rahman, ayat 60)

---

[33] Adopted according to the pre-Islamic customs.

The best amongst people is the one who benefits people the most.[34]

Islamic Principles of Universal Social Goodness

Recognizing the need for harmonious interaction, Islam promotes a system of high social values and ethics, and establishes the rights of humans and all other living things. It inspires God-consciousness and discipline, and induces moral and social responsibility. The qualities of a true believer (mu'min) include God-consciousness in all affairs, always being mindful of not displeasing God, kindness and generosity, compassion and mercy towards all, desire for peace, fairness and truthfulness in all situations, and responsible behavior towards all others, including animals, vegetation and the environment.[35] These are qualities from which only good may be expected.

Social responsibility includes due consideration for the rights of all people, irrespective of religious persuasion and social status, and also the rights of all other living creatures. For example, hunting for the sake of sport is prohibited. Hunting is permitted only for food. The cutting of fruit-bearing trees and plants is forbidden unless there is a compelling reason. Giving in charity, caring for the poor, the sick and elderly, for orphaned children, widows, and relatives are greatly encouraged.

The benefits of responsible conduct are social harmony and prevention of abuse and injustice. Every act of good social behavior, no matter how trivial appearing, if performed with a sincere purpose, is considered an act of charity. For example, greeting another person with a pleasant demeanor or removing a potentially harmful object from the sidewalk are all acts of charity.

Care of Relatives

None of you is a true Believer, until he likes for his brother what he likes for himself. [36]

---

[34] Dar Qutni, Jami us Saghir. Muntakhab Ahadith, Kandhlavi MY. Annayyar, Karachi, Pakistan. Hadith 161, page 449.

[35] Everything in the universe was created for the benefit of man. Thus, appreciating and caring for these God-given benefits constitutes an act of gratitude and worship.

[36] Reported by Al Bukhari. Muntakhab Ahadith. Kandhlavi MY. Annayyar, Karachi, Pakistan. Hadith 138, page 442. The term brother is generally understood as meaning a fellow Muslim.

The family is the recipient of the greatest attention: spouse, parents, children, grandparents, and other close and distant relatives. However, Islamic social responsibility extends beyond the immediate family and the Muslim community. Discrimination on the basis of religious persuasion is prohibited. Giving in charity is not restricted to Muslims, and under certain conditions, even *Zakat* may be given to non-Muslims. For additional information on Zakat, see Chapter 1, Islam.

The Arabic words for relationship, kinship and uterus (womb) are derived from same root *(rahima)* which means *to have mercy, compassion. Ar Rahman* (The Merciful), which is an Attribute of God, is also derived of the same root word. Hence, ties of kinship (especially with close relatives) are valued and there is prohibition of severing relationships. The uterus is the initial place of rest, security and development of an individual. Thus, the reverence for the mother and also relatives from her side, eg., maternal aunts. In the broader context, it includes all relatives.

The laws of inheritance are specified in the Qur'an and only close relatives are eligible to inherit after the demise of a person. However, if others (orphans, poor, distant relatives are present) at the time of distribution of a deceased's property, God has prescribed that a share be given to them. This is in keeping with the basic Islamic principles of compassion and generosity.

And when kinsfolk and orphans and the needy are present at the division (of the heritage), bestow on them therefrom and speak kindly unto them.
(Surah 4, An Nisa', ayat 8)

And give the relatives their due rights, and to those in need, and to the wayfarer; but do not squander your wealth in the manner of a spendthrift (wastefully).
(Surah 17, Al Isra', ayat 26)

Sick, Elderly and Neighbours

Visiting the sick, respect for elders, kindness towards neighbours, help and compassion for the poor and those in need are some of the characteristics of the faith in practice. The following Hadith explain the importance and benefits of some social practices.

Whoever visits a sick person enters into the Mercy of God, and when he sits with the sick, he is completely immersed in His Mercy [37]

He is not a believer who eats his fill while his neighbour is hungry [38]

He will not enter Paradise whose neighbours feels unsafe from his injurious conduct [39]

Allah is kind and loves kindness. [40]

Social Interaction, Mingling of Women and Men

Islam guides to a "middle" path. It shuns extremes and blindly adapting permissive practices far removed from Islamic norms. Complete separation of men and women with restriction of the movement of latter, which is practiced by some cultures, does not find its source (ruling) in the Shari'ah. On the contrary, there is ample historical evidence dating back to the time of the Prophet ﷺ, of women's participation in public meetings, congregational prayers, education, and in a supportive role in social and military undertakings.

The Shari'ah evaluates such issues from the following perspective: objectives, potential benefits and potential harm to the individual and societal structure. The meeting of men and women in a public forum is acceptable provided the objective is a good cause, eg., an acceptable (under Shari'ah rules) undertaking which would provide benefit by combining the efforts of men and women or to acquire useful knowledge. Additionally, it is permissible in the setting of an educational institution and the work place. In all such meetings, the individuals (both men and women) must adhere to the Islamic rules of conduct.

---

[37] Musnad Ahmad. Muntakhab Ahadith. Kandhlavi MY. Annayyar, Karachi, Pakistan. Hadith 123, pages 436-437.

[38] Reported by At Tabarani. Muntakhab Ahadith. Kandhlavi MY. Annayyar, Karachi, Pakistan. Hadith 229, page 472.

[39] Reported by Muslim. Muntakhab Ahadith. Kandhlavi MY, Annayyar, Karachi, Pakistan. Hadith 227, page 471.

[40] Reported by Muslim. Muntakhab Ahadith. Kandhlavi MY. Annayyar, Karachi, Pakistan. Hadith 76, page 421.

Western style social mixing of women and men without a necessity is not desirable. Such interaction has the potential to exceed the limits prescribed by Shari'ah, with all of its repercussions for the individuals, their families and society as a whole. Adherence to Islamic principles is necessary for participation in mixed gatherings. These include an appropriate, unprovocative attire, avoidance of drawing attention towards oneself, avoiding the use of excessive perfume or make up, and lowering of the gaze (see footnote 42 for an explanation of the expression *lower their gaze*). It is also forbidden for a Muslim woman or man to be alone with a non-mahram.[41] Dating and mixed parties are not permitted.

Tell the believing men to lower (restrain) their gaze and be modest: that is purer for them: Allah is aware of what they do.[42]
And tell the believing women to lower their gaze and be modest; that they should not display their beauty and ornaments except what (must ordinarily) appear thereof; that they should draw their veils over their bosoms and not display their beauty except to their husbands, ...
(Surah 24, An Nur, ayaat 30-31)

Physical contact between women and men

Physical contact between a non-mahram woman and man such as an embrace at the time of greeting, or dancing, etc., is strictly prohibited. This practice does not find its roots in Islam. Such non-Muslim practices often creep into Muslim society, being the norm for a non-Muslim majority population, or are condoned and promoted by some socialites in Muslim majority populations. Sexual contact outside of marriage and homosexuality are strictly forbidden.

Say, my Lord forbids only indecencies (shameful deeds), whether open or secret, and sin and wrongful oppression ...
(Surah 7, Al A'raaf, ayat 33)

---

[41] This includes traveling privately. A non-mahram is a person to whom marriage is permitted (provided that the other Shari'ah requirements are fulfilled).

[42] *Lower their gaze and be modest (or guard their modesty)*, Surah 24, An Nur, ayaat 30-31. This applies to both men and women and advises Islamic etiquette, ie., other than an innocent glance, do not look or stare at another person (or at any part of another person's body, including the face).

Intoxicants, Gambling and Betting

O you who believe! Khamr (intoxicating drink) and games of chance (gambling) and sacrifices on altars (al ansab) dedicated to idols and divining arrows (for seeking luck) are only an abomination of devil's handiwork. Avoid them in order that you may be successful.[43]
The devil seeks only to cause enmity and hatred among you by means of khamr (intoxicating drink) and games of chance (gambling), and hinder you from remembrance of Allah and from prayer. Will you then not abstain?   (Surah 5, Al Ma'idah, ayaat 90-91)

For reasons discussed below, Islam forbids the use of all intoxicants: beverages and drugs, including those smoked, sniffed, ingested, injected or taken by any other route. The Arabic word *khamr* means an intoxicating alcoholic beverage or *wine* in the generic sense. However, the Shari'ah definition of *khamr* includes any substance that inebriates or intoxicates. This includes all alcoholic beverages and mind altering substances.

Prophet Muhammad ﷺ said: *Every intoxicant is khamr, and every intoxicant is unlawful...*[44] Further elaborating on the definition, Umar Ibn al Khattab ؓ, the second Khalifah, said: *...khamr is that which clouds the mind ('aql).*[45,46] Thus, it includes any substance which alters the mind in such a fashion so as to cause impairment of the cognitive functions and alertness, and inhibits the normally present ability of discernment between right and wrong. This prohibition applies uniformly to all Muslims, irrespective of the age of the consumer and irrespective of amount of intoxicant. Prophet Muhammad ﷺ said: *Of that which intoxicates in a large amount, a small amount is unlawful.* He ﷺ also said:

---

[43] Intoxicants and gambling are been placed in the same category as sacrifices on altars in the name of deities, omens and superstition. They are termed *rijs* which means atrocious, dirty, filthy. This term is derived from from *rajisa* which means to do something shameful or disgraceful.

[44] English Translation of Jami At-Tirmidhi, Darussalam, Riyadh, S Arabia, 2007. Volume 3, hadith 1861, page 547.

[45] *'aql*: its meanings also include reason, understanding, comprehension and intellect.

[46] Sahih Muslim, Al-Jami'-us-Sahih by Imam Muslim. M Matraji. Darul-Isha'at, Karachi, Pakistan, 1998. Volume IV-B, Hadith 3032, page 404.

...a sip of it is unlawful.[47] Therefore, there is neither a "safe" drinking amount (legally "acceptable" blood alcohol level) nor a "safe" drinking age.

Alcohol and non-Alcoholic Intoxicants

They ask you (Muhammad) about khamr (intoxicating drink) and gambling, say: In both is great harm and some benefit for mankind; but their sin is greater than their benefit. ...

(Surah 2, Al Baqarah, ayat 219)

Alcohol is consumed for social reasons, or as in the case of recreational drug use, as an escape from reality. Studies have suggested some beneficial effect of certain alcoholic beverages, when consumed in small amounts, in reducing heart disease. However, for most people and society at large, as shown by healthcare and mortality statistics, the harms associated with alcoholic beverage consumption outweigh the relatively trivial benefits.

Alcohol dulls the senses, it alters perceptions, impairs the ability to make sound decisions and judgements, impairs coordination, and suppresses naturally occurring inhibitions against immoral and wrongful activity. It has been linked to numerous problems, personal, familial, occupational and societal, and chronic alcohol consumption in larger amounts has been associated with numerous mental and somatic ailments.

Remembrance of God and His worship are central to the Islamic faith. The remembrance of God instills a state of consciousness which prevents an individual from straying from the path of goodness and facilitates avoidance of acts that are prohibited by Shari'ah. An altered state of mind with dulled senses and impaired judgement cannot provide such protection. Furthermore, it may hinder fulfillment of religious obligations. Additionally, the concentration required during prayer is not possible in an altered state of mind.

Dealing and handling Alcohol and Non-alcoholic Intoxicants

The purchase, sale, serving, receiving or the giving of an alcoholic

---

[47] English Translation of Jami At-Tirmidhi, Darussalam, Riyadh, S Arabia, 2007. Volume 3. Hadith 1865 and 1866, pages 550-551.

beverage or any intoxicant as a gift to anyone (including non-Muslims), are all unlawful for Muslims. The Prophet ﷺ said: ...*He who has forbidden its drinking (consumption) has also forbidden selling it.*[48]

Non-alcoholic versions of traditional Alcoholic Beverages

The process for making alcoholic and non-alcoholic beers and wines is similar. The alcohol is subsequently extracted to make the beverage "non-alcoholic". Since the entire alcohol content cannot be removed, these products usually retain between 0.2 to 0.5 percent alcohol by volume. Although they may be labeled as "non-alcoholic", Muslims are prohibited from consuming them because of the residual alcohol content and the principle cited in the Hadith: *Of that which intoxicates in a large amount, a small amount is unlawful.*

Cooking with Alcoholic Beverages

There is a common myth that alcohol evaporates completely after cooking. While it is correct that a longer duration of cooking or baking diminishes the percentage of retained alcohol, it is never eliminated. For example, baking or simmering for two hours removes up to ninety percent of the alcohol, while the same for thirty minutes, removes about sixty-five percent of the alcohol. Thus, Muslims are not permitted to use wines, beers or other alcoholic beverages for cooking or baking.

Gambling and Betting

There are two interrelated issues, namely, unfair acquisition of wealth and its effects upon the individual, family and society. Islam prohibits the acquisition of large sums without making any effort. It also prohibits acquisition by means that are illicit or depend on "chance". The latter includes gambling, betting, raffle and lottery.[49] These are unlawful, irrespective of the amount, as wealth or property acquired through such means is considered unearned since no labour or effort was involved. Islam requires that income and/or acquisition

---

[48] Sahih Muslim, Al-Jami'-us-Sahih by Imam Muslim. M Matraji. Darul-Isha'at, Karachi, Pakistan, 1998. Volume III-A, Hadith 1579, page 44.

[49] Competitive sport between individuals and teams with subsequent awarding of prizes to the winners is not considered betting. Making bets on competitive events (sports, animals, cars, teams, etc.) are forms of gambling and are prohibited.

of property be through pure and lawful means, such as labour or service, purchase, uncoerced exchange or barter, gift or charity. Gambling and betting are the equivalent of unlawfully taking money or property from others.

In both gambling and betting, there are some winners and a multitude of losers. Gambling and betting are often associated with other prohibited activities such as consumption of intoxicants and illicit social behavior. Losses through gambling may destroy the person and family. Gambling may addict, sow discord, cause neglect of responsibilities (towards family and community) and obligations (including prayers and other religious duties) and even lead to criminal activity, eg., stealing and embezzlement. While there are clear repercussions from substantial gambling losses, there are also detrimental effects of winning, such as the emboldening to repeat the gambling process with the hope of further gains. As a social order, Islam does not allow illicit gains or illicit losses, because both have adverse effects upon the individual, the family and society.

Consumption of intoxicants, gambling and betting (games of chance) are placed in the same category as idolatry and superstitions. Belief in omens and superstitions asserts the reliance on powers besides God for the disposition of affairs with the ultimate result of straying off the right path (Surah 5, Al Ma'idah, ayaat 90-92).

Concluding Summary

Invite (all) to the Way of your Lord with wisdom and beautiful preaching; and reason with them in ways that are best and most gracious. For your Lord knows best, who have strayed from His Path, and who receive guidance.   (Surah 16, An Nahl, ayat 125)

But if they turn away, your duty (O Muhammad) is only to convey the clear message.   (Surah 16, An Nahl, ayat 82)

Islam discourages celibacy or living in seclusion. Marriage and family are a sunnah and participation in the community and society is encouraged: *The believer who mixes with people and endures any harm that they cause him has a greater reward than a believer who does not mix with people and does not endure the harm they cause him.*[50]

The family is at the center of society and Islam makes a tremendous effort towards protecting its integrity. Besides the spouse and children, parents, grandparents, other near and distant relatives are included in this definition of the Muslim family. Additionally, in the broader context, the term is used to include Muslims all over the world.

A family that is intact and thriving is the institution which makes the single most important contribution to the moral and social well-being of society. To a great extent, the integrity of the family depends upon the relationships between men and women. In a society which permits or condones unrestricted male-female interaction, both family and society suffer from the consequences. To protect society from moral decay and preserve the sanctity of the family, the Shari'ah has established rules and guidelines. These guide personal conduct as well as interpersonal and inter-gender interaction and seek to preserve a strict system of morals and values. Since all interactions between people (of both genders) are regulated by Shari'ah rules, the extent and the types of interaction permitted between the genders may differ from Western practice, in one or more ways.

Unrestricted male-female interaction is prohibited by Shari'ah.[51] While observing their own rules, Muslims are obliged to respect and tolerate the customs of other societies, as long as these do not infringe upon their own rights, and also expect reciprocal understanding and respect for esteemed Islamic values.

In addition to a strict moral and social code, there are other requirements that seek to further strengthen the family and society. These include the responsibilities and duties of parents, those of children towards their parents, and the maintaining of family ties. The latter has broad implications as all Muslims constitute one Ummah and its wider definition includes all the relationships under Islam, ie., those

---

[50] Reported by Ibn Majah. Muntakhab Ahadith. Kandhlavi MY, Annayyar, Karachi, Pakistan. Hadith 82, page 422.

[51] In this discussion, the reference is to non-mahram male-female interaction. A non-mahram person is one to whom marriage is permissible provided all other Shari'ah requirements have been fulfilled.

with all others, including social, business or otherwise.

Parents have a significant responsibility towards their children. Adult behavior is learned in childhood. Therefore, proper upbringing (education, moral and social etiquette, stable home environment, etc) not only benefits the children as they venture on their own and the society in which they live, it also rewards the parents in an ongoing basis, even after their death, through the good deeds of their children.

Islamic laws consider child abandonment a major sin. Legislation enacted in some states legalized abandonment of babies and infants. Nebraska State Law (a safe-haven law, 2008) also allowed abandonment of older children at hospitals. Something of this kind is unthinkable under Shari'ah.

The children's duty to reciprocate and care for their parents sets an example for future generations, to continue the cycle of compassion: *My Lord! Have mercy on them both as they did care for me when I was small* (Surah 17, Al Isra', ayat 24). In the context of caring for parents, efforts limited to an occasional visit, celebration of a parent's birthday, mother's or father's day, as a means of appreciating parents, carries little meaning in Muslim society. Muslims are obliged to look after aging parents and assure their comfort and safety. Parents are remembered many times each day. In the last portion of each prayer (*salat*), a supplication is often made for parents.[52]

Social appropriateness requires tolerance, which is acceptance and respect for diversity and overlooking of differences, faults and shortcomings of others. This is of particular importance when the principle of tolerance is applied to those of a different culture, religious, racial or social background. The perceived shortcomings of others, in such settings, may in fact be a manifestation of one's own inability to know, understand and appreciate diversity, or it may be the expression of an imagined cultural superiority.

Since Islam is for all of mankind, without exception, it seamlessly incorporates tolerance into its messages and practice. Tolerance of others is one of the fundamental morals underlying the Islamic social teachings. This includes tolerance of belief, opinion, expression and deeds, so long as the latter do not adversely effect the rights of others

---

[52] There are five obligatory daily prayers at fixed times of the day and night. The supplication recited in prayer occurs in Surah 14, Ibrahim, ayaat 40-41.

(individuals and society). No one may be compelled to any religious observance.

Intolerance is at the heart of most conflicts and the effects are often severe on the victims. Racial intolerance, bigotry and prejudice are incompatible with Shari'ah. They often involve personal issues or a regional cultural phenomenon. Islam, on the other hand, advocates concern for the welfare of all, irrespective of gender, race, religion or social status. Injustice to others, regardless of its nature or instigating factors, is a serious misdeed, a sinful act which is subject to accountability. For every ill deed perpetrated against others, there is retribution to be paid during this life and/or on the Day of Reckoning, unless forgiven by God.[53] There is no escape. Therefore, it is the fairness of conduct and the purity of intentions that matter, for in the end, it is these that must pass the test of accountability.

The principles of tolerance are provided in the Qur'an and the practical examples are found in the Sunnah of Prophet Muhammad ﷺ. They are enforceable through the Shari'ah which establishes human dignity and honour and provides basic rights through justice (adl) and equality (qist). Without tolerance for differences in religious persuasion, race, language, culture, gender, etc., there cannot be justice or equality, nor can the rights of individuals and societies be upheld.

Islam is the complete submission to the Will of God. It is established as His final, all-encompassing message to all of mankind. Accordingly, there is no place for any other religious belief before God. Despite this, Islam accepts the freedom of all individuals to believe in any other religion or to not believe in any religion. A manifestation of this tolerance is the prohibition of forced or coerced conversion to Islam or injustice in any form. However, concern for the welfare of others necessitates that the message of Islam be conveyed to all. Whether the person receiving the Message of Islam accepts and follows it or rejects it, is a matter of the individual's choice.

---

[53] English Translation of Sahih Muslim. Darussalam, Riyadh, S Arabia, 2007. Volume 6, Hadith 6579, page 447. On the Day of Judgement, those who were wronged will be given from the accumulated good deeds of the perpetrator, until nothing remains with the latter, resulting in that person being cast into Hell.

Say, It is the truth is from your Lord. Then whosoever will, let him believe, and whosoever will, let him disbelieve.

(Surah 18, Al Kahf, ayat 29)

Chapter Nine

Women's Issues

Introduction

O mankind! Reverence your Guardian Lord Who created you from a single soul (nafsin wahida) and from it created its mate of like nature (minha) and from the two of them spread countless men and women ...

(Surah 4, An Nisa', ayat 1)

The mention of the word women in the context of Islam frequently brings up the stereotypical and distorted image cast by the prolific Western media, feminists and right's activists, who judge the world through their own, often misplaced "liberal" beliefs, as if others have no right to an existence of their choosing. Is this distorted image a reflection of their ignorance about other cultures, a reaction which betrays the conditions prevalent in these "liberated" societies or a manifestation of the neocolonial urge to impose the Western way of life upon others?

Historically, in Western society women were considered inferior to men, and to an extent, that viewpoint persists even today. Discrimination of women finds its beginnings in the scriptures with the creation of Eve.[1] She is said to have given the fruit from the forbidden tree to Adam. Accordingly, Adam blamed Eve (and also God

---

[1] Bible, King James Version. Genesis 2:22-23. *And the rib, which the Lord God had taken from man, made he a woman, and brought her unto the man. And Adam said, this is now bone of my bones, and flesh of my flesh: she shall be called Woman, because she was taken out of Man.*

indirectly) for his own action.[2] After giving birth to a child, women were considered unclean, requiring purification (twice as long after the birth of a girl) and atonement.[3]

It was not until the mid nineteenth century that women were permitted to make business transaction and own property independently and not until 1920 that they were allowed to vote in the United States of America.[4,5] By comparison, Islam truly liberated women from the very beginning (some fourteen hundred years ago), established their rights, provided respect and dignity, and elevated their status in society. Any attempted judgment of the treatment of women in Islam must consider the Islamic laws and the Islamic social order and exclude regional customs. This requires familiarization with Islamic laws and rules published by scholarly Muslim sources and not from the writings of Orientalists and self-styled "experts" on Islam.

Women's Rights in Islam

The Shari'ah applies equally to all Muslims, men and women. There are no restrictions on what a Muslim woman may choose to do as long as she remains within the limits prescribed by Shari'ah. Contrary to prevailing misconceptions and some regional cultural peculiarities, there are absolutely no restrictions on women's education or employment. Islam gives women the right, the freedom and the choice to own property, own and operate businesses, pursue a profession or career, hold public office, vote, etc.

---

[2] Bible, King James Version. Genesis 3:6, 3:12 and 3:16.
...she took of the fruit thereof, and did eat, and gave also unto her husband with her; and he did eat. And the man said, The woman whom thou gavest to be with me, she gave me of the tree, and I did eat. Unto the woman He said, I will greatly multiply thy sorrow and thy conception; in sorrow thou shalt bring forth children; and thy desire shall be to thy husband, and he shall rule over thee.

[3] Bible, King James Version. Leviticus, Chapter 12: 6-8 ...for a sin offering: and the priest shall make an atonement for her, and she shall be clean.

[4] Married Women's Property Act: 1848, New York State.

[5] Seneca Falls Declaration 1848: Woman's Rights Convention in Seneca Falls, New York that started the Woman Suffrage Movement. In 1971, a joint resolution of Congress designated August 26 as Women's Equality Day.

Spiritual

Both men and women were created equal and endowed with similar qualities. There is no distinction between the spiritual status of men and women. This is stated lucidly in the Qur'an:

O mankind! Reverence your Guardian Lord Who created you from a single
soul (nafsin wahida) and from it created its mate of like nature (minha)
and from the two of them spread countless men and women. Reverence
Allah in Whose name you demand your mutual rights, and reverence the
wombs (that bore you). For Allah ever watches over you.

(Surah 4, An Nisa', ayat 1)

In addition to stating the common origin of men and women *(nafsin wahida)*, this verse refers to *mutual rights* that are established through the Shari'ah and prescribes reverence for *the wombs that bore you*. The latter phrase and its use in this connection highlights the esteemed status of women, not only as mothers, but also their important role in preserving family relationships.

The concept of the *Original Sin,* with blame being placed on women, does not exist in Islam. Both Adam and Eve shared the responsibility for disobeying God. As a result, both were expelled from Paradise.[6] In contrast to the Biblical view, the guilt of disobedience is placed upon both Adam and Eve.[7] Both of them repented[8] and were forgiven.[9] Furthermore, for all generations (past, present and future), without exception, every person is responsible only for his or her own deeds. Assigning the blame to others for one's deeds or that *she* or *he made me do it* simply does not exist in Islam.

Every soul will be (held) in pledge for its own deeds.

(Surah 74, Al Muddathir, ayat 38)

And whoever does good deeds, whether male or female (and he or she is
a believer) they will enter paradise and not the least injustice will be done
to them.   (Surah 4, An Nisa', ayat 124)

---

[6] Surah 2, Al Baqarah, ayat 36; and Surah 7, Al A'raaf, ayat 24.
[7] Surah 20, Ta Ha, ayat 121: *...And Adam disobeyed his Lord, so went astray.*
[8] Surah 7, Al A'raaf, ayat 23. *They said: Our Lord! We have wronged ourselves.*
[9] Surah 2, Al Baqarah, ayat 37; Surah 20, Ta Ha, ayat 122.

... Never will I suffer to be lost the work of any of you, whether male or female. You proceed one from another [10] *...*

(Surah 3, 'Al Imraan, ayat 195)

Equal but not Identical

Men and women were created equal but they are not identical. There is equality with respect to rights, responsibilities and spiritual obligations. There are also undeniable physical, physiological and emotional differences. These differences have advantages in some ways as the Shari'ah rulings take them into account.

Exemption from the daily prayers is provided during the menstrual periods and immediately after childbirth for the duration of the postpartum bleeding. The menstrual periods are considered a hurt and an inconvenience and the missed prayers do not have to be made up. By contrast, prayers missed as a result of an illness must be made up by both women and men. While women are not required to go to the mosque for congregational prayers on Fridays, this is mandatory for men.

Menstruating women are exempted from the obligatory fasting during the month of Ramadan. They are also exempted from fasting during pregnancy, after childbirth and while nursing. However, the missed obligatory fasts must be made up at a later date, before commencement of the next Ramadan. Pregnancy is considered a struggle and a hardship and if a woman dies during pregnancy she is considered a martyr, a highly esteemed status, and is granted Paradise.

As Wife and Mother [11]

Marriage is viewed as a companionship based upon love, mutual respect, care and compassion. Kindness, obedience and respect for parents is next to the worship of God. Between the parents, there is particular reverence for the mother.

And of His Signs is this, that He created for you mates from among

---

[10] *You proceed one from another.* This expression reaffirms that both men and women are from the same source, *nafsin wahida* (created from one soul) and thus equals.

[11] The rights of the wife and mother are discussed in Chapter 7, Marriage and in Chapter 8, Family and Social Issues.

yourselves that you may dwell in tranquillity with them and He has put love and mercy between your (hearts); verily in that are signs for those who reflect. (Surah 30, Ar Rum, ayat 21)

And We have enjoined upon man concerning his parents: his mother bears him in weakness upon weakness, and his weaning is in two years. Give thanks to Me and to your parents. To Me is (your final) journey. (Surah 31, Luqman, ayat 14)

And We have enjoined on man kindness towards parents. In pain did his mother bear him and in pain did she give him birth... (Surah 46 Al Ahqaf, ayat 15)

Socioeconomic Issues

Education
It is only those among His servants who have knowledge that fear God ... (Surah 35, Al Fatir, ayat 28)

Islam has made it a duty for every Muslim, male and female, to seek knowledge. Educated women are a great and desirable asset to society. Emphasizing the importance of women's education, Prophet Muhammad ﷺ insisted that women be educated, especially about Islam.

As mothers, women are the first educators of children, leaving a lasting imprint on the developing minds. They are an important source for knowledge about Islam (faith and practice). However, only an informed mother can educate her children. For this very reason, women's education is not just desirable, but a necessity. Islam encourages women to seek education in any field of their choice. Denial of education to women, as practiced in some cultures, does not find its basis in the Shari'ah.

Dating back to the early years of Islam, women have been notable educators. The yearning for knowledge that was instilled by Islam produced numerous women scholars in diverse fields. Scholars of

Hadith and Fiqh (Jurisprudence) were the sources of guidance and education for latter generations. Many of them tutored male jurists who later achieved distinction. Notable Muslim women scholars include jurists, narrators of Hadith, mystics, writers, poets, etc. Below are a few names. A more detailed listing is beyond the scope of this text.

A'isha ﷺ

She was a wife of Prophet Muhammad ﷺ. A very gifted person with an extremely sharp memory and an equally keen mind, she was an educator with unmatched eloquence, a scholar of law, and a source of guidance [through transmission of Hadith and independent rulings (fatwas)].[12] She provided an important source of knowledge of the sunnah with respect to personal and family matters. She was also versed in traditional medicine, spiritual healing, poetry, history and mathematics. She died in Madinah in 58 AH.

Umm Salama ﷺ

She was also a wife of Prophet Muhammad ﷺ. She is a source of many Hadith and provided guidance to the Muslim community in matters of Fiqh. Several scholars learned Hadith from her. She died in Madinah in 63 AH, at the age of 84 years.

Sayyida Nafisa

She was the great granddaughter of Hasan ibn Ali, grandson of Prophet Muhammad ﷺ. She lived in Fustat, Egypt. She was known for piety and scholarship and taught a large number of pupils, including the Jurist Imam al-Shafi'.

Some of the other Muslim women intellectuals were: A'isha bint Sa'ad ibn Abi Waqqas, Umm Atiyyah of Basrah, and Rabi'ah Bint Mu'awwad of Madinah (notable Jurists and educators); Rabia al Adawiyya al Qadsiyya, also known as Rabia of Basrah (mystic), and Nana Asma'u Fodio of Sokoto, Nigeria [(1793-1864 CE), scholar, educator, public figure and social reformer].

---

[12] A'isha ﷺ is the source of over 2200 authentic Hadith.

Politics

The participation of women in public affairs had already started during the lifetime of Prophet Muhammad ﷺ. Muslim women entered into politics during the Caliphates of Damascus (Umayyads), Baghdad (Abbasids), and the Ottomans. Women played political leadership roles in Persia, India (eg., Empress Nur Jehan 1577-1645 CE, Queen Razia Sultana 1205-1240 CE), Egypt (Sultana Shajar ad-Durr, died 1259 CE), and have continued to do so in many other Muslim countries.[13] In more recent years, women served as prime ministers in Bangladesh and Pakistan, and as head of state in Indonesia.

Social Issues

Men and women have different but naturally complementary roles in society. Equality between men and women must incorporate fairness while keeping in perspective their respective roles in society. In Western societies, changes in these roles have been spurred by liberal ideologies, economic greed and rights movements. While many necessary changes were long overdue, there has been a pendulum swing to the opposite extreme.

The family is at the center of Islamic society and women are the center point of the family. While there is spiritual equality, Islam recognizes the different societal roles of men and women, and all rulings of Shari'ah are based upon fairness first but also upon equality within the societal framework. In many cases, women come out ahead because their interests are protected by Divine injunctions and the Sunnah of Prophet Muhammad ﷺ.

In an Islamic society, the most important role for a woman is that of wife and mother. Although her economic security is guaranteed, she may opt to work or pursue a career. However, a married woman must not neglect the responsibilities towards her family or subordinate them to a job or career.

Historically, Muslim women have been active participants in social affairs since the time of Prophet Muhammad ﷺ. Muslim women were involved in numerous private and state social and welfare activities,

---

[13] Shajar ad-Durr. Her troops defeated the army of the seventh Crusade and captured its leader, King Louis IX of France, at the Battle of Fariskur in April 1250 CE.

nursing of the sick and caring for those wounded in battle, long
before Florence Nightingale. They arranged rations and supplies for
soldiers and occasionally participated in actual combat. In so far, there
are no restrictions on women's activities, as long as these do not
violate the rules of Shari'ah.

Economic Issues

Western societies deprived women of their economic rights for
centuries. Before marriage, property rights often belonged to the
woman's father, and after marriage, they passed on to the husband.
Before the 1848 Married Women's Property Act, married women
were restricted from independently owning property or operating a
business enterprise.[14]

In the early seventh century CE, Islam removed the economic
restrictions and provided women freedom from financial worries. In an
Islamic society, there is provision for all of the needs of women and
their interests are protected from the cradle to the grave.
Responsibility for the financial and other needs of the family is
assigned to the male members. That includes the extended family, ie.,
uncles and nephews, if there are no close relatives such as father,
brother or an adult son. At the same time, the Shari'ah neither
restricts nor obliges women to work.

A father's responsibility of caring for daughters has no age limitation.
If the father has passed away, the brothers assume the responsibility
of caring for the unmarried or widowed sisters. If there is no male
sibling, uncles and nephews have that responsibility. If there are no
male relatives, this obligation falls upon the Muslim community. After
marriage, this responsibility passes on to the husband. At the time of
marriage, the husband is obliged to make a gift (mahr), in proportion
to his means.[15] The mahr remains the wife's personal property. If the
husband dies without fulfilling this obligation (ie., before he has paid
the mahr), it is considered a debt and must be paid out of his estate.
In addition, the wife is entitled to a share in the husband's estate in

---

[14] Married Women's Property Act, New York State, 1848.
Married Women's Property Act of 1882 (England).

[15] The terms and amount are by mutual consent and fixed prior to marriage. Also
see Chapter 7, Marriage.

accordance with the Islamic rules of inheritance. Islam considers debts a very serious matter, to the extent, that: *Every sin of a martyr is forgiven except his debt.*[16]

Any property or money that a woman acquires through her own efforts, such as through employment, business, inheritance, or as a gift, belongs solely to her. Her husband has no claim over it and she may do with it as she pleases. Household expenses are the husband's responsibility and a woman with an independent source of income is under no obligation to contribute towards those expenses.

Inheritance

To the men (of a family) belongs a share of that which parents and near kindred leave, and to the women a share of that which parents and near kindred (near relatives) leave, whether it be little or much, a legal share.

(Surah 4, An Nisa', ayat 7)

Laws of inheritance in previous Scriptures differ from those of Shari'ah. According to the Bible, daughters of the deceased are entitled to inheritance only if there is no male heir.[17] In contrast, the Shari'ah laws of inheritance take into account the needs of all heirs. In addition, if unrelated poor persons, distant relatives and orphans are present at the time of property distribution, it is encouraged that they also be given a share. In all cases, distribution is after payment of debts, legacies and funeral expenses. The basic rules are as follows:

From a married man's property
   • the wife inherits one eighth (if they have children)
   • each male child gets the equivalent of two females
   • if there is only one female child, she gets one half
   • if there are two or more daughters, they share two-thirds of the inheritance

---

[16] Until payment of the debt. Reported by Muslim. Muntakhab Ahadith, Kandhlavi MY, Annayyar, Karachi, Pakistan. Hadith 203, page 464.
  Also see Definition of a Martyr (*shaheed*) in Chapter 24, Suicide, Killing and War.
[17] Bible, New International Version. Numbers 27:1-11.

From the wife's property
  • the husband gets one-half, if there are no children
  • the husband gets one fourth if they have children

At first glance, these laws may seem inequitable, providing the male more than the female heir. In order to understand the rationale, one must study and also understand the Islamic social system. Only a third of the property may be bequeathed through a Will, to any person and/or for any other legitimate purpose.[18] Two thirds of the property remains subject to the mandatory Shari'ah laws. Favoring one child over another or the exclusion of an eligible person from his/her share of the inheritance are prohibited.

The distribution takes into account that female heirs are under no obligation to earn a living. The responsibility for their needs lies with the father or with other male members of the family, if the father is deceased and they are unmarried. After marriage, women are recipients of the mahr (marriage gift). The amount and composition are negotiable. Additionally, their husbands are responsible for all of their needs. Conversely, the male must care for the family after the father's death, including his mother, sisters and other siblings who are unable to provide for themselves. The male is also responsible for his own family (wife and children).[19] Taking all of these into consideration, the female child is financially better off than her male sibling.

... Who is better than Allah for judgment for a people who have certainty in their Faith ?   (Surah 5, Al Ma'idah, ayat 50)

Equitable or Unfair ?
These rules are structured for a society that complies with the Islamic Shari'ah. In order to understand the wisdom and appreciate the fairness of the Islamic rules of inheritance, one has to look beyond the numbers. While it may appear that males are favored in some cases, their financial responsibilities are far greater. On the other hand, there is provision for all the financial needs of women. They are under

---

[18] Any purpose that is permissible under the Shari'ah.
[19] If both parents of the husband are alive and old or sick, the responsibility for their care (physical and financial) also falls upon his shoulders.

no obligation to work for the purposes of earning a living or to cover domestic expenses. Divorce does not absolve the husband of his financial responsibilities. Thus, in the final analysis, women are assured greater financially security.

Testimony

The meanings of the Arabic word *shahida* include: *to witness (with one's eyes)*, and *personally experience*, and *shahada* means: *to bear witness, to testify/give testimony, to sign as a witness*. The meanings of the English term *testimony* include: *attestation, statement under oath by a witness, proof, evidence, etc.* In the context of this discussion, *testimony* will be used as meaning both *to witness* and *give evidence*.

Testimony is an issue where unfamiliarity with the rationale breeds the impression of discrimination against women. Those making such allegations quote ayat 282 of Surah 2, Al Baqarah which states:

> ... *And call to witness from among your own men, two witnesses. And if two men are not at hand, then a man and two women, of such as you approve as witnesses, so that if one of them errs (through forgetfulness) the other will remember. And the witnesses must not refuse when summoned.*

The meaning of this verse has been subjected to misinterpretations and/or misinformed representations. This verse addresses specifically the witnessing of business debt/obligation transactions and may not be used to generalize that the testimony of two female witnesses is equivalent to that of one male or that the testimony of a male is superior to that of a female.[20]

In situations that necessitate testimony, the objectives of Islamic law are to ascertain the truth and impart justice in the fairest manner. The Shari'ah mandates fairness and justice in every case. Therefore, Islamic law is very particular about testimony, to the extent, that a Muslim is required tell the truth even if goes against his/her own interests: *Stand firmly for justice, as witnesses to Allah, even though it be against yourselves, or your parents, or your kindred, and whether it be against rich or poor, ...* (Surah 4, An Nisa', ayat 135).

---

[20] Surah 2, Al Baqarah, ayat 282: *...a debt for a fixed term or transaction involving future obligations....*

As a general rule, to safeguard the interests of all involved parties, Islamic law requires that all agreements and transactions be written down and witnessed. In most instances in the Qur'an, the reference to witnesses does not specify gender. The general rule is to have a minimum of two witnesses. Some situations require four witnesses. While no verse in the Qur'an assigns more weight to the testimony of a man over that of a woman, one verse clearly assigns equal or greater weight to the testimony of women in certain matters.[21]

Why are two women required in lieu of one man as witness in ayat 282, Surah 2, Al Baqarah?

The ultimate knowledge is with God alone. However, He has also provided a reason for this requirement in the same verse: ...*so that if the one errs (through forgetfulness, tadil-la ihda' huma) the other can remind her.*[22] That is, providing assistance in remembering the facts in order to prevent unintended errors in the understanding of the terms of the agreement. That is the only reason given and there is no reference to gender superiority.

Why is only the woman in need of assistance in remembering?

Islam purposefully balances everything, and in order to understand that purpose, each Divine injunction or Shari'ah ruling must be viewed in the overall context. While these rulings may date as far back as the seventh century CE, the Shari'ah is a living law which cannot be confined by time or geography. It is endowed with the ability to effortlessly adapt to changing times without ever compromising its core values. In the early Islamic society, the roles assigned to women provided little experience or exposure to the intricacies of complex business financial transactions. The requirement for two female witnesses relates to a specific matter, ie., the witnessing of financial agreements, namely loans, debts and promissory commitments for repayment of those debts. It relates to issues which can be very

---

[21] Surah 24, An Nur, ayaat 6-9. If a man accuses his wife of adultery and cannot produce witnesses, he is required to solemnly affirm five times that what he says is true, ie., that his wife committed adultery. If the wife denies it and solemnly affirms five times that what she is accused of is untrue, her oath carries more weight and she is exonerated.

[22] *tadil-la* means to err through forgetfulness, be confused or lose the way.

involved and contentious, and inaccuracies could incur significant financial hardship, injustices and discord, or even enmity between the parties. Thus, as the verse indicates, there is the requirement for two female witnesses so that if one of them errs (forgets, becomes confused) the other can remind her, meaning that even though the recollection of one of them was lacking, together they could provide testimony which would be both accurate and admissible.

This is the only verse specifying such a witness composition and does not constitute a general rule that all cases require two women in lieu of one male witness. Today, women are increasingly involved in financial matters and also possess the qualifications and expertise for overseeing complex business and financial transactions. Therefore, utilizing the ability of the Shari'ah to adapt to changing times, Islamic scholars have concluded that the testimony of one woman with the appropriate business experience is to be considered equivalent to that of one man.

In all such matters of witnessing and providing testimony, the core issue is justice for the involved (contractual) parties, for which accuracy is imperative. Commentators may provide explanations such as women's perceived propensity to forget, lack of business experience, inundation with responsibilities, familial or emotional issues, etc. However, the reason for this Divine injunction is stated in the same verse (Surah 2, Al Baqarah, ayat 282), and in essence, this provision has a positive implication rather than the apparent negative connotation assigned to it after cursory interpretation. In the end, this injunction serves women's interest insofar, that the joint testimony of the two women stands even though one of them may have forgotten or misunderstood and needed to be reminded by the other, while an error on the part of a male witness results in the disqualification or invalidation of his testimony. Any other interpretation of this requirement, such as reflection of the worth of women's testimony, is incorrect.

Simply stated, had Islam ever considered the worth or the credibility of a woman's testimony to be inferior to that of a man, women would have neither been allowed judgeships or independent rulings (fatwas), nor would the Hadith transmitted by them be accepted. In addition, they would not have been allowed as educators. Clearly, this has never been the case.

Hijab

And tell the believing women to lower their gaze and be modest, and to display of their adornment only that which is apparent,[23] and to draw their veils over their bosoms.[24] And not to reveal their adornments save to their own husbands or fathers ... or small children who know naught of women's nakedness.[25]   (Surah 24, An Nur, ayat 31)

Hijab refers to modest dressing. It is commonly identified with the head cover or the scarf used by Muslim women to cover the head and neck. Until the mid-twentieth century, the head scarf was commonly used in European society. Even to this day, it is used in many regions of Europe, Africa and Asia and is accepted by the West as a cultural phenomenon or an expression of religious persuasion in many cases, eg., catholic nuns.

The literal meaning of *hijab* is a cover, curtain, screen, or veil.[26] While the head cover or scarf is part of hijab, by itself, this may not fulfill the requirements. Various cultures have adopted different dress forms such as the *burqa* in South Asia and the *niqab* (face veil) in some Asian and Arab countries. The latter have no basis in the Shari'ah. Thus, when discussing the *hijab* as required by Shari'ah, all regional, cultural and national practices of dressing/clothing must be separated out.

The rules for hijab are strict for women of marriageable and childbearing age. They are less stringent for older women, ie., who are

---

[23] Adornments or *zeenat* only applies to those parts of the body that are visible even when a person is clothed. It does not mean nudity.

[24] In addition to bosom or chest, the meaning of the Arabic word *juyub* includes the upper body.

[25] *nakedness* here means being *without outer attire that covers the body contours.* It does not mean *nudity.*

[26] The word *hijab* is derived from *hajaba* which means to obscure, hide from sight or conceal. The Hans Wehr Dictionary of Modern Written Arabic. Spoken Language Services, Ithaca, NY. 4 th Edition, 1994. Page 184.
In the Qur'an, the term *hijab* is also used for a visual and/or auditory barrier, ie., one that separates the Divine from the world of mankind.

past the childbearing age and no longer have the desire for marriage. Nakedness, such as being scantily clad, and nudity in public, which is accepted in many Western societies and exists in some primitive tribal societies, is strictly prohibited.[27] Nudity in private is also discouraged.[28]

Injunctions for Hijab

O Prophet! Tell your wives and your daughters and the women of the believers to draw over themselves some of their outer garments (when they go out). That will be better, so that they may be recognized and not annoyed (or molested). (Surah 33, Al Ahzaab, ayat 59)

And it is not becoming for a believing man or a believing woman, when Allah and His messenger have decided a matter for them that they should (after that) claim any say in their decision. And whoever disobeys Allah and His Messenger, goes astray in a manifest error. (Surah 33, Al Ahzaab, ayat 36)

Implications of Hijab

In the context of religious practice, the actual implications of *hijab* extend beyond the modest attire to include the individual's behavior and mannerism in public. The dress is only one aspect. Required modest behavior includes not staring at others: ...*Tell the believing men to lower their gaze and be modest....; And tell the believing women to lower their gaze and be modest...*[29] The Arabic term *ya-ghuddu* means to reduce the intensity of gaze, ie., looking to see only and not stare lustfully or to observe details of another persons body. It may also require looking away. In this context, it should be noted that staring at another person's body with lust is considered adultery of the

---

[27] The Arabic term for nakedness is *awraat* (from *awraah*), which means naked and unprotected and something when exposed would be embarrassing. *Awraah* refers to those parts of the body that may be exposed only to one's spouse.

[28] Sunan Abu Dawud. English Translation with Explanatory Notes. A Hasan. Kitab Bhavan, New Delhi, 1997. Volume 3, Hadith 4006, pages 1123-1124.

[29] Surah 24, An Nur, ayaat 30 and 31. *ya-ghuddu* (from *ghadd, ghadada*) means to cast down, lower eyes or glance out of modesty, to lower or lessen something in intensity. The Hans Wehr Dictionary of Modern Written Arabic. Spoken Language Services, Ithaca, NY. 4 th Edition, 1994, page 791.

eyes.[30] *Hijab* is an expression of modesty (*haya*), it displays an Islamic identity and preserves privacy.[31,32]

Islamic Dress Requirements

These dress requirements apply when men or/and women are in the presence of other adult individuals who are non-mahram or when going out of the home.

For Women

... When a girl reaches the age of menstruation, it does not suit her that she displays her body parts except this and this, and he (Prophet Muhammad ﷺ) pointed to the face and hands.[33]

The modest attire as understood by *hijab* covers that which the modest person wants to obscure from the sight of others. No particular form of dress is specified in the Shari'ah, other than it should cover those areas of the body that could attract lustful attention. It should be loose and opaque clothing which covers the entire body, eg., a large shawl or some outer garment. It is not necessary to cover the face, hands and feet. A loose cloak or similar outer garment may be worn over other clothing. However, if the clothing is loose and opaque, an outer garment is not necessary.

For Men

Prohibited are tight fitting or attention attracting clothing. Men are also prohibited from wearing silk (except for medical reasons) and

---

[30] The Translation and Meanings of Sahih Al-Bukhari. MM Khan, Kazi Publications, Lahore, Pakistan, 1979. Volume VIII, Hadith 260, page 171.

[31] Prophet Muhammad ﷺ said: *Faith (Belief) consists of more than sixty branches (parts) and haya is a part of faith.* The Translation and Meanings of Sahih Al-Bukhari. MM Khan, Kazi Publications, Lahore, Pakistan, 1979. Volume I, Hadith 8, page 18.

[32] Here *haya* is translated as *modesty*. However, the term *haya* has a broad meaning. It covers a large number of concepts which are to be taken together. These include: self respect, modesty, bashfulness and scruple, etc. In addition, a person with *haya* will be ashamed to do something that was forbidden by God or to not do something that was ordered to be done by God.
The Translation and Meanings of Sahih Al-Bukhari. MM Khan, Kazi Publications, Lahore, Pakistan, 1979. Volume I, Glossary, page ixx.

[33] Sunan Abu Dawud. English Translation with Explanatory Notes. A Hasan. Kitab Bhavan, New Delhi, 1997. Volume 3, Hadith 4092, pages 1144-1145.

gold in any form. As a minimum, the clothing must cover the areas between the navel and the knees.

The Veil

A veil that covers the face partially or completely is a purely social or cultural phenomenon and has no basis in the Shari'ah. The latter requires that the face and hands remain uncovered. Certainly, gloves and a scarf to cover the face, may be used for other reasons, eg., in cold climates.

Is Hijab Oppression or Liberation?

Hijab is worn in voluntary obedience to God.[34] There is no element of compulsion or oppression. It is an individual's expression of modesty (*haya*), inspiring self-confidence and providing distance from frivolous social practices. For some women it is empowerment. *Hijab* does not hinder work or other activities, including sports, and in the true meaning of the word, the Muslim woman in *hijab* may be more liberated than her Western counterpart.

Female Circumcision

Circumcision of males is a sunnah which is practiced in Muslim societies all over the world. It was prescribed for the followers of Prophet Abraham ﷺ, and as such, it was endorsed by Prophet Muhammad ﷺ.[35] Circumcision of females is a cultural practice in a few parts of the world, particularly in northeast Africa. Its goal was to lessen women's sexual desire in order to ensure chastity. It was also practiced in some Arab societies before Islam.[36] Hadith that have been attributed to the Prophet ﷺ as having recommended or condoned female circumcision are considered weak or inauthentic because the sources and/or chain of transmission are either unreliable or not

---

[34] Surah 24, An Nur, ayat 31.

[35] Prophet Muhammad ﷺ said: *Ibrahim was circumcised at the age of eighty years...* Al Adab al Mufrad, Imam Bukhari's Book of Muslim Morals and Manners. Translation by YT DeLorenzo. Al Saadawi Publications, Alexandria, VA. 1997. Hadith 1249, page 535.

[36] This practice was known to exist since the times of the Pharaohs.

known.[37]

In the male, circumcision involves surgical removal of the prepuce (foreskin). Male circumcision has proven benefits. Amongst others, it reduces the incidence of sexually transmitted diseases and there is reduced incidence of cervical cancer in spouses of circumcised males.

Anatomically, women also have a prepuce. Some forms of female "circumcision" reportedly involve the removal of more than just the prepuce. The latter forms have been termed *female genital mutilation*. Under Islamic Law, any practice that harms the person is not permissible. The Shari'ah aims to preserve life and well-being (mind and body) of the person, and therefore, anything that is harmful is unlawful. Consequently, the Shari'ah neither permits nor condones *female genital mutilation*.

Concluding Summary

Fictitious inequalities

Shari'ah Laws are of Divine inception, and indisputably, there is no injustice in Divine rulings. On many occasions, the human mind is unable to understand the reasons for a certain injunction which may then appear as being discriminatory against one or the other. This is the case when a ruling is given only a cursory reading or it is taken out of the overall context without attempting to understand the purpose and/or the Islamic social structure.

Piety and virtuous conduct, irrespective of gender, race or social standing, constitute the only basis for superiority of one individual over another:

O mankind! We created you from a single (pair) of a male and a female and made you into nations and tribes that you may know one another. Verily, the noblest of you in the sight of God is (one who is) the best in conduct. And God has full knowledge and is well acquainted (with all things).   (Surah 49, Al Hujuraat, ayat 13)

In an Islamic society, the roles of men and women are different but

---

[37] Sunan Abu Dawud. English Translation with Explanatory Notes. A Hasan. Kitab Bhavan, New Delhi, 1997. Volume 3, Hadith 5251, page 1451.

complementary. There is equality where it is essential (spiritual, human rights, ownership rights, etc) and there are differences where other contributing factors come into play (eg., inheritance). There cannot be a one-to-one parity in every respect, simply because men and women are different and also have different societal roles. However, given their individual needs and considering their differences, Islam balances their rights and duties in the most perfect way possible.

In many Muslim societies, women remain subordinated because of a pre-Islamic patriarchal societal structure has either persisted or was reintroduced. This practice finds its roots in the regional cultures that predated Islam. The Shari'ah aims to eliminate practices which induce inequality, abuse and exploitation of women.

Chapter Ten

Business Ethics
and Financial Dealings

Introduction

Both lawful and unlawful things are clear, and between them are doubtful matters. So whoever rejects those doubtful things lest he commit a sin, will definitely avoid what is clearly unlawful: and whoever indulges in these doubtful things is likely to commit what is clearly unlawful. Sins are Allah's hima[1] and whoever pastures near it, is likely to get in it at any moment.[2]

Islam seeks to establish fairness and justice in society and Muslims are obliged to high ethical standards in all activities. Since economic issues can be quite contentious, disrupting relationships at all levels of society, Islam established rules for fairness in trade and commerce. As in all other cases, the primary sources of guidance are the Qur'an and Sunnah.

Prophet Muhammad ﷺ was an ideal human being in every respect, the best source of inspiration and the best example to follow. He was also a very successful businessman who started his career long before he received the first Divine Revelation which marked the beginning of

---

[1] *Hima*: private pasture or a prohibited area. Something that is out of bounds. Paraphrased, it means that the transition from the doubtful to the forbidden may not be obvious and one can easily and unknowingly slip into doing something forbidden. Therefore, doubtful things should be avoided.

[2] The Translation of the Meanings of Sahih Al-Bukhari. MM Khan, Kazi Publications, Lahore, Pakistan, 1979. Volume III, Hadith 267, pages 151-152.

prophethood.[3] He entered into business activity during his youth and established himself by virtue of his honesty and highly successful business skills.[4] His conduct provides the best example for all Muslims:

> ﷺ In the messenger of Allah you have a good example for him who looks towards Allah and the Last Day and remembers Allah much.
>
> (Surah 33, Al Ahzab, ayat 21)

General Rules Governing Business Transactions

All business transactions must distinguish between *halal* and *haram.*[5] Islamic rules of ethics for business and commerce are strict and take into account multiple factors, including the rights of others and those of society at large. They require honesty and fairness, full disclosure, and the fulfillment of commitments and obligations.

Prohibited are all unfair and usurious practices. This includes any form of cheating, fraud, deceit, bribery (giving and receiving), false testimony, betrayal of trust, usurping or encroaching upon another's rights by any means (including litigation), and profiteering at the expense of people's needs or hardships, hoarding, exploitation, undermining of the competition, price fixing, and price gouging. Usury (*riba*) in any form is prohibited.

Both the requirements and prohibitions apply to all dealings, irrespective of religious persuasion, ethnic origin, etc., of the other party. All earnings and profits must be through honest means and from *halal* sources. In addition, leniency and kindness are strongly encouraged. Leniency towards the debtor includes facilitation of debt rescheduling and easing of the terms of debt repayment. Prophet Muhammad ﷺ said: *Whoever is deprived of kindness is deprived of all good.*[6] He also said: *May God's mercy be on him who is lenient in his*

---

[3] He received the first Divine Revelation at the age of 40 years.

[4] Impeccable honesty and integrity earned him the title of *as sadiq al amin,* the truthful and the trustworthy.

[5] *Halal* means lawful or permissible under the Shari'ah. *Haram* is that which is unlawful and not permissible.

[6] Reported by Muslim. Muntakhab Ahadith, Kandhlavi MY, Annayyar, Karachi, Pakistan. Hadith 77, page 421.

buying, selling, and in demanding back his money.[7]

Lawful (*halal*) Income

In Islam, worship and duty to God are central. The goal of every believing Muslim is to gain God's acceptance of his/her worship and deeds. Since, Islam has linked the purity of the sources of earnings to acceptability of worship, no matter how "pious" a person may appear, if the sources of income are not lawful (*halal*) as defined by Shari'ah, his/her worship may not be accepted by God. Therefore, all earnings must be through honest and legitimate means, regardless of whether it is an investment, physical labour, management, or business.

Investment income is permitted from sources where the principal is subject to both profit and loss. Income from the following sources is prohibited (*haram*): interest and usury, betting and gambling, bribes and kickbacks, embezzlement, theft, dishonest transactions, and dealing in forbidden items such as alcohol, recreational drugs, pornographic materials and items that may harm others, including weapons that cause massive loss of life and destruction of property and environment.

Honesty and Fairness

... Give just measure and weight, nor withhold from the people the things that are their due. And do not commit evil in the earth, causing corruption.   (Surah 11, Hud, ayat 85)

Honesty, fairness and reliability are expected in all dealings, business and also otherwise. Today's business world has witnessed an erosion of many such values, something that Prophet Muhammad ﷺ had predicted when he said: *A time will come when one will not care how one gains one's money, lawfully or unlawfully.*[8]

Forbidden are unfair marketing practices, concealing of defects in items being sold or traded, use of inaccurate weights and measures, or delivering goods inferior in quality to what was shown as sample. A

---

[7] *demanding back his money* from the debtor. The Translation of the Meanings of Sahih Al-Bukhari. MM Khan, Kazi Publications, Lahore, Pakistan, 1979. Volume III, Hadith 290, page 164.

[8] The Translation of the Meanings of Sahih Al-Bukhari. MM Khan, Kazi Publications, Lahore, Pakistan, 1979. Volume III, Hadith 275, pages 156-157.

Hadith states:[9] *He who deceives people does not belong to us,* meaning that individual is not following Islam.

Also prohibited is the use of coercion and/or intimidation by any method (including litigation) as a tool of business. While these may achieve the intended material goals, the adverse consequences are far reaching and dwarf the perceived benefits. A Hadith states:

> *... maybe someone amongst you can present his case more eloquently than the other, whereby I may consider him true and give a verdict in his favour. So if I give the right of a Muslim to another by mistake, then it is really a portion of Hellfire. He has the option to take it or give it up.*[10]

> *O believers ! Do not devour one another's property by unlawful (unfair) means; instead do business by mutual consent. And do not kill yourselves.*[11] *Surely, God is Most Merciful to you.*
>
> (Surah 4, An Nisa', ayat 29)

As the Hadith and verse indicate, the consequences of knowingly pursuing the rights of others by any means, including a judge or jury decision, can be severe. Furthermore, it is a serious offense for a judge to pronounce a ruling in favour of a particular individual, group or entity, knowing that the ruling was not impartial. This is similar to being an accomplice in usurping some other person's rights. This topic is discussed further in the section Rights of Others.

> *O you who believe! Stand firmly for justice, as witnesses to God, even though it be against yourselves, or your parents, or your kindred, and whether it be against rich or poor, for God is nearer to you both. So do not follow your own desire lest you deviate from doing justice. If you*

---

[9] Reported by Muslim. Muntakhab Ahadith, Kandhlavi MY, Annayyar, Karachi, Pakistan. Hadith 300, p 497.

[10] The Translation of the Meanings of Sahih Al-Bukhari. MM Khan, Kazi Publications, Lahore, Pakistan, 1979. Volume III, Hadith 638, page 381.

[11] *and do not kill yourselves (each other):* This has a broad meaning. In the context of this discussion, it means: *the one who unlawfully takes the property of others, leads him- or herself to self-destruction by being disobedient to God (by violating the sanctity of what God has made unlawful) and will suffer the consequences in the Hereafter.*
Tafsir ibn Kathir. Al-Firdous Ltd, London. 2000. Part 5, pages 37-40.
Maududi SAA. The Meaning of the Qur'an, Volume II. Islamic Publications Ltd., Lahore, Pakistan, 1976. Pages 108-119.

distort your evidence or refrain from the truth, know it well that God is
fully aware of what you do.   (Surah 4, An Nisa', ayat 135)

Fulfillment of Oaths, Commitments and Trusts

And those who keep their pledges and their covenants. And those who
stand by their testimony. And those who are guard their prayers. These
will dwell in the Gardens (of Paradise), honoured.
(Surah 70, Al Ma'arij, ayaat 32-35)

God commands you to restore deposits to their owners[12] and if you judge
between people that you judge with justice.
(Surah 4, An Nisa', ayat 58)

Islam requires fulfillment of all contractual obligations, honouring of
pledges and the payment of debts. Considerable importance is
attached to debts as these also involve the rights of others. A debt or
loan is a contractual obligation, even if it was a verbal agreement. It is
considered a greater sin if a person should die without making
arrangements for the repayment of his/her debt.[13] Prophet Muhammad
☆ said:[14] *A believer's soul is attached to his debt till it is paid*, meaning that
the unpaid debt prevents the believer's entry into Paradise.

Payment for services provided is due upon completion of the job.[15]
This contrasts sharply with aspects of the current system in some
societies where payment may be delayed for weeks or even months.[16]
In cases where there is disagreement in business matters, arbitration
and not litigation, is the solution.

---

[12] to give back to the owners that with which one was entrusted (*amanaat*) for
safekeeping.

[13] Reported by Abu Dawud. Muntakhab Ahadith. Kandhlavi MY, Annayyar, Karachi,
Pakistan. Hadith 200, pages 463-264.

[14] Reported by Tirmidhi. Muntakhab Ahadith. Kandhlavi MY, Annayyar, Karachi,
Pakistan. Hadith 201, page 464.

[15] The Prophet ☆ said: *Pay the labourer his wages before his sweat dries.* Reported by Ibn
Majah. Muntakhab Ahadith, Kandhlavi MY, Annayyar, Karachi, Pakistan. Hadith 252,
page 479.

[16] For example, it is not unusual for health care insurance companies in North
America to take several weeks, and often months, to "process" claims before
making payments for services rendered.

Rights of Others

If anyone acquired what rightly belongs to another Muslim by a false oath, then God has made Hell obligatory for him and prohibited his admission to Paradise.[17]

Respecting the rights of others is a part of Islamic ethics. Personal or corporate interest may not be placed above the rights of others, ie., those of other individuals, society, environment, etc. Usurping the property or rights of others by any means, including force, defrauding, litigation, eminent domain, compulsory acquisition, etc., is forbidden. False testimony has been made equivalent to *shirk* (ascribing partners to God), which is a major sin.[18]

Parties entering into a contract must be provided all information and given the right and the freedom to make choices in the spirit of a true mutual agreement. Under the Shari'ah, a contract does not resort to the use of "fine print" as there is requirement for full and unambiguous disclosure. Bribes and kickbacks (a form of bribery) also infringe upon the rights of others in a free market. Both the giving and receiving of bribes is prohibited.[19]

For all conduct there is accountability. The present day social and geopolitical setup may allow a person, an organization, corporation or governmental body to illicitly acquire something that belongs to others or a nation may occupy and plunder the wealth and resources of another without being held accountable because of military, financial or political weight. However, each person, irrespective of worldly status, is accountable for all of his/her actions and stands all alone in the ultimate court of justice to answer to the ultimate Judge. It may be interesting to know that God, whose attributes include *The Most Merciful* and *The Most Forgiving,* indeed forgives the supplicant for violations and infringements upon His (God's) rights but He does not forgive the violation against the rights of His creatures. The transgressions against the rights of others must be settled here, before

---

[17] This includes things/matters that may appear trivial. Reported by Muslim. Muntakhab Ahadith. Kandhlavi MY, Annayyar, Karachi, Pakistan. Hadith 345, pages 509-510.

[18] Sunan Abu Dawud. English Translation with Explanatory Notes. A Hasan. Kitab Bhavan, New Delhi, 1997. Volume 3, Hadith 3592, page 1022.

[19] Sunan Abu Dawud. English translation with Explanatory Notes. A Hasan. Kitab Bhavan, New Delhi, 1997. Volume 3, Hadith 3573, page 1015.

the Day of Accountability. (Also see the hadith in the section that follows)

Bankruptcy

Bankruptcy as a result of financial insolvency is the inability of an individual or business to pay the creditors. Consequently, legal proceedings are initiated to obtain "relief" from the debt(s). Bankruptcy may involve liquidation (Chapter 7, US Bankruptcy Code) or permit continued operation after financial restructuring and scheduled debt repayment (Chapters 11 and 13). With the former, the debtor's property not exempted under state or federal law is liquidated and the proceeds distributed among the creditors. In return, certain debts are *erased*, namely, credit card debts, medical bills, and unsecured loans. Chapter 11 allows businesses (and individuals with substantial debts and assets) to reorganize. Chapter 13 is available to individuals with a regular income. A portion of that income is used to repay some or all of the debt over a three to five year period while retaining ownership and possession of the assets/property. Thereafter, the debt is formally discharged.

Islamic Perspective on Bankruptcy

Islam recognizes two forms of bankruptcy, moral and financial. Both are interrelated in many ways. Financial bankruptcy is a consequence of being in insurmountable debt. In order to make debt payments or in an attempt to delay or avoid making payments, the debtor may occasionally resort to illicit practices such as lying, misappropriation, defrauding, etc. Such behavior reflects moral bankruptcy and is prohibited by Shari'ah.[20] Moral bankruptcy and its consequences are explained in a Hadith:

> The one who is bankrupt among my Ummah is the one who would come on the Day of Resurrection with prayer, fasting, and charity (ie., with abundant good deeds); but would have exhausted his fund of virtues because he will come having insulted others, slandered others, unlawfully

---

[20] The Prophet ﷺ said: *If a person is in debt, he tells lies when he speaks, and breaks his promises when he promises.* The Translation of the Meanings of Sahih Al-Bukhari. MM Khan, Kazi Publications, Lahore, Pakistan, 1979. Volume III, Hadith 582, page 342.

consumed the wealth of others, shed the blood of others, and beat others.
They will each be given from his good deeds, and if his good deeds run
out before the scores have been settled, some of their bad deeds will be
taken and cast upon him, then he will be thrown into the Fire.[21]

The Islamic Shari'ah recognizes that unanticipated events may bring
about changes which adversely affect the financial well-being of
individuals and businesses. Therefore, it provides remedies to protect
the debtor and also satisfy the interests of the creditor. It is worthy of
note, that these rules were promulgated over fourteen hundred years
ago. The essentials of these Shari'ah laws find themselves incorporated
into the current bankruptcy laws of several Western countries.

As a principle, the Shari'ah requires that all debts be paid in
accordance with the agreement(s) between debtor and creditor.[22] It
also encourages the creditor to be lenient and considerate of the
debtor's circumstances, and when necessary, facilitate adjustments or
renegotiation of the terms of repayment.

If the debtor is in a difficulty, grant him time till it is easy for him to
repay. But if you remit it by way of charity, that is best for you if you only
knew.[23]   (Surah 2, Al Baqarah, ayat 280)

In the case of a genuine inability to repay debts from assets and
income, the Shari'ah allows erasure of debts after distribution of the
debtor's assets between the creditors, to satisfy the debt in
proportion to the amounts owed. This is also what some of the
present day bankruptcy proceedings aim to accomplish. However,
seeking bankruptcy "protection" for the purpose of avoiding
repayment of personal or other nonbusiness debts/loans is forbidden
by Shari'ah. Even though a court may provide "protection" and "relief"

---

[21] English Translation of Sahih Muslim, Darussalam, Riyadh, S Arabia 2007. Volume 6,
Hadith 2581, page 447.

[22] *O you who believe! Fulfill your obligations....* Surah 5, Al Ma'idah, ayat 1.
Also see under Fulfillment of Oaths, Commitments and Trusts; Rights of Others.

[23] *This verse empowers an Islamic court of law to compel the creditors to give more time to*
the debtors for the payment of debts, if they are in straightened circumstances that they
cannot pay back their debts. Under certain circumstances the court is entitled to write off
the debt altogether or a part of it. Maududi SAA, The meaning of the Qur'an. Islamic
Publications Ltd., Lahore, Pakistan, 1978. Volume 1, pages 203-207.

in the form of a settlement with partial payments, etc., the Shari'ah requires that these debts be paid in full, unless there is a genuine inability to pay. A Hadith of Prophet Muhammad ﷺ states: *Whoever takes the money of the people with the intention of repaying it, Allah will enable him to pay it back, and whoever takes it in order to spoil it, then Allah will spoil him.*[24]

Hoarding, Price-fixing, Market-manipulation and Monopoly

Withholding essential commodities such as foods and other basic necessities from the market to drive up prices and increase profits or attempting to control certain aspects of the market to alter the nature of a free market economy, are considered sinful and are prohibited.[25] Similarly, price-fixing (with exception of rare crisis situations where the price is fixed to protect the consumer), monopoly, and destruction of crops (or other forms of wasting) to stabilize market prices are prohibited by Islam.

Interest and Ambiguous Transactions

... God has permitted trade and forbidden usury. ...
But those who return to usury, such are the rightful owners of the Fire. They will abide therein for ever. God will deprive usury of all blessings but will give increase for deeds of charity ...
(Surah 2, Al Baqarah, ayaat 275-276)

O you who believe! Do not devour usury, doubled and multiplied; But fear God that you may prosper.
(Surah 3, 'Al Imraan, ayat 130)

[24] The Translation of the Meanings of Sahih Al-Bukhari. MM Khan, Kazi Publications, Lahore, Pakistan, 1979. Volume III, Hadith 572, page 336.
[25] Musnad Ahmad, Majma uz-Zawaid. Muntakhab Ahadith, Kandhlavi MY. Annayyar, Karachi, Pakistan. Hadith 294, page 495.

Usury (*riba*) and interest based financial dealings are prohibited.[26] This prohibition includes most of the dealings of non-Islamic financial institutions, namely those profiting from interest based lending. Under the Islamic system, lending is permitted where the borrower pays back what he/she had borrowed. The prohibition of interest is out of concern for social injustice as the interest accumulating lendings (usury) enrich the lender and impose hardship upon the borrower.

Another type of prohibited transaction is that of uncertainty or ambiguity. One may not buy or set a price for something that is undefined. For example, trading in futures and options, buying fish that has not yet been caught or fruit that has not ripened, ie., ready for harvesting and consumption.[27] Such transactions are called: *ghabn* and *al gharar - something that is not present*. Also along these lines, resale of foodstuff is not permitted until the buyer has received it, ie., taken possession of it.[28]

Islamic Banking, Loans and Financing

The Islamic socioeconomic order is an ethically and socially responsible form of capitalism. It permits accumulation of legitimately acquired wealth, prohibits the ills of Western capitalism and corporatism by forbidding economic inequities and other prohibited activities (those that are unfair, unjust, morally or socially harmful), and it promotes social justice and equitable wealth distribution.

True Islamic banking is one step in that direction. It is a system that conforms to the principles of Shari'ah and incorporates social justice by eliminating usury and introducing a system of profit-and-loss sharing. Usury not only overburdens the debtor and unfairly enriches the lender but also empowers the latter over the socio-financial well-

---

[26] This prohibition also includes the writing and/or witnessing of usurious transactions.

[27] Fruit that has not ripened could be damaged or destroyed by disease, weather, etc. The seller and not the buyer should bear the loss. The Translation of the Meanings of Sahih Al-Bukhari. MM Khan, Kazi Publications, Lahore, Pakistan, 1979. Volume III, Hadith 400, page 221.

[28] The Translation of the Meanings of Sahih Al-Bukhari. MM Khan, Kazi Publications, Lahore, Pakistan, 1979. Volume III, Hadith 343, page 194 and Hadith 345, page 195.

being of the debtor.[29]

The basic features of a Shari'ah compliant banking system include the following:

- Elimination of interest/usury (*riba*). This includes its paying and/or receiving
- Profit and loss sharing. Unlike the average commercial bank with interest based operations, Shari'ah compliant banks have an interest-free operation. Instead of a fixed return (interest), depositors share the investment risks, ie., profits as well as losses
- Islamic ethics and morals must be followed in all undertakings. This includes the prohibition of investment in businesses and enterprises that are unlawful (haram), ie., that deal in anything that the Shari'ah has prohibited. This includes financial institutions engaged in usurious lending (eg., banks and mortgage companies), liquor (production, buying, selling and serving), pork, gambling, and media that propagate immorality, gossip and/or pornography
- Prohibited are undertakings that deal with contractual uncertainty and/or ambiguity
- If the Shari'ah compliant services are only one product of a conventional commercial financial institution, there must be strict segregation of funds. Funds for Islamic investments must not be co-mingled with those of non-Islamic investments. This requirement is based on the principle, that in order to maintain purity as required by Shari'ah, all necessary precautions must be taken to prevent the funds from being mixed with others which may have involvement in prohibited activities, eg., interest/usury, gambling, and others

---

[29] Usury is the exorbitant interest on loans that is charged by banks and some financial institutions. In some cases, the charges (interest and other fees) for credit card use may reach or exceed an annual rate of 50 %. This falls under the classic description of usury as it was practiced in the dark days of human civilization. It is unfair and barbaric, and exploits the weakness and/or misfortune of fellow humans.

Concluding Summary

Islamic banking, which is based upon Shari'ah compliant financial dealings, is not a new phenomenon. Its initial applications date back to the seventh century CE. It is a system which is based upon fairness and transparency of operations. Shari'ah compliant transactions deal in real assets and the risk is shared by both the bank and depositors.

By and large, Islamic banking and finance have survived the fallout from the global financial crisis because the Shari'ah based guiding rules provide an inherent protection against practices which were responsible for the 2008-2009 economic downturn. This has attracted attention in several European countries where even non-Muslims have started to utilize the Shari'ah based banking system and there are also calls for conventional banks to incorporate some of these principles into their dealings.

Shari'ah rules are uniformly applicable. These forbid both payment and collection of interest in any form, trading in derivatives, futures, and other speculative and creative transactions that were inspired by the capitalist financial system. Paper transactions are prohibited and there is requirement for actual goods to be traded on the market.

There is prohibition for investment in companies and/or industries whose products are detrimental to the social fabric of society. Herein included are conventional banks, casino and gaming enterprises, alcoholic beverage production (also prohibited is its marketing, distribution, and serving), pornography, and also such industries that produce instruments of destruction or products that are otherwise detrimental to welfare and survival of life, such as weapons of mass destruction and other offensive military products.

Islamic moral codes regulate all aspect of a Muslim's life. Unethical behavior in one situation is often reflective of similar conduct in other situations. Therefore, proper conduct is a requirement for all dealings. Uncontrolled greed disrupts world peace, destroys societal structures and has contributed to damaging the environment. In an economic system that complied with Islamic Shari'ah, there would be no usurpation of the rights of others. There would not have been the merciless assault by financial institutions and other corporate entities upon individuals and families already suffering economic hardships consequent to an economy in recession. Shari'ah promotes goodness and compassion and an economic system that complied with the Islamic Shari'ah would have prevented the scale of home foreclosures and evictions of families in straightened financial circumstances and the untold misery associated therewith.[30]

---

[30] Foreclosure and eviction condemns individuals and families to an existence on the streets or in tent cities.
Foreclosures soar 76% to record 1.35 million (December 5, 2008)
http://money.cnn.com/2008/12/05/news/economy/mortgage_delinquencies/index.htm?postversion=2008120512
Economic casualties pile into tent cities (May 4, 2009) "The National Alliance to End Homelessness predicted in January that the recession would force 1.5 million more people into homelessness over the next two years".
http://www.usatoday.com/news/nation/2009-05-04-new-homelessN.htm

Chapter Eleven

Minorities
under Muslim Rule

Introduction

O mankind! We created you from a male and a female and made you nations and tribes, that you may know one another. Verily, the noblest of you in the sight of Allah, is the best in conduct. Allah is Knower, Aware of all things. (Surah 49, Al Hujuraat, ayat 13)

Islam views diversity as a gift from the Creator and as a sign of His Wisdom. If all people were alike, with an identical culture and spoke the same language, this world would have been truly monotonous. Differences in the people enriches the global community and it is only through these differences that we are able to recognize others. Once predominantly racial and cultural, increasing these differences are being assigned a religious connotation.

Smaller groups of people with distinct ethno-cultural characteristics are found in virtually every part of the globe. In some regions, what constitutes a minority today, may have been the dominant culture in the past. Examples are native Americans and Aborigines of Australia. Similarly, religious minorities are distributed throughout the world.

Major sources of disharmony between a minority and the majority population are discrimination and persecution. To an extent, both are driven by greed with the desire to displace, subdue, or even decimate the minorities for usurpation of their lands and resources.[1] Occasionally, the reverse is also true that a minority with a distinct philosophy or political motivation may hold the reins of power and seeks to control a majority population, often against their will.

Discrimination may be defined as any distinction, exclusion, restriction or preference based on race, religion, language, ethnicity, social origin, or birth, with the purpose of curbing or denying freedom and/or basic rights. It may be exercised in one or more areas such as political, social, cultural or economic. Extreme forms of discrimination have led to ethnic cleansing and genocide.

Secular Definition of a Minority

The term *minority* is used for any group of people(s) that are identified as having their own ethnic, linguistic and/or religious identity which is different from that of the majority population.

International Declarations

While there are provisions in various international declarations which target discrimination against minorities, these have often been non-binding.[2] Furthermore, some of the key players in the formulation of these declarations have been the worst offenders. A few of these declarations are listed below:

- The Universal Declaration of Human Rights (1948, Article 2) (http://www.un.org/events/humanrights/udhr60/hrphotos/declar ation%20_eng.pdf)
- International Covenants on Civil and Political Rights (1988, Article 27) (http://www.unhchr.ch/html/menu3/b/a_ccpr.htm)
- International Covenant on Economic, Social and Cultural Rights (1966, Article 2) (http://www.unhchr.ch/html/menu3/b/a_cescr.htm)

---

[1] Roy A: The heart of India is under attack: To justify enforcing a corporate land grab, the state needs an enemy and it has chosen the Maoists. Last accessed May 2011. http://www.zmag.org/znet/viewArticle/23013 October 31, 2009.

[2] On 23 March 1976, a binding provision on minorities entered into force. It placed the responsibility of protecting and promoting minorities rights on individual states.

- International Convention on the Elimination of All Forms of
  Racial Discrimination (1965, Article 1)
  (http://www.unhchr.ch/html/menu3/b/d_icerd.htm)
- UNESCO Declaration on Race and Racial Prejudice (1978,
  Articles 1-3)
  (http://portal.unesco.org/shs/fr/files/3958/10771110281decl_on
  _race_and_racial_prejudice.pdf/decl%2Bon%2Brace%2Band%2B
  racial%2Bprejudice.pdf)
- Declaration on the Elimination of All Forms of Intolerance and
  of Discrimination based on Religion or Belief (1981, Article 2)
  (http://www.unhchr.ch/html/menu3/b/d_intole.htm)
- United Nations Declaration on the Rights of Persons Belonging
  to National or Ethnic, Religious and Linguistic Minorities [3]

Islamic Definition of a Minority

The Arabic term used for minorities living in an Islamic state is *ahl
al-dhimmah or dhimmi* which means *protected people. Dhimmah* means a
covenant (an agreement, contract, pact or pledge) and refers to a
covenant that has been made with God. Thus, the *dhimmi* is a
covenanted person, ie., has the pledge of the Prophet ﷺ and of the
Islamic community to safeguard their legitimate rights. The rights of
dhimmis are irrevocable because they are guaranteed by Shari'ah.

---

[3] http://www.un.org/documents/ga/res/47/a47r135.htm Last accessed May 2011
Adopted by General Assembly resolution 47/135 of 18 December 1992.
Article 1: States shall protect the existence and the national or ethnic, cultural,
religious and linguistic identity of minorities within their respective territories and
shall encourage conditions for the promotion of that identity.
Article 2:1 ...the right to enjoy their own culture, to profess and practice their
own religion, and to use their own language, in private and in public, freely and
without interference or any form of discrimination.
2.3 ...the right to participate effectively in decisions on the national and, where
appropriate, regional level concerning the minority to which they belong or the
regions in which they live, in a manner not incompatible with national legislation.
2.4 ...the right to establish and maintain their own associations.
2.5 ...the right to establish and maintain, without any discrimination, free and
peaceful contacts with other members of their group and with persons belonging to
other minorities, as well as contacts across frontiers with citizens of other States to
whom they are related by national or ethnic, religious or linguistic ties.
Article 3.1 ...may exercise their rights, including those set forth in the present
Declaration, individually as well as in community with other members of their group,
without any discrimination.

By definition, a *dhimmi* is one who has chosen to live in harmony and peace with fellow citizens and does not harbor any ill-will or hostility towards the majority Muslim community. A *dhimmi* enjoys full citizenship rights in an Islamic state. These rights are identical to those of the Muslim citizens and include access to all state services and benefits.

Non-Muslim Minorities living among a Muslim Majority Population

From the very beginning, Islam established strict rules that governed the interaction between Muslims and non-Muslim communities. In general, no distinction is made between a Muslim and non-Muslim citizen of a Muslim-ruled state. Exceptions due to a religious necessity are discussed below. All discussions in this section refer to states with Muslim majority populations that are ruled in conformity with the Islamic Shari'ah.

In Muslim ruled states, there are no restrictions which target minorities for any reason and there is nothing in the Shari'ah that can be construed as being discriminatory towards minorities. The Shari'ah is specific in granting minorities freedom of religion, speech, and thought. It assures their individual and collective rights, safety, protection of their properties and places of worship. These rights were assigned over thirteen centuries before any human rights groups or other international organizations conceived of any minority rights declarations.

Islam came to mankind as a choice. People are free to accept or reject it.[4] Prophet Muhammad ﷺ was the Messenger whose duty was only to convey the Message of Islam.[5] His uncle Abu Talib, who was also his guardian, did not accept Islam and was under no obligation to do so. Coercion or compulsion, by any means, to convert someone to Islam is prohibited. Besides, to be a Muslim requires a conscious and

---

[4] Surah 18, Al Kahf, ayat 29: *Say the truth is from your Lord. Then whosoever will, let him believe, and whosoever will, let him disbelieve (reject it).*
Surah 10, Yunus, ayat 99: *And if it had been your Lord's will, all who are on the earth would have believed. Will you then force the people to become believers?*
[5] Surah 42, Ash-Shura, ayat 48: *If then they turn away, We have not sent you (O Prophet) as a warder over them. Your only responsibility is to convey the message...*

uncoerced acceptance. The misconception that force was used to spread Islam is discussed in Chapter 22, Islamic History and Chapter 23, Crusades and Holy War.

Rights of Minorities under Shari'ah

Minority rights under Muslim rule can be summarized as follows: for the minorities are rights like ours and on them are responsibilities like ours.[6] The rights of minorities include the following:[7]

- Freedom of belief, ie., to choose and practice any faith. There may not be any pressure to embrace Islam since that is prohibited by the Shari'ah [8]
- Freedom of expression and association
- Right to build places of worship and the protection of those places of worship
- Protection from injustice and/or oppression by the state or from external aggression. This includes the protection of life and body
- Protection of honour (from verbal injustices or vilification)
- Protection of wealth and property. The latter includes anything that is considered valuable by the *dhimmi*. If any such belonging is taken without permission or damaged by a Muslim, compensation is required
- Right to justice and equality under the law
- Right to jobs (including civil and military service) and business, except those prohibited by Shari'ah. Prohibited are usury (*riba*), interest-based businesses, alcoholic beverages, lottery, gambling, etc.
- Provision of social services, financial, disability and senior citizens benefits similar to those provided to all other citizens

---

[6] Dr. Jamal Badawi, Islamic Teachings.

[7] The Prophet ﷺ said: *Beware, if anyone wrongs a dhimmi or diminishes his right, or forces him to work beyond his capacity, or takes from him anything without his consent, I shall plead for him on the Day of Judgment.* Sunan Abu Dawud. English Translation with Explanatory Notes. A Hasan. Kitab Bhavan, New Delhi, 1997. Volume 2, Hadith 3046, page 866.

[8] Surah 2, Al Baqarah, ayat 256: *There is no compulsion in religion. The right direction is henceforth distinct from error. And he who rejects false deities and believes in Allah has grasped a firm handhold which will never break. Allah is Hearer, Knower.*

The protection afforded non-Muslims under the Islamic Shari'ah makes it a duty to help them and save them from oppression, even if the offender is a Muslim, because Islam opposes oppression in every form:

> *And if anyone of the idolators seeks your protection, then protect him so that he may hear the word of God and afterward convey him to his place of safety ...*   (Surah 9, At Taubah, ayat 6)

Dhimmis are not permitted certain posts and assignments which have specific Islamic religious responsibilities. These include Head of State or of the military, charge of departments dealing with Zakat and Sadaqa (charity), or a judgeship presiding over disputes between Muslims and cases requiring Shari'ah rulings. In the first instance, the Head of an Islamic State is also the spiritual leader (*Imam*). Jihad may be assigned to the military and a non-Muslim may not be forced to participate. Zakat and Sadaqa are religious obligations and judicial rulings may require interpretation of Shari'ah laws.

Responsibilities of the Minorities

While minorities enjoy rights they also have responsibilities such as respect and tolerance for the majority community's religious, cultural, and other esteemed values. Additionally, loyalty to the nation/country of residence from which they draw all kinds of benefits, must be unconditional. Betrayal (especially in conjunction with foreign elements) constitutes a major crime.

Each minority may have its own peculiarities. Therefore, blanket statements such as those issued by international bodies and formulated in Western societies, may be culturally insensitive and also misplaced in some cases, if not in most. Importantly, minority rights cannot be at the expense of the majority.

Jizya

This word is derived from *jazah* which means to give something in return for something. It occurs in a commonly used phrase expressing appreciation for a favour or kindness: *Jazakum Allahu khairan.*[9] Thus,

---

[9] Meaning *may Allah reward you with goodness.*

jizya as a term, is neither impolite nor derogatory. However, like many topics connected to Islam, the meaning and implication of jizya have been subjected to misrepresentation and it has been portrayed as a "burdensome tax" imposed upon non-Muslims.

Today, jizya is no longer in use. It has been superseded by the taxation systems that were developed by Westerners and adopted by governments in Muslim countries.

The Basis for Jizya

The Muslim state is required to provide certain social welfare benefits to all of its citizens. Amongst others, these include public amenities, schools, orphanages, financial help (social security) for the elderly and needy, food for the indigent, shelter for the homeless and the travelers, health care, and security services (police and military). In order to fund such services which benefit all citizens, Muslim are required to pay the compulsory Zakat which is a form of tax.[10] Since Zakat is a religious obligation and Islam may not be imposed upon any non-Muslim, a different system of taxation was enacted. This is the jizya. Contribution to the state treasury by the non-Muslim minority is not only necessary for solvency of the system, but it is also equitable, allowing all beneficiaries endowed with that ability to participate in the expense-sharing.

Was the Jizya unfair ?

There is virtually nothing in Islam that overburdens an individual, spiritually or otherwise. All Muslims are required to pay Zakat. Non-Muslim citizens are also required to pay taxes. The only difference is in the name assigned to that tax. Additionally, jizya is collectable only from those who are financially able to pay it, ie., those who have a certain minimum income/savings. Poor and indigent non-Muslim citizens are not only exempted from paying jizya but are entitled to state financial support. Non-Muslims voluntarily serving in the defense forces are exempted from the jizya.

With the imposition of income and other taxes by the present day

---

[10] This is also called *obligatory alms* or a *wealth tax* and is an amount equivalent to 2.5 % of a person's savings. It is paid to the State Treasury or other Islamic agency authorized to collect Zakat. Also see Chapter 1, Islam.

governments, payment of jizya may no longer be a requirement. However, the payment of Zakat (in addition to government imposed taxes) is not waived for Muslim citizens.

Apostasy

Accepting another faith by abandoning Islam is defined as apostasy. From the religious standpoint, it is a major sin. However, Islam is a choice and no one may be forced to follow its tenets. According to Islamic scholars, punishment for apostasy, if any, depends upon whether Islam is abandoned for personal reasons or to challenge Islam as a faith and the Islamic society. The former being a personal matter and the individual's exercise of freedom of choice, it carries no prescribed punishment under the Shari'ah. In the latter case, when the person challenges the Islamic society after converting to another faith, it is considered as being betrayal or high treason. The prescribed punishment for high treason is death. Importantly, in such cases, the prescribed punishment is not for the change to another religion, ie., not for apostasy, but for the high treason of attacking the Islamic society and/or State.

Mutual Respect and Harmony

Islam does not permitted double standards of behavior at any time. When interacting with non-Muslims socially or during the course of business, all Islamic rules of general conduct must be observed including morality, honesty, compassion, fairness, justice, etc. Oppression is strictly prohibited and so is discrimination, especially because of religion. There are no prohibitions on friendship or social interaction between Muslims and non-Muslims as long as the Shari'ah rules of social behavior and marriage are not violated.

Members of a minority may freely preach their faith and culture to other members of their persuasion. However, it is not permissible for minorities to exploit illiteracy, poverty, financial or other needs of any segment the majority Muslim community and manipulate, entice or induce them into adopting a different faith. That is essentially what foreign Christian Missionaries have been doing in impoverished

Muslim countries. This is not only improper behavior towards the host country and an abuse of the tolerance, but it also jeopardizes the rights and status of their co-religionists.

From the very beginning, Islam required tolerance and respect for all religious and ethnic minorities. History is replete with examples which include the Muslim periods in Jerusalem, Spain, India and the Balkans. Had the converse been true, there would have been no Hindu, Christian or Jew in any Muslim land today. It was this tolerance that elevated Muslim Spain out of the darkness that engulfed Europe in the Middle Ages. Until today, Christians, Jews and other minorities live among Muslims, well integrated into society, centuries after Islam came to their lands. The Copts of Egypt, Christians in Palestine, Syria, Jordan and Iraq, and Hindus in Malaysia and Indonesia are examples. Descendants of the Spanish Jews who fled the Catholic Inquisition still prosper in North African Muslim lands. Maltreatment of Muslims at the hands of the Christian, Jews and others has not brought about any retribution against these minorities, simply because Islam prohibits harming innocents and also strictly prohibits collective punishment.

The relationship of Muslims with those of other faiths is predicated upon mutual tolerance, respect, kindness, and justice.[11] Muslims are under obligation to respect the choice of faith of fellow citizens and all others.

> *Revile not those to whom they pray besides God, lest they wrongfully revile God through ignorance. Thus to every nation We have made their conduct seem fair ...*   (Surah 6, Al An'aam, ayat 108)

The Islamic state has to guarantee protection for the life, property, and places of worship of all minorities. While this injunction has been respected by Muslim rulers, the same cannot be said for many others who profess high moral ground. In a short period of time, the Catholic Inquisition in Spain erased almost eight hundred years of harmony, peaceful coexistence and prosperity. Similar religious fanaticism and intolerance by the Serbs destroyed five centuries of harmonious coexistence in the Balkans. Other examples are the targeted

---

[11] Surah 31, Luqman, ayat 17: ...*Establish worship and enjoin kindness and forbid inequity, and persevere whatever may befall you...*

destruction and desecration of countless Muslim places of worship by non-Muslims in the former Yugoslavia, occupied Iraq and Afghanistan.

In Muslim ruled countries, churches and temples have remained undamaged during centuries of Muslim dominance, because Islam protects non-Muslim places of worship and allows minorities to observe their religious rites. After the surrender of Jerusalem to Umar ibn al Khattab ﷺ and the recapture of Jerusalem by Salahuddin Ayyubi from the Crusaders, the citizens were guaranteed religious freedom and protection of the their places of worship.[12] (Also see Chapter 23, Crusades and Holy War).

Are non-Muslims Persecuted and Oppressed in Muslim Countries?

Today, in every country that is called a "Muslim" country, other faiths were dominant prior to Islam. Conversion to Islam was by choice, unlike the Spanish Inquisition. In every one of those countries (except for Saudi Arabia and perhaps some Persian Gulf states) there are non-Muslim citizens: Christians, Jews, Hindus, Zoroastrians, Sikhs, Buddhists, etc. Their lives and businesses remain well protected. Had there been persecution and oppression, these minorities would have migrated to other lands.

Factors Responsible for Disharmony

For centuries Christians, Jews and other minorities have lived and prospered in Muslim Lands. Problems of a serious nature which disrupted the existing harmony between the minorities and the Muslim majority can be traced back to a few sources, none of which are local. Major causes are the intrigues and manipulations by foreign based and foreign funded agencies which operate under the guise of missionaries or aid programs. Another significant cause is the fallout from the new crusades. For example, in Iraq there were no problems

---

[12] A Decree was issued by the Khalifah Umar Ibn al Khattab ﷺ which safeguarded the entire community, their lives, properties, churches, religious objects, and other belongings from occupation, damage and destruction. The same was repeated by Salahuddin Ayyubi. That latter decree came with full knowledge of what the Christian Crusaders had dealt the Muslim inhabitants of Jerusalem.

between Christians and Muslims before March 2003. Similarly, in South Asia, Christians and Muslims lived in peace until missionaries from nations with a colonial past polluted their relationships. When members of minorities fall prey to the intrigues of outsiders, they also become instruments of their own hardships.

Concluding Summary

Do not judge, or you too will be judged.
For in the same way you judge others, you will be judged, and with the measure you use, it will be measured to you.
Why do you look at the speck of sawdust in your brother's eye and pay no attention to the plank in your own eye?
How can you say to your brother, 'Let me take the speck out of your eye,' when all the time there is a plank in your own eye?
You hypocrite, first take the plank out of your own eye, and then you will see clearly to remove the speck from your brother's eye.
                              Matthew 7, verses 1-5 [13]

There is an incredible amount of disinformation and gross misrepresentation about the status and treatment of minorities in Islam. Printed and cybermedia are replete with erroneous representations from sources as diverse as Islamophobes and self styled "experts" on Islam to poorly informed individuals with Muslim names.

Throughout ages minorities have had a difficult time simply because they are different from the dominant culture in which they live. The latter would prefer to have them assimilate into a bland melting-pot or into the dominant culture and thereby relinquish any heritage, culture, language or the religion they may cherish. Some dominant cultures openly persecuted minorities. Today, in some parts of the world, this practice continues with the utilization of a variety of subtle but also overt methods.

Islam took the lead in granting official recognition to minorities about fourteen hundred years ago and provided them rights, benefits

---

[13] BibleGateway.com New International Version. Last accessed May 2011.

and protection as citizens, through the state apparatus. The Islamic State is obliged to honour these commitments which are prescribed by the Shari'ah. However, the right to such benefits is forfeited if a member of the minority community indulges in any act of treason against the state or its other citizens.

Chapter Twelve

Human, Environmental,
Animal and Other's Rights

Introduction

᷈᷈᷈ You are the best community that has been raised up for mankind.
You enjoin what is good and forbid what is evil, and you believe in Allah ...

(Surah 3, 'Al Imraan, ayat 110)

Thus We have made you a just nation,[1] that you may be witnesses over
mankind, and the Messenger a witness over you.

(Surah 2, Al Baqarah, ayat 143)

There is no separation of state and religion in Islam. It is one system
with one set of laws. There are no special privileges for anybody,
including the wealthy, the ruler, judge, politician, or the scholar. The
absence of such privileges set Islamic Laws apart from all other man-
made laws or laws claimed in the name of Divine Authority, both in
theory and in practice. The Shari'ah is God's Law and believing men

---

[1] *Ummah wasat. Ummah* means nation or community and *al wasat* means *of preference,*
the best of a kind, most honored, of the middle course. Thus, *ummah wasat* is a *just nation*
and God *bestowed upon this nation (Muslims) the most perfect laws, the most correct*
methods and the clearest creeds.
Tafsir ibn Kathir. Al-Firdous Ltd, London, 1998. Part 2, pages 21-29.
SAA Maududi's commentary on this verse states: *A virtuous and noble community*
which does not go beyond proper limits but follows the middle course (without extremes)
and deals out justice... and bases its relations with other nations on truth and justice.
The Meaning of the Quran. Maududi SAA. Islamic Publications Ltd, Lahore, Pakistan,
1978. Volume I, pages 114-120.

and women are obliged to obey. Islam mandates justice and respect for life. Justice is one of the cornerstones of Shari'ah and protection of life and granting of rights to all living creatures is one of its fundamental purposes. These rights were accorded over fourteen centuries ago. They remain in force today as they did at the time of their promulgation during the lifetime of Prophet Muhammad ﷺ.

Unlike man-given rights, which are subject to alteration, God-given rights are inalienable. Furthermore, the latter are a part of Islamic belief and acceptance is obligatory for all believing men and women. In Islamic belief, the *right to life* is not restricted to humans. It also applies to all other forms of life. By respecting the *rights* of others, Islam is inherently at peace with all other life-forms and also with the environment.

Human Rights

Islamic teachings establish the intrinsic value and dignity of humans. Man is the best of all creation.[2] The main purpose of his creation was worship of the Creator. In order to fulfill that purpose, life must be of quality. The designation of man as a *khalifah* on this earth (a vicegerent, a chosen representative of God) in itself indicates the high value that has been assigned to man.

There is much criticism of Islamic laws in the Western media and assertions of harshness of punishments prescribed by Shari'ah (see Chapter 4, Islamic Law, Shari'ah and Fiqh). These criticisms come from same sources that proclaim high morals only to flout those very principles whenever it suits their purpose, in an unabashed display of hypocrisy. Those condoning or tacitly accepting rendition flights, incarceration without a charge or trial, killing of civilians, destruction of civilian infrastructure, and torture of innocents, including women and children, have just as little moral or religious consciousness as the perpetrators of such conduct. Thus, any criticism of Islamic laws or allegations of human rights violations by Muslims who truly understand and faithfully adhere to the principles of Islam, must begin with a

---

[2] Surah 95, At Tin, ayat 4: *Surely, We created man of the best stature.* Humans are the best of creation endowed with intellect and ability to choose. Consequently, they face accountability for every action.

critical and unbiased assessment of the credibility of the party making such allegations.

Vigilante sentencing after summary judgement, carried out by un- or poorly qualified individuals and practiced in certain parts of the world, has absolutely nothing to do with implementation of Islamic laws. Shari'ah mandates justice. Punishment may be carried out only after a fair and unbiased trial and sentencing is based upon hard evidence and not merely suspicion or circumstantial indicators.

Human Rights Declarations

Human Rights proclamations by the United Nations have fundamental flaws. They advocate the imposition of Western norms upon people of other faiths and cultures. Additionally, they failed to recognize, and consequently failed to include in their declarations, Human Rights issues covered exhaustively by the Islamic Shari'ah.

Secular Western Perspective on Human Rights

The *United Nations Universal Declaration of Human Rights* (UN-UDHR), a document containing 30 Articles, was published in 1948, soon after the end of the Second World War. The document was drafted, to the largest extent, by nations with a colonial past. The atrocities committed against ethnic and religious minorities before and during the Second World War are reprehensible. However, those are dwarfed by the centuries of oppression, repression, genocide and exploitation meted out by the colonialists throughout the world.

The UN-UDHR is deficient as it does not speak for all segments of the global human community. It is not "universal" as it failed to address the issue from the perspective of large segments of the global population, including that of Islam.[3] It is essentially an expression of Western perspectives and can be equated with those secular values. The latter are often at odds with religious views. In the following, a discussion of two articles of the UN-UDHR serves to illustrate the lack of universality of that document.

---

[3] About one out of every four persons inhabiting the globe is a Muslim (23 % of the global population is Muslim, based on a conservative estimate from in 2009).
Mapping the Global Muslim Population. A report on the size of the World's Muslim population. Pew Research Center, Forum on Religion and Public Life, 2009.

Freedom of Opinion and Expression

Article 19 of the UN-UDHR states:
Everyone has the right to freedom of opinion and expression; this right includes freedom to hold opinions without interference and to seek, receive and impart information and ideas through any media and regardless of frontiers.

This relatively one-sided declaration permits freedom of expression without any consideration of its consequences, ie., on the rights and sensitivities of others that might be adversely affected by such expression. There is also no mention of socially responsible behavior. Therefore, it can neither be considered universal nor promoting Human Rights. Freedom of expression must be exercised in a responsible fashion and not by disregarding and trampling upon the rights, feelings and cherished values of others.

Such one-sided "freedom of opinion and expression" finds extensive utilization in Western media with reckless disregard for the sensitivities and values of others, especially when the issue is Islam and/or Muslims. For example, in the case of the offensive caricatures published by the Danish newspaper Jyllands Post in September 2005, the "right to freedom of expression" was proclaimed by Fogh-Rasmussen, the Danish prime minister at the time and was supported by several others in the Western hemisphere. The consequences of that regretful stance, which showed utter disregard for the sensitivities of Muslims all over the world, was directly responsible for inciting violence and the loss of human life and property in several countries.

Right to Life

Article 3 of the UN-UDHR states:
Everyone has the right to life, liberty and security of person.

Although it does not define or explain the meaning of life, the inclusion of *liberty* and *security* in that definition could imply that *life* should be understood as meaning more than what the standard definition implies, ie., *a characteristic state or a mode of living, state of being alive*. It would be meaningless if only the *state of being alive* (physical, vegetative living) is afforded a right and protection and does not include other factors necessary for functional human existence, ie., all that which contributes to the quality of life.

Ascribing a proprietary position to the UN-UDHR as the charter of freedom and equality for all humans is not only unrealistic but also unnatural given the diversity of religions, races, languages and cultures. While humans are indeed one community, each nation, religion and civilization has its own rights and must be free to exercise them. Needless to say, there should not be any attempt of reimpose Western values upon the rest of the global community.

And of His Signs is the creation of heavens and the earth, and the differences of your languages and colors: verily in that are Signs for those who know.   (Surah 30, Ar Rum, ayat 22)

Islamic Perspective on Human Rights

The issues fundamental to Human Rights were not only introduced by Islam but also implemented under Islamic law as early as the seventh century CE. These apply to all, without discrimination, and include the rights of the individual and society as a whole. They address all aspects of life and living and are clearly established under Shari'ah. These rights are carefully balanced so that they do not encroach upon those of others. Additionally, as these are God-given rights, it becomes incumbent upon individuals and society to uphold them.

Right to Life: Islamic Perspective

The Shari'ah protects and preserves the five essentials which are necessary for a life of quality: *deen*,[4] *nafs*,[5] family, intellect, and

---

[4] For many terms used in the Qur'an, a simple translation of the Arabic into English is not sufficient as their meanings are frequently comprehensive. *Deen* means a *way of life*. It is living a life in compliance with the Will of God and includes faith/religion in the traditional sense.

[5] Here, *nafs* is translated as meaning life, incorporating the physical as well as spiritual and moral aspects.

property. Each one of these essentials is inseparable from the others. Thus, from the outset, Shari'ah guaranteed not only the right to life but also its quality through protection of the elements which contribute to a meaningful life and living. Taking a life without just cause is a major sin.

> ... and that you slay not the life which Allah has made sacred, except in the course of justice ...   (Surah 6, Al An'aam, ayat 151)

> ... who ever kills a person for other than manslaughter or spreading mischief in the earth, it shall be as if he had killed all mankind, and whoso saves the life of one, it shall be as if he had saved the life of all mankind...   (Surah 5, Al Ma'idah, ayat 32)

Cairo Declaration on Human Rights in Islam

The UN-UDHR was the first international effort to establish rights for humans.[6] Primarily from a Western perspective, it did not take into consideration values esteemed by many others. In August 1990, the Organization of the Islamic Conference (OIC) published the *Cairo Declaration on Human Rights in Islam*.[7] This is a document of 25 articles which reiterates the Islamic position on this issue.

In essence, true human rights are not just the rights of one individual, community or nation. They are mutual rights of all peoples. This is what the Islamic Shari'ah promotes: *to be mindful of the rights of others when exercising your own rights*. This consideration is absent in the UN-UDHR.

Rights of the Environment

Environment can be defined as our surroundings which consist of all naturally occurring things, living and inanimate. This includes the atmosphere, water, ice bodies and the earth. From the beginning, the environment sustained itself because of a delicate balance and

---

[6] The Universal Declaration of Human Rights.
http://www.un.org/en/documents/udhr/index.shtml Last accessed May 2011.
[7] Cairo Declaration on Human Rights in Islam. Last accessed May 2011.
http://www.oic-oci.org/english/article/human.htm

harmony between its components. Contributing to this balance and working in superb harmony are countless creatures, from the large to the minutest forms invisible to the naked eye. Despite the many discoveries, counting the number of life-forms in existence remains an unrealistic dream.

Nothing that is naturally occurring is ever wasted. Recycling is the law of nature. It regenerates the elements necessary to sustain life and establishes an ecobalance. Factors that overwhelm this balance throw off course the natural cycles. The water cycle and the natural atmospheric gases are examples of two simple, yet most vital processes. The water cycle continues but the purity is compromised by human-industrial pollution which also alters the ecobalance. Similarly, oxygen continues to be replenished in the atmosphere by natural sources, yet pollution from industry and fossil fuels has significantly altered the natural balance, leading to climatic changes, amongst others.

Islamic Perspective

From the Islamic perspective, everything in the universe belongs to God.[8] Man, who was placed on the earth as vicegerent (*khalifah*), is only one of its countless inhabitants. Man is the best creation and everything in the universe was made available for his use.[9,10] The earth was destined as *...a habitation and a repository.*[11] Man was given the choice and accepted the trusteeship of the earth and of all of its inhabitants.

> *We offered the trust to the heavens and the earth and the hills, but they shrank from bearing it and were afraid of it. And man assumed it. Lo! he has proved a tyrant and a fool.*
>
> (Surah 33, Al Ahzab, ayat 72)

---

[8] Surah 2, Al Baqarah, ayat 284: *To Allah belongs whatever is in the heavens and whatever is in the earth...*

[9] Surah 45, Al Jathiyah, ayat 13: *And has made of service to you whatever is in the heavens and whatever is in the earth. It is all from Him. Lo! herein are signs for people who reflect.*

[10] Surah 31, Luqman, ayat 20: *Do you not see that God has subjected to your use whatever is in the skies and whatever is in the earth and has loaded you with His favours, seen and unseen?*

[11] Surah 6, An An'aam, ayat 98: *(fa mustaqarrunw wa mustawdaun)* The earth is both a place of habitation in this life as well the final resting place, ie., the grave(repository).

Man's honored status of being the best of creation came with the endowed ability to choose between right and wrong, good and bad, and the accountability for all actions. Guidance was provided by God's messengers. The essence of all previous messages was unified into the final Divine Message, ie., *Al Islam*, the conscientious and willful subservience to God, and was delivered through Prophet Muhammad ﷺ.

The Islamic Shari'ah provides guidance for every sphere of life, for the facilitation of man's assumed responsibilities as God's trustee on earth. Included therein is the respect for the rights of all living creatures. The Shari'ah also teaches purity of intention, physical cleanliness, avoidance of excesses and waste, and encourages overall goodness. Prophet Muhammad ﷺ stated: *There will be nothing heavier on the Scale than good conduct.*[12]

All creatures live in communities of varying sizes. Just like humans, they care for their young and seek sustenance from what is provided in nature. Human actions that alter the environment can deprive other creations of their habitats and food and endanger their existence. Therefore, actions that may be detrimental for the environment are discouraged, unless they constitute a necessity for human survival. Examples of human actions with adverse consequences are deforestation driven by economic greed and some forms of commercial fishing.[13]

While man was given the ability to choose, all other creatures submit willingly to the Commandments of God. By definition, they are all Muslims. What Islam also teaches is that every one of these creatures glorifies God. Thus, by destroying a colony of ants or a nest of wasps, for whatever reason, one kills creatures that unconditionally worship the Creator. Such killing is prohibited unless clearly warranted for human safety or well-being. By harming these creations unnecessarily man infringes upon God's Rights.

The seven heavens and the earth and all that is therein praise Him, and there is not a thing but hymns His praise; but you do not understand their praise.   (Surah 17, Al Isra', ayat 44)

---

[12] Scale of accountability on the Day of Judgement. Reported by Abu Dawud. Muntakhab Ahadith, Kandhlavi MY, Annayyar, Karachi, Pakistan. Hadith 48, p 413.

[13] Also see Chapter 18, Bioengineering.

In the environment are things that humans do not know and life forms that have not been discovered by man. The rulings of Shari'ah also take into account their rights and prohibit actions that may be harmful to them or any other community.

Vegetation

Vegetation is a part of the environment and an important contributor to the ecosystem and is subject to rules of preservation and protection. Plants are responsible for replenishing the atmospheric oxygen and removal of carbon dioxide. Both processes are essential for life. Vegetation also counters soil erosion, provides food and habitat for numerous creatures.

Islam discourages needless destruction of vegetation. Unnecessary cutting of trees, in particular fruit-bearing trees, is prohibited. Similarly, systematic deforestation which creates an imbalance in nature and contributes to the global climatic changes, is prohibited. Cultivation is encouraged. If birds and animals eat away the seeds or the leaves and fruits from plants and trees, it is accepted as having been given in charity.[14] Even in conflict situations, needless destruction of vegetation, crops and orchards is prohibited. Such an act is tantamount to collective punishment with destruction of life, forage and habitat of numerous creatures. Collective punishment is strictly prohibited by Shari'ah.[15]

Water

See the water which you drink? Do you bring it down in rain from the cloud or do We? If We willed, We could make it bitter. Why then do you not give thanks?   (Surah 56, Al Waqi'ah, ayaat 68-70)[16]

Water is a gift from God, a resource that is essential for life on

---

[14] The Prophet ﷺ said: *There is none amongst the Muslims who plants a tree or sows seeds, and then a bird, or a person, or an animal eats from it, but is regarded as a charitable gift for him.* The Translation of the Meanings of Sahih Al-Bukhari. MM Khan, Kazi Publications, Lahore, Pakistan, 1979. Volume III, Hadith 513, page 295.

[15] Also see Islamic Rules of Warfare in Chapter 24 Suicide, Killing and War.

[16] This verse makes reference to the water cycle. There are only a few places on earth where rain water is collected for drinking purposes. Most of the drinking water has its source in the earth and is replenished by rain water. For additional discussion on this subject see Chapter 13, Science and Islam.

earth.[17] It is such a substantial component of all life-forms, that without it, all their functions would cease. Its addition promotes life out of dormancy.[18] Water scarcity in several parts of the globe serves as a reminder of our dependance on God for this essential gift. No one person or nation has exclusive rights to water sources and it must be shared equitably. Historically, usurpation of other's rights to water have had serious consequences.[19]

Water conservation and preservation of the purity of water sources is a requirement under Shari'ah. There are several Hadith of Prophet Muhammad ﷺ that provide instructions for the preservation of public water sources. Additionally, conservation is encouraged and wasting is prohibited even during the course of required practices such as the wudu (washing in preparation for prayer). These rules are applicable even where water is plentiful.

Rights of Animals and Other Living Creatures

The number of different species that inhabit the earth and contribute to the ecosystem to sustain the balance is known only to the Creator. Each creature fulfills a specific purpose, although that purpose may not be known to us. Nothing was created in vain. The precision and physical detail endowed to each species for the fulfillment of their particular roles is truly amazing, representing signs of God's greatness.

The earth We have spread out (like a carpet); set thereon mountains firm and immovable: and produced therein all kinds of things in due balance.

(Surah 15, Al Hijr, ayat 19)

---

[17] Surah 21, Al Anbiya', ayat 30: *...and We made every living thing from water...*

[18] Surah 2, Al Baqarah, ayat 164: *...and the water which Allah sends down from the sky, thereby reviving the earth after its death,...*
Surah 36, Yaseen, ayat 33: *A token for them is the dead earth, We revive it and bring forth from it grain so that they eat thereof.*

[19] Surah 54, Al Qamar, ayat 28: *And tell them that the water is to be shared between them.* While this injunction was for the Thamud, the people of Prophet Saleh ﷺ, its applicability is universal because of the nature of water as being essential for life. The Thamud disobeyed God's Commandment by preventing an animal sent as a test, from drinking. As a consequence, they perished.

This balance not only benefits all the earth's inhabitants but is essential for their survival. Thus, anything that creates an imbalance in the system infringes upon the God-given rights of those affected by that change.

Behavioral observations have shown that animal species display emotion. Some are also perceptive to human emotions and reactions. In the absence of inter-species communication, it is virtually impossible for humans to determine the extent and the types of emotions experienced by other species, with some exceptions such as the apes. Pain and distress are experienced by animals and possibly by other species.

Certain social behavioral patterns are found in animal species and fowl, such as seeking a partner/spouse, existence of communities, protection and care for offspring. While humans generally assign these activities to instinct, an emotional component cannot be excluded. Additionally, animals possess certain audiovisual abilities that are well beyond human comprehension. Barking of dogs in the evening or at other times without a humanly perceptible cause or exhibition of fright by some animals without an obvious external stimulus are indicators that they see and/or hear what humans cannot perceive.[20]

It is also known from the devastating Asian Tsunami of December 2004, that animals and birds left for the high ground well before the tidal waves appeared. Similarly, wild animals are absent and birds are silent before a severe thunderstorm or tornado. Is this instinctive or what did the animals and birds hear or see that humans are unable to discern?

Islamic Perspective

There is not an animal in the earth nor a flying creature flying on two wings, but they are peoples like you. We have neglected nothing in the Book (of Our Decrees)...   (Surah 6, Al An'aam, ayat 38)

The Shari'ah assigns rights to all creatures. These include access to food and water, security, and safety from harm and destruction of

---

[20] Prophet Muhammad ﷺ said: *...they see what you do not.* Al Adab al Mufrad, Imam Bukhari's Book of Muslim Morals and Manners. Translation by DeLorenzo YT. Al Saadawi Publications, Alexandria, VA. 1997. Hadith 1239, page 531.

habitat. Cruelty to animals is prohibited. This includes indefinite captivity in cages, deprivation of food or drink, physical or emotional injury (eg., beating, overwork, animal and bird fights). Killing animals is permitted only for food or if and when they endanger human life. Hunting for sport is prohibited. Even cursing animals is prohibited. The rights of animals and other creatures were unequivocally established at the instruction of Prophet Muhammad ﷺ. By doing so, he was fulfilling his role as a *mercy for all worlds*.[21]

Animals are God's creation and must therefore be cared for appropriately. The basic rules of general Islamic conduct apply: do good and refrain from every evil. It follows that if a person owns animals, he/she must take care of their needs even when they are old, sick, or no longer of benefit to the owner. While kindness to animals is a part of faith, cruelty or abuse is a crime which may be punished by being condemned to fire of Hell.[22]

Animals used for work may not be burdened beyond capacity, abused or mutilated in any way, or exposed to situations where they could be injured. They may not be deprived of food, drink or isolated during their mating times.

Slaughtering Animals for Food

For animals that are slaughtered for food or those that must be culled because of disease, the process must be humane. While there is criticism about the Islamic method of slaughtering, there is no scientific substantiation that this method is either painful or less humane than any of the other methods employed by the meat industry. On the contrary, there is indication that stunning and other similar ways of attempting to render the animals unconscious may actually be more traumatic and cruel.[23]

For the Islamic method of slaughtering (*zabihah*), specific guidelines have been provided. It requires the use of a sharp knife to sever the neck blood vessels in a single, swift stroke to facilitate exsanguination.

---

[21] Surah 21, Al Anbiya', ayat 107: *We have only sent you as a mercy for all worlds.*

[22] The Translation of the Meanings of Sahih Al-Bukhari. MM Khan, Kazi Publications, Lahore, Pakistan, 1979. Volume IV, Hadith 689, page 456.

[23] Benlafquih C: Ritual Slaughter in Islam (Zabihah). Islamic Slaughter is Humane and Produces Healthy Halal Meat. October 2008. Last accessed May 2011. http://www.suite101.com/content/ritual-slaughter-in-islam-dhabihah-a73803

Furthermore, it is forbidden to display the knife or sharpen it in the presence of the animal. It is also forbidden to sacrifice an animal in the presence of another that is also to be sacrificed.

Composition of Animal Feed

Dietary laws of the Shari'ah require that Muslims refrain from consuming certain foods and food products. Prohibited are pork and other pig-derived products, blood, meat from carnivorous animals, carrion, birds of prey as well as several others. Meat from appropriately raised herbivorous animals such as cows, sheep, goats and camels are permitted.

To a large extent, industrialized beef production has not only changed the diet of these herbivorous animals (made them omnivores, ie., plant and meat eaters) but also relegated them to a life of captivity. Industrially manufactured animal feed may contain body parts from a variety of other animals, including meat products, blood, fat, ground bone, intestines, neural organs, etc. This is a gross violation of the rights of these animals who are herbivores. Such composition of feed has been linked to Bovine Spongiform Encephalopathy (BSE), also known as Mad Cow Disease. Thus, herbivorous animals that would have otherwise been permitted as food under Islamic law, may no longer be permissible, if they were consistently fed on a diet containing blood, meat and/or other animal products in substantial proportions.[24]

Concluding Summary

And to Allah belongs whatsoever is in the heavens and the earth. And it is Allah that encompasses all things.

(Surah 4, An Nisa', ayat 126)

An individual's conduct and sense of responsibility determines the relationship with fellow humans, other creatures and the environment. More importantly, these are a reflection of his relationship to God. If the relationship to God is sincere, he will follow God's injunctions of

---

[24] www.islam-qa.com/en/ref/148665 Last accessed July 2011.

kindness, compassion and care for all of God's creation. If the relationship is superficial or pretentious, man could care less about anything but himself.

Subservience to God is at the center of Islamic belief. The universe was created flawless and balanced to exist in perfect harmony. Of all creations, man singularly possesses the ability to maintain or disturb the ecobalance and destroy life and the environment to an extent that the self-repairing processes may falter. Islam places obligations which prohibit such wantonness.

As trustee/caretaker of the earth and its inhabitants, man is responsible for the protection and preservation of his environment and maintenance of the balance that existed. By doing so, he also insures his own survival. As indicated by the above verse, everything in the universe belongs to God. That includes everything man claims to be his own. In Islamic belief, a person's own body is also considered a part of the Divine Trust (amana) which man has accepted. Thus, insuring his/her own physical well-being is a central part of each individual's responsibility, and if dutifully executed, it is considered an act of worship. This is also a reason why Shari'ah prohibits anything that may harm the individual.

Islam also assigns rights: an individual's rights upon others and other's rights upon an individual. The latter play an important role in formulating behavior. The rights of others upon an individual are numerous and include the right of the person's own body for care, rest and nourishment, rights of the family for time, attention, affection etc., rights of other persons, living creatures, job and environment and those responsibilities that come with such rights. Wrapped around all of these rights is the responsibility and duty towards God. Although it may appear very complex, it easily and intuitively falls into place by observing the duty towards God and following the Sunnah of Prophet Muhammad ﷺ.

Islam obliges mankind to certain responsibilities. As a way of life, it is the unconditional submission to God, to do as commanded, to worship[25] and revere God,[26] to show kindness and compassion towards God's creations. Misuse or abuse of any of His creations, whether living or inanimate, is a wrong. Included in these obligations are the rights of others. Every believer must be mindful of the rights of others and strive to avoid violating them. Every action, no matter how proper, must weight the consequences and repercussions on others and on their rights. This stands in contrast to the *freedom of expression* championed by the UN-UDHR which ignores the rights of others who may be affected during the process of protecting the rights of a few.

Extremes and excesses of any kind are prohibited. This includes excess in worship.[27] Moderation and modesty are strongly encouraged while extravagance and wastefulness are discouraged. Waste deprives others of the benefit of the wasted item(s) and pollution harms the environment and all inhabitants. Both are undesirable.

Built-in checks and balances encourage behavior modification as there is accountability for literally every action. This includes things such as the amount of water used, food consumed or wasted, clothing, etc. What is reasonable consumption per judgement of the individual, is acceptable. Extravagance and waste may incur God's displeasure with the potential for severe consequences. This is something opulent societies must take into serious consideration and it should serve as an inducement to behavior modification.

When We decree to destroy a population, We first warn and command those among them who are given the good things of this life and yet transgress (persist in sin), so that the word is proved true against them and then We destroy them utterly (Surah 17, Al Isra', ayat 16).

---

[25] *Ibaadah,* often translated as worship, has a very broad meaning. It includes the physical rituals of worship, ie., prayers, fasting, zakat, etc., but also means the complete obedience to God by following all His Injunctions.

[26] *Taqwa* is usually translated as piety. It is closely linked to *ibaadah.* Its meaning also includes to be mindful and ever-conscious of God, to obey Him and fear His displeasure, ie., to do what pleases Him and avoid that which may incur His displeasure.

[27] This is an example of the *middle path* of Islamic guidance. Prophet Muhammad ﷺ prohibited continuous fasting or praying (both acts of piety and worship of God) for longer periods. The reasons were that the individual's body, with is a trust (*amana*) of God, also had rights which need to be respected, ie., for rest and nourishment. In addition, the individual's family (ie., spouse and children) have rights that may be infringed upon by such extensive worship.

III. Science and Bioethical Issues

Chapter Thirteen

Science and Islam

Introduction

🌸 *Your Lord is Allah, Who created the heavens and the earth in six periods (ayyaam)[1] and is firmly established on the throne of authority. He draws the night as a veil over the day, each seeking the other in rapid succession. And has made the sun and the moon and the stars subservient by His command. His is all creation and command. Blessed be Allah, the Cherisher and Sustainer of all the Worlds!*

(Surah 7, Al A'raaf, ayat 54)

A revelation from Him Who created the earth and the high heavens. The Beneficent One, who is firmly established on the throne of authority.[2] To Him belongs what is in the heavens and on earth and all between them, and all beneath the soil.

(Surah 20, Ta Ha, ayaat 4-6)

---

[1] *ayyaam* is usually translated as *day*. However, it indicates *a period of time* without specifying its duration. Time as understood in human terms has no meaning with regard to God. Thus, *in relation to Him, one day and a thousand years are alike*. The implied meaning is that this period cannot be calculated in human terms.
The Message of the Qur'an, Translated and Explained by Muhammad Asad, The Book Foundation, Bristol, England, 2008. Page 571.
Surah 22, Haj, ayat 47: *...A day with your Lord is like a thousand years of your reckoning;* Surah 70, Ma'arij, ayat 4: *The angels and the Spirit (ruh) ascend to Him in a day the measure whereof is as fifty thousand years.*

[2] *On the throne of authority (alal 'arsh istawa).* The use of the term throne ('arsh) is metaphorical and expresses *God's absolute sway over all His creation.* The Message of the Qur'an, Translated and Explained by Muhammad Asad, The Book Foundation, Bristol, England, 2008. Pages 240-241.

The Qur'an is the Word of God and every word, phrase and sentence is purposeful. The descriptions of many scientific phenomena eluded comprehension at the time it was revealed (ca 610-632 CE) and some continue to be beyond human imaginative grasp. As the sciences advanced and human knowledge increased, the meanings of some of these verses became clear.

While there is a lot of scientific information in the Qur'an, simply reading it like any other book may not always expose it to the reader's perception. That is not because the information is hidden but because of the literary style. Also, this information is interspersed throughout the book. Furthermore, widespread accessibility to present day scientific knowledge may lead the reader to discount the importance of a statement that was made fourteen centuries ago. In addition, translations may overlook some of the relevant intricacies. For those and many other reasons, the reader or listener of the recited verses is asked to contemplate, reflect, and ponder over the meanings. Not only the literal but also the implied.

For example, the second verse cited above states: *To Him belongs what is in the heavens and on earth and all between them, and all beneath the soil* (Surah 20, Ta Ha, ayat 6). Today, it is common knowledge that vast resources exist under the surface of the earth. At the time the Qur'an was revealed, no one had a clue about the presence of any resources beneath the surface of the earth other than water which appeared as springs or was brought out through a well.

The following will briefly explore four subjects mentioned in the Qur'an, namely, the universe and celestial bodies, some geological information, pairs and opposites and human reproductive physiology. Discussion of a few other science related topics may be found in subsequent chapters in this section. Some of the earlier Muslim scientists and their works are listed in Chapter 22, Islamic History.

The Universe

The very first Surah of the Qur'an (*Al Fateha*) states in the opening verse: *Praise be to Allah, Lord of the worlds (alameen)*. The word *alameen* is plural for *alam* which means *world*. This informs us of the existence of one or more worlds besides the one we inhabit. In addition, the

Qur'an states that its message is for all of *mankind* and not only for the human race, implying the existence of other life-forms endowed with qualities and abilities similar to those of humans.

Revealed over fourteen centuries ago, well before any of the sciences as we know them today existed, the Qur'an continues to inform us that there is still much more in existence in the universe than what is known to us.

Creation of the Universe: Scientific Explanation

Modern science has provided some understanding about the creation of the universe. The popular theory is that of the Big Bang which is said to have occurred close to fourteen billion years ago. Initially, it was believed to be a tremendous explosion, a primordial fireball from a point source, ie., an atomic nucleus containing all of the matter and energy of space before which space and time did not exist. This event led to the filling of space with particles of the embryonic universe dispersing away from each other.[3] The observation that the universe is continuously expanding in every direction with increasing distances between clusters of galaxies and the discovery of cosmic background microwave radiation, a noise of extraterrestrial origin similar to radio static, supported the Big Bang theory.[4,5] Interestingly, not all of the known elements in the universe appear to have originated from the perceived primordial source.

According to another explanation, the Big Bang did not occur at a single point in space like an explosion, but as the simultaneous appearance of space everywhere in the universe and that there is no *center of expansion* ie., there is no point from which the universe is

[3] Creation of a Cosmology: Big Bang Theory. http://ssscott.tripod.com/BigBang.html Last accessed May 2011.

[4] Doppler Red Shift: Light from distant galaxies and stars shows distinct spectral characteristics because of the composition of the surrounding gases. Spectral analyses reveal a shift toward the red end of the spectrum which indicates that galaxies are receding, ie., moving away. As expected from an expanding universe, the distant ones move faster than those closer.
http://hyperphysics.phy-astr.gsu.edu/hbase/astro/redshf.htm Last accessed May 2011.

[5] Discovery of the Cosmic Microwave Background.
http://map.gsfc.nasa.gov/universe/bb_tests_cmb.html Last accessed May 2011.

expanding.[6] This theory follows the description provided in the Qur'an in Surah 41, Fussilat, ayat 11. (see below)

Creation of the Universe: Qur'anic Explanation

In the Qur'an, the creation and expansion of the universe are described as follows: the existence of an initial gaseous mass (*ad dukhan,* smoke) whose elements were fused together and subsequently separated. The scientific concept of the *primary nebula[7] (initial mass)* and secondary separation leading to the formation of galaxies corresponds with the information provided in the Qur'an.[8] A sequence for the creation of the heavens and earth is not given which suggests that it occurred simultaneously. Additionally, in the Qur'an there is no mention of a point source such as the *primordial atomic nucleus*, which also indicates that it was a simultaneous appearance everywhere.

Then He turned to the sky [9] which was smoke, and said to it and to the earth: Come (into being) both of you, willingly or unwillingly ...
(Surah 41, Fussilat, Ayat 11)

Do the unbelievers not know that the heavens and the earth were one single entity (ratqan), then We parted them (fataq), and made every living thing from water? Will they not then believe?
(Surah 21, Al Anbiya', ayat 30)

It is He who created the heavens and the earth and all that is between

---

[6] Foundations of Big Bang Cosmology. Last accessed May 2011 . http://map.gsfc.nasa.gov/universe/bb_concepts.html

[7] *nebula* means cloud.

[8] Galaxies, first discovered after the invention of the telescope are enormous systems of stars and interstellar matter. Typically, they can contain trillions of stars, each having a mass that is several million to trillion times larger than that of the Sun. Their size can be from a thousand to several hundred thousand light years. They are also separated by distances of millions of light years.

[9] Commonly translated as *sky* or *heaven,* the Arabic word *samaa* refers to something that is spread out like a canopy, like the skies form a canopy over the earth. Its wider meaning includes the all of the extraterrestrial worlds (the cosmic system), ie., the Universe. The Message of the Qur'an, Translated and Explained by Muhammad Asad, The Book Foundation, Bristol, England, 2008. Pages 15 and 917.

them in six periods[10] *then He established Himself on the throne of authority ...*   (Surah 25, Al Furqan, ayat 59)

Expansion and Evolution of the Universe

Theoretical predictions put forward by Aleksander Friedmann, a Russian mathematician, were corroborated several years later by G. Lemaître and E. Hubble that the universe was forever in a state of expansion. These predictions were supported by observational data that galaxies were receding, ie., that the universe was indeed expanding and in a state of evolution. While this information was derived only recently, in the twentieth century, this fact was stated in the Qur'an over fourteen hundred years ago: *We built the Universe (samaa) with power and We are extending it (inna la musioon)* (Surah 51, Ad Dhariyat, ayat 47).

Commonly translated as *heaven* or *sky,* the meaning of the word *samaa* includes all of the extraterrestrial worlds (also see footnote 9). *Musi'oona* (from the verb *ausa'a*) means *to widen, to make more spacious, to extend,* and *to expand.* Thus, *wa inna la musioon* stated that which we are only now discovering about the universe, ie., that it is expanding.

The Sun

The evolution of the sun, our solar system's largest object, is also mentioned in the Qur'an (see below). The sun, which is a star, comprises mainly of Hydrogen (~71%) and Helium (~27 %). Deep inside its core, nuclear fusion reactions convert Hydrogen into Helium with production of energy. This energy is emitted in the form of visible light and infrared radiation. Like other stars, the sun is in a state of evolution. Present estimates of its age put it at about 4.5 billion years. It has used about half of the Hydrogen in its core, giving it a scientifically calculated life of another five billion years at the present rate of conversion. Its light output is expected to increase (approximately double by that time).

---

[10] See footnote 1 for explanation of the meaning of *ayyaam*. Here, the reference is probably to the six stages in which the earth, its vegetation and inhabitants (exclusive of man), the solar system and galaxies were created.

And the sun runs its course to a resting place. This is the decree of the All-Mighty, the All-Knowing.   (Surah 36, Yaseen, ayat 38)

Resting place is the translation of the Arabic word *mustaqarr* which means an exact or a specific location, a particular destination. The above verse can be translated in two ways with both translations meaning the same: *The sun runs its course to a resting place* and *The sun runs its course for a period determined.* There are two pieces of information, ie., *runs its course* and *to a resting place (for a period determined).* These refer to the movement of the sun to its final location over a predetermined period of time and its finite life span. The evolution of the sun will end (*runs its course*) once it reaches the destined place. That life span may well be the predicted ten billion years by human calculation. Scientific information now available indicates that as the sun undergoes the process of evolution in space, it is indeed moving towards a point in the constellation of Hercules known as the solar apex (*runs its course to a resting place*).

Celestial Bodies and Orbits

In the Qur'an, the moon (*al qamar*) is referred to as a light (*an nur*). In distinction, the sun (*as shams*), is referred to as a lamp (*siraj*), a source of light. Scientific information available to us corresponds to these descriptions. Energy produced by the nuclear fusion reactions inside the sun's core is emitted mainly in the form of visible light, ie., making the sun a source of light. The planets are referred to as *kawkab* and do not produce but reflect light.

We now know that the celestial organization is balanced with harmonious interplay between forces of gravity, mass and speed of movement of each celestial body by its own motion. Scientific data show that both the sun and the moon rotate, each by its own motion: the sun rotates around the galactic center and on its own axis. The latter takes between 25 days at its equator to 36 days, as different parts rotate at different speeds. The moon rotates on its axis in 29 1/2 days as it revolves around the earth. The rotation of the earth results in night and day. This information is also provided in the Qur'an.

*It is not permitted for the sun to overtake the moon, nor does the
night outstrip the day. Each just swims along (yasbahoon) in its own
orbit (falak).*   (Surah 36, Yaseen, ayat 40)

*And He it is Who created the night and the day, and the sun and the
moon. Each of them (the celestial bodies)[11] swims in its orbit (fee falaki
yasbahoon).[12]*   (Surah 21, Al Anbiya', ayat 33)

Earth's Resources

And to Allah belong the treasures of the heavens and the earth ...
                    (Surah 63, Al Munafiqoon, ayat 7)

*... To Him belongs what is in the heavens and on earth and all between
them, and all beneath the soil.*
                    (Surah 20, Ta Ha, ayat 6)

Since an enormous amount of geological data is available today,
information about the earth and subterranean resources provided in
the Qur'an may not come across as being striking. However, the
Qur'an and Hadith provided information about the existence of such
resources long before any of these discoveries were possible. Today,
we know of the existence of large underground water reservoirs
(aquifers) and of vast underground gas, oil and mineral wealth, ie.,
treasures.

Water

... and made every living thing from water ...
                    (Surah 21, Al Anbiya', ayat 30)

Water is quantitatively the major component of all living systems.
About 70 % of each body cell comprises of water. Deprivation of

---

[11] That is, each celestial body moves in its own orbit.
   Maududi SAA. Towards Understanding the Qur'an. The Islamic Foundation,
   Leicester, England, 1995. Volume V, page 264.
[12] *Yasbahoon* expresses movement of its own accord, ie., *self-propelled* like in running
   or swimming. *Falak* means orbit or sphere.

water results in the slowing or ceasing of cell and organ function.

While farmers and common people may have long suspected that rain water percolated through the soil and resurfaced as springs and streams, established scientists often theorized that springs and streams originated from condensations in underground caverns or from influx and desalinization of sea water.[13] The water cycle is described in the Qur'an as follows: *Do you not see that Allah sends down water from the sky and causes it to penetrate the earth as water springs, ...* (Surah 39, Az Zumar, ayat 21).

Pairs

> *Glory to God Who created in pairs all things that the earth produces as well as their own kind (humans) and other things of which they have no knowledge.*   (Surah 36, Yaseen, ayat 36)[14]

Zauj (plural azwaaj) which means both *a pair* and *one of a pair*, refers to polarity or opposites which exists in virtually everything, ie., in all of creation, living and inanimate.[15] It indicates the existence of counterparts or counteracting forces, each having a defined and often complementary relationship with the other and function to maintain an equilibrium.[16]

While gender differentiation in animals may be obvious, differentiation of male and female in the plant kingdom was not known to exist at the time of revelation of the Qur'an and for many centuries thereafter. The existence of distinct sexual pairs (male and female) in plants is described in Surah 13, Ar Ra'ad, ayat 3: *...and fruit of every kind*

---

[13] Brutsaert, W: Physics Today. Letters. Science and common beliefs. http://ptonline.aip.org/journals/doc/PHTOAD-ft/vol_60/iss_1/17_1.shtml

[14] Some of the other verses that also make this statement are:
Surah 78, An Naba', ayaat 6-8: *...And We have created you in pairs.*
Surah 51, Ad Dhariyat, ayat 49: *And all things We have created by pairs (khalaqna zawjaini), that haply you may reflect.*
Surah 43, Az Zukhruf, ayat 12: *...has created pairs in all things...*

[15] Zauj refers opposites and not duplicates. Besides gender, these exist in everything, from all living things to inorganic matter such as ions, magnetism and electricity.

[16] The Message of the Qur'an, Translated and Explained by Muhammad Asad, The Book Foundation, Bristol, England, 2008. Pages 761-762.

He made in pairs (zawjain ithnain), two and two...;[17] Surah 20, Ta Ha, ayat 53: *With it have We produced divers pairs of plants each separate from the others (azwajam min nabatin shata);* and Surah 36, Yaseen, ayat 36 *...created in pairs all things that the earth produces...*

Pairs also exist at the molecular and submolecular level. DNA and the chromosomes exist in pairs. If things with opposite reactions which facilitate a balance are included, such as specific systems, forces, enzymes, etc., that counter the effects of others, then *pairs* exist virtually everywhere. Hormones and enzymes acting in an antagonistic fashion (as opposites) serve to regulate numerous body functions in order to maintain a balance. Many such discoveries have been made only within the past few decades, including those in the scientific and medical fields. Despite our widening knowledge, there will remain many *other things of which* we still have no knowledge.

Reproduction and Development

Verses describing human reproduction and embryological development are found in several surahs of the Qur'an. The specificity of those descriptions could be understood only after microscopy became available, with the help of advanced methods for laboratory analysis and knowledge of modern physiology. Below is a very basic description of the process as understood today followed by verses from the Qur'an and explanation of the Arabic terms which described this same process over fourteen centuries ago.

Current understanding of Reproductive Physiology

In humans, fertilization of the ovum (egg) requires only a small amount of fluid. Of the millions of active spermatozoa in the ejaculate, only a fraction make it to the ovum and only one of them is responsible for fertilization which then leads to the development of an embryo.[18] Most of the fluid in the ejaculate serves other purposes, including that of providing the appropriate pH and medium for the

---

[17] *zawjain ithnain* indicates *a pair comprising of both sexes,* i.e., *that there are two sexes to every kind of plant.* The Message of the Qur'an, Translated and Explained by Muhammad Asad, The Book Foundation, Bristol, England, 2008. Pages 399-400.

[18] Rarely, more than one sperm is able to penetrate the ovum (polyspermy). The product of polyspermy is not viable.

movement of spermatozoa. In the following is a brief description of the process:

1. The male ejaculate (2-5 ml) is a mixture of liquids comprising of spermatozoa, prostatic and other glandular secretions. The process of fertilization requires only a tiny fraction of this fluid
2. After the ejaculate is deposited, it mingles with the secretions of the female. The cervical mucus, under the influence of the hormone estrogen, plays an important role in facilitating the ascent of spermatozoa through the uterine cervical canal
3. The spermatozoa travel to the Fallopian tube to fertilize the ovum (egg). This journey may takes several minutes to hours. Only a single sperm is allowed to fertilize the egg. The sperm binds to receptors in the wall of the egg. An enzymatic reaction allows the egg wall to be pierced and the sperm head is incorporated into the egg cytoplasm. The genetic information (pronucleus) is extracted from the sperm and condenses with that of the egg to form chromosomes
4. About four days after fertilization, the ovum enters the uterus where it becomes firmly implanted (day 5-7) until the time of birth, with the exception of extrauterine pregnancy and abortion
5. The fertilized egg undergoes multiple cell divisions and grows in size, assuming a shape which is likened to that of a leech. This occurs about 2.5-3.0 weeks after fertilization. At this stage, the embryo measures between 1.5 and 2.5 mm
6. Alterations occur in its shape and appearance [due surface prominences (somites)]. This occurs at about 3-4 weeks. At this stage, the embryo measures between 2.0-3.0 mm
7. The skeletal elements are formed followed by formation of skeletal muscles (flesh)
8. The fetal stage begins at nine weeks

Description in the Qur'an and its Correlation

1. *He created man from a drop of fluid (nutfa) ...*

(Surah 16, An Nahl, ayat 4)

Nutfa describes a very small amount of fluid, like the residual in a glass after it is emptied. As this term indicates, only a small fraction of the ejaculate is needed for the actual process of fertilization.

2.   *We create man from a drop of mingled fluid (amsaj) ...*
     We gave him (the gifts of) hearing and sight.

     (Surah 76, Ad Dahr, ayat 2)

Mingled fluid (amsaj) applies to both the composition of the ejaculate which consists of spermatozoa, prostatic and other glandular secretions and also to the mixing of male and female fluids. This mixing of male and female fluids is essential for facilitating the ascent of spermatozoa into the uterus and Fallopian tube.

We gave him (the gifts of) hearing and sight. These senses develop in that very order. The primordia of the internal ears develop first, followed by those of the eyes.

3.   *Then He made his progeny from an extract (sulala) of a humble fluid.*

     (Surah 32, As Sajdah, ayat 8)

Sulala (extract or essence) describes the process in which the best component is extracted. The spermatozoa *extract* themselves from the ejaculate and travel upstream into the Fallopian tubes. Additionally, after fertilization of the ovum, there is *extraction* of the genetic information contained in the sperm head. This condenses with that of the ovum.

4.   *... and We cause whom We will to remain in the wombs for an appointed term ...*   (Surah 22, Al Haj, ayat 5)

     Then placed him as a drop of seed in a safe lodging (in a place of rest firmly fixed).   (Surah 23, Al Mu'minoon, ayat 13)

The expression, *an appointed term*, is very pertinent since not all fetuses make it to maturity. The second verse, *...in a safe lodging (or a place of rest firmly fixed)*, complements the meaning of the first one in that the implantation is secure (see footnote 19), except for those that are aborted. However, they still rest in the uterus for *an appointed term*. Additionally, the fertilized egg is likened to a seed which grows only after implantation.

5. *Created man from a clinging clot (alaqa).* (Surah 96, Iqra', ayat 2)

   We have created you from dust, then from a drop of fluid, then from a clot, then from a little lump of flesh partly formed and partly unformed, ... (Surah 22, Al Haj, ayat 5)

These and the verses cited below describe the appearance and stages of development of the embryo. The word *alaqa* means something that clings or has an attachment, like a clot of congealed blood attached to a wound or a clinging leech. This is a precise description of the early embryo and of its attachment to the uterus.[19] Like the leech, the embryo derives its nutrition from the host, the uterus. The description of the embryo as being *partly formed and partly unformed (mukhallaqah wa ghair mukhallaqah)* is discussed below.

6. *Then We made the drop (nutfa) into a clot (alaqa), then We made the clot into a shapeless lump (mudgha), then We made bones within the little lump, then We clothed the bones with flesh (lahm), and then produced it as another creation. So blessed be Allah, the Best of Creators!* (Surah 23, Al Mu'minoon, ayat 14)

Mudgha is translated as a *shapeless lump, chewed flesh,* or a *morsel,* which the embryo indeed resembles, ie., a piece of meat that has been chewed upon. This distinct appearance is due to the presence of the surface prominences (somites) and has been likened to teeth marks. *Lahm* means flesh or meat which constitute the skeletal musculature. The sequence stated in the verse is precisely the way the musculoskeletal system develops, ie., formation of bones which are subsequently covered by musculature: *...then We clothed the bones with*

---

[19] Already at the blastocyst stage (about one week after fertilization), the outer cells (trophoblast) adhere to the inner surface of the uterus and begin to erode and invade the endometrial epithelium. Subsequently, it becomes embedded (buried) in the endometrium, providing it a *safe lodging*. Finger-like projections develop through which it derives its nourishment from the uterus. Later, these form the placenta.

flesh.

7.   *... and He gave you the faculties of hearing and sight and al af'ida
      (mind, feeling and understanding).* (Surah 32, As Sajdah, ayat 9)

This verse and Surah 76, Ad Dahr, ayat 2 [*We gave him (the gifts of)
hearing and sight*] describe the senses in the very order they develop.
First the internal ears, followed by the eyes and the brain [*feeling
(emotion) and understanding*].

8.   *He created you (all) from a single being, then from that being, He
      made its mate... He created you in the wombs of your mothers, in
      stages, one after another, in three veils of darkness.*
                                            (Surah 39, Az Zumar, ayat 6)

The process of organogenesis and development takes place in stages
(*in stages, one after another*) inside the body of the mother, unlike the
egg of a bird or reptile. There are different interpretations of *three
veils of darkness* (*zulumaatin salasa*). In the first case, it may be referring
to the anatomic layers surrounding the embryo/fetus (abdominal wall,
uterus, chorion/amnion). Alternatively, it may be referring to the
actual stages of embryonic-fetal development and the uncertainty
surrounding survival and/or normal prenatal development. However,
the true meaning of this and other verses is known only to God. The
usual calculation of pregnancy is also in trimesters.

9.   *...then from a little lump of flesh partly formed (mukhallaqah) and
      partly unformed (ghair mukhallaqah).*
                                            (Surah 22, Al Haj, ayat 5)

In addition to *partly formed and partly unformed*, the meanings of
mukhallaqah and *ghair mukhallaqah* include *in proportion and out of
proportion, partly complete and partly incomplete, shaped and unshaped.*
This verse provides an intriguing description of the anatomic
peculiarities of the embryo at this stage of development. The organ
systems find themselves at different stages of development, ie., some
tissues have already undergone differentiation into organs (neural,

cardiovascular, cartilage), while others have not yet matured (*partly complete and partly incomplete*).[20] Additionally, during the early phases of development, certain body parts are disproportionate in size to others, eg., neural and central circulatory systems (*in proportion and out of proportion*). Later, proportionality is established. These developments occur at a stage when the embryo is barely visible to the naked eye.

Concluding Summary

This is absolute Truth with certainty.

(Surah 56, Al Waqi'ah, ayat 95)

It should not come as a surprise that scientific information is present in the Qur'an. It is information that could have been provided only by the One who made it all happen. The meaning of many verses comes to light as scientific advancements increase our knowledge and understanding of those matters. Some of the verses may seem to say something we already know because these discoveries were made in the relatively recent past and this information is now widely available. However, it is inconceivable that such knowledge was in the possession of mankind at the time the Qur'an was revealed, in the seventh century CE.

The Qur'an is not a tutorial but a source. Therefore, information must be extracted by reflecting upon the words, by contemplating, trying to understand and searching for the meaning. The message contained in many verses may never be understood. Yet, there are others whose meanings become evident as we reflect, research and progress in the sciences.

Islam is a way of life which teaches reliance on God, acceptance of destiny (what was ordained by God) and living in peaceful harmony with fellow creatures and the environment. It encourages the continuous quest for increasing knowledge and endorses beneficial

---

[20] Blood cells are formed by about 17-19 days and vascular channels begin to develop. A fetal heart and rudimentary circulation are formed as early as 3 weeks after fertilization. Doppler ultrasound can detect fetal heart motion by about 5 weeks.

research in virtually all fields. The greater the acquired knowledge, the closer the individual comes to the truth and to God. Whether that is recognized as such is another issue.

And that man has only that for which he makes effort.

(Surah 53, An Najm, ayat 39)

Additional Reading

Moore KL. A scientist's Interpretation of References to Embryology in the Qur'an. J Islamic Med Assn 18:15-17,1986.

Chapter Fourteen

Reproductive Issues
Abortion, Contraception and Sterilization

Introduction

≈ Say: Come, I will recite to you that which your Lord has made a sacred duty for you: that you do not join anything in Worship with Him; and that you be good and dutiful to your parents, and that you do not kill your children because of poverty, We provide sustenance for you and for them, and that you do not come near shameful deeds, whether open or secret. And you do not take life which Allah has made sacred (forbidden), except in the course of justice. This He has commanded you, so that you may understand. (Surah 6, An An'aam, ayat 151)

Islam regards every child as a trust and a gift from God which is to be cherished. In a true Islamic society, every conception occurs under legitimate circumstances and every pregnancy is desired. There is no *unwanted* pregnancy. In addition, the question of abortion, other than for the few reasons discussed later in this chapter, would not arise as the factors leading up to such situations would be absent, ie., sexual relationships out of wedlock, concern for financial hardship, career, etc.

Islam strictly prohibits taking innocent human life. For taking a person's life, a clear and justifiable reason must exist, eg., carrying out an approved punishment for murder or major treason, or during the course of a just and legal war. Even during war it is prohibited to harm noncombatants, children, women and the elderly. The killing of one's own children is explicitly prohibited. The consequences of intentionally killing an innocent person can be enormous.

Whoever kills a believer intentionally, his recompense is Hell forever, and the wrath and curse of Allah are upon him, and a dreadful penalty is prepared for him. (Surah 4, An Nisa', ayat 93)

Do not kill your children fearing a fall to poverty. We shall provide for them and for you. Indeed, their killing is a great sin.
(Surah 17, Al Isra', ayat 31)

While this verse (Surah 17, Al Isra', ayat 31) was revealed to end the pre-Islamic practice of killing infants (frequently females), the message of Islam is universal and for all times. The message states clearly *Do not kill your children...* By any definition, the conceptus (embryo, fetus) is a child and a life at a given stage of intrauterine development. Thus, the killing of children, born and unborn, is prohibited. Additionally, the believing woman pledges not to kill her children:

O Prophet! If believing women come to you, taking oath of allegiance to you that they will ascribe nothing as partner unto Allah, and will neither steal nor commit adultery, nor kill their children, nor produce any lie that they have devised between their hands and feet, nor disobey you in what is right, then accept their allegiance and ask Allah to forgive them. Indeed, Allah is Forgiving, Merciful. (Surah 60, Al Mumtahanah, ayat 1)

Abortion

Each year approximately forty-two million abortions are performed world wide.[1] Over eighty percent of them are performed in developing countries. In India, it is reported that over half a million female fetuses

---

[1] Sedgh G, Henshaw S, Singh S, et al: Induced abortion: estimated rates and trends worldwide. Lancet 2007; 370:1338–45.

are aborted each year.[2] In the United States of North America, 1.31 million abortions were performed in 2001 and 1.21 million abortions were performed in 2005.[3] For 2007, 827,609 abortions were reported to the CDC.[4] For American women, it is estimated that about half of the pregnancies are unintended, and of these, forty-two percent are aborted.[5] In 2000, about half of the American women undergoing an abortion were less than than twenty-five years of age, nineteen percent were teenagers, over two thirds were never married, and sixty percent of abortions seekers had one or more children.[6] The stated reasons were socioeconomic in the vast majority of cases: financial concerns, interference with job, career or education, unwanted pregnancy, unmarried, and husband or partner wanted the abortion. An abortion was sought for rape in one percent (amounting to around 12,000 cases) and incest in less than 0.5 % of cases.[7]

Islamic Perspective

With the exceptions discussed below, Islam forbids abortion at any stage of pregnancy. This includes all circumstances such as undesired or unplanned pregnancy, for social, financial and other reasons. The further the pregnancy has advanced, the greater the wrong in carrying out an abortion. After one hundred and twenty days of pregnancy (timing of the ensoulment of the fetus), abortion is considered

---

[2] A girl's right to live: Female Foeticide and Girl Infanticide.
http://www.wunrn.com/news/2007/03_07/03_12_07/031707_female.pdf
Last accessed May 2011.

[3] Jones RK, Zolna MRS, Henshaw SK, et al: Abortion in the United States: incidence and access to services, 2005. Perspectives on Sexual and Reproductive Health, 2008, 40:6–16.

[4] Pazol K, Zane SB, Parker WY, et al. Abortion Surveillance - United States, 2007. Morbidity and Mortality Weekly Report (MMWR).   Last accessed May 2011.
http://www.cdc.gov/mmwr/preview/mmwrhtml/ss6001a1.htm?s_cid=ss6001a1_w

[5] Finer LB and Henshaw SK, Disparities in rates of unintended pregnancy in the United States, 1994 and 2001. Perspectives on Sexual and Reproductive Health, 2006, 38:90–96.

[6] Jones RK, Darroch JE, Henshaw SK, Patterns in the socioeconomic characteristics of women obtaining abortions in 2000–2001. Perspectives on Sexual and Reproductive Health, 2002, 34:226–235.

[7] Finer LB, Frohwirth LF, Dauphinee LA, et al., Reasons U.S. women have abortions: quantitative and qualitative perspectives. Perspectives on Sexual and Reproductive Health, 2005, 37:110–118.

equivalent to murder.[8] The prescribed penalty for unjustified abortion after one hundred and twenty days of pregnancy is the payment of compensation (*diya*) which is also an option in cases involving murder. The recipients of such payment are those who would normally inherit from the child under Shari'ah rules, exclusive of those involved in the decision making or facilitating the abortion. An abortion performed before the one hundred and twentieth day of pregnancy requires no such compensation.[9]

Permitted Exceptions

The only exception permitting abortion (at any stage of pregnancy) is when continuing the pregnancy would result in the mother's death. This determination must be made by medical experts and requires that all available options be exhausted to save both mother and the unborn child.

In cases of rape, both in the civilian setting or during war and occupation, the victim of rape is not considered guilty of sin since the act was forced upon her and was beyond her control. In such cases, early medical intervention is recommended to avoid pregnancy and abortion. If the rape victim becomes pregnant, she has the option to keep the child or undergo an abortion within the first forty days.[10] Under such circumstances, permission for abortion is given because of necessity. Other circumstances may arise for which a ruling may be sought from Islamic Scholars. In such cases, each situation is to be considered individually.

Abortion in Multi-gestational Pregnancy

For abortion in multi-gestational pregnancy see the Chapter 15, Reproductive Issues: Infertility, Assisted Reproduction, and Surrogacy.

Abortion for Fetal Abnormalities

Genetic counseling can usually identify the risk of conceiving a child with chromosomal or other genetically transmissible abnormalities. If

---

[8] European Council for Fatwa and Research, First Collection of Fatwas, Fatwa 22. www.e-cfr.org/data/cat30072008113814.doc   Last accessed May 2011.

[9] Some scholars consider all abortions to be akin to murder.

[10] Abortion of pregnancy resulting from rape http://www.islam-qa.com/en/ref/13317/abortion   Last accessed May 2011.

medical tests obtained during pregnancy detect a fetal abnormality may the fetus be aborted? Some Islamic scholars have indicated that it would be permissible in the presence of compelling medical evidence suggesting significant neurological and physical abnormalities which would deprive the child of a normal life.[11] In such situations, each case is assessed on its individual merits by seeking expert medical advice and the opinion of Shari'ah Scholars.

Contraception

The Shari'ah permits the prevention of pregnancy for valid reasons, for a finite period, through mutual agreement between husband and wife. An exception permitting unilateral decision by the wife is the determination that a pregnancy would endanger her life. Acceptable reasons for contraception include the following:

- Pregnancy or parturition may adversely affect the health of the mother or endanger her life, as determined by a qualified medical practitioner
- Sickness that would be aggravated by pregnancy
- Desire for spacing pregnancies in the interest of the children
- Young age of the couple who are unprepared for parental responsibilities
- Overwhelming responsibilities such as caring for a sick child, older parents or grandparents
- To facilitate breast feeding[12]

In addition, contraception is permitted for the couple who are concerned that they might resort to unlawful means in order to fulfill the family's needs because of the added responsibility of children.

Types of Contraception Permitted

Only methods for temporary birth control are permitted. Any birth control method which could harm the body or is irreversible, ie.,

---

[11] Ruling on aborting a deformed foetus.
http://www.islam-qa.com/en/ref/12289/abortion Last accessed May 2011.

[12] After childbirth, usually only the first 3-4 menstrual cycles are anovulatory which means that a pregnancy is possible thereafter. That may also shorten the duration of lactation.

results in sterilization, is not permitted. The latter includes, irreversible tubal ligation and vasectomy. Both of these are not permitted since reversal procedures cannot reliably reestablish fertility.

Sterilization

One of the purposes for the creation of the sexes was procreation to inhabit the earth. Sterilization interrupts this natural function and also unnecessarily alters God's creation. The Shari'ah prohibits procedures that cause irreversible infertility or prevent pregnancy on a permanent basis. Exceptions to this rule are situations where a critical necessity exists (darurah) to protect a woman's life and health. An example is the case where an underlying cardiac or other disease may be aggravated by pregnancy. This necessity must be established by expert medical opinion. In the absence of a compelling reason, sterilization is considered a major sin.[13]

An argument expressed in favour of mass sterilization is the perceived need for the containment of a predicted global overpopulation. This viewpoint is sponsored by some nations and organizations and is encouraged, and even imposed upon poorer segments of society, in some developing countries.[14] Neither individual emotions nor the uncertainty of life with respect to the family's existing children are given any consideration. In most of the countries where sterilizations are imposed, life expectancy is shorter than in the industrially developed countries, health care is lacking, and there is significant infant and childhood mortality. Loss of a child through sickness or accident and the inability to have additional children is significant and unnecessary emotional trauma. Additionally, the sterilized individual would rarely possess the resources to have the sterilization reversed. Such practices disregard the rights of individuals, violate their bodies, and are prohibited by Shari'ah.

---

[13] M Al-Munajjid: Fiqh of the family, Sterilization. Fatwa # 47196.
   http://www.islam-qa.com/en/ref/47196   Last accessed May 2011.
[14] For example, the forced sterilizations which were carried out in India.

Concluding Summary

... And whoever keeps his duty to Allah, He will appoint a way out for him.
(Surah 65, At Talaq, ayat 2)

The rulings of Shari'ah take into account all aspects of human ability and weakness. Strict as they might appear at first glance, on closer examination, these rulings are universally just and equitable. Islam requires the believers to adhere to the highest moral standards. Situations that may cause a person to unwittingly stray off course must be avoided. This is one of the reasons for prohibiting free mixing of men and women and other irresponsible forms of social liberty. It is stated in the Qur'an:

... do not come near shameful deeds, whether open or secret.
(Surah 6, An An'aam, ayat 151)

The statistics on abortion are very disturbing, yet they tell only a small part of the story. The long-term effects, including emotional and somatic problems, remain largely unreported. In the majority of cases, the abortion serves to remove the consequence of irresponsible behavior.[15] Considering the published statistics, well over eighty-seven percent of abortions would be avoided if the society were to accept and implement Islamic norms for social and moral conduct. This is a conservative estimate based on a 2004 survey of over twelve hundred abortion patients in which only thirteen percent of women seeking abortion cited medical reasons and health *concerns*.[16] In the absence of compelling evidence, many of these health *concerns* may not qualify as being legitimate reasons for having an abortion.

Abortion is prohibited under Islamic law. Since Islam prescribes a non-extreme middle course, there is built-in flexibility. If there is a genuine need for termination of pregnancy, the individual situation is reviewed, and if certain necessity criteria are met, it is permissible to abort the embryo or fetus. In such cases, the permission for abortion

---

[15] About every other American woman having an abortion is younger than than 25 years and over two thirds were never married.

[16] Finer LB, Frohwirth LF, Dauphinee LA, et al.: Reasons U.S. women have abortions: quantitative and qualitative perspectives. Perspectives on Sexual and Reproductive Health, 2005, 37:110–118.

is based upon the Shari'ah principle of choosing the lesser of two harms because God does not intend hardship on the believers and Islam represents mercy and compassion.

By prohibiting abortion as a rule and permitting it only as an exception for justifiable and legitimate reasons, Islam seeks to inspire moral and social responsibility. Furthermore, it requires that any conduct which could lead to a prohibited act, be avoided.

Programs for the curtailment of global population growth with doomsday predictions of overpopulation and scarcity of food stem from the same sources that attempt to wrestle control of the world's resources and dominate the global political scene. These predictions do not appear to have taken into account population attrition through natural calamities, genocide and other conflicts. From the Islamic perspective, only the Creator knows what lies ahead for His creation and He has clearly promised to provide for them.

... do not kill your children because of poverty, We provide sustenance for you and for them, ...   (Surah 6, An An'aam, ayat 151)

Chapter Fifteen

Reproductive Issues
Infertility, Assisted Reproduction, and Surrogacy

Infertility

*To Allah belongs the Sovereignty of the heavens and the earth. He
creates whatever He wills. He gives daughters to whomever He wills and
sons to whomever He wills. Or He gives both sons and daughters to
whomever He wills and leaves barren whomever He wills. Indeed He is
all-knowing, infinite in His power.* (Surah 42, Ash Shura', ayaat 49-50)

Infertility is an age old problem. It is a disease that afflicts up to ten
percent of couples worldwide and can be associated with significant
psychological and psychosomatic morbidity.[1] While enduring destiny
with patience and prayer, Muslims are encouraged to seek treatment
for whatever ailments befall them. The desire to seek treatment for
infertility is no exception. It is encouraged as newer treatments make
conception possible by using therapies permitted by Shari'ah. For
every Muslim suffering from infertility, the following statement of
Prophet Muhammad ﷺ provides the hope for fulfillment of the joys
and blessings of children:[2]

---

[1] Recent advances in medically assisted conception. Report of a WHO Scientific
Group. WHO technical report series 820. World Health Organization, Geneva,
1992.

[2] Sunan Abu Dawud. English Translation with Explanatory Notes. A Hasan. Kitab
Bhavan, New Delhi, 1997. Volume 3, Hadith 3865, page 1087.

Allah has sent down both the disease and the cure, and He has
appointed a cure for every disease, so treat yourselves medically, but
use nothing unlawful.

Assisted Reproduction

This is a technique which facilitates reproduction in couples who are
unable to have children naturally. It involves several processes and
procedures which are used in managing infertility and include an in-
depth evaluation of the infertile couple, induction of ovulation or
spermatogenesis, harvesting gametes, fertilization and embryo
transfer.

In vivo assisted reproduction facilitates fertilization within the female
reproductive tract (eg., intrauterine or intratubal insemination). In the
in vitro procedures, the fertilization occurs outside the body and the
embryo is transferred into the uterus [in vitro fertilization and embryo
transfer (IVF-ET)]. Additionally, several other techniques may be used,
such as intracytoplasmic sperm injection, micromanipulation of
spermatid cells, injection of round spermatid nuclei into oocytes, etc.

In IVF-ET eggs are harvested after ovulation and are fertilized by
sperm outside the body. They are allowed to divide for a few cycles
and are then transferred into the uterus. The technique is inefficient
and necessitates the fertilization of several eggs. Thus, several
embryos (also described as pre-embryos) are produced in the
anticipation that at least one will successfully implant in the uterus and
result in pregnancy. The unused embryos are either cryopreserved for
later use or destroyed. Some embryos may be used for harvesting
stem cells. The success of assisted reproduction techniques in
achieving a pregnancy depends upon multiple factors and can be as
low as thirty percent per treatment cycle.

Islamic Perspective

Islam has established rules for social behavior. The family is a key
component of Muslim society, its importance extending well beyond
the social aspects. This includes a clear identity of lineage. This is
necessary, amongst other reasons, for the purposes of inheritance and

permissibility of marriage (mahram status). Social morality, marriage and procreation are inseparable. In addition, marriage and children are a Sunnah of Prophet Muhammad ﷺ. All believers strive to incorporate sunnah into their lives and marriage is encouraged. The Prophet ﷺ advised: *Marry women who are loving and are able to bear children.*[3]

Motherhood is awarded a very special, revered status in Muslim society. Proper upbringing of children is a religious responsibility, not just the extension of a biological function. Children are not only a blessing and an adornment in their parent's lives but also a test of responsibility.[4,5] A virtuous child benefits the parents both in this world and in the Hereafter as his/her virtuous deeds continue to benefit the parents even after their death.

The moral and social codes of Islam require purity and unambiguity of genes and lineage. It follows that each child must be able relate to his/her biological parents united by marriage. According to the Shari'ah, marriage is not only a contract but a solemn pledge (*misaakun ghaleeza*) between the husband and wife which excludes any third party intrusion into the marital functions and procreation. Therefore, adoption as practiced in Western society and some other parts of the world, is not permitted under Shari'ah as it conceals the true identity, genetic lineage and heredity of the adopted child. For the Islamic view on marriage and adoption see Chapter 7, Marriage and Chapter 8, Family and Social Issues.

Rules guiding assisted reproduction have been established by Muslim jurists, medical specialists and scientists.[6,7,8] The Islamic Shari'ah permits assisted reproduction [*in vivo* and *in vitro fertilization* (IVF)] for married

---

[3] Bulugh Al-Maram. Dar-us-Salam Publications, Riyadh, S Arabia, 1996. Hadith 826, pages 342-343.

[4] Surah 18, Al Kahf, ayat 46: *Wealth and children are an ornament of the life of this world.*

[5] Surah 64, At Taghabun, ayat 15: *Your wealth and your children are only a trial ...*

[6] Human Reproduction in Islam. Islamic Organization for Medical Sciences. Publication Series Fiqh Medical Seminar. 11 Shaban,1403 AH (24 May 1983). http://www.islamset.com/bioethics/firstvol.html Last accessed May 2011.

[7] Sharmin I, Rusli BN, Rani A, et al. Ethics of Artificial Insemination: An Islamic Perspective. J Islamic Med Assoc 2007 39:29-32. jima.imana.org/article/download/5264/3610 Last accessed May 2011.

[8] Siddiqi M: An Islamic Perspective on Stem Cells Research. http://www.islam101.com/science/stemCells.htm Last accessed May 2011

couples under the following conditions:

- Only within a marriage (while married and not after divorce or after the husband's death) and as long as no other party is introduced (sperm, egg, embryo or surrogate uterus)
- The egg is fertilized with the sperm of the lawful husband and is put into the uterus of the wife whose egg was fertilized in vitro (not into a surrogate)
- Since death of the husband or divorce terminate the marriage contract, assisted reproduction is not permitted on the divorced wife or widow. This includes the use of cryopreserved sperms or embryos of the couple
- There must be strict procedural safeguards to protect against mingling or substitution of the sperms and eggs of the couple with those of other sources

Cryopreserved sperm or embryos

The husband's sperm or embryos of the couple that were cryopreserved may be used only if the marriage contract is valid, ie., they are not divorced and the husband is alive. Use of the husband's sperm that was obtained and cryopreserved prior to marriage is prohibited.[9] Similarly, sperm obtained from a deceased husband may not be used.[10]

Donor Sperm or Egg

Under Shari'ah, IVF is permissible only when both sperm and egg originate from a legally married couple. The use of sperm or egg from a third person is considered as being similar to adultery (zina) and is

---

[9] A. Kutty: Using Sperm Frozen before Marriage.
http://www.islamonline.net/servlet/Satellite?pagename=IslamOnline-English-Ask_Scholar/FatwaE/FatwaE&cid=1119503548564
http://www.islamonline.net/livefatwa/english/ Last accessed May 2009.

[10] Sharmin I, Rusli BN, Rani A, et al. Ethics of Artificial Insemination: An Islamic Perspective. J Islamic Med Association 2007 39:29-32.
jima.imana.org/article/download/5264/3610 Last accessed May 2011.
Ash-Shareef A-K H: Artificial Insemination from an Islamic Perspective.
http://www.islamonline.net/servlet/Satellite?pagename=IslamOnline-English-Ask_Scholar/FatwaE/FatwaE&cid=1119503545560 Last accessed May 2009.

strictly prohibited. A child conceived through the use of donated sperm or egg is considered to be out of wedlock.

The thrust of these rules is to prevent pollution of the family's genetic makeup and lineage by preventing the introduction of an outside the marriage source. By prohibiting the use of third person gametes, the Shari'ah keeps the family's lineage unambiguous.

Multigestation Pregnancy and Pregnancy Reduction

During IVF, several fertilized eggs (pre-embryos) are implanted (usually between two and four). This can result in a multiple fetus pregnancy which may pose an increased health risk for both the mother and the fetuses (spontaneous abortion, prematurity and associated problems).[11] Aborting some of the fetuses is permitted by Shari'ah if there is a real threat to maternal life.[12] Pregnancy reduction in a multiple fetus pregnancy is not permissible if the sole indication is to improve survivability of the fetuses or any other *perceived* risk. However, it is permitted to selectively remove unhealthy embryos that might cause death to others, if there is evidence to that effect.[13] This permission is based on the Shari'ah principle of choosing the lesser of two harms (*akhaff ad-dararayn*) and requires appropriate testing to determine which of the embryos is unhealthy and the involvement of experienced physicians in the decision making process.

Preimplantation Genetic Diagnosis

Pre-implantation genetic diagnosis can be used in conjunction with IVF to test embryos for certain inherited disorders prior to transferring them into the uterus. This is useful in X-linked disorders, single gene defects, mutations, and hereditary cancers. Diseases that can be diagnosed include the trisomies (including Down's Syndrome),

[11] Strauss A, Paek BW, Genzel-Boroviczény O, et al: Multifetal gestation maternal and perinatal outcome of 112 pregnancies. Fetal Diagn Ther 2002;17(4):209-217.

[12] http://www.islam-qa.com/en/ref/11047/abortion Last accessed May 2011

[13] Siddiqi M: Abortion in Case of Multiple Embryos.
http://www.islamonline.net/servlet/Satellite?pagename=IslamOnline-English-AskScholar/FatwaE/FatwaE&cid=1119503543076 Last accessed May 2009.

hemoglobinopathies and hemophilias, cystic fibrosis, Marfan's syndrome, neurofibromatosis, polycystic kidney disease, x-linked immune deficiency, retinitis pigmentosa, fragile X syndrome and muscular dystrophies.

Long term care of a physically or mentally handicapped child can be extremely testing for parents and other caregivers. Islam being logical and rational, not only guides to a middle course but endeavors ease for the believers.[14] Thus, preimplantation genetic diagnosis is permitted and also rejection (for implantation) of genetically defective embryos.[15] Permissibility of preimplantation genetic treatment (when available) for correction of an abnormality remains to be determined.

Gender Selection

Gender selection prior to fertilization or embryo implantation may prevent several debilitating genetic diseases which are sex-linked. Therefore, the Shari'ah permits gender selection for that particular purpose, ie., where gender predisposes to a serious condition.[16] Gender selection for non-medical reasons is permissible only in cases of necessity (darurah) and that determination is made on an individual basis.[17] In Islamic belief, nothing in the universe ever happens without God's permission. Therefore, the outcome of any gender selection attempt remains in accordance with God's Will:

And your Lord creates whatever He wills and chooses. No choice have
they (in the matter) ...   (Surah 28, Al Qasas, ayat 68)

Allah knows what every female bears (in her womb and what takes shape
in it) and by how much the wombs fall short (of their time or number) or
exceed. And everything with Him is measured. (Surah 13, Ar Ra'ad, ayat 8)

---

[14] Surah 22, Al Haj, ayat 78: *He has chosen you and has not laid upon you in religion any hardship ...*

[15] Serour GI. Opinion. Religious perspectives of ethical issues in ART.
1. Islamic perspectives of ethical issues in ART. M E Fertil Soc J: 2005,10(3),185-190.
http://www.bioline.org.br/pdf?mf05030   Last accessed May 2011.

[16] Al Azhar Likely to Allow Restricted Gender Choice. Last accessed May 2009.
http://www.islamonline.net/English/News/2005-03/28/article03.shtml

[17] Al-Qaradawi Y: Choosing the Sex of the Child.
http://www.islamonline.net/servlet/Satellite?pagename=IslamOnline-English-Ask_Scholar/FatwaE/FatwaE&cid=1119503546928 Last accessed May 2009.

Pregnancy after Menopause

While post-menopausal women can be prepared hormonally for pregnancy and childbirth, relevant health issues and risks must be given due consideration. There is nothing in the Shari'ah that prohibits pregnancy after menopause as long as it involves a married couple and no other Shari'ah rules are violated. Surrogate pregnancy is not permitted.

Research on Fetal Tissue

Research is permitted on unused embryos that were obtained during the course of IVF and are donated for research purposes. This requires informed consent from the couple to whom the embryos belonged and they may not be implanted into any body.[18] Also see Chapter 18, Genetic Engineering: Gene Therapy, Stem Cell Research and Cloning and Chapter 19, Bioengineering: An Islamic Perspective.

Surrogate Pregnancy

In surrogate pregnancy, a woman carries in her womb the fetus of another couple placed through IVF-ET. The egg and sperm may come from a legally married couple, or either or both may have been *donated* or *procured*. The surrogate carries the pregnancy to term and the newborn child is given to its *genetic parent(s)*, or in the case of *donated* or *procured* sperm or egg, to the party that initiated the surrogacy process.

Sperm donation and cryopreservation for use in IVF has become accepted practice in some cultures. Similarly, egg donation makes it possible for a woman to procreate without going through a pregnancy and child birth. However, the question of parentage remains unanswered. Is it the one donating the egg or the surrogate to whom belong neither the egg nor the embryo?

Does surrogacy affect the fetus and in what ways? This question too, remains far from being answered. While the DNA makeup of the fertilized egg does not change, the placenta is not impervious to fetal

[18] Siddiqi M: An Islamic Perspective on Stem Cells Research.
   http://www.islam101.com/science/stemCells.htm Last accessed May 2011.

and maternal blood elements, making pregnancy a very intimate relationship between mother and child. The potential long term social and psychological effects on the involved individuals (especially the children) and society are not known.

From the Shari'ah perspective, surrogate pregnancy (surrogate motherhood) is an illegitimate pregnancy, falling outside the established limits of a marriage. It is strictly prohibited since it involves a third party and introduces alien elements into a marriage.

Concluding Summary

... And whoever keeps his duty to Allah, He will appoint a way out for him.
(Surah 65 At Talaq, ayat 2)

Advancements in the assisted reproductive technologies in the era of changing societal norms have redefined the meanings of parenthood and motherhood. Sperm and egg donation and surrogate pregnancies attempt to defy naturally defined limits. From a simple desire for having children, some have embarked upon out-sourcing or even commercialization of reproduction by essentially purchasing embryos through third party sperms and eggs and/or renting a uterus to carry the child. While such practice may be permitted in Western society, it is strictly prohibited in Islam.

Islam requires that the relationship of the child to its parents be unambiguous. The parents must be both its legal and biological parents. Thus, the gametes (egg and sperms) must be from the married couple desiring assisted reproduction and implantation of the fertilized egg is permitted only into the uterus of the wife who was also the source of the egg. Involvement of another person (as donor or surrogate) is strictly prohibited by Shari'ah.

Chapter Sixteen

Euthanasia and Related Issues

Introduction

... My Lord is He who gives life and causes death ...
(Surah 2, Al Baqarah, ayat 258)

God gives life and He takes it at the time of death. Despite the advances in biological sciences, neither do we know when life begins nor do we know when it actually ends. At the time the fetal heart starts to beat, brain development is at a very early stage.[1] After extensive brain injury, the heart may continue to beat even after all chances of cerebral function recovery have ended. But life consists of much more that the mere physical, biological state of vegetative living.

In Muslim belief, life begins with the ensoulment of the fetus and life ends when the soul leaves the body. Neither of these times has been scientifically established with any certainty. Hadith from Prophet Muhammad ﷺ indicate that the ensoulment of the fetus occurs about one hundred and twenty days after implantation in the uterus.[2] However, it is not known exactly what constitutes the soul or where it resides in the body. It is assumed to have a physical presence in the

---

[1] A rudimentary circulatory system begins to form as early as 3 weeks after fertilization. Fetal heart motion is present at about 4 weeks and can be detected by Doppler ultrasound as early as 5 weeks.

[2] The Translation and Meanings of Sahih Al-Bukhari. MM Khan. Kazi Publications, Lahore, Pakistan, 1979. Volume VIII, Hadith 593, page 387.

human body since it is extracted at the time of death: *...when the soul of the dying reaches the throat* (Surah 56, Al Waqi'ah, ayat 83).

In Muslim belief, a person has no more right or control over his/her own life than he/she has over death. The time, place and mode of death have been predetermined. Since only God gives life and also takes it, any unnatural event which appears to have contributed to an individual's death, is purely a means.

God is the most Merciful and the All-Knowing. Therefore, it improper that any human should assume to know what is best for a very sick or an old person and take it upon him/herself and decide to terminate the life of that innocent individual. Pain and suffering from a sickness or injury, whether treatable or terminal, carries a different implication in the Muslim mind and contributes to the lack of expressed interest in euthanasia (so-called *mercy killing*) in Muslim society. It is in this context that the Islamic view on euthanasia must be understood.

The Value of Life

Islam views human life as being sacred and the value attached to life goes far beyond the ability of an individual to make tangible contribution to society. In this way, Islamic values differ from those acceptable to some facets of contemporary Western society. The elderly and the sick are not perceived as a burden on the family or society.[3] On the contrary, emphasis is placed on caring for the elderly (especially parents), widows and the sick.[4] These efforts are also well rewarded.

In Islamic belief, this worldly life is a transition period. The next life, after resurrection on the Day of Judgment, is eternal. Whatever transpires in this life is in preparation for the next life. Any suffering in this world is transient while the situation in the next life is long lasting. Whatever befalls them, Muslims must endure with patience and

---

[3] Prophet Muhammad ﷺ said: *Blessings are with your elders*. Mustadrak Hakim. Muntakhab Ahadith. Kandhlavi MY, Annayyar, Karachi, Pakistan. Hadith 148, page 445.

[4] See Chapter 8, Family and Social Issues.

perseverance,[5] for whatever befalls a person, happens only with God's permission.[6] Every suffering carries a benefit, although it might not be apparent in this worldly life. In this regard, Prophet Muhammad ﷺ said: ... *No Muslim is afflicted with any harm, even if it were the prick of a thorn, but that Allah expiates his sins because of that, like a tree sheds its leaves.*[7]

Additionally, the process of accountability which may include punishment, already begins in the grave.[8] Thus, from the Islamic point of view, euthanasia only expedites the process and cannot be considered a *mercy* by any definition. The living can still pray for God's forgiveness but death seals the accounts. Islam prohibits even wishing for death.[9]

Euthanasia

The word *euthanasia* means *good death, merciful* or *facilitated death/killing*, ie., facilitating the death of an individual with an incurable illness to end pain and/or suffering. As of 2008, euthanasia is legal in three states of the United States of North America (Oregon, Washington and Montana) and several European countries, namely, Belgium, Holland, Luxembourg, and Switzerland.

Euthanasia may be carried out at the individual's request (*voluntary*) or the decision may be made by a caregiver, guardian or family member who believes that killing the individual would be in his/her best interest (*involuntary*). Such a process may be enacted through an action of a caregiver such as a lethal dose of drug(s) (*directly*) or *indirectly* by giving large doses of medications which compromise vital functions and thereby induce death, and as *assisted suicide* where the individual ends his/her own life using instructions and material

---

[5] Surah 2, Al Baqarah, ayat 153: *O you who believe! Seek help in steadfast patience and prayer.*

[6] Surah 64, At Taghabun, ayat 11: *No kind of calamity can occur except by the permission of Allah ...*

[7] The Translation and Meanings of Sahih Al-Bukhari. MM Khan, Kazi Publications, Lahore, Pakistan, 1979. Volume VII, Hadith 551, page 374.

[8] English Translation of Jami' At-Tirmidhi. Darussalam, Riyadh, S Arabia, 2007. Volume 2, Hadith 1071, pages 443-445.

[9] Prophet Muhammad ﷺ said: *None of you should long for death because of a calamity that has befallen him...* The Translation and Meanings of Sahih Al-Bukhari. MM Khan, Kazi Publications, Lahore, Pakistan, 1979. Volume VIII, Hadith 362, page 242.

provided by another.

Islamic Perspective on Euthanasia

Say: Come, I will recite to you that which your Lord has made a sacred duty for you: that you do not join anything in Worship with Him; and that you be good and dutiful to your parents, and that you do not kill your children because of poverty, We provide sustenance for you and for them, and that you do not come near shameful deeds, whether open or secret. And you do not take life which Allah has made sacred (forbidden), except in the course of justice. This He has commanded you, so that you may understand.   (Surah 6, An An'aam, ayat 151)

And do not take the life which Allah has forbidden,[10] except for a just cause.[11] And whoever is killed unjustly, We have given his heir authority...[12]
                              (Surah 17, Al Isra', ayat 33)

The above cited verse from Surah An An'aam which directs Muslims to be *good and dutiful* towards parents follows the commandment to worship only One God.[13] This sequence emphasizes the importance assigned to parents. This verse is ever so pertinent since the old and sick, who are the focus of euthanasia, are often someone's parents.

Euthanasia, voluntary or involuntary, including assisted suicide, is strictly prohibited by Shari'ah.[14,15] Neither the individual seeking euthanasia nor any other person, including physician, caregiver, guardian or family member, has any right to terminate life without a legitimate and justifiable reason. Old age, physical incapacitation, terminal illness, pain and suffering provide absolutely no justification

---

[10] *harram Allah: forbidden* or *made sacred by Allah.* This includes suicide.

[11] In the course of justice. For example, death sentence for a justly convicted murderer, for treason and during a legal and morally justified war.

[12] *qisas:* The principle of just retribution, ie., death sentence for the murderer. The heirs also have the right to forgive the murderer or demand compensation, *diya.*

[13] That is, do not ascribe divinity, in any way, to any other beside God.

[14] Siddiqi M: Is Euthanasia Allowed in Islam? Last accessed May 2011.
    http://infad.usim.edu.my/modules.php?op=modload&name=News&file=article&sid=9079

[15] Al-Qaradawi Y: Islam's Stance on Euthanasia. Last accessed May 2011.
    http://infad.usim.edu.my/modules.php?op=modload&name=News&file=article&sid=10561

for killing a person. Indeed, killing a person only because he/she is suffering from an incurable or crippling illness, is equivalent to the killing any other innocent person, ie., murder. Islam considers unjustified killing a major sin. Similarly, suicide (including assisted suicide) is not permitted under any circumstances.[16] Prophet Muhammad ﷺ said: *A man was inflicted with wounds and he committed suicide, and so Allah said: My slave has caused death on himself hurriedly, so I forbid Paradise for him.*[17]

Islam recognizes that pain and chronic debilitating illnesses can be extremely difficult to endure. Therefore, it encourages the individual to seek medical attention for alleviation of pain and relief of symptoms. Enduring patiently and seeking help through prayer is a part of faith. Additionally, although difficult for the one afflicted and hard to comprehend for others, death which is not sudden has its merits for a believer. A sudden death may deprive an individual the chance for reaffirmation of faith and repentance. A painful death or a severe illness is equated with lessening of the burden of sin which is carried over for the final reckoning on the Day of Judgment. A Hadith states: *The believer's soul seeps out ...*[18]

Withdrawal of Life Support

Life is considered sacred and the Shari'ah seeks the preservation of life whenever possible. Therefore, all available methods, including resuscitation, should be used in any given emergency situation. If subsequent assessments reveal an absence of improvement and negligible chances of recovery (eg., extensive brain damage), resuscitative measures may be discontinued. Similarly, in irreversible coma associated with a severe chronic illness, mechanical life support and certain medication (eg., chemotherapy) may be discontinued.[19]

---

[16] A person who commits suicide is punished in Hell-Fire perpetually reenacting the suicide. The Translation and Meanings of Sahih Al-Bukhari. MM Khan, Kazi Publications, Lahore, Pakistan, 1979. Volume II, Hadith 446, page 252.

[17] The Translation and Meanings of Sahih Al-Bukhari. MM Khan. Kazi Publications, Lahore Pakistan, 1979. Volume II. Hadith 445, page 251.

[18] English Translation of Jami' At-Tirmidhi. Darussalam, Riyadh, S Arabia, 2007. Volume 2, Hadith 980, page 372.

[19] Siddiqi M: Is Euthanasia Allowed in Islam? Last accessed May 2011. http://infad.usim.edu.my/modules.php?op=modload&name=News&file=article&sid=9079

These should be informed, consensus decisions based upon expert medical opinion.

In severe, chronic illnesses with a remote chance of recovery, seeking medical treatment is not obligatory. Faced with the diagnosis of an incurable or terminal disease, an individual has the freedom to accept or decline medical treatment, including the initiation of life support measures. However, food, drink, pain relief and general nursing may not be withheld.

Discontinuation of life support is not considered equivalent to *euthanasia* or *mercy killing* as no one actively or indirectly induces death but the disease process is allowed its natural course. Islamic scholars accept the medically established criteria of death: irreversible cessation of respiratory and cardiovascular activity and/or the complete and irreversible cessation of brain function, including the brain stem.[20,21]

---

[20] Siddiqi MH: Questions of Life and Death.
(3/26/2005, Article Ref: IC0503-2653) Last accessed May 2011.
http://www.islamicity.com/Articles/articles.asp?ref=IC0503-2653
(http://www.pakistanlink.com/Religion/2005/04082005.htm)

[21] Resolutions and Recommendations of The Council of the Islamic Fiqh Academy,1985-2000. Resolution No: 26 (1/4), pages 51-54. From the fourth Session, Jeddah, S. Arabia, 18-23 Jumada II, 1408 AH (6-11 February,1988). The Medical Definition of Death.
http://www.islamset.com/bioethics/death/index.html Last accessed May 2011.

Chapter Seventeen

Organ Donation and Transplantation

Introduction

Allah has sent down both the disease and the cure, and He has appointed a cure for every disease, so treat yourselves medically, but use nothing unlawful.[1]

Islam seeks the preservation of human life and well-being. The Shari'ah recognizes the diverse problems and needs of individuals and society and seeks to provide meaningful solutions. It lays down explicit rules about the permitted and the prohibited, and as a living law, it remains in harmony with the changing times. Thus, issues that become relevant with advancement of knowledge, beneficial scientific progress and technical accomplishments, are easily reconciled. Organ donation and transplantation is one such issue.

After death, the human body is inviolable to the extent that autopsy is disallowed (unless required for legal reasons) and mutilation and cremation are strictly prohibited by Shari'ah. Yet it allows exceptions like organ harvesting for transplantation, if the purpose is driven by a necessity, for the treatment of an otherwise incurable ailment or it is deemed essential for the survival of another person. Under such circumstances, a principle of Fiqh is invoked which states: *Necessity*

---

[1] Sunan Abu Dawud. English Translation with Explanatory Notes. A Hasan. Kitab Bhavan, New Delhi, 1997. Volume 3, Hadith 3865, page 1087.

makes prohibition lawful.[2] Here, the *necessity* is determined by Islamic Scholars after a study of the pertinent issues.

The human body is a trust (*amana*) from God and the trust comes with a responsibility. The latter includes protecting against harm (self inflicted or external) and the encouragement to pursue all permissible options for health care needs. Caring for the indigent and the sick is a part of the Islamic faith and applies to all, irrespective of religion, race, gender, ethnic origin, etc.

Organ Procurement

Organ donation for transplantation is permitted from living donors and organs may also be harvested from deceased individuals.[3,4,5] The latter is subject to Shari'ah rulings which govern necessity and require that certain preconditions be fulfilled. These include obtaining consent from heirs or other individuals endowed with the responsibility. Furthermore, organ harvesting is permitted only after medically established criteria of death are evident, ie., irreversible cessation of respiratory and cardiovascular activity and/or complete and irreversible cessation of brain function (including the brain stem).[6,7]

Organ procurement from living donors has the following

---

[2] Ibn Nujaym: al-Ashbah wa al-Naza'ir, page 85. Cited in: *Is organ donation permissible?* ibn Adam al Kawthari M, Darul Iftaa (Leicester, UK). Last accessed June 2011. http://www.themodernreligion.com/misc/hh/organ-transplant.html

[3] The Fiqh Academy of the Muslim World League, 8 th Session, Makkah, 28 Rabi ul Thani - 7 Jumada I, 1405 and Supreme Council of Ulama', Riyadh, resolution no. 99 dated 6 Dhul Qa'dah 1402, AH. (Cited by Siddiqi MH: Issues and Questions. http://www.pakistanlink.com/Religion/2005/09092005.htm). Siddiqi MH: Organ Donation. Last accessed June 2011. http://www.saudigazette.com.sa/index.cfm?method=home.regcon&contentID=200805126216

[4] Resolutions and Recommendations of The Council of the Islamic Fiqh Academy, 1985-2000. Resolution No: 26 (1/4), pages 51-54. From the fourth Session, Jeddah, S Arabia,18-23 Jumada II, 1408 AH (6-11 February,1988).

[5] Yaseen MN: Sale of Human Organs. Medical Jurisprudence, Third Symposium on The Islamic Vision of Some Medical Practices, 18-21 April, 1987 CE. http://www.islamset.com/bioethics/organ/index.html Last accessed June 2011.

[6] Siddiqi MH: Questions of Life and Death. March 25,2005. Last accessed June 2011. http://www.islamicity.com/Articles/articles.asp?ref=IC0503-2653

[7] Resolutions and Recommendations of The Council of the Islamic Fiqh Academy, 1985-2000. Resolution No: 26 (1/4), pages 51-54. From the fourth Session, Jeddah, S Arabia, 18-23 Jumada II, 1408 AH (6-11 February,1988).

requirements:
- Informed donor consent without coercion
- The organ donation must not pose a risk to the life or health of the donor and only non-vital organs may be donated
- There must be a verifiable necessity based upon expert medical opinion that there is no other reasonable alternative for saving the recipient's life or for the restoration of health
- The sale of body parts is strictly prohibited

Thus, it is permissible for a Muslim to donate blood, bone marrow, and organs such as a kidney or a portion of the liver, provided it does not compromise the donor's life or well being. Muslims are allowed only to donate organs and are prohibited from selling their body parts. Similarly, receiving compensation for blood and bone marrow is prohibited.

It is permissible to receive organ transplantation provided there is a medical necessity. This also includes skin and cornea from tissue banks. For the donation of blood and the receiving of blood transfusions, there are no restrictions (ethnic, religious, etc) on the source of the donated blood or it's recipient.

Buying of organs for transplantation is also prohibited. In the presence of a critical need for an organ and absence of availability from regular channels, with purchase being the only means of obtaining the organ, it becomes permissible to pay for procurement of the organ for transplantation or blood for transfusion.[8,9]

Not permitted for transplantation are organs which propagate the donor's genetic code, ie., the ovary and testicle.[10] A child born subsequent to such a transplantation will carry the genetic code of the donor and will not be a true biological offspring.

---

[8] Abul-Fotouh M Y: Sale of Human Organs in the Balance of Legitimacy. Medical Jurisprudence, Third Symposium on The Islamic Vision of Some Medical Practices, 18-21 April, 1987 CE.
http://www.islamset.com/bioethics/organ/index.html Last accessed May 2009.

[9] ibn Adam al-Kawthari M: Is blood Blood Donation permissible ?
http://www.themodernreligion.com/misc/hh/blood-donation.html
Last accessed June 2011.

[10] Resolutions and Recommendations of the Council of the Islamic Fiqh Academy 1985-2000. Transplant of Genital Organs. Resolution No: 57/8/6, Page 114.

Status of the Human Body in Islam

The sanctity of the human body, also after death, is the issue at the heart of the discussion on organ donation and harvesting from cadavers. While the brief discussion that follows is in this context, the basic Islamic perspectives also apply to other situations, such as those that occupy present world and media attention, specifically torture, mutilation and killing of innocents.

Islam views the human body as a sacred gift which must be handled with respect both in life and after death, whether it belongs to a Muslim or to a non-Muslim. It is prohibited for any person to inflict harm upon him/herself, and for this very reason, suicide by any method is strictly prohibited.

The dead body must be handled gently and mutilation is prohibited. In Islamic belief, death occurs when the soul exits the body. It is not known whether this coincides with ceasing of any of the known signs of life, ie., beating heart, breathing or brain stem activity. The dead feel pain and hear what is being said with the difference being their inability to respond.[11] In addition, on the Day of Resurrection, an individual will be raised in the same state that was present at the time of death.

Concluding Summary

Organ donation and transplantation have been extensively debated by contemporary Islamic Scholars. There are two opinions: a majority ruling permits organ donation and transplantation while some consider it prohibited. This difference highlights one of the many elegant features of Islamic Shari'ah. These rulings are made by knowledgeable scholars and were expressed after exhaustive research of the sources of Shari'ah and the authoritative and classical works of earlier scholars. Their rulings are in essence opinions based upon general Shari'ah guidelines. Although the two viewpoints are opposites, they are derived on the basis of analytical and logical deduction, and therefore, each opinion is correct in its own right. Here, Shari'ah permits the individual to make the choice based

---

[11] Prophet Muhammad ﷺ said: *Breaking a dead man's bones is like breaking it when he is alive.* Sunan Abu Dawud. English Translation with Explanatory Notes. A. Hasan. Kitab Bhavan, New Delhi, 1997. Volume 2, Hadith 3201, page 912.

upon his/her own inclination.

The permission to receive blood provides another insight to the working of these Islamic rules. Blood contains essential elements that fulfill multiple vital functions and at the same time blood carries impurities and substances which the body seeks to eliminate. While the intake of impurities is prohibited, blood transfusion becomes permissible as a necessity, by virtue of the Fiqh principle that a *necessity makes a prohibition lawful.*

Chapter Eighteen

Bioengineering
Genetic Engineering, Gene Therapy, Stem Cell Research and Cloning

Introduction

In the creation of the heavens and the earth; and in the alternation of night and day; and in the sailing of the ships upon the sea with that which is of benefit to mankind; and in the water which Allah sends down from the sky, thereby reviving the earth after its death, and dispersing over it all kinds of living creatures; and in the blowing of the winds and in the clouds obedient between the sky and earth: are signs for people who are wise.

(Surah 2, Al Baqarah, ayat 164)

Science has always been accorded a front row seat in Islamic society. Islam and science have never been at odds and science has never been able to contradict anything in the Qur'an.[1] The acquisition of knowledge is a greatly encouraged religious obligation for every Muslim and science provides a means for acquiring such knowledge. Numerous scientific phenomena are described in the Qur'an with the encouragement to reflect and to understand the wonders of creation and its Source. Scientific advancements continue to be studied by Muslim jurists to determine their implications in light of the Islamic

---

[1] There are contradictions in the books of other monotheistic faiths. The reader is referred to: *Bucaille M: The Bible, The Qur'an and Science.* North American Trust Publications, Indianapolis, IN, 1978. (CCN 77-90336)

laws.

While scientific advancements bring benefits, there may also be applications with potentially detrimental effects. Examples are nuclear technology and bioengineering. Therefore, the Shari'ah maintains a policy which facilitates progress and encourages beneficial scientific research while prohibiting pursuits that are potentially harmful to life and the environment. This is based upon the Shari'ah principles: *do no harm* and *weigh the potential benefits (good) against the harmful effects*.

The rules that guide Muslims (Shari'ah and Fiqh) are remarkably adaptable and without temporal or geographic limitations. These are derived from four sources, namely the Qur'an, Sunnah (traditions of Prophet Muhammad ﷺ), Ijma' and Ijtihaad. The two latter sources provide the vehicle for adaptability. The rulings are objective and universally applicable. It is this adaptability which allows Islam to deal with any contemporary issue, irrespective of its nature and complexity.

Genetic Engineering

O Mankind, eat of that which is lawful and wholesome (tayyib)[2] on the earth, and do not follow the footsteps of the devil, for indeed he is an avowed enemy to you. (Surah 2, Al Baqarah, ayat 168)

Genetic engineering (GE), genetic modification or manipulation, recombinant DNA technology,[3] and gene splicing are terms used to describe procedures that manipulate and alter genetic structure. Essentially, this involves the transfer of genetic material from one organism into another through molecular cloning and transformation. This process transforms the cells of the recipient organism leading to creation of a genetically modified organism.

Applications of Genetic Engineering

This technology (also known as bioengineering or biotechnology) has been used in a variety of plants, microbes, insects, fish, animals and

---

[2] *tayyib:* means wholesome, good, agreeable, healthy.

[3] DNA: deoxyribonucleic acid.

also in humans. In the United States of America, there is a significant acreage of genetically modified (GM) soya bean, corn (maize), canola, rape seed and cotton crop.[4] Genetic modification of food crops is said to improve taste, nutritional value and yield, provide disease resistance and a longer shelf-life. Other uses include the manufacture of medicines, eg., insulin, erythropoietin (stimulates red blood cell production), tissue plasminogen activator (TPA) to dissolve blood clots, and drugs used in cancer and immunology. It is also used in research. In humans, it is anticipated to be applied to a potentially long list of diseases including the treatment of genetic disorders and some forms of cancer.

Potential Adverse Environmental Effects of GE Products

Secure methods for controlling or preventing the spread of GE products or their genes are lacking.[5] GE organisms may survive longer than expected and there is the possibility of cross fertilization (and transfer of genes) with those occurring naturally, with the potential for unintended environmental and public health effects.[6,7,8,9] Long-term effects on the environment and humans have not been adequately assessed because of the relatively recent introduction of such products.

Like nuclear weapons, genetically engineered biological weapons

---

[4] Cotton is genetically engineered to kill insects. A majority of processed foods contain one or more of the following as ingredients which may be derived from genetically engineered crops: corn, soybeans and canola.

[5] Rice "Mystery" Illustrates Potential for Food Contamination with Unapproved, Genetically Altered Crops.
http://www.ucsusa.org/food_and_agriculture/science_and_impacts/impacts_genetic_engineering/rice-contamination-a-mystery.html Last accessed June 2011.

[6] Kapuscinski A R, Hallerman E M: Transgenic Fish and Public Policy: Anticipating Environmental Impacts of Transgenic Fish. Fisheries 15 (1):2–11, January 1990.

[7] Ingham E: Ecological Balance and Biological Integrity. Good Intentions and Engineering Organisms that Kill Wheat. Synthesis/Regeneration. 18 /Winter 1999.
http://www.greens.org/s-r/18/18-14.html Last accessed June 2011.

[8] Mellon M, Rissler,J: Environmental Effects of Genetically Modified Food Crops -- Recent Experiences
http://www.ucsusa.org/food_and_agriculture/science_and_impacts/impacts_genetic_engineering/environmental-effects-of.html Last accessed June 2011.

[9] Risks of Genetic Engineering
http://www.ucsusa.org/food_and_agriculture/science_and_impacts/impacts_genetic_engineering/risks-of-genetic-engineering.html Last accessed June 2011.

would pose a very serious threat to global security. Additionally, agroterrorism through sabotage of non-modified crops in an effort to promote pest and herbicide resistant products, is a distinct possibility.

Potential Adverse Effects on Human Health

Absence of a strict GE product labeling requirement raises human health concerns in the form of unexpected allergic reactions, toxins, and antibiotic resistance.[10,11,12] For example, foods using GE products may contain genes from substances known to be associated with allergy.[13] Reports indicate an increase in childhood allergies over the past decade.[14] Although that is probably coincidental, it parallels the increasing use of GE products in foods. In the absence of appropriate labeling, the unsuspecting consumer may be at risk.

Gene Therapy

Genes are carried on chromosomes and consist of DNA sequences with specific encoded instructions on how to make specific substances that regulate body functions. If a gene is defective or altered, the encoded instructions result in the production of abnormal proteins that are unable to carry out their normal functions. The goal of gene therapy is to attempt correction of the loss of function caused by a

---

[10] About 12 million Americans and up to 4 % of US children have allergy to commonly eaten foods.

[11] Kraft Recalls Biotech Taco Shells.
http://abcnews.go.com/Health/story?id=117944&page=1
Safeway Recalls it's Taco Shells.
http://articles.cnn.com/2000-10-12/health/safeway.taco.shells_1_taco-shells-starlink-taco-bell?_s=PM:FOOD   Last accessed June 2011.

[12] GE uses an *antibiotic resistance gene* as marker to identify success of gene transfer. Cells that do not take up the transferred DNA are killed by antibiotic treatment. *The Rest Of The Story Behind Genetic Engineering.* An interview with Brian Tokar by M Oshinskie. http://online.sfsu.edu/%7Erone/GEessays/tokarinterview.htm Last accessed June 2011.

[13] Nordlee JA, Taylor SL, Townsend JA, et al: Identification of a Brazil-Nut Allergen in Transgenic Soybeans. New Engl J Med 334 (11):688-692,1996.

[14] Food Allergies increased by 18% among U. S. children. Those with food allergies were also at higher risk for asthma, other respiratory problems and skin allergies. Branum AM, Lukacs SL: Food allergy among US children: Trends in Prevalence and Hospitalizations. NCHS Data Brief, No. 10, October 2008.
http://www.cdc.gov/nchs/data/databriefs/db10.htm Last accessed June 2011.

defective or missing gene by inserting normally functioning or *corrected* genes. This can be accomplished by using a carrier (often a virus) to deliver the new genes into the cells. These carriers (also called vectors) are injected into the patient in need of such therapy. Another way is to use therapeutic cloning on a sample of the patient's cells which are then returned to the patient.

Gene therapy for somatic cell diseases is being evaluated for application in single gene defects such as cystic fibrosis, hemophilia, muscular dystrophies and sickle cell disease. It may have potential application in some forms of inherited blindness and deafness, treatment of acquired diseases such as ischemic cardiovascular diseases, hematological and other cancers.[15] Treatment of inherited diseases associated with germ line cells has also been considered, ie., the replacement of defective genes responsible for the transmission of disease to offspring. The latter would alter the genetic pool of future generations. Presently, gene therapy is considered experimental.

Stem Cell Research

Stem cells are undifferentiated cells that have the capability for developing into specialized body cells. There are two main types, embryonic and adult stem cells.

Embryonic Stem Cells

The existence of embryonic stem cell is transient and occurs during the early phase of the development of the embryo. These cells possess the capability of maturing into all types of body tissues. Embryonic stem cells are extracted from the inner cell mass of the fertilized egg (human pro-embryo) after about five days (blastocyst stage). Usually several embryos are produced during in vitro fertilization (IVF) procedures. Embryos that are not implanted are either cryopreserved, destroyed or become the source for stem cells.

Adult Stem Cells

Also known as somatic stem cells, these are self-renewing cells that

---

[15] Bainbridge JWB, Smith AJ, Barker SS, et al: Effect of Gene Therapy on Visual Function in Leber's Congenital Amaurosis. N Engl J Med (2008), 358(21):2231-2239.

exist in all body tissues and produce the cell lineage of the tissue (or organ) in which they are located. They are used for the replacement of aging and damaged cells of that particular tissue type. Sources of adult stem cells include bone marrow, peripheral blood, small blood vessel wall pericytes and skin. Their acquisition is inefficient. Therefore, newer approaches are being used to *induce* adult cells into behaving like embryonic cells (induced pluripotent stem cells) by manipulating genes through viruses and other methods that *reprogram* adult cells (reprogrammed adult cells).

Potential uses of Stem Cells

The potential use of stem cells includes the generation of cell lines for researching diseases and treatments, eg., to test the effectiveness and safety of new drugs and treatments, production of individually tailored organ specific cells for replacement of damaged or diseased tissue (eg., liver, pancreas, brain, heart muscle, etc). This would potentially bypass problems resulting from organ shortages and transplant rejection.

Other potential uses include insulin producing cells for Type I diabetes, treatment of certain autoimmune diseases (multiple sclerosis, systemic lupus erythematosus, rheumatoid arthritis, systemic sclerosis), chronic vascular diseases (including coronary and cerebrovascular diseases), cardiomyopathy and spinal cord injury.

Cloning

Cloning is a biotechnological process which duplicates biological material. A process of naturally occurring asexual reproduction is observed in bacteria, fungi, insects, certain species of vertebrates and plants.[16] This naturally occurring asexual reproduction or duplication occurs without a known extrinsic stimulus or initiating factor. On the other hand, cloning in biotechnological laboratories is the result of human intervention and should not be equated with the naturally occurring process. Several terms are used to describe the cloning procedures, often resulting in a confusing mix of terminology.

---

[16] Agametogenesis, duplication of an organism without a male, vegetative reproduction. It is also referred to as *parthenogenesis* or *of virgin origin*.

Molecular Cloning

Also known as recombinant DNA technology, DNA cloning, and gene cloning, it refers to the process of making multiple copies of a defined DNA sequence. DNA fragment that is to be replicated is transferred to a self-replicating genetic sequence in a cloning vector (a carrier molecule).[17] This new DNA (recombinant DNA molecule) is then inserted into into suitable host cells for duplication. Recombinant DNA technology finds its use in the production of drugs, vaccines, research and gene therapy.

Reproductive Cloning

Also known as ordinary cloning, it is used to make a genetic twin of another organism. Genetic material from the nucleus of a donor adult cell (somatic cell) is transferred to an egg that has had its nucleus removed. The egg is transferred into a surrogate uterus once it begins to divide normally after being stimulated. This process is also known as somatic cell nuclear transfer (SCNT) and produces animals that are close genetic copies of the donor.[18] Since it was first reported, this process has been used to clone several species including frog, fish, mice, rabbit, cat, goat, sheep, cattle, pig, monkey, horse and dog.[19,20] Identical human twins have also erroneously been referred to as clones. As noted above, cloning does not occur naturally and is a procedure that requires external assistance. There have been some reports of alleged human cloning but proof has not been made available. Anticipated applications of cloning include creating genetically altered animals to serve as study models for human diseases, genetic engineered animals (eg., cows and sheep) for the production of drugs (Pharming) and for food.

---

[17] Cloning vectors that are used to carry the foreign DNA include bacterial plasmids, viruses, bacteria and yeast artificial chromosomes, and cosmids. Bacteria are often used as host cells for recombinant DNA molecules.

[18] Such clones are not strictly identical because of the presence of mitochondrial DNA in the host cell.

[19] Briggs R, King TJ: Transplantation of living nuclei from blastula cells into enucleated frogs' eggs. Proc Natl Acad Sci USA 38:455-463,1952.

[20] Campbell KHS, McWhir J,Ritchie WA, et al. Sheep cloned by nuclear transfer from cultured cell line. Nature 380:64-66,1996.

Therapeutic Cloning

This is a type of stem cell therapy that utilizes SCNT. Its goal is to grow biologically compatible tissues and organs for use in humans. Healthy adult cells (usually from the skin) taken from a patient have the DNA extracted and inserted into a donor egg that has had its own nucleus removed. These cells are stimulated to divide, forming an embryo (blastocyst). The stem cells from this blastocyst are removed, cultured and induced to differentiate into mature cell types required for transplantation to treat diseased tissues and organs. Since these cells are copies the patient's own cells, they match for transplantation.

Problems associated with Cloning

Presently, reproductive cloning is inefficient and expensive. Cloned animals have multiple problems such as compromised immune function, high infection rates, tumors, developmental abnormalities (from genome dysfunction), placental, respiratory, digestive, cardiovascular, neural and musculoskeletal abnormalities, as well as increased rates of mortality and deformities at birth.

An embryo created through a natural union of sperm and egg gets working copies of genes from both parents. *Imprinting* is a process through which genes from the either the mother or father are chemically marked so that there is only one active copy (either from the mother or father) and the other is epigenetically silenced. Imprinting is a normally occurring process. However, improper imprinting may result in two active or two silenced copies which may then cause severe abnormalities, including tumors.

In uniparental disomy, the offspring receives two copies of a chromosome from one parent and none from the other. In such cases imprinting, may silence an essential gene with resulting loss of gene function also leading to developmental abnormalities and other medical issues. Both uniparental disomy and errors in genomic imprinting are responsible for certain genetic disorders. Examples are the Prader-Willi, Angelman and Beckwith-Wiedemann Syndromes.

Defects related to the genetic imprinting process in the donor cell are the likely cause of some of the developmental abnormalities seen in cloned embryos. Some abnormalities manifest early while others of hitherto undetermined seriousness may show up later, and in either case, they have the potential to be passed on to future generations. This *imprinting* highlights the molecular/submolecular level intricacies associated with reproduction and the importance of mechanisms that safeguard the natural process which cloning attempts to replace.

Cloning Animals for Food

Cloning of animals for food and dairy production utilizes the SCNT process. As noted, cloned animals have demonstrated multiple problems and reports indicate, that despite an exhaustive search for possible causes, there are few clues. Animals that survive the first few months after birth, *appear* to be normal. Food safety evaluation studies have looked at numerous known parameters (from genes to hormone levels) and have reported not finding any abnormalities.[21]

Although some concerns about safety and ethics remain, food derived from cloned animals and their offspring has been declared as being as safe as other food.[22,23] Additionally, the U. S. Food and Drug Administration will not require mandatory labeling for clone-derived foods.

Synthetic Biology

This involves the application of engineering principles to biological research for the development of new biological systems utilizing genetic engineering technologies. It enables design and construction (synthesis) of new (artificial) biological systems [genomes, genetic circuits and metabolic pathways in cells and microorganisms (artificial

---

[21] Fox M: Long study led to U. S. cloned food safety decision. January 15, 2008.
http://www.reuters.com/article/2008/01/16/idUSN1553700520080116
Last accessed June 2011.

[22] The US FDA considers food derived from cloned animals to be safe for human consumption: *Meat and milk from cow, pig, and goat clones, and the offspring of any animal clones, are as safe as food we eat every day.* Furthermore such food does not require special labeling. FDA Consumer Health Information. January 15, 2008.
http://www.fda.gov/consumer/updates/cloning011508.pdf
Animal Cloning and Food Safety.
http://www.fda.gov/ForConsumers/ConsumerUpdates/ucm148768.htm

[23] Doering C: Timeline and facts about animal cloning. The U. S. Food and Drug Administration has ruled that milk and meat from certain cloned animals and their offspring are safe to eat. Last accessed June 2011.
http://www.reuters.com/article/2008/01/15/us-cloning-food-factbox-idUSN1551320720080115

genes)]. It also enables the redesign of naturally existing biological systems to modify behavior of organisms to perform specified tasks or for other, new purposes.

Applications of Synthetic Biology

Bioengineered microorganisms have many potentially useful applications. They may be able to process information, detect toxic chemicals, fabricate materials (eg., pharmaceuticals), produce energy (biofuels), break down environmental pollutants, repair defective genes, and seek and destroy cancer cells.[24]

Potential Adverse Effects of Synthetic Biology

Risks associated with this technology include unintended harmful effects on human health and environment. There is also the possibility of deliberate misuse, ie., development of synthetic organisms designed to produce toxins, resynthesis of known pathogens (eg., Ebola, smallpox, polio, Spanish influenza viruses, etc) or the creation of new, specifically designed and more virulent biological agents.[25,26,27,28,29] Additionally, the economic impact on developing nations that depend upon production and export of materials which may be laboratory manufactured as a result of Synthetic Biology, cannot be discounted.

---

[24] Ro D-K, Paradise EM, Ouellet M, et al., Production of the antimalarial drug precursor artemisinic acid in engineered yeast. Nature 2006: 440, 940-943.

[25] Wheelis M: Will the New Biology Lead to New Weapons? Arms Control Today (July/August 2004), http://www.armscontrol.org/act/2004_07-08/Wheelis.asp Last accessed June 2011.

[26] In 2002, synthesis of the infectious polio virus was reported. Cello J, Paul AV, Wimmer E: Chemical synthesis of polio virus cDNA: Generation of infectious virus in the absence of natural template. Science 2002: 297 (no. 5583),1016-1018.

[27] In 2005, the Spanish influenza virus that was responsible for the 1918-19 pandemic (over 50 million deaths) was reconstructed by collaborative effort of the Centers for Disease Control and Prevention, Armed Forces Institute of Pathology, Department of Agriculture (USDA), and Mt. Sinai School of Medicine. Tumpey TM, Basler CF, Aguilar PV, et al.: Characterization of the Reconstructed 1918 Spanish Influenza Pandemic Virus. Science 2005: 310 (no. 5745), 77-80.

[28] Security fears as flu virus that killed 50 million is recreated. Last accessed June 2011. http://www.guardian.co.uk/society/2005/oct/06/health.medicineandhealth3 Shreeve J. Why Revive a Deadly Flu Virus? January 29, 2006 http://www.nytimes.com/2006/01/29/magazine/29flu Last accessed June 2011.

[29] Wimmer E: The test-tube synthesis of a chemical called polio virus. The simple synthesis of a virus has far-reaching societal implications. http://www.nature.com/embor/journal/v7/n1s/full/7400728.html

Chapter Nineteen

Bioengineering
An Islamic Perspective

Knowledge as the Basis for Understanding

... Can those who know and those who do not know ever be equal ?
But only they who are endowed with insight keep this in mind.
(Surah 39, Az Zumar, ayat 9)

The pursuit of knowledge is an obligation for every Muslim. It is only knowledge that brings the understanding of the beauty and wonders of Creation and it is only through knowledge and understanding that a person draws closer to God. As a religion whose basis is knowledge, Islam promotes the sciences and encourages research. At the same time, Islam seeks to preserve life, human health and well-being and seeks to avoid harm, particularly one that is self-inflicted (purposeful or unintentional). Therefore, it restricts research and the application of scientific knowledge to beneficial uses. The Qur'an states:

Spend your wealth for the cause of Allah, and do not cast yourselves into ruin by your own hands, and do good. For Allah loves those who do good.
(Surah 2, Al Baqarah, ayat 195)

Harmony with Scientific Advancements

The question at the heart of this discussion is whether such research and its applications are permissible under Shari'ah? To make this determination, all issues are evaluated in light of the sources of Shari'ah: the Qur'an, Sunnah of Prophet Muhammad ﷺ, Ijma' and Ijtihaad. The key to permissibility under the Shari'ah is *do no harm* and *weigh the potential benefits (good) against the harmful effects*. Thus, the issues of safety and of fairness towards others become pertinent. The latter includes all of creation that inhabits the universe and also the environment.

The Shari'ah is flexible, living and adaptable to all times. In the context of scientific research, its objective is to create a fair and healthy balance between the benefits and harms by facilitating the former and curtailing the latter. This role gains particular significance because of the numerous remarkable advancements in biological and biomedical research. It fulfills its objectives using the following reasoning:[1]

- A true necessity is not bound by any laws
- Avoiding a harm has priority over a potential benefit
- A harm of lesser intensity is acceptable if it can avoid a greater harm
- An individual harm is acceptable if it can avoid harming the general public
- Harm should neither be inflicted nor reciprocated
- The end does not justify the means and
- If the means is prohibited, it must be avoided
- The strictness of the rules is relaxed to accommodate cases of bona-fide necessity or hardship

A means that is prohibited must be avoided. However, under certain circumstances, exceptions are permitted. This is in keeping with the compassionate basic principles of Islam which aim to preserve meaningful life. Each new situation is addressed individually, with due consideration of the immediate as well as the long term

---

[1] Al-Qara Daaghi AM: Gene Therapy: Islamic Rules and Regulations. (http://www.islamonline.net/servlet/Satellite?pagename=IslamOnlineEnglishAsk_Scholar/FatwaE/FatwaE&cid=1119503545702) 12 December 2004.

benefits and detrimental effects. The determination of permissibility is made by the Shari'ah scholars working in conjunction with experts in the respective fields.[2]

Harnessing Resources

O mankind, eat of that which is lawful and wholesome (tayyib)[3] on the earth, and do not follow the footsteps of the devil, for he is indeed an avowed enemy to you. (Surah 2, Al Baqarah, ayat 168)

Humans have been making changes to virtually everything they could in order to harness and maximally utilize resources. Since all things in the universe were placed at the service of man, it follows that developments and changes that enhance beneficial utility cannot be considered a deviation from proper use.[4] However, there have been deviations from the *lawful and wholesome* in the utilization of resources and knowledge. Examples include the development, and in some cases also the use, of weapons of mass destruction (including thermonuclear, chemical, biological and electromagnetic).

With the foregoing in mind, there is nothing in the Qur'an or the sunnah that specifically prohibits the development and beneficial utilization of biotechnology. Since there exists the possibility for countless applications, subversion for illicit or harmful uses is a distinct possibility. Consequently, no blanket statement has been issued by learned Islamic scholars and they recommend that each issue be evaluated individually, with analysis of its benefits, potential risks and established harms.

Before discussing some of the issues associated with biotechnology and the consequences of their applications, attention is drawn to the the following verses from the Qur'an which essentially predict events

---

[2] *Mujtahid* is a Muslim jurist who is qualified to interpret the law (to deduce Islamic rulings from the primary sources of Shari'ah using his own independent reasoning) and thus generate an *ijtihaad*.

[3] *tayyib* means wholesome, good, agreeable, healthy.

[4] Surah 31, Luqman, ayat 20: *Do you not see that God has subjected to your use all things in the heavens and on earth and has made His bounties flow to you in exceeding measure, both seen and unseen?*

that may be unfolding:

> ... *Satan, the persistent rebel. Whom Allah cursed, and he said: I will take an appointed portion of your servants. And I will mislead them, and I will entice them by vain desires and I will command them and they will slit the cattle's ears,[5] and I will command them and they will change and corrupt Allah's creation (change the nature created by Allah). And whoever takes Satan for a friend instead of Allah has surely suffered a manifest loss. He promises them and stirs up desires in them and Satan promises them only to deceive. For such people, their dwelling place will be Hell, and they will find no escape therefrom.* (Surah 4, An Nisa', ayaat 117-121)

Genetic Engineering

Safety of bioengineered products should be of concern to all as materials used to facilitate repair and regeneration of all body cells (including those responsible for reproduction) are derived from consumed products which have been exposed to the environment. If bioengineered substances are incorporated into genetic material and passed on to subsequent generations, it may alter the existing natural biological makeup. Whether the effects will be detrimental, beneficial or just tolerated through an adaptation process, can only be assessed in later generations through unbiased, independent studies.

Even at the intracellular level, God created a delicate balance through interaction of various enzymes and chemicals that exist in minute quantities. Removing one segment of DNA (deoxyribonucleic acid) and replacing it with a different one (as is the case in genetic engineering) invariably alters that delicate and often fragile balance. The endowed ability to adapt may well compensate for the changes. However, technology and scientific knowledge have not advanced to the level where subtle alterations in all interactions and reactions resulting from genetic manipulation can be identified and the impact accurately assessed. Thus, the effects of altering DNA may not become apparent during a relatively short observation period.

There are also environmental concerns. Produce that spoils, does so under the influence of numerous microorganisms. This is essentially

---

[5] This refers to a practice among the pre-Islamic Arabs. Small cuts were made in the ears of certain animals as a distinguishing mark for dedication to various deities.

a process of composting which returns elements back to nature through a series of natural biological cycles. These involve other living creatures who benefit from the process. In addition, it contributes to the ecologic balance. Food that does not decay interrupts those natural phenomena. Many of the genetically engineered products no longer depend upon insects for pollination and may be engineered to kill or repel insects, disrupting naturally occurring cycles. However, God had endowed living creatures with remarkable adaptability which may minimize many detrimental effects.

Genetically engineered seed may have a *terminator gene*. Unlike natural seed which can be replanted to grow crops, the genetically engineered seed is for one time use, compelling the farmer to buy new seed each season. This creates financial hardships for farming families. In India, this has been linked to a very high suicide rate amongst farmers.

With some known rare exceptions,[6] genetically engineered food products that have been allowed on the market have not shown short-term safety concerns. Long-term effects, if any, remain to be determined. Benefits vary with the type of product and are said to include a longer shelf-life, improved taste, increased nutritional value, higher crop yields, disease resistance, etc.

Biomedical products such as those used in diagnosis and therapy (insulin, TPA, etc) have generally been very beneficial with little or no harmful effects. Consequently, based on currently available information, medical applications of genetical engineering have been approved by Muslim jurists.[7] As newer products and therapeutic applications become available, permissibility of use for each one of them will need to be assessed individually. While this approach may appear restrictive, it provides an opportunity for the efficacy and safety of a product or therapy to be established before permitting its use in the general population.

Agricultural applications of genetic engineering are permissible as long as they are beneficial to humans and do not pose a hazard to the

---

[6] Nordlee JA, Taylor SL, Townsend JA, et al: Identification of a Brazil-Nut Allergen in Transgenic Soybeans. New Engl J Med 334 (11):688-692,1996.

[7] Al Qaradawi Y: How Does Islam View Genetic Engineering? http://infad.usim.edu.my/modules.php?op=modload&name=News&file=article&sid= 10276&mode=thread&order=0&thold=0 Last accessed June 2011.

present and also subsequent generations of humans, animals, other living creatures and the environment. Laboratory experiments, also on animals, are permitted if they are intended to provide information that may benefit humans.

Gene Therapy

Gene Therapy is approved by Muslim jurists as long as it remains within the limits established by Shari'ah.[8,9] Accordingly, is should benefit the individual by preventing a disease, mitigating the effects of disease or provide a cure and inflict no harm. Restoration of altered genes or treatment of a genetic defect responsible for significant physical or psychological suffering is also permitted.[10] Prohibited is gene therapy that aims to alter the whole body or one or more body parts such as changes in appearance and/or color. Similarly, gene therapy to effect changes in offspring is prohibited. This latter ruling is subject to reconsideration as additional research results become available and the absence of ill effects of such therapy are established.

Below are excerpts from the statement issued at the conclusion of the seminar *Genetics, Genetic Engineering, the Human Genes, and Genetic Treatment - An Islamic Perspective:*[11]

The outcome and the conclusion from such research should not, however, find their way into implementation before having considered in the light of Islamic legal principles and so long as they do not violate these principles they should be permitted. Genetic science and all its ramifications are, like any other field of knowledge, encouraged and supported by Islam, and Muslim scientists should be at the forefront of research and inquiry in this field. Furthermore, treatment is specifically urged by Islam for hereditary

---

[8] Al-Qara Daaghi AM: Gene Therapy: Islamic Rules and Regulations. (http://www.islamonline.net/servlet/Satellite?pagename=IslamOnline-English-Ask_Scholar/FatwaE/FatwaE&cid=1119503545702) 12 December 2004.

[9] Al Qaradawi Y: How Does Islam View Genetic Engineering? http://infad.usim.edu.my/modules.php?op=modload&name=News&file=article&sid=10276&mode=thread&order=0&thold=0 Last accessed June 2011.

[10] 15th session of The Islamic Fiqh Academy (IFA) of the Organization of the Islamic Conference (OIC) 11 Rajab 1419 AH (31 October 1998 CE).

[11] Genetics, Genetic Engineering, the Human Genes, and Genetic Treatment - An Islamic Perspective. 23-25 Jumada al-Akhirah 1419 AH (13-15 October 1998). http://www.islamset.org/bioethics/genetics/index.html Last accessed June 2011.

as well as acquired diseases and ailments. This in no way conflicts with the Islamic teachings of perseverance and acceptance of God's will. Genetic engineering should not be used on germ cells, due to certain reservations from the Islamic legal point of view.

Embryonic Stem Cell Use and Research[12,13]

Permissibility of harvesting embryonic stem cell for research and disease treatment depends upon whether, at this given stage of development, the embryo is considered a person. Islam permits in-vitro fertilization (IVF) where the embryo initially develops outside the uterus.[14] Without intrauterine implantation, its chances of survival and developing into a person are nil. At the stage of development when stem cells are harvested, the Shari'ah does not assign the embryo the status of a person.[15]

Hence, stem cells derived from surplus embryos (from IVF) may be used for research directed towards finding treatments and cures for human diseases. Some scholars consider it be an obligation (*fard kifayah*) to pursue such research with the goal of alleviating human suffering.[16] This ruling is restricted to the use of those embryos which were developed specifically for IVF and would otherwise be destroyed. It also requires donor consent for use in research and requires safeguards against creation of excessive numbers of embryos with the intention of using them for research. Donor compensation is prohibited.

---

[12] Siddiqi M: Stem Cell Research in Shari`ah Perspective.
http://infad.usim.edu.my/modules.php?op=modload&name=News&file=article&sid=9785&mode=thread&order=0&thold=0   Last accessed June 2011.

[13] Human Genetic and Reproductive Technologies: Comparing Religious and Secular Perspectives. 6-9 February 2006, Cairo, Egypt.
http://www.islamset.org/ioms/cairo2006/index.html Last accessed June 2011.

[14] For the rules governing use of IVF see Chapter Fifteen: Reproductive Issues: Infertility, Assisted Reproduction, and Surrogacy

[15] Had the embryo been considered a human being at this stage of development, the production of only one embryo would have been permitted as the destruction of superfluous embryos would have been prohibited. Siddiqi M: Stem Cell Research in Shari'ah Perspective. See footnote 12.

[16] Siddiqi M: Stem Cell Research in Shari'ah Perspective.
http://infad.usim.edu.my/modules.php?op=modload&name=News&file=article&sid=9785&mode=thread&order=0&thold=0   Last accessed June 2011.

Cloning Issues

Verses in the Qur'an are explicit about the origins of creation and of humans. The latter were created from a single pair of a male and a female,[17,18] through the mingling of the male and female fluids[19] and the embryo/fetus rests and develops in a womb.[20,21] Additionally, it is only God who produces and reproduces the individual.[22] It is also known from the Qur'an, that man will follow Satan's promptings and cause changes in God's creation:

> ... and I will command them and they will change and corrupt Allah's creation (change the nature created by Allah).
>
> (Surah 4, An Nisa', ayat 119)

The phrase ...change and corrupt Allah's creation or change the nature created by Allah (fala yughayyi runna khalq allahi) has been interpreted differently, each addressing a particular aspect of creation. According to Ibn Kathir, it refers to changing the Fitrah, the intrinsic pure faith (belief in the Oneness of God, ie., Islamic monotheism) into which God has created mankind.[23] The meaning of changing the Fitrah would include deviating from the path of true faith because of worldly allurements. Another interpretation is that it refers to alterations, for the purpose of making wrong and improper use of things against human nature and against their natural functions.[24]

---

[17] Surah 4, An Nisa', ayat 1: O mankind! Reverence your Guardian Lord Who created you from a single soul (nafsin wahida) and from it created its mate of like nature (minha) and from the two of them spread countless men and women ...
Surah 53, An Najm, ayat 45: And that He created the two spouses, the male and the female.

[18] Surah 78, An Naba, ayat 8: And We have created you in pairs.

[19] Surah 76, Al Insan, ayat 2: We create man from a drop of mingled fluid... The mingled fluid (amsaj) refers to the composition of the ejaculate and the mixing of the male and female fluids carrying the gametes which facilitates fertilization.

[20] Surah 23, Al Mu'minoon, ayat 13: Then placed him as a drop of seed in a safe lodging (in a place of rest firmly fixed).

[21] Surah 39, Az Zumar, ayat 6: ... He created you in the wombs of your mothers, in stages, one after another, in three veils of darkness.

[22] Surah 85, Al Buruj, ayat 13: He it is Who produces, then reproduces.

[23] Tafsir ibn Kathir. Al-Firdous Ltd., London, 2000. Part 5, pages 179-182.

[24] Maududi SAA: The Meaning of the Qur'an. Islamic Publications Ltd., Lahore, Pakistan. 1976. Volume II, pages 164-167.

Islam prohibits human cloning.[25] According to Sheikh Al Qaradawi:[26] cloning *contradicts the diversity of creation* as *Allah has created the universe on the base of diversity.* Human cloning only replicates the characteristics of the original. In addition, cloning *contradicts the pattern of creating things in pairs* since it depends only on one gender. While the use of whole body cloning is prohibited, utilization of cloning techniques for the treatment of organ specific disorders (eg., of the heart, kidney, liver) is not only permitted but recommended. The use of cloned infants as a source for transplant organs is prohibited.

Muslim scholars are unanimous about the negative social implications of human cloning including confused parentage and confused family relationships, inheritance issues, and other psychological and social problems.[27] While prohibiting human cloning, Muslim scholars concluded that cloning was permissible in microbes, plants and animals, as long as it was for beneficial uses and did not violate the Shari'ah. The Islamic Organization for Medical Sciences at the 9th Fiqh-Medical Seminar in Casablanca, Morocco (1997), provided the following statement:[28]

> Islam imposes no restrictions on scientific research, but considers it a religious duty and encourages it as a means of understanding God's traditions in His creation. However, Islam advocates that the doors of scientific study should not be left wide open for the application of the results of research in the public domain without proper examination by Shari'ah experts. Not everything that is practicable is necessarily applicable, but should be free of any harmful effects and in line with the rules of Shari'ah. Since some of the untoward effects do not become apparent until some time later, it is important to give full consideration and adequate time to the issues involved and take all possible precautions.

---

[25] Islamic Fiqh Academy. Tenth Session, Jeddah, Saudi Arabia. 23-25 Safar AH (28 June-3 July 1997,CE). Resolution N° 100/2/10 on Human Cloning, pp 209-214.

[26] Al Qaradawi Y: Cloning and Its Dangerous Impacts. 29 December, 2002. http://infad.usim.edu.my/modules.php?op=modload&name=News&file=article&sid=10553&mode=thread&order=0&thold=0   Last accessed June 2011.

[27] Cloned individuals would not have a father or mother in the traditional sense.

[28] An Islamic View of Certain Contemporary Medical Issues. Islamic Organization for Medical Sciences 9th Fiqh Medical Seminar, Casablanca, Morocco. 8–11 Safar, 1418 AH (14–17 June 1997 CE). http://www.islamset.org/bioethics/9thfiqh.html

Concluding Summary

And of mankind there is he whose conversation on the life of this world
pleases you (Muhammad), and he calls Allah to witness as to that which
is in his heart; [29] *yet he is the most rigid of opponents.*
And when he turns away (from you) his effort in the land is to make
mischief therein and to destroy the crops and the cattle; and Allah does
not like mischief.   (Surah 2, Al Baqarah, ayaat 204-205)

In keeping with its responsibility as lawgiver and caretaker, Shari'ah
establishes basic principles from which rulings are derived. With
respect to scientific research and its applications, Islam imposes no
restrictions as long as its purpose is beneficial but requires that results
be scrutinized by Shari'ah scholars before being permitted for
application. Key determinants of permissibility are that the application
of research and its products be devoid of harmful effects (for the
consumer and environment) and the benefits must outweigh the
harmful effects. Additionally, the process must be permissible (as
determined by Shari'ah) because the end result does not justify the
means.

In the context of modern research and permissibility of its
application, one of the many notable features of the Islamic faith and
the Shari'ah is highlighted. At the time when the Shari'ah laws were
established, no person had any clue (perhaps with the exception of the
Prophet of God, Muhammad ﷺ) as to the kinds of circumstances for
which it would be required to provide rulings. As questions dealing
with genetic engineering and cloning show, it provides practical and
logical rulings which seek to allow the maximal benefit to individuals
and society while prohibiting the harmful.

---

[29] *That he cherishes good intentions in his heart when in fact he is the deadliest opponent*
of the Truth. When he returns to everyday life, he directs all his efforts towards spreading
corruption in the land, destroying harvests and killing the human race...
Maududi SAA. The Meaning of the Qur'an. Islamic Publications Ltd., Lahore,
Pakistan, 1978. Volume I, pages 151-153.

IV. Contemporary Issues

Chapter Twenty

Common Islamic Terms
and their Meanings

Introduction

This chapter provides information about a few commonly used Islamic terms so that their true meanings and implications can be understood and put into proper context. This has become necessary because of the extensive media coverage Islam and Muslims have been receiving, frequently from sources with superficial or absent knowledge of Islam.

Islam is a comprehensive code of living based upon Divine Guidance. It includes the virtuous beliefs and codes of virtuous social conduct that may be found in other Abrahamic Traditions. While it incorporates rules to guide all aspects of human conduct, Islam is not embodied in any human form. Consequently, Islam is not responsible for any untoward acts committed by individuals professing this faith. This reasoning follows the same logic that the responsibility for undesirable or criminal acts perpetrated by individuals of Hindu, Christian, Jewish or other persuasions cannot be placed upon their respective faiths.

The basic message of Islam is very simple: believe in One God, shun evil and indulge in good deeds. Human nature is diverse and motivation is frequently nurtured by circumstances. What leads a person to an act of goodness or what motivates another to evil and violence is very individual, even in an ethnically and racially homogeneous society.

Common Islamic Terms

Arafat

Arafat is a plain which lies about twenty kilometers southeast of Makkah, Arabia. During Haj, all pilgrims gather here on the ninth day of the month of Dhul Hijjah. This day is considered the crowning point of the pilgrimage as God has promised to answer the supplication of each and every person who is present.

One of the small hillocks bordering Arafat is known as *Jabal ar Rahmah* or the Mount of Mercy. While it carries no religious importance, this place has witnessed several significant historical events. It was here that Adam and Eve came down to earth after they were cast from Paradise. They were also on *Jabal ar Rahmah* when God forgave them. This was the place where Prophet Muhammad ﷺ delivered the Farewell Sermon (see Chapter 3, Muhammad ﷺ).

Also see under Haj and Umrah.

Ashura

This is the tenth day of Muharram, the first month of the Islamic calendar. Three events of major historical importance occurred on this day. The Ark of Nuh ؑ (Noah) rested upon the mountain as the flood waters receded and Musa ؑ (Moses) crossed the sea ahead of the pursuing armies of the Pharaoh. In commemoration of the latter event, Muslims are encouraged to fast two consecutive days (the tenth and either the ninth or eleventh of Muharram) as a token of gratitude to Allah for delivering Moses ؑ and his believing followers from the hardships imposed upon them by the Pharaoh.

This day also marks a very tragic event in Muslim history. Hussein ؓ, the grandson of the Prophet ﷺ, his family and other companions were martyred in Karbala (Iraq) on this day.

Fasting (*Sawm*) (also see under Ramadan)

During the month of Ramadan, fasting is obligatory for all adult

Muslims and children past puberty. Fasting is one of the Five Pillars of Islam together with the Shahadah, daily obligatory prayers, Zakat and Haj. Excused from fasting are those who have attained fragile old age, the sick, menstruating and nursing women, and travelers. With the exception of the elderly and chronically ill, all others must make up the missed days of fasting before the next Ramadan.

The fast begins before dawn and ends immediately after sunset. A predawn meal (*suhoor*) is encouraged. The fast is ended with *iftar* consisting of water or dates or a light snack and supper is partaken after the Maghrib prayer. Each night, there are extraordinary congregational prayers (*tarawih*). Eid ul Fitr is celebrated upon completion of the month of fasting.

Purpose of Fasting

Fasting during the month of Ramadan, for the expiation of some sinful actions or neglect is by Divine injunction. It is by no means unique to Islam as it was also prescribed for the followers of other prophets:

> ... *fasting is prescribed for you as it was prescribed for those before you that you may become al mutaqoon.*[1] (Surah 2, Al Baqarah, ayat 183)

There are two aspects to the Muslim Fast. It induces self-discipline and facilitates self-purification. A part of the former is the physical self-restraint, ie., abstaining from food, drink, smoking and sexual activity.[2] The other is spiritual. The fasting person must exercise patience and self-control in all affairs including business dealings, language and actions, no matter how insignificant these may appear.

Since the month of Ramadan brings immense blessings, actions that provide maximal benefit are encouraged. This includes all good deeds, spiritual devotion, charity, socially beneficial activity, etc. Importantly, these actions and activities serve as an initial exercise for maintaining such behavior throughout the year, as an ongoing effort for self-improvement. Fasting without observing the spiritual aspects is

---

[1] May acquire *taqwa*, ie., piety, self-restraint.

[2] Islam prohibits extramarital sex and homosexuality.

meaningless.[3]

There are also several non-obligatory fasts. These represent either the Sunnah of Prophet Muhammad ﷺ or of other prophets ﷺ. The sole purpose of observing these fasts is that of seeking God's pleasure, forgiveness and protection.[4] Fasting may also be used as expiation for breaking a promise.

Fatwa

This constitutes an independent opinion given by a learned Islamic scholar on a religious or other matter. A fatwa is sought for unusual situations where a solution cannot be found through the regular methods provided by Shari'ah. It is a *personal opinion*. It does not constitute a religious ruling and there is no obligation to follow it. This is an important distinction because Shari'ah provides religious rulings which must be obeyed.

The principle source of guidance for Shari'ah is the Qur'an. If an answer to a question or solution to a problem cannot be found in the Qur'an, the Sunnah of Prophet Muhammad ﷺ (the Hadith) is searched. The third source is *ijma'* or opinion by consensus. It is a ruling based upon the *unanimous* opinion and practices of the companions of the Prophet ﷺ (the sahabah) and also the consensus of learned Muslim scholars after an in-depth study of the issues. The fourth source of guidance for the Shari'ah is *ijtihaad* or personal reasoning. This is an opinion of Muslim scholars derived in conformity with the Qur'an, Sunnah and Ijma'.

Also see Chapter 4, Islamic Law, Shari'ah and Fiqh.

Festivals and Holidays

Muslim festivals are both family and community oriented with a distinct social purpose. A spiritual event serves as the basis and is combined with social activities. To the casual observer, the festivities may appear conventional with food, fun, sporting events, games for children, etc., however, the purpose is to bring together people from

---

[3] Prophet Muhammad ﷺ said: *Whoever does not give up false words and deeds, Allah has no need for his giving up his food and drink.* Sunan Ibn Majah, Darussalaam, Riyadh, S Arabia, 2007. Volume 2, Hadith 1689, page 498.

[4] *Fasting is a shield against the Fire (Hell)...* Sunan Ibn Majah, Darussalaam, Riyadh.

all walks of life, without segregation. Such integration is an essential component of the Islamic social order where ethnicity, social or economic status play no role. In different countries, often local ethnic festive customs have been incorporated.

There are two main Islamic festivals: Eid ul Fitr and Eid ul Adha. The word Eid means to celebrate, day of feast, or festival. In addition to sharing the festivities with family and friends, provision has been made by Shari'ah, to extend the circle of joy and festivities to include the poor, needy and underprivileged.

Eid ul Fitr occurs on the first day of the month of Shawwal, the tenth month of the Islamic calendar. This commemorates the successful completion of Ramadan, the month of Fasting (ninth month of the Islamic calendar). A special one time tax becomes due every Ramadan. This is the zakat ul fitr. The amount is roughly equivalent to the cost of a simple meal.[5] It is due from every Muslim, irrespective of age and economic status. This money is collected during the month of Ramadan, and before the Eid, it is distributed among those in need so as to facilitate for them the joys of Eid.

Eid ul Adha (Festival of the sacrifice) occurs at the conclusion of the Haj, on the tenth day of the month of Dhul Hijjah. This event commemorates the sacrifice of Prophet Ibrahim (Abraham) and his son Ismail (peace be upon them).

As a test of faith, God commanded Ibrahim ﷺ to sacrifice his only son Ismail ﷺ.[6] Ibrahim ﷺ told Ismail ﷺ about the vision, to which the young child replied: *Do that which you are commanded. Inshallah, you shall find me of the steadfast.*[7] As Ibrahim ﷺ readied his son for the sacrifice by placing him face down, God revealed to him that he had already passed the test: *O Ibrahim! You have already fulfilled the vision...*[8] and he was told to sacrifice an animal.

Thus, on the day of Eid ul Adha, a lamb, goat or other animal is

---

[5] For 2011 in North America, the zakat ul fitr is between 8-10 US Dollars. Each year the amount is determined by religious scholars. It may vary with changing economic situations and locality.

[6] Issac ﷺ was born several years later.

[7] Surah 37, As Saffat, ayat 102.

[8] Surah 37, As Saffat, ayaat 104-105.

sacrificed.[9] The meat from the sacrificed animal is divided into three portions: one portion is given to the poor and needy to facilitate their joy and celebration. The second portion is either given to friends and/or relatives or it is served to them in the form of a cooked meal. The third portion may be retained by the family that sacrificed the animal.

Both Eids begin with an early morning congregational prayer which is followed by a short sermon. According to the tradition of the Prophet ﷺ, every Muslim should attend these services. The remainder of the day is spent with family and friends. The giving of gifts is traditional for Eid ul Fitr.

Haj and Umrah

... And pilgrimage to the House (Ka'ba) is a duty to Allah for mankind, for those who can afford the journey ... (Surah 3, 'Al Imraan, ayat 97)

Haj is the pilgrimage to the sacred places in and around Makkah. It is an annual event which occurs during the first ten days of the month of Dhul Hijjah, the twelfth month of the Islamic calendar. It is the fifth of the five basic tenets of Islam (also known as The Five Pillars) (see Chapter 1, Islam). It is a requirement that every adult Muslim perform Haj once during life, provided he/she can afford it (physically and financially). Like the sacrifice of Eid ul Adha, the Commandment for Haj was delivered through Prophet Ibrahim ﷺ: *And proclaim to mankind the pilgrimage.*[10]

In addition to being an extraordinary spiritual experience, Haj is a social event on a massive scale. During Haj, between two to three million Muslims come to Makkah from every corner of the globe and are integrated in a friction-free manner. Here, the common denominator is the singularity of faith and acceptance of the equality of mankind before God. The only thing that elevates one individual above another is piety (*taqwa*), not wealth, social standing nor secular education.

---

[9] Larger animals (eg., a cow) can be shared by several families. Islamic dietary laws prohibit consumption of pork and other pig derived products, animals and birds of prey.

[10] Surah 22, Al Haj, ayat 27.

Umrah is also called the lesser pilgrimage. This may be performed at any time of the year and there are no prerequisites like those for Haj (see below). For Umrah, only the first three steps listed below are required (*ihram, tawaf and sa'ee*).

Prerequisites for Haj

While Haj is an obligation, certain financial requirements must be fulfilled before one is permitted to embark upon this journey. In addition, certain social obligations take precedence. These are:

- The person intending to go for Haj must be able to afford the travel financially, as this may not be through borrowed money
- The person traveling for Haj must be free from debt and financial obligations as repayment of debts takes precedence
- Certain social matters also take precedence. Tending to the needs of older parents is a moral obligation for Muslims and takes precedence over going for Haj, even though the latter is was Divinely ordained

The following are the basic steps for Haj with an explanation of their significance:

- Donning the *ihram* before entering Makkah. *Ihram* refers to both a physical attire and also the spiritual state of preparedness for Haj and Umrah. For women, there is no specific dress other than the usual Islamic attire. For men, the *ihram* consists of two sheets of unstitched, opaque, white cloth. One piece is wrapped around the lower body while the second one covers the upper body. This cloth signifies simplicity. A similar cloth is used to shroud the dead body for burial.[11] During the state of *ihram*, hair or nails may not be cut. In addition, hunting, killing insects, cutting trees, shaving, use of perfume, and sexual activity are not permitted
- Once in Makkah, *Umrah* is performed at the Sacred Mosque (*Al Masjid al Haram*). This consists of circumambulating the Ka'ba seven times (*tawaf*), praying, and walking seven times

---

[11] For Muslim burial, stitched clothing (shirt, dress, suit, socks, etc) or shoes are not permitted.

between the two hillocks, Safa and Marwa (sa'ee)

- On the eighth day of Dhul Hijjah, the pilgrims proceed to Mina which is located about six kilometers from Makkah
- On the ninth day of Dhul Hijjah, the pilgrims proceed to Arafat which is located about twenty kilometers southeast of Makkah. After spending the day in Arafat, they proceed to Muzdalifah to spend the night. Muzdalifah is located about eight kilometers from Arafat
- The next morning (tenth day of Dhul Hijjah), they return to Mina. Here they cast pebbles at the Jamarat. These consist of three pillars erected at the sites where Satan attempted to dissuade Ibrahim and Ismail (peace be upon them) from obeying the Commandment to sacrifice Ismail (see under Festivals and Holidays, Eid ul Adha). Pebbles are cast at these three pillars, reenacting what was done by Ibrahim and Ismail (peace be upon them)
- The sacrifice of Eid ul Adha is performed (see under festivals), and upon completion of the Haj rites, men shave their heads (or trim the hair) and return to wearing regular clothing. Women trim about 1 cm length of hair. The pilgrims return to Makkah for tawaf and sa'ee. Before returning home, they usually travel to Madinah

During the days of Haj, the time is spent in prayer and other devotional activity. Additionally, learned scholars from all over the world present lectures on religious topics. There is also ample time for social activity which provides the unparalleled opportunity to interact with Muslims from all parts of the world. At the end of the Haj, if performed sincerely and in conformity with the rules, the person emerges purified of all previous sins, just like a newborn.

Imam

Imam means leader, spiritual and political. An imam is also the person who leads congregational prayers. During the early periods of Muslim rule, ie., of the early khalifahs, the Head of State was also the imam. Later, with growth of the Islamic Commonwealth, the khalifah retained duties of the Head of State and another individual assumed the role of spiritual leader, ie., that of the imam.

In the Shia tradition, the original concept of imam continues, ie., that of both a spiritual and political leader. In the Sunni traditions, today this designation is retained for a spiritual leader, an individual given the responsibility for religious matters in the community, Mosque, or religious institution. This position is assigned only to individuals with appropriate education and experience. Historically, all prophets were designated imams of their respective peoples.

Inshallah

This means *if Allah Wills*. This phrase is very commonly used, for in Muslim belief, nothing ever happens without the permission from God. The best of human plans cannot materialize without God's permission, therefore, every *halal* plan of action is prefaced with this phrase.[12] It also asserts an individual's subservience to the Will of God and dependence upon Him for the conduct of all affairs.

Isa (Jesus) ﷺ

Isa ﷺ is a revered prophet of Islam. Of all prophets and messengers, Jesus ﷺ brought an explicit message about the coming of the Final Messenger of God, Muhammad ﷺ (see Chapter 3, Muhammad ﷺ). In the Qur'an, Prophet Jesus and his mother Mary (peace be upon them) are described as a symbol of God's grace to all people (*ayaatal lil alameen*).[13] Muslims believe in the miraculous conception of Mary ﷺ,[14] however, Islam does not assign divine status to Jesus ﷺ.

The likeness of Jesus with Allah is as like the likeness of Adam. He created him of dust, then He said to him: Be! and he was.

(Surah 'Al Imraan, ayat 59)

---

[12] *Halal* indicates that which is permissible under the rules of Shari'ah.

[13] Surah 21, Al Anbiya', ayat 91. Isa ﷺ is referred to as *ayatal lin nas,* a sign or symbol to mankind in Surah 19, Maryam, ayat 21.

[14] Surah 19 of the Qur'an titled Maryam (Arabic for Mary), gives the description of Mary's ﷺ conception and the birth of Jesus ﷺ. The lifting of Jesus ﷺ to the heavens is described in Surah 4, An Nisa', ayaat 157-158.

The Messiah, son of Mary, was no other than a messenger, messengers
the like of whom had passed away before him. And his mother was a
saintly woman. And they both used to eat earthly food ...

(Surah 5, Al Ma'idah, ayat 75)

Islam

Islam is the complete submission to God. It is a way of life, a
complete and comprehensive *code of living (deen)*. It prescribes all
goodness and prohibits all evil. The word Islam is derived from *silm*
which means peace, to be safe, secure, protected from harm, and to
surrender.

Also see See Chapter 1, Islam.

Islamic Calendar and New Year

The Islamic calendar is based on the lunar cycle. There are twelve
months in the year. Each month has either twenty-nine or thirty days,
depending upon the lunar cycle. The total number of days in a lunar
year is 354. The emigration of Prophet Muhammad ﷺ from Makkah to
Madinah (*the Hijrah*) marks the beginning of the Islamic calendar. The
months are as follows: Muharram, Safar, Rabi' al Awwal, Rabi' al Thani,
Jumada al Awwal, Jumada al Thani, Rajab, Sha'ban, Ramadan, Shawwal,
Dhul Qa'dah, Dhul Hijjah. Four of these months are sacred:
Muharram, Rajab, Dhul Qa'dah, Dhul Hijjah.

Why do Muslims have a different calendar ?
The number of months with Allah is twelve (in a year). So ordained by
Him the day He created the heavens and the earth ...

(Surah 9, At Taubah, ayat 36)

While the wisdom behind the decision to use the lunar calendar is
known only to God as it is per His injunction, there are some obvious
practical benefits. This calendar is about 11 days shorter than the solar
(Julian) calendar which permits rotation of the months through the
seasons. Thus, with passage of time, the month of fasting (Ramadan)
and the Haj (Dhul Hijjah) occur during different seasons. If Ramadan
were to occur only during the summer months, the days would be

very long in regions that witness the midnight sun. Additionally, fasting would be very hard in hot climatic regions. The same also applies to Haj. If the Haj season were to occur only in the summer months, it would be very strenuous because of the hot summer temperatures in Arabia. With the lunar calendar, in some years the days in Ramadan will be long while in others they will invariably be shorter, providing equality for inhabitants of all regions.

Islamic New Year

The Islamic new year starts on a different date than the Christian or Jewish new year. Muharram is the first month of the Islamic calendar. Since the latter is a lunar calendar, each subsequent year, the months occur about 11 days earlier. New Year's day has no special significance in Islam other than it marks the beginning of the sacred month of Muharram.

Jesus 🕊

See under Isa 🕊

Jinn

Adam, the first human being, was created out of *potter's clay*. Eve was created from the body of Adam, thus giving all humans this singular origin (*nafsin wahida*). The Jinn were created from *smokeless fire*. Like humans, the Jinn possess intellectual abilities and a free will to determine individual paths. Furthermore, they have been endowed certain powers that far exceed those possessed by humans. Under normal circumstances, Jinn are not visible to the human eye. They may be seen by animals. One of the abilities of the Jinn is to transform themselves into human form. Like humans, they are male and female Jinns. Iblees (Satan) is from the Jinn.

Ka'ba

The Ka'ba is the first house on earth which was dedicated to the worship of the One and Only God of the universe. It was originally built by Adam and rebuilt by the Prophet Ibrahim 🕊, together with his first born son Ismail ﷺ.[15] It is a stone building located in Makkah, Arabia. This was about the site to which Ibrahim ﷺ brought his second wife Hajar (Hagar) and their infant son, Ismail. As people settled in the valleys around Makkah, the Ka'ba remained a center of worship. With the influx of pagans, dozens of idols were introduced into the sanctuary and remained there until the liberation of Makkah by Prophet Muhammad ﷺ in 8 AH (630 CE).

The Mosque which is built around the Ka'ba is called *Al Masjid al Haram*, which means the *sacred place of worship*. Together, the Ka'ba and this Mosque are the most sacred Muslim sanctuary. There are several other sacred places in the region which are visited during Haj. The second most sacred Muslim sanctuary is the Mosque of the Prophet ﷺ in Madinah, the *Masjid al Nabwi*. The Al Aqsa Sanctuary in Jerusalem which includes the Al Aqsa Mosque, the Al Buraq Wall and the Dome of the Rock Mosque (site of the Isra' and Miraj of the Prophet ﷺ) is the third most sacred sanctuary for Muslims.

Khalifah

The Arabic term *khalifah* means successor or deputy.[16] After the death of Prophet Muhammad ﷺ, the men who were elected to be Heads of State as his successors were called *Khalifat ur Rasoolillah (successors of the Messenger of Allah)*. The shortened title, *Khalifah* (Caliph), has subsequently found widespread use. This title carries a specific implication. It identifies the Head of State of an Islamic country who governs in accordance with the guidance provided by the Qur'an and Sunnah, ie., Shari'ah.

The four men elected to be khalifahs after the death of Prophet Muhammad ﷺ were also called the *ar rashidoon* (the Rightly Guided) and governed the Muslim Commonwealth from Madinah. These were: Abu Bakr as Siddiq ﷺ, Umar ibn al Khattab ﷺ, Uthman ibn Affan ﷺ, Ali ibn Abu Talib ﷺ. Thereafter, the center of governance shifted to Damascus with the Umayyad khalifahs and subsequently to Baghdad with the Abbassids. With the shift of the center of governance from Madinah, the khilafat (caliphate) saw a transformation into monarchy.

---

[15] The History of al-Tabari. SUNY Press Albany, NY, 1989. Volume 1, pages 216-217.

[16] The plural of *khalifah* is *khulafah*. For the sake of simplicity, *khalifahs* has been used.

The designation, *Rightly Guided,* stems from their commitment to continue governing in accordance with the rules and regulations established by Prophet Muhammad ﷺ. Since the death of the Prophet ﷺ had brought to an end all Divine guidance, all subsequent laws enacted by the *Rightly Guided* khalifahs were in accordance with the Qur'an and Sunnah. The position of khalifah was only that of a ruler and not that of a sovereign. Sovereignty is attributed only to God. Reiteration of this position is found in the words of the first khalifah, Abu Bakr ؓ, in his acceptance address:

> ... *Obey me as long as I obey God and His Messenger (Prophet Muhammad ﷺ). When I disobey Him and His Messenger, then do not obey me.*

Lord

This is the usual translation of the Arabic word *Rabb.* As is frequently the case with many Arabic words, a single English word does not communicate the full meaning. The literal meanings of *Rabb* include God, Creator, Master, Lord, Owner of the universe, etc.

In Islam, *Rabb* is used only when referring to God. Unlike the use of the word Lord in Christianity for both God and Jesus ؑ, *Rabb* is not applicable to any being other than the One and Only God. In distinction, Allah is the name God has given Himself. Thus, when referring to Lord (*Rabb*), it carries the same meaning as Allah.

Madrassah

A madrassah is a public school, an educational institution. The only difference between a European or American public school and a madrassah is the inclusion of religious education in the curriculum. In addition to religion classes, the madrassah's curriculum includes subjects such as reading, writing, mathematics, geography, science, etc., subjects that are taught in secular schools.

The word madrassah is the Arabic equivalent of the English word school. Its meaning and implications are no different than what is understood by school in English, ecole in French, skole in Danish, or schule in German. There are hundreds of thousands of madrassahs in Muslim lands in all corners of the globe providing essential basic education. Unlike the managed media misrepresentations, these are ordinary schools, just like any public or private school in the United States or Europe and are not associated with any unusual or sinister activity.

Muslim

A Muslim is one who has willingly and by choice *submitted to the Will of God* and follows Islam as *a way of life (deen)*. A believer (*mu'min*) is a person whose submission to God is conscientious, willful, whole-hearted and complete. Also see under Muslims in Chapter 1, Islam.

World Muslim Population

Conservative estimates put the world Muslim population at 1.57 billion in 2009, constituting about 23 % of the estimated total global population of 6.8 billion.[17] Muslims live in all five continents and there are over fifty countries with a majority Muslim population.

Muslim Greeting

As salaam u alaikum (*may peace be upon you*) is the universal greeting used by all Muslims. It is replied to by saying: *wa alaikum as salaam* (*and may peace also be upon you*).

This greeting is of significance. The meanings of *salaam* include: peace, to be safe, secure, and protected from harm. This includes both inner peace and peace with everything around (all creatures, plants, and environment, etc). *As Salaam* is also one of the Attributes of God and the word *Islam* is derived from the same root. Islam is peace and seeks to instill that condition into every believer. *Salaam* is repeated on every pertinent occasion and serves to instill the consciousness of peace in every Muslim mind. The Prophet ﷺ encouraged it. He said: *Spread salaam amongst yourselves.*[18]

Muslim Festivals

See under Festivals and Holidays.

---

[17] Mapping the Global Muslim Population. A report on the size of the World's Muslim population. Pew Research Center, Forum on Religion and Public Life, 2009.

[18] Reported by Muslim. Muntakhab Ahadith. Kandhlavi MY, Annayar, Karachi, Pakistan. Hadith 89, page 427.

Prayer (Salat)

There are five daily obligatory prayers. *Fajr* prayer (at dawn), *Zuhr* (mid day), *Asr* (mid afternoon), *Maghrib* (soon after sunset) and *Isha* (late evening or night prayer). The time for *Isha* is about 90 minutes after sunset. Muslims are requires to complete these prayers at their stated times. Prayers are shortened and certain prayers may be combined while traveling. Menstruating women and the seriously ill (who are unable to pray) are exempt from the obligatory prayers. While women do not have to make up the missed prayers, the sick are required to make up the missed prayers as soon as they are able to.

The obligatory prayers may be offered individually or in congregation. It is preferable to pray in congregation even if there are only two persons. Prayer is permitted only in a state of physical cleanliness. During the prayer, the individual is before God. It follows a prescribed routine which includes standing, bowing and prostration. The latter are in subservience to God and indicate humbleness before Him.

Prophets

Muslims believe in all prophets that were sent to mankind. These include Noah, Abraham, Lot, Ismail, Issac, Jacob, Joseph, David, Solomon, Moses, Aaron, John, Jesus, and Muhammad ﷺ as the final Prophet (peace and blessings be upon them all). The names of twenty-five prophets are mentioned in the Qur'an. All of God's prophets are revered. They were all mortals and none possessed divine powers. Whatever miracle any one of them performed was with the permission and help of Almighty God. With the exception of Jesus ﷺ, all have died. According to Muslim belief, Jesus ﷺ was not crucified. He was taken up to heaven by God and will return to earth and live amongst the people for a couple of decades before this world comes to an end.

Prophet Muhammad's ﷺ Birthday

The focus of Islam is on the Divine, the One God of the universe. Unlike the Christian tradition, the birthday of the Prophet ﷺ is not a holy day. However, it is celebrated with focus on learning about his life and teachings, ie., Islam.

Rabb
See under Lord

Ramadan (also see under Fasting)
Ramadan is the ninth month of the Islamic calendar. This is the month during which the first verses of the Qur'an were revealed to Prophet Muhammad ﷺ. Fasting during this month is obligatory for all adult Muslims and children past puberty. *Lailatul Qadr (Night of Power or Destiny)* occurs during this month. This night is of particular significance because worship during this night is immensely rewarded: *Lailatul Qadr is better than a thousand months* (Surah 97, Al Qadr, ayat 3). The exact occurrence is not known but it is one of the odd nights during the last third of Ramadan.

Each year, during the month of Ramadan, the angel Gabriel ؈ would visit Prophet Muhammad ﷺ and go over the verses of the Qur'an that had been revealed up to that time. During the last Ramadan, before the Prophet ﷺ died, Gabriel ؈ rehearsed the entire Qur'an twice.

Ramadan is also the month during with the Battle of Badr took place. This battle was one of the most significant events and a turning point in the history of the nascent Islamic community in Madinah. A well equipped, numerically superior force (pagan Quraish from Makkah) had set out to destroy the Muslim State. They lost the battle and the establishment of the Islamic State became irreversible.

Safa and Marwa
These are the names of the two small hillocks adjacent to the Ka'ba. Walking between these two hillocks is requirement for the Umrah. Historically, these are the two hillocks between which Ismail's ؈ mother Hajar (Hagar) scurried back and forth seven times looking for help. During Umrah, pilgrims walk seven times between these two hillocks, in commemoration.

Schools of Islamic Jurisprudence

These are also known as *madhabs*. There are four Sunni madhabs, namely, Hanafi, Shafi'i, Maliki, and Hanbali, and the Jafari madhab which is Shia. These were established by the third century AH (about the ninth century CE) in response to the growing and diverse needs and issues faced by Muslims in the different areas of the Commonwealth. They carry the names of the learned scholars who took the initiatives in addressing the issues and finding solutions.

Shirk

Associating partners with God is called shirk. There are different levels of shirk. A major form is that of setting idols and icons as representations of God or assigning divine status to any other being. At the other end of the spectrum are lesser forms of shirk which include things like giving priority or importance to material objects (wealth, business, etc) over and above that given to God. For example, routinely missing obligatory duties while tending to business and other worldly activities.

Umrah

See under Haj and Umrah

Zakat

This is the obligatory alms required of all Muslims possessing savings/property over and above a certain minimum. It is one of the five basic tenets of Islam. Zakat is collected by the Islamic State or other authorized Islamic organizations and distributed to the poor and those in need. There are several categories of individuals who are eligible for Zakat. It facilitates distribution of wealth in the society, providing for those in need and for alleviation of poverty.

Zakat is payable upon the net worth of an individual's assets that reach or exceed a minimum threshold (minimum wealth). It is payable in the amount of 2.5 % of their value. The assets must be in the individual's possession for twelve consecutive months before Zakat becomes due. The home, furnishings, personal apparel and means of transportation (car, truck, horse, etc) are exempted.

Chapter Twenty-One

Creative Terminology
for Islam and Muslims

Introduction

✥ O you who believe! Be steadfast witnesses for Allah in equity; and let not hatred of any people make you swerve from justice. Deal justly, that is next to piety. Observe your duty to Allah. Indeed, Allah is Informed of what you do. (Surah 5, Al Ma'idah, ayat 8)

Geopolitical events, both current and of the recent past, have kept media attention on Islam and Muslims. Violence against civilians or an act of terrorism anywhere in the world elicits a relatively predictable reaction from certain sections of the Western media, ie., that of pointing at Muslims and Islam, even before the facts have been ascertained. In such reporting, objectivity is frequently overshadowed by prejudice and confabulation, making it quite necessary to critically assess before accepting anything as being factual.

In the following are two examples of such journalism. On 1 June 2009, Air France Flight 447 crashed into the Atlantic Ocean. The tragedy may have had any number of causes, including mechanical problems or atmospheric occurrences, and numerous computer error messages were received prior to the crash. Yet the media lost little time in linking two passengers with common Muslim names to alleged terrorist groups.[1] More recently, after the 22 July 2011 tragedy in Norway, the self-styled experts[2] blamed Muslims even before the dust had settled in Oslo, and the shooting had barely stopped.[3,4,5,6] Is it simply poor and irresponsible journalism or is it purposeful?

The following will discuss a few of the creative terms from the media's popular lexicon for Islam and Muslims. This terminology is often illogical and betrays the user's ignorance about Islam.

Holy War

Like Crusade, the term *holy war* finds its origins with Pope Urban II (1088-1099 CE) who pronounced that it was *a new remedy for human sin,*[7] *journey for the remission of your sins,*[8] and *journey for all penance for sin.*[9] The Crusaders were *the army of the living God*[10] and the Christian warriors were called *pilgrims.* Unlike the Crusades which were

---

[1] On 6 June 2009, The Christian Science Monitor reported: Terror link to Air France crash? Two passengers' names match those of Al Qaeda suspects, reports say. But experts caution that it's too early to tell if the link is legitimate.
http://www.csmonitor.com/2009/0610/p02s08-usgn.html

[2] Norway bombing. By Jennifer Rubin. Posted at 05:06 PM ET, 07/22/2011.
http://www.washingtonpost.com/blogs/right-turn/post/norwaybombing/2011/03/29/gIQAB4D3TI_blog.html Last accessed July 2011.

[3] The Washington Post Owes the World an Apology for this Item. James Fallows, 23 July 2011.
http://www.theatlantic.com/international/archive/2011/07/the-washington-post-owes-the-world-an-apology-for-this-item/242400/ Last accessed July 2011.

[4] The Norway Massacre and the nexus of Islamophobia and Right-wing Zionism
http://www.informationclearinghouse.info/article28669.htm Last accessed July 2011.

[5] From Pamela Geller to Anders Behring Breivik - how Islamophobia turned deadly in Norway. Paul Woodward, 23 July 2011.
http://warincontext.org/2011/07/23/from-pamela-geller-to-anders-behring-breivik-how-islamophobia-turned-deadly/ Last accessed July 2011.

[6] Jihad Against Islam - The Anti-Muslim Inner Circle. Activists attacking Muslims and Islam are springing up around the country. But there's a core group of 10 hard-liners. Robert Steinback, 23 July 2011.
http://www.informationclearinghouse.info/article28671.htm Last accessed July 2011.

[7] The First Crusade. E Peters. Second Edition. University of Pennsylvania Press, 1998, page 16. ISNB 0-8122-1656-3

[8] The First Crusade. E Peters. Second Edition. University of Pennsylvania Press, 1998, page 28.

[9] The First Crusade. E Peters. Second Edition. University of Pennsylvania Press, 1998, page 37.

[10] The First Crusade. E Peters. Second Edition. University of Pennsylvania Press, 1998, page 20.

officially designated *holy wars*, Islam does not assign warfare or any other form of violence, the status of being holy. Furthermore, there is nothing in Islamic teachings or practice that can be likened to the medieval *holy wars*.

The uninformed frequently refer to Jihad as being a *holy war*. While the Crusades were *holy wars* since they had been sanctioned by the Pope and the Crusaders were called *the soldiers of God*,[11] when used for Jihad, the term *holy war* is given a negative connotation, perhaps reflecting upon a deep seated guilt that the Crusades were not that holy after all. There is absolutely no similarity between Jihad and the medieval holy wars. Jihad is a *struggle against evil*, both inner and external. While the external struggle could entail warfare, that constitutes only a small portion and it is also restricted by narrowly defined guidelines. Islam considers the taking of any innocent life to be a major sin and the equivalent of a crime against all of humanity, irrespective of the faith of the victim. It is stated in the Qur'an: *...who ever kills a person for other than manslaughter or spreading mischief in the earth, it shall be as if he had killed all mankind,...* (Surah 5, Al Ma'idah, ayat 32). In addition, Prophet Muhammad ﷺ said: *Allah will not be merciful to those who are not merciful to mankind.*[12]

For an additional discussion on Holy War see Chapter 6, Jihad, The Struggle to Self-discipline and Chapter 23, Crusades and Holy War.

Islamic Extremism, Islamic Extremist[13]

Extremism is exaggeration. It is also defined as *the quality or state of being extreme; advocacy of extreme measures or views; radicalism* (Merriam-Webster Dictionary). *Extreme* is defined as *existing in a very high degree: going to great or exaggerated lengths: exceeding the ordinary, usual, or expected* (Merriam-Webster Dictionary). And an *extremist* is the one who advocates *extreme (or radical) measures or views* (Merriam-Webster Dictionary).

From these definitions, it is difficult to understand or extrapolate

---

[11] *...let this one cry be raised by all soldiers of God: It is the will of God! It is the will of God!* The First Crusade. E Peters. Second Edition. University of Pennsylvania Press, 1998, pages 28-29.

[12] The Translation of the Meanings of Sahih Al-Bukhari. MM Khan, Kazi Publications, Lahore, Pakistan, 1979. Volume IX, Hadith 473, page 351.

[13] Also see Religious Extremism in Chapter 24, Suicide, Killing and War.

what is really meant by *Islamic Extremism* and *Islamic Extremist.* Such allegations of *extremism* seem to appear mainly in the Western media and the actual issues, statements and grievances of those being accused of expressing "extremist" views are rarely disclosed.

There is no place for extremes in Islam. It is a *middle course* that prescribes a life of high ethical and moral standards with fairness and justice when dealing with all others. Islam does not allow extremes in worldly or religious matters. Had there been any extremes in Islam, it would have been difficult to follow. Prophet Muhammad ﷺ cautioned against extremism when he said: *Those who go to extremes are doomed.*[14] He also said:[15] *...do good deeds properly, sincerely and moderately, and worship Allah in the forenoon and in the afternoon and during a part of the night, and "always adopt a middle, moderate, regular course" whereby you will reach your target (Paradise).*[16]

Consequently, believing Muslim men and women steer clear of what could be considered an extreme practice and follow only the middle path. In the Qur'an it is stated:

Thus We have appointed you a middle nation ...
(Surah 2, Al Baqarah, ayat 143)

You are the best community that has been raised up for mankind. You enjoin what is good and forbid what is evil, and you believe in God.
(Surah 3, 'Al Imraan, ayat 110)

Islamic Fascism, Islamic Neofascism

Fascism is an authoritarian political ideology in which the individual is *subordinated to the interests of the state or a given social order.* It's features include *racism, nationalism, religious, ethnic and cultural purity, intolerance for political opposition* and *imposition of economic control.*

Fascism was prevalent in several European countries prior to the Second World War: Italy under Mussolini, Germany, Spain, Portugal, Hungary and Romania. Although the fascist label was accepted, they

---

[14] English Translation of Sahih Muslim. Daruussalam, Riyadh, S Arabia, 2007. Volume 7, Hadith 6784, page 44.

[15] The Translation of the Meanings of Sahih Al-Bukhari. MM Khan, Kazi Publications, Lahore, Pakistan, 1979. Volume VIII, Hadith 470, page 313.

[16] emphasis added.

were never called "Christian fascists" or "Christian Nazis". Today, this designation is used for disparagement.

By it's very definition, Islam can never be fascist and *fascism* can never be connected to Islam as they are diametrical opposites. The Islamic system of conducting affairs (personal and public) is through *shura'* and not authoritarian.[17] There is no place for *racism* in Islam because all of mankind was created equal and only *piety (taqwa)* enhances an individual's stature. The absence of racism is displayed during Haj (the pilgrimage to Makkah) where people of all races and diverse social backgrounds come together without any barriers. Also, people of all races and social backgrounds stand next to each other for the Muslim congregational prayer.

Nationalism is a creation of the colonialists and has served to divide the previously colonized peoples. Extreme *nationalism* as sponsored by *fascism* is irreconcilable with Islam as all Muslims constitute one community (ummah), irrespective of race, language, ethnic origin and geographic location.

The other characteristics of *fascism* are also incompatible with Islam: *subordination* is to God and not to a state or sociopolitical order. *Religious, ethnic and cultural purity* which are key elements of *fascism* contradict the laws of nature, ie., diversity of creation and can therefore never be linked to Islam.

> *And of His Signs is the creation of heavens and the earth, and the differences of your languages and colors: verily in that are Signs for those who know.*   (Surah 30, Ar Rum, ayat 22)

> *... We created you from a male and a female and made you nations and tribes, that you may know one another ...*
> (Surah 49, Al Hujuraat, ayat 13)

Intolerance to opposition and *economic control,* which are also features of *fascism,* are associated with aggression, oppression and usurpation of the rights of others. All of these are strictly forbidden by Islam and

---

[17] Surah 42, Ash Shura, ayat 38. Shura' means *through mutual consultation.*

such conduct has consequences.[18,19]

> *... The blame is only against those who oppress mankind, and wrongfully rebel in the earth. For such people there is a painful torment.*
>
> (Surah 42, Ash Shura, ayaat 41-42)

Islam teaches peace. Not peace at any price but a just and equitable peace. Peace through justice and equality is also longer lasting. Sustainable peace cannot be achieved by giving up legitimate rights or through surrender to injustice and oppression. Islam protects the rights of the oppressed. As the final resort, it permits the oppressed to exercise their rights to secure freedom and justice. There can be no blame on the victims if they respond to injustices and violence that are unleashed upon them.

Islamic Fundamentalist, Islamic Fundamentalism

In the context of religion, the fundamentalist is a person devoted to following the fundamentals of his/her faith. Such persons are found in all faiths. A strong belief coupled with an understanding of the faith and adherence to its virtuous tenets is a desirable state. This is particularly true for Islam because those who understand and conscientiously follow the pristine teachings of Islam (ie., adopt the fundamentals) are undoubtedly amongst *the best of mankind*. Thus, anyone who is a true *Islamic Fundamentalist* can do no evil, because the fundamentals of Islam which include only goodness, ie., peace, equality, fairness, kindness, justice, etc., for all (mankind, animals, vegetation and environment) instill consciousness for the rights of others and the fear of God's wrath should those rights be violated. Consequently, if everyone were to become an *Islamic Fundamentalist*, the world would be at peace, there would be no injustice, no usurpation of the rights of the weak, no exploitation of people or nations, and the environment would be protected, to name just a few benefits. Thus, any negative connotation that is assigned to this term is misplaced.

---

[18] Surah 2, Al Baqarah: ayat 190: *Allah does not like aggressors.*

[19] Prophet Muhammad ﷺ said: *If anyone acquired what rightly belongs to another Muslim by a false oath, then God has made Hell obligatory for him and prohibited his admission to Paradise.* Reported by Muslim. Muntakhab Ahadith. Kandhlavi MY, Annayyar, Karachi Pakistan. Hadith 345, pages 509-510.

Islamic Terrorism, Islamic Terrorist

Of the many definitions of *terrorism*, three are reproduced below:

- *Violence against civilians to achieve political or ideological objectives by creating fear.* The perpetrator may be an individual, organization or state
- *Any act intended to cause death or serious bodily harm to civilians or non combatants with the purpose of intimidating a population or compelling a government or an international organization to do or abstain from doing any act* (United Nations, 2004)
- *Calculated use of unlawful violence or threat to unlawful violence to inculcate fear; intended to coerce or to intimidate governments or societies in the pursuit of goals that are generally political, religious or ideological* (U.S. Government's definition)

Acts of terrorism perpetrated by a Christian individual or group are not labeled *Christian* terrorism. Acts of terrorism perpetrated by a Jewish person or group are not labeled *Jewish* terrorism. Similarly, an act of violence committed by individuals or groups calling themselves Muslims cannot, and must not, be called *Islamic*. The use of Islamic slogans by perpetrators of terrorism neither legitimizes their actions nor makes them Islamic by any stretch of the imagination.

Islam is peace. Terrorism is at the opposite end of the spectrum. Islam and terrorism are simply incompatible. These terms, *Islamic terrorism* and *Islamic terrorist* are not only ill-conceived but also disclose the ignorance of those using them.

In Islam, the prohibition for acts of terrorism and wanton violence is unequivocal. Islam forbids harming innocent people and it forbids oppression in any form. Even during war, noncombatant women, children, elderly and clergy may not be harmed. Besides, with the intensive activity of foreign agencies in Muslim lands, nothing can be taken for granted, ie., those who proclaim to be Muslim may well be otherwise.

Moderate Islam, Moderate Muslim

The term *moderate* has been defined as: *a person who is moderate in opinion or opposed to extreme views and actions, especially in politics or religion;* and *professing or characterized by political or social beliefs that are not extreme* or *limited in scope or effect* (Merriam-Webster Dictionary).

The use of the term *moderate* Islam betrays the user's misplaced belief in the existence of different grades of Islam (see Chapter 1, Islam). *Moderate* Muslim is used to identify an individual who is willing to comply with secular wishes, to bend Islamic rules in order to appease and blend into non-Muslim society.

There is only one Islam and it is a middle course, free of extremes. As stated in the Hadith quoted earlier, the injunction for all believers is to ...*always adopt a middle, moderate, regular course...* Had it been otherwise, Islam would have either been secularized like many of the other faiths or it would have been so difficult to follow so that it could not retain but a handful of followers. God says: *Allah desires for you ease: He does not desire hardship for you.*[20] This is applicable to every obligation.

Islam incorporates the teaching of all prophets, including Abraham, Issac, Jacob, Moses and Jesus (may peace be upon them). No matter how knowledgeable humans may become or how great their political, scientific or military prowess, they cannot alter what is Divine. It is mankind that must change to conform to God's Laws.

Spread by Violence

There an erroneous notion that Islam was *spread by the sword*, ie., by violence. This is false both historically as well as in the context of the present times. Islam prescribes peace, justice, and tolerance. There is no place for forceful conversion as compulsion in religion is strictly prohibited.[21]

Historically, as with most other nations, wars were fought by Muslims. They were military encounters and not missionary in nature. Many of them were defensive or preemptive, while others were in response to foreign incursions or call for help by oppressed native populations (eg., Coptic Christians of Egypt, Berbers of North Africa). The acquired lands were neither subjected to loot, plunder or massacre, nor was the population forced to convert to Islam. One of the manifestations of the latter is that virtually every Muslim country has non-Muslim citizens. Conversion to Islam was voluntary as the

---

[20] Surah 2, Al Baqarah, ayat 185.
[21] Surah 2, Al Baqarah, ayat 256: *There is no compulsion in religion.*

high morals and ethical standards embodied in Islam appealed to the local people. Furthermore, after the first one hundred years of Muslim rule in greater Syria and Palestine, only about six percent of the population was Muslim.[22] Forced conversion would have resulted in a much higher number.

The deliberate, misleading notion that *Islam was spread by the sword* also does not apply to the present day in which the world is witnessing a steady conversion to Islam despite sustained negative propaganda and the numerous military campaigns being waged against Muslims.

For an additional discussion on this and related topics see Chapter 1, Islam; Chapter 6, Jihad, The Struggle to Self-Discipline and Chapter 23, Crusades and Holy War.

Violent Islam

Violence may be defined as *an illegitimate use of force or an excessive use of legitimate force.* It is a worldwide phenomenon and may be perpetrated by individuals, groups, organizations or states. Violence has no nationality or religion. Historically, violence has been perpetrated in the name of religion (see Chapter 23, Crusades and Holy War).

Islam is peace. Violence is not an Islamic phenomenon as there is no place for *an illegitimate use of force* in Islam. On the contrary, Islam specifically prohibits all injustices, oppression and aggression, and promotes peace, equality, justice, and tolerance. Therefore, the term *violent Islam* is illogical. The *illegitimate use of force* is also incompatible with Islam as it goes against its basic principles. There is also never any permission for *the excessive use of legitimate force.*

Violence as defined above must be differentiated from the legitimate right to self-defense by people(s) subjected to oppression, military occupation, exploitation, economic and other injustices. Islam prescribes restraint and patience but it also permits legitimate self-defense against oppression, aggression and injustices. That is a right which has also been officially recognized by the rest of the world through the United Nations. For an additional discussion on this topic

---

[22] Courbage Y, Fargues P. Christian and Jews under Islam. Translated by Judy Mabro. IB Tauris Publishers, London, 1997. Page 11.

see Violence and Islam in Chapter 1, Islam and Violence in Perspective in Chapter 24, Suicide, Killing and War.

Concluding Summary

While fascism, terrorism and the likes can become a religion for certain types of people, an established, centuries old faith cannot be assigned such a label by any stretch of logical imagination. A faith is judged by it tenets and its followers are judged by their compliance. The reverse is illogical.

People professing to follow any established religious belief come with different strengths of faith and a wide spectrum of practices. While most humans, with or without strong opinions, find themselves going about their business in a peaceful manner, there are those who attempt to impose their views and doctrines upon others. The latter come in various forms, ie., as individuals, groups, organizations, and even governments. The forceful imposition of one set of values upon others carries the exact same implications, whether it is perpetrated by an individual, a group of individuals, an outlawed group, an organization, or a state.

Anyone, including all non-Muslim groups, governments and spy agencies, can use the name of any religion as front for any type of activity, including violence and terrorism. There is no international law prohibiting or stopping it. Therefore, any activity carried out in the name of Islam must be critically evaluated to identify the actual perpetrator(s) before making any judgement. Furthermore, anything that stands in contradiction to its principles, can never be condoned by Islam since there is no dichotomy between Islamic belief and practice.

A believer who follows Islam stands in awe of the consequences of any unbecoming act. Violence and terrorism could not be far enough from him or her. At the end of the day, there is accountability for all individuals, whether the individual's belief encompasses it or not, and at the time of that accountability, only genuine goodness prevails.

Surely, this Qur'an guides to that which is most right, and gives good tidings to the believers who do good works that theirs will be a great reward.   (Surah 17, Al Isra', ayat 9)

Allah has promised those who believe and do good deeds; theirs will be forgiveness and an immense reward.
                                                    (Surah 5, Al Ma'idah, ayat 9)

The promise to *those who believe and do good deeds* is *forgiveness* and *an immense reward* is eternal bliss in Paradise. It is clearly established what is meant by *believing*. This includes following the letter and spirit of God's injunctions. However, by itself, *believing* is insufficient. The believer also has to do *good deeds*. These *good deeds* are clearly and unmistakably identified by God and His Prophet ﷺ and are defined in the Shari'ah and not left up to the discretion of humans. These include general goodness, honesty, fairness, justice, equality, generosity, compassion, politeness, etc., towards all.[23] The following verse from the Qur'an summarizes it:

Is the reward of goodness anything but goodness?
                                                    (Surah 55, Ar Rahman, ayat 60)

---

[23] The list is very long and only a few are listed here.

Chapter Twenty-Two

Islamic History

Historical Dates[1]

570	Birth of Muhammad ﷺ in Makkah, Arabia
	Invasion of Makkah by Abraha from Yemen[2]
576	Death of Amina, Muhammad's ﷺ mother
578	Death of Abd al-Muttalib, Muhammad's ﷺ grandfather and guardian
595	Marriage of Muhammad ﷺ to Khadeeja ◈
610	First revelation of the Qur'an
613	First Hijrah to Abyssinia (Ethiopia) by a group of Muslims because of persecution by the pagan Quraish
619	Year of sorrow. Death of Abu Talib, the Prophet's ﷺ uncle and his wife Khadeeja ◈
620	Isra' and Miraj
622	Hijrah, Emigration to Madinah. This marks the beginning of the Islamic Calendar
623	Battle of Badr against invading Makkan pagans (Friday, 16 Ramadan, 2 AH)

---

[1] These dates are in CE (Current Era). The CE and Hijrah (AH) calendars are difficult to synchronize over successive years because of the differences in the number of days in each calendar. See Islamic Calendar and New Year in Chapter 20, Common Islamic Terms and their Meanings.

[2] Also known as *The Year of the Elephant* as Abraha, the Abyssinian ruler of Yemen, invaded with an army which included elephants.

624	Battle of Uhud against attacking Makkan pagans (Saturday, 11 Shawwal, 3 AH)
627	Battle of Khandaq (al-Ahzab) against Makkan and allied pagans (Shawwal-Dhul Qa'dah, 5 AH)
628	Treaty of Hudaibiya' (1 Dhul Qa'dah, 6 AH)[3]
630	Liberation of Makkah (Ramadan, 8 AH)
632	Farewell pilgrimage, Death of Prophet Muhammad ﷺ (11 AH) Election of Abu Bakr ؓ as the first Khalifah
634	Election of Umar ibn al Khattab ؓ as the second Khalifah after the death of Abu Bakr ؓ
635	Surrender of Byzantine-ruled Damascus
636	Battle of Yarmuk (Syria). Defeat of Heraclius and the Byzantines by Muslim armies
637	Surrender of Jerusalem (16 AH)
644	Uthman bin Affan ؓ became the third Khalifah after the death of Umar ibn al Khattab ؓ
656	Ali ibn Abu Talib ؓ became the fourth Khalifah after the death of Uthman bin Affan ؓ
661	Death of Ali ibn Abu Talib ؓ Mu'awiyah became the Khalifah in Damascus
680	Tragedy at Karbala. Martyrdom of Hussain ؓ, grandson of the Prophet ﷺ (10 Muharram, 61 AH)
711	Invasion of Spain by Tarik bin Ziyad
712	Muslims reach India under Muhammad bin Qasim
750	End of the Umayyad Caliphate Beginning of Abbasid Caliphate
786	Haroon al Rashid (763-809 CE) became the Khalifah in Baghdad
1095-1099	First Crusade
1099	Fall of Jerusalem to the Crusaders
1147-1149	Second Crusade

---

[3] The Prophet ﷺ accompanied by a group of about 1400 people set out towards Makkah to perform the pilgrimage. They were refused entry to the Sanctuaries by the Quraish. Uthman ibn Affan ؓ was sent into Makkah and after intense negotiations a treaty was signed which, among other things, would permit them to perform the pilgrimage in the following year. Hudaibiya' is on the outskirts of Makkah.

1187	Surrender of Jerusalem to Salahuddin Ayyubi (27 Rajab, 583 AH)
1188-1192	Third crusade
1202-1204	Fourth Crusade
1217-1221	Fifth Crusade
1228-1229	Sixth Crusade
1248-1250	Seventh Crusade, Louis IX of France
1258	Occupation and destruction of Baghdad by the Mongols under Halagu Khan End of the Abbasid Caliphate
1260	Defeat of the Mongols by Mamluke Sultan Mahmood Saifuddin Qutuz at Ain Jaloot in Palestine
1267	First Muslim state in Indonesia. Islam first came to this nation of islands in the eleventh century
1255-1270	Mansa Wali Keita, first Muslim ruler of Mali
1270	Eighth crusade. The second for Louis IX of France
1271-1272	Ninth crusade. Edward I of England
1389	First Battle of Kosova
1448	Second battle of Kosova
1453	Constantinople (Istanbul) came under Turkish rule, Sultan Mehmet II
1492	End of Muslim rule in Spain
1520-1566	Rule of Sulaiman the Magnificent
1526-1530	Zahiruddin Muhammad Babur, first Mughal King of India
ca. 1612	Establishment of a British trading post in India during the reign of Mughal Emperor Jahangir
1658-1707	Aurangzeb, last great Mughal Emperor of India
1710-1711	Russo-Turkish war, defeat of the Russians at the Battle of Pruth
1824	Anglo-Dutch Treaty (Treaty of London). Malaya (Malaysia) came under British occupation
1830	French invaded and occupied Algeria (until 1962)
1857	British captured Delhi ending Mughal rule in India
1881-1956	French occupation of Tunisia
1882	Anglo-Egyptian War, British occupation of Egypt

1914-1918	First World War
1918-1922	Partition of the Ottoman Empire into several countries. Syria and Lebanon came under France, the British controlled Iraq and Palestine. Further partitioning of Palestine to create Jordan. Installation of monarchies in the newly created Arab countries
1923	Turkish Republic declared by Mustafa Kemal
1939-1945	Second World War
1941	Anglo-Russian invasion of Iran to secure Iranian oil fields and supply lines, Shah forced to abdicate
1944-1947	Independence of Jordan, Syria and the new Islamic State of Pakistan
1953	Coup facilitated by the C.I.A. toppled the elected Iranian government of Mohammad Mossadegh in response to the nationalization of the Iranian oil fields
1951-1962	Independence of several Mediterranean-North African countries
1962-2011	Independence from colonial rule for several other Muslim countries. Wars for the reoccupation of Iraq, Afghanistan and Libya

First Islamic State

After the emigration in 622 CE (The Hijrah), Prophet Muhammad ﷺ established the first Muslim State in Madinah, Arabia. After his death, there were four Khalifahs. These were from amongst his closest companions and are also known as *ar Rashidoon,* the Rightly Guided.

Abu Bakr as Siddiq ؓ (632-634 CE) was the first Khalifah after the death of Prophet Muhammad ﷺ. He was elected to this post by consensus of the people of Madinah. He died at the age of 63, after a short illness.

Umar ibn al Khattab ؓ (634-644 CE) was elected as the second Khalifah after the death of Abu Bakr ؓ. He died at the age of 61 years, after being stabbed by a Magian named Abu Lulu. His time as Khalifah is considered as *The Period of Justice.*

Uthman ibn Affan ﷺ (644-656 CE) was elected Khalifah after the death of Umar ibn al Khattab ﷺ. He was also a son-in-law of the Prophet ﷺ.

Ali ibn Abu Talib ﷺ (656-661 CE) was elected as the fourth Khalifah. Ali ﷺ was the first cousin of the Prophet ﷺ and also a son-in-law by virtue of his marriage to Fatima' ﷺ, the Prophet's ﷺ youngest daughter.

Also see under Khalifah in Chapter 20, Common Islamic Terms and their Meanings.

The Umayyad and Abbasid Caliphates

After the death of Ali ibn Abu Talib ﷺ, the administrative responsibility of the Muslim Commonwealth was taken over by the Umayyads. The Umayyad caliphate (661-750 CE) had its capital in Damascus. By the end of this period, Islam had spread from the Atlantic coast of Africa to western China. The Umayyads were succeeded by the Abbasid Caliphs, who ruled from 750 until 1258. Their capital Baghdad became a center for culture and learning with its libraries, observatories and other educational institutions such as the *Bayt al Hikma* (House of Wisdom)[4] and produced a large number of great scholars such as: *al-Khwarizimi* who coined the term *algebra* [(Arabic *al jabr*), derived from his work Al Kitab al mukhtasar fi hisab al-jabr wal muqabala], *al-Kindi, ibn Qurra, al-Farghani* (Alfraganus), *Banu Musa*, and *al-Farabi* (Alpharabius).

The authority of the Abbasid Caliphs gradually waned, giving rise to smaller, powerful sultanates and principalities. The Abbasid caliphate ended in 1258 with the destruction of Baghdad by the Mongols. The Mongols subjected the city to barbaric massacre and widespread destruction. The city was rampaged for about six weeks and everything was burned to the ground. It is estimated that over one and a half million people perished. The Mongols continued their rampage westward into Syria and the mediterranean coastal regions until they were stopped in 1260 at Ain Jaloot, Palestine.

---

[4] *Bayt al Hikma* was a center of excellence for the study of the humanities and sciences, including mathematics, basic sciences, medicine, and astronomy.

While the Abbasids ruled the middle east, the Umayyads established themselves in Spain, bringing to it a golden age. Cordoba, the capital of Muslim Spain, became one of Europe's greatest cities for culture and learning. The nearly eight hundred year Muslim rule ended with the fall of Granada in 1492. During this period, Muslims intellectuals made immense contributions to advancements in many fields, including the sciences, medicine and philosophy, and to the renaissance of Europe. In essence, Islam brought what is called "freedom and democracy" to Europe which had been in its dark ages.

In the following are the names of a few of the notable Spanish Muslim intellectuals.

Abu Ishaq Ibrahim al Zarqali (1029–1087 CE) of Toledo (also known as Arzachel). A leading Muslim mathematician, inventor and foremost astronomer of his time. His works included the compilation of the first almanac (*Almanac of Azarqueil*). The Latin translation and adaptation of his work became the *Tables of Toledo*.

Abu al Qasim Khalaf ibn al Abbas al Zahrawi (936-1013 CE) (also known as Albucasis).[5,6] Renown surgeon and inventor also referred to as being the *Father of Surgery*.

Abu Muhammad Ali ibn Ahmad bin Said ibn Hazm (994-1064 CE) of Cordoba. He was a philosopher, psychologist, theologian, and historian.

Abu Bakr Muhammad ibn Yahya ibn al Sayigh at Tujibi ibn Baja (1095-1138 CE) of Zaragoza (also known as Ibn Bajjah, or Avempace). A leading scientist, astronomer and philosopher whose achievements include the definition of the *law of motion* and the *law of reciprocal actions*. The latter forms the basis of what is known as Newton's third law of motion.

Abu Marwan Abdal Malik ibn Zuhr (1091-1161 CE) of Seville (also known as Avenzoar or Abumeron). He was a notable physician, parasitologist, and educator. He is credited as being the pioneer of experimental surgery. His numerous achievements include

---

[5] Hajar R: History of Medicine, Al Zahrawi: Father of Surgery.
Heart Views Dec 2006–Feb 2007; 7(4):154-156. Last accessed June 2011.
http://www.hmc.org.qa/heartviews/vol7no4/pdf/history_med.pdf

[6] Ahmed M: El Zahrawi (Albucasis) - father of surgery.
http://www.ummah.net/history/scholars/el_zahrawi/ Last accessed June 2011.

the establishment of surgery as an independent specialty and the establishment of a supervised training program for surgeons similar to today's residency training programs.[7] He is also credited with first application of surgical tracheotomy for the emergency management of upper airway obstruction and the use of inhalation anesthesia for surgical procedures.[8]

Abu Bakr Muhammad ibn Abd al Malik ibn Muhammad ibn Tufail al Qaisi al Andalusi (1105-1185 CE) of Guadix (also known as Ibn Tufail or Abubacer). He was writer and philosopher whose thought and works significantly influenced European literature and philosophy. His novel *Hayy ibn Yaqzan* (translated as *Philosophus Autodidactus*) may have been the first philosophical novel ever written. His works distinctly influenced, and may also have served as a template, for the writings of some, including Defoe (Robinson Crusoe), Kipling (The Jungle Book), and Rousseau (Émile).[9,10]

Abu al Walid Muhammad ibn Ahmad ibn Rushd (1126-1198 CE) of Cordoba (also known as Averroes). He was a notable Spanish Muslim scientist [master mathematician, physicist, astronomer (celestial mechanics)], physician, and philosopher. Ibn Rushd was the first to suggest the presence of photoreceptors in the retina and also ascribed to it the function of sight. His works influenced the likes of Thomas Aquinas and Johannes Kepler.

Nur al Din Ibn Ishaq al Bitruji (died ca. 1204 CE) of Seville (also known as Alpetragius) was an astronomer and philosopher.

---

[7] Abdel-Halim RE: Contributions of ibn Zuhr (Avenzoar) to the progress of surgery. A study and translations from his book Al-Taisir. Saudi Med J 2005;26(9):1333-1339.
http://www.rabieabdelhalim.com/01Contribution20050521.pdf
Last accessed June 2011.

[8] Shehata M: The Ear, Nose and Throat in Islamic Medicine. J of the Internat Soc for the History of Islamic Medicine. 2003; (1): 2-5.
http://www.ishim.net/ishimj/3/01.pdf   Last accessed June 2011.

[9] Attar S: The Vital Roots of European Enlightenment: Ibn Tufayl's Influence on Modern Western Thought, Lexington Books, ISBN 0739119893.

[10] Wainwright M: Desert island scripts. Martin Wainwright happily follows the footprints of a 12 th-century Muslim Robinson Crusoe. The Guardian, 22 March 2003. Last accessed June 2011.
http://www.guardian.co.uk/books/2003/mar/22/featuresreviews.guardianreview1

The Uthmania Turks

The name Uthmania (Ottoman) is derived from the name of the man, Uthman Khan, who united the Turkish tribes around 1300 CE. From the late fourteenth century onwards, the Turks ruled much of eastern Europe, Arab lands, and large parts of North Africa. In 1453, Sultan Mehmet II captured Constantinople, bringing an end to the Byzantine empire. Their glory peaked during the reign of Sulaiman, the Magnificent (1520-1566 CE). The Uthmanian Turkish empire gradually declined and the almost six hundred year caliphate ended with declaration of the Turkish Republic in 1923.

The East

After their rampage through Persia and Iraq, the Mongols settled down and ruled for several decades. Their interaction with the remaining local populations led to their conversion to Islam. In India, like in Malaysia and Indonesia, Islam came with the traders whose high morals and ethics attracted the locals. In a similar fashion, Islam spread from Indonesia to the Philippines and all countries of Indochina. Muslims also entered India from the northwest (Afghanistan and Persia). In 1526, Zahiruddin Muhammad Babur[11] established Mughal rule in Northern India. The Mughal rule ended in 1857 when the English overthrew the last Mughal Emperor, Bahadur Shah Zafar. They executed virtually all the male members of his family and sent the eighty year old monarch into exile, in chains.[12] Ironically, the English had also come to India as traders (East India Company) but their conduct contrasted very significantly from that of the peaceful Muslim traders.

Africa

In the central, western and southern parts of the African continent, Islam spread through the amicable interaction of travelers and traders.

---

[11] Babur was a descendant of Timur. He left his home in Farghana, Central Asia and came to Afghanistan in 1502.

[12] He was exiled to Rangoon (now Yangon), Burma (Myanmar).

Several Muslim states were established from the fourteenth century onwards. Timbuktu, on a caravan and trading route, was a thriving center for Islamic learning.

The Postcolonial Period

The major colonizers of Muslim lands were the English, French, Italians, Dutch, Spaniards, and Portuguese. For the most part, their rule was that of cruel repression and exploitation. Most of the Muslim lands have been either under European colonial occupation or their influence. As the occupiers withdrew in the aftermath of the Second World War, they fragmented the Muslim lands with the creation of numerous new entities like Lebanon, Jordan, Kuwait and Gulf Emirates. In addition, interjection of large numbers of European and Russian Jewish immigrants and the creation of Israel further complicated the status quo in Palestine and the remainder of the middle east, changing forever the religious and ethnic harmony and peaceful coexistence.

The British occupation of India was no less gruesome than the French occupation of North Africa and the Dutch occupation of Indonesia.[13] Most propagated history books have been written by the colonialists and are amnesic, at the very least. Indian Muslims spearheaded the unsuccessful freedom movement against British[14] long before independence became a reality in 1947. After independence, the colonialists and their surrogates succeeded in further partitioning the country in 1971. The eastern province of Pakistan became Bangladesh.

In North and Central Africa, the majority of the population is Muslim. In west Africa, many countries have either a large Muslim minority or a majority Muslim population. By the beginning of the twenty-first century, most parts of the Islamic world had officially

---

[13] Dutch state found liable for 1947 massacre of 431 men and boys in Java.
http://www.irishtimes.com/newspaper/world/2011/0916/1224304195266_pf.html

[14] The Sepoy War of 1857. Mutiny or First Indian War of Independence?
http://english.emory.edu/Bahri/Mutiny.html Last Accessed September 2011.
That uprising, similar to the American war of Independence, was called the the Indian Mutiny by the colonialists.

become independent. Some Muslim states of the former Soviet Union and China remain under occupation. Some countries in west Asia have been reoccupied and others in north Africa are in the process of being reoccupied in 2011.

After independence from colonial occupation, the goals were political independence, freedom to assert Islamic religious and cultural identity, build a society based upon Islamic values and coexist peacefully with the rest of the world. Those were never achieved because of the cancer left behind by the colonialists. As Western influence continued to penetrate into Islamic societies, attempts were made to preserve Islamic values and prevent secularization by placing emphasis on education. The greater the pressure from the outside world, the stronger became the rejection of the negative aspects of Western thought and culture and the desire return to an Islamic society based upon Shari'ah.

Concluding Summary

But for him who is a greedy miser and deems himself independent (self sufficient). And disbelieves in goodness. We will ease his way into adversity. His riches will not save him when he perishes

(Surah 92, Al Lail, ayaat 8-11)

Therefore I have warned you of the blazing Fire. Which only the most wretched must endure.   (Surah 92, Al Lail, ayaat 14-15)

Muslims live in virtually every corner of the world. Like all other people, ie., non-Muslim communities, there is a wide spectrum of opinions and intensity of practice of the faith, from the casual to the very strict. Like every other community, the middle of the road Muslims constitute the majority. This majority seeks to maintain its Islamic identity. It wants to adapt to the changes occurring in the world without having to blindly imitate or unconditionally adopt the ways of non-Muslim societies, especially those of the West.

Peace is what all Muslims seek and like all other communities, they wish to maintain the freedom to practice their faith and live by the culture of their choosing, free of external domination and coercion. Muslims, like all other people, will respond to oppression. Fate has it that many Muslim countries are endowed with vast stores of natural wealth or find themselves in strategic geographic locations. This has been rediscovered by the colonialists, old and new. Thus, it is no coincidence, that Muslim lands are targeted for political turmoil, economic coercion and subjugation, clandestine or outright occupation under one pretext or another. Like any other community in the world, they seek to resist recolonization.

Muslims are quite content with their belief and ways of living. The notion that they are somehow envious of the Western way of life is false and baseless. For world peace, it would be a significant starting point, if today's world leaders were to hearken and contemplate upon the words that the greatest leader known to mankind spoke at the Farewell Pilgrimage:

... so regard the life and property of every Muslim as a sacred trust.
Return the goods entrusted to you to their rightful owners.
Hurt no one so that no one may hurt you.
Remember that you will indeed meet your Lord, and that He will indeed reckon your deeds.

Chapter Twenty-Three

Crusades and
Holy War

The Original Holy War

Holy War, like *Crusade*, was the brainchild of Pope Urban II (1088-1099). In an attempt to consolidate papal power and unite the fragmented Christians of Europe, he embarked upon an ominous plan. Utilizing Christian emotions, false and malicious propaganda against Muslims who were ruling Jerusalem, he skillfully rallied European Christianity for the invasion and occupation of Jerusalem and Palestine. A systematic vilification of Muslims was initiated with fabrication of horror tales about the treatment of Christians. His plans succeeded in inciting the faithful against an enemy created by imagination and culminated in the Crusades and the European occupation of Palestine and adjacent territories.

Fighting and its ultimate goal, ie., that of killing Muslims in Palestine, was depicted as *a penitential and spiritually meritorious act.* The evolving creed glorifying militancy gave birth to the concept of *holy war.*[1] The Crusaders, who were called pilgrims, were told that *the journey to free the church of God in Jerusalem* would be *...penance for sin.*[2]

Urban II made his allegations and the case for the invasion of Palestine at the Council of Clermont on 27 November 1095 CE.

---

[1] The First Crusade. The chronicles of Fulcher of Chartres and other source materials. E Peters. Second Edition. University of Pennsylvania Press, 1998, pages 7-16. ISBN 0-8122-1656-3

[2] The First Crusade. E Peters. Second Edition. University of Pennsylvania Press, 1998, page 37.

There are four or five versions or translations of his speech and it is uncertain which one is the most authentic. Suffice it to say, there was no truth to the allegations. The purpose was to unite the European Christians by distracting them from the realities at home and to consolidate power by focussing on a concocted external threat. Excerpts from three versions are reproduced below.

> ... a race from the kingdom of the Persians, an accursed race, a race utterly alienated from God...
> ... has invaded the lands of those Christians and has depopulated them by the sword, pillage and fire ...[3]

> ... we cannot recount without deep sorrow - how, with great hurt and dire suffering our Christian brothers, members in Christ, are scourged, oppressed, and injured in Jerusalem, in Antioch and other cities of the East. ... Christian blood, redeemed by the blood of Christ, has been shed, and Christian flesh, akin to the flesh of Christ, has been subjected to unspeakable degradation and servitude. Everywhere in those cities there is sorrow, everywhere misery, everywhere groaning (I say it with a sigh). The churches ... to our sorrow, used as stables for the animals of these people! Holy men do not posses those cities; nay base and bastard Turks hold sway over our brothers. ... and rush as quickly as you can to the defense of the Eastern Church. ...it is less wicked to brandish your sword against Saracens. It is the only warfare that is righteous, ... [4]

> The noble race of Franks must come to the aid their fellow Christians in the East. The infidel Turks are advancing into the heart of Eastern Christendom; Christians are being oppressed and attacked; churches and holy places are being defiled. Jerusalem is groaning under the Saracen yoke. The Holy Sepulchre is in Moslem hands and has been turned into a Mosque. Pilgrims are harassed and even prevented from access to the Holy Land. The West must march to the defense of the East. All should go, rich and poor alike. The Franks must stop their internal wars and

---

[3] The First Crusade. E Peters. Second Edition. University of Pennsylvania Press, 1998, pages 26-29. The Speech of Urban: Version of Robert of Rheims.

[4] The First Crusade. E Peters. Second Edition. University of Pennsylvania Press, 1998, pages 29-33. The Speech of Urban: Version of Baldric of Dol.

squabbles. Let them go instead against the infidel and fight a righteous war. God himself will lead them, for they will be doing His work. There will be absolution and remission of sins for all who die in the service of Christ. Here they are poor and miserable sinners; there they will be rich and happy. Let none hesitate; they must march next summer. God wills it! [5]

For an additional discussion on this topic see Chapter 6, Jihad, The Struggle to Self-Discipline and Chapter 21, Creative Terminology for Islam and Muslims.

The Crusades

First Crusade	1095-1099 CE	
Second Crusade	1147-1149 CE	
Third Crusade	1188-1192 CE	
Fourth Crusade	1202-1204 CE	
Fifth Crusade	1217-1221 CE	
Sixth Crusade	1228-1229 CE	
Seventh Crusade	1248-1250 CE	(Louis IX of France)
Eighth Crusade	1270 CE	(Louis IX of France)
Ninth Crusade	1271-1272 CE	(Edward I of England)

The term crusade is derived from *crucesignati* which means *those marked by the cross*. There were nine medieval Crusades from the eleventh through the thirteenth centuries. Unacknowledged are crusades which continue up to this day under the guise of combating terrorism, spreading democracy, etc. The latter day crusades unfold in exactly the same fashion and also place the blame squarely upon the victims.

The medieval Crusades were a series of Christians *holy war* campaigns in the middle east (present day Lebanon, Syria, Palestine) and later spread to Egypt and North Africa. They resulted in European occupation of the conquered territories and the establishment of

---

[5] Skip Knox EL. http://gbgm-umc.org/UMW/bible/crusades.stm Last accessed June 2011.

numerous kingdoms (colonies). These Crusades were directed primarily towards capturing territories and the city of Jerusalem from Muslims who were portrayed as *infidels*.

Crusader conquest of Jerusalem

The First Crusade began in 1095 CE and Jerusalem fell to the invaders on 15 July 1099 CE (492 AH). Pillage, death, and destruction were commonplace in the cities and countryside that came under the Crusaders. The capture of Jerusalem and subsequent gruesome acts of the invaders are documented by the eyewitness accounts of the Christian historian Raymond d'Aguilers.

But now that our men has possession of the walls and towers, wonderful sights were to be seen. Some of our men (and this was more merciful) cut off the heads of their enemies; others shot them with arrows, so that they fell from the towers; others tortured them longer by casting them into the flames. Piles of heads, hands and feet were to be seen in the streets of the city. It was necessary to pick one's way over the bodies of men and horses. But these were small matters compared to what happened at the Temple of Solomon, a place where religious services are ordinarily chanted. What happened there? If I tell the truth, it will exceed your powers of belief. So let it suffice to say this much, at least, that in the Temple and porch of Solomon, men rode in blood up to their knees and bridle reins. Indeed, it was a just and splendid judgement of God that this place should be filled with the blood of the unbelievers, since it had suffered so long from their blasphemies. The city was filled with corpses and blood.[6]

In addition, crops were destroyed, religious shrines were desecrated, including the Dome of the Rock Mosque, the tomb of Abraham ☙, and the synagogue was burnt with the Jews inside.[7] By some accounts, 70,000 people who had sought refuge, and had also

---

[6] The First Crusade. E Peters. Second Edition. University of Pennsylvania Press, 1998, pages 256-260.

[7] The First Crusade. E Peters. Second Edition. University of Pennsylvania Press, 1998, pages 274-277.

been assured protection, were treacherously massacred in the Al Aqsa Sanctuary.[8,9]

Muslim Conquests of Jerusalem

The conduct of the Muslim conquerors of Jerusalem stands in sharp contrast to that of the Crusaders. Long before the Crusades began, Muslim armies had defeated the numerically superior Byzantine armies in the Battle of Yarmuk (Syria) in 636 CE.[10] Subsequently, they besieged Jerusalem. The citizens of Jerusalem agreed to a surrender provided the Khalifah, Umar ibn al Khattab ﷺ, himself oversaw the process. This was a very significant and a calculated request. The period of Umar ibn al Khattab's ﷺ caliphate is also known as *The Period of Justice*. Thus, by requesting Umar ﷺ to personally oversee the surrender of the city, the citizens of Jerusalem were securing their own safety.

Umar ibn al Khattab ﷺ traveled from Madinah to Jerusalem and accepted the surrender in 637 CE (16 AH). Entering Jerusalem, the Khalifah was accompanied by the Greek Orthodox Patriarch. While visiting the Church of the Holy Sepulchre, it became time for prayer. The Patriarch invited Umar ﷺ to pray in the Church. However, he declined and instead went out of the Church to pray. This foresight on his part prevented his followers from taking over the church. Had he prayed inside the church, Muslims could have built a mosque at that site, in commemoration. Later, a Mosque was constructed at the site where Umar ﷺ had prayed.

After the surrender and occupation of Jerusalem by Muslims, general amnesty was proclaimed and there was no bloodshed, no rape or pillage. All religious sanctuaries were protected and remained protected under each and every successive Muslim administration.

This example was followed by Salahuddin Ayyubi (Saladin) who retook Jerusalem from the Crusaders on Friday, 27 Rajab 583 AH

---

[8] J Arthur McFall. Taking Jerusalem, Climax of the First Crusade. Last accessed June 2011. http://www.historynet.com/first-crusade-siege-of-jerusalem.htm/1

[9] Maalouf A: The Crusade through Arab eyes. Schocken Books, New York. 1984, pages 50-52.

[10] The troops were commanded by the generals Abu Ubaidah ibn al Jarrah, Amr ibn al 'Aas, Khalid ibn al Walid, Yazid ibn Abi Sufiyan, and Shurahbil ibn Hasanah.

(1187 CE). With the surrender of Jerusalem to Salahuddin, thousands of enemy combatants were arrested. They were released after payment of tribute, some of which came from Salahuddin's personal funds. Those citizens wishing to leave the city were granted free passage. There was no revenge taking, killing, rape or plunder. All religious sites remained untouched.

There was tolerance and respect for the other faiths, as required by Islam. The Jews, who had been evicted by the Crusaders, were invited back and the Jewish places of worship were rebuilt. This tolerance and accommodation included the Latin Christians and was exercised by successive Muslim rulers of Jerusalem. Until 1948, the followers of all faiths lived in peace and harmony.

Christian and Muslim Occupation of Jerusalem: a comparison

As Christian historians have recorded, after the fall of Jerusalem, the Orthodox Christian priests had possession of the Church of The Holy Sepulchre and all Christian and Jewish places of worship had not been harmed under Muslim rule. Subsequent to the capture of Jerusalem by the Crusaders, the Greek and Armenian Orthodox and Coptic priests were evicted from the city after having been tortured into revealing the location of the *True Cross* which they had hidden, to prevent it from falling into the hands of the Crusaders. Tens of thousands Muslims were massacred, not even sparing the women and children and the Jews were burned alive in the main Synagogue (see quotation from the historian Raymond d'Aguilers). Muslim and Jewish places of worship, including the Dome of the Rock Mosque, were pillaged. The Crusaders even destroyed the monuments sacred to Orthodox Christians and desecrated the tomb of Abraham ﷺ. J Arthur McFall writes:[11]

The Crusaders spent at least that night and the next day killing Muslims, including all of those in the al-Aqsa Mosque, where Tancred's banner

---

[11] J Arthur McFall. Taking Jerusalem, Climax of the First Crusade. (http://www.thefreelibrary.com/TAKING+JERUSALEM+CLIMAX+OF+THE+FIRST+CRUSADE.-a054994230)
http://www.historynet.com/first-crusade-siege-of-jerusalem.htm/1 Last accessed June 2011.

should have protected them. Not even women and children were spared. The city's Jews sought refuge in their synagogue, only to be burned alive within it by the Crusaders. Raymond of Aquilers reported that he saw "piles of heads, hands and feet" on a walk through the holy city. Men trotted across the bodies and body fragments as if they were a carpet for their convenience. The Europeans also destroyed the monuments to Orthodox Christian saints and the tomb of Abraham.

History shows that even though Jerusalem had been under Muslim rule since 637 CE, Christian pilgrims were not restricted from visiting the city. Christian places of worship were safe under all Muslim administrations. The Crusades destroyed the mutual respect, harmony and peaceful coexistence that existed between Muslims and Christians.

Viewed by the light of their original purpose, the Crusades were failures. They made no permanent conquests of the Holy Land. They did not retard the advance of Islam. Far from aiding the Eastern Empire, they hastened its disintegration. They also revealed the continuing inability of Latin Christians to understand Greek Christians, and they hardened the schism between them. They fostered a harsh intolerance between Muslims and Christians, where before there had been a measure of mutual respect. They were marked, and marred, by a recrudescence of anti-Semitism ...[12]

At Homs the large church provided shelter for the services of the two religions for four centuries. It was not until the Crusades, and the atmosphere of suspicion they generated, that this practice, which testified to the great tolerance of the early Islamic rulers, ceased.[13]

Holy War in Perspective

War is an act of violence. It invariably results in the loss of innocent life, of the defenseless, elderly, women and children. Pronouncements

---

[12] A History of the Christian Church, Fourth Edition. Walker W, Norris RA, Lotz DW, Handy RT, Editors. Scribner (Simon & Schuster), New York 1985, page 290.

[13] Sauvaget J: Les Monuments historiques de Damas, Beirut, 1932. Cited by Courbage Y, Fargues P. Christian and Jews under Islam. Translated by J Mabro. IB Tauris Publishers, London, 1997. Pages 10-11.

by the pope, Urban II, elevated the status of this act of violence to that of *a penitential and spiritually meritorious act providing atonement for sin and* thus the *Holy War* was born.

There is nothing in Islamic teachings and practice that can be likened to *holy war*. Calling Jihad a *holy war* is not only an absurdity but also betrays ignorance. Unlike the Crusades, which were designated *holy wars*, Islam does not assign warfare the status of being holy. It considers war to be a deceit, something that should be avoided. While Islam conditionally permits warfare, it also requires that efforts be made to avoid it. Warfare is only an act of necessity and it is permitted under the aegis of Jihad only for specific situations and sets forth strict preconditions (see Chapter 6, Jihad, The Struggle to Self-Discipline).

Jihad is a unique and unquestionably noble undertaking with the purpose of striving for overall goodness which benefits all of mankind. It is primarily an *inner struggle* of the individual for betterment in all affairs, religious and worldly. This involves following the principles of Islam and by avoiding everything that is evil and doing and encouraging everything that is good: living a life of morality, honesty, integrity, fairness, exercising compassion for others and doing general goodness. Jihad is the purification of the self to make every action acceptable and pleasing to God. It pursues the true meaning of Islam, ie., *submission to the Will of God*, which is the ultimate goal of every believing woman and man. Jihad cannot be linked to *holy war,* even remotely.

For an additional discussion on this topic see Chapter 6, Jihad, The Struggle to Self-Discipline and Chapter 21, Creative Terminology for Islam and Muslims.

Concluding Commentary

Surely We created man of the best stature. Then We reduced him to the lowest of the low, Except those who believe and do good works, and theirs is a unfailing reward. (Surah 95, At Tin, ayaat 4-6)

The precedent set by Urban II was followed by others, beginning with the subsequent medieval Crusades to Palestine, the Spanish

Inquisition, the national-socialistic movement leading to the Second World War, the Serbian genocide, to the twenty-first century crusades. Amazing is the unabashed use of the same terminology, ie., *crusade*, and replication of the conduct of the medieval Crusaders with no less intensity.

Islam strictly prohibits torture of the living and mutilation of the dead. History confirms that people of other faiths have lived in peace and harmony under Muslim rule. This is no coincidence. Muslim rulers had to abide by strict Islamic laws dictating conduct towards non-Muslims. The magnitude of destruction or desecration of edifices sacred to Muslim during the Crusades, the Serbian genocide, Afghan and Persian Gulf wars has no parallel in Muslim history. Islamic law prohibits the desecration of non-Muslim places of worship. There are hundreds of churches with tall spires scattered throughout the Muslim world where Christian still live or once lived. No indigenous or naturalized Christian was ever prohibited from building a church. However, there is often no reciprocity for Muslims who are citizens of predominantly Christian states.[14]

Islam reveres all prophets that were sent by God to guide mankind. As recipients of earlier Scriptures, both Jews and Christians are referred to as *Ahl al Kitaab or People of the Book,* and as such, they are assigned a privileged status. No Muslim ever calls a Christian or Jew an infidel or unbeliever since they believe in the same God, the Creator and Owner of the universe.

Additional Reading

Maalouf A. The Crusade through Arab eyes. Schocken Books, New York. 1984. ISBN 0-8052-0898-4

Armstrong K: The curse of the infidel. A century ago Muslim intellectuals admired the west. Why did we lose their goodwill? http://www.guardian.co.uk/world/2002/jun/20/religion.september11

---

[14] Examples are Spain, Italy, and Greece. Additionally, the construction of minarets was banned by Switzerland in December 2009.

Chapter Twenty-Four

Suicide, Killing and War

Introduction

> *And do not take the life which Allah has forbidden,[1] except for a just cause [2]...* (Surah 17, Al Isra', ayat 33)

Life is sacred and the protection of life is one of the purposes of Shari'ah. Islam does not permit aggression, oppression, or injustice in any form but requires peace, tolerance and justice. While Islam permits self-defense for the individual, group, or nation, the Shari'ah has laid down explicit rules for what is permitted and prohibited in conflict situations. These surpass those established by any international organization in the aftermath of the world wars. Compliance with these Shari'ah rules is required of all believers.

Every believer knows that the Day of Judgement is a certainty and fears that day. When that inevitable Event occurs, each person will be held accountable for his/her deeds with no excuses accepted (eg., that superiors ordered it) nor will there be any plea bargaining.[3] No one will carry the burden of another's deeds. Only those who obeyed God's laws and complied with His directives (the Shari'ah) will have little to fear. It is this fear of standing before God and having to

---

[1] *harram Allah*: forbidden or made sacred by Allah. This includes suicide.

[2] *... except for a just cause ...* meaning in the course of justice.

[3] Surah 56, Al Waqi'ah, ayaat 2-3. *There is no denying that it will occur. Abasing some, exalting others.* The Day of Reckoning (Judgement) is coming whether one believes in it or not.

account for each and every action, dreading the consequences of any wrongdoing, especially towards others, that makes a believer carefully choose a path which avoids even coming close to the possibility of a wrongful action.

> *And each one of them will come to Him (God) on the Day of Resurrection, alone.*   (Surah 19, Maryam, ayat 95)

> *Your Lord is best aware of those who stray from His way and of those who are rightly guided.*   (Surah 68, Al Qalam, ayat 7)

Persons involved in killing or other forms of systematic violence causing destruction of life and property may justify their intentions and their actions through a process of rationalization. However, through acts of injustice, indiscriminate violence and terror, they become renegades, deviating from pristine nature in which man was created, ie., the *fitrah*.

Religious Extremism

When attempting to identify *religious extremism*, several factors must be taken into consideration, especially when the focus is on people in foreign lands. Language barriers, an alien culture, and unfamiliarity with their religious practices increase the likelihood for misinterpretation of expression. Furthermore, the Westerner is often overwhelmed by the exhibited religious devotion and is unfamiliar with its implications which may also lead to misinterpretation of intent. Finally, the intensity or the lack of religious zeal and observance of the one attempting judgement must be factored into the analysis as it inherently biases the opinion.

In the context of Islam, does religious extremism really exist or is it a manifestation of extremist human behavior under the guise of religion? Those endowed with a true knowledge of Islam can never be extremists because Islam imbibes humility, distances a person from every extreme and teaches respect and tolerance for diversity of opinions and beliefs. An example is found in the founding scholars of the four Sunni schools of jurisprudence, Imams Abu Hanifa, Shafi,

Malik and Hanbal (may God's Blessings be upon them). Each one of those imams was a very learned scholar and accepted the opinions of the others while maintaining his own.

By definition and by requirement, Islam is peace and a middle course. It discourages extremes in behavior as well as in religious observances. Prophet Muhammad ﷺ said: *Those who go to extremes are doomed.*[4] Furthermore, there cannot be any compulsion in religion nor imposition of one's belief upon others. Therefore, regardless of the fervor of belief of an individual or group, it may not be imposed upon others.

In light of the foregoing, who are the so-called *religious extremists?* Are they the learned scholars (ulema), educators or students in schools, colleges and universities, imams at religious institutions, farmers, members of the Muslim militaries, or the hundreds of millions of other ordinary persons in different professions and walks of life who observe their religious duties conscientiously? While none of these people qualify for this media propagated distinction, much of the ongoing violence in several middle eastern countries and south Asia continues to be attributed to "Islamic extremists" by the media and those directing it. An analysis of the facts shows otherwise.

What is portrayed as being *religious extremism* by Western media is the expression of a certain type of human behavior that uses religion as a front to achieve its goals, political, social, or otherwise. It is by no means peculiar to Muslims.[5] Those pursuing acts of "extremism" are rarely, if ever, motivated by genuine religious beliefs or even posses a true understanding of the religion they profess to follow. This is particularly true for Islam and it may or may not have the same applicability for other faiths.

Those tasked with carrying out the actual acts of violence in pursuit of "extremist" beliefs are unfortunate, often uneducated, and misguided individuals who understand little, if anything, about the consequences of their actions, especially for themselves. As many historical and also recent events have shown, such ordinary persons

---

[4] English Translation of Sahih Muslim. Daruussalam, Riyadh, S Arabia, 2007, Volume 7, Hadith 6784, page 44.

[5] When actual numbers are considered in relation to total populations, extremism, religious intolerance and prejudice are far more common among non-Muslims.

are used as tools by the masterminds of terrorism and violence.

Violence in Perspective

On the Day when every soul will be confronted with all the good it has done, and all the evil it has done, it will wish that there were a great distance between it and its evil. Allah warns you to fear Him; and Allah is full of kindness to those that serve Him (ibaad).

Surah 3, 'Al Imraan, ayat 30

Violence is a complex, multifaceted problem with multiple forms of expression.[6] Instigating factors include socioeconomic and political issues, both from external and internal sources. Violence and terrorism exist everywhere and are perpetrated by individuals, groups, organizations, and also states who use it for political and economic goals. Significantly, reactive violence is a consequence of economic and social injustices. While the acts of reactive violence receive full media attention, the causes are frequently ignored or understated.

In virtually every society there are elements who are prone to violent reaction. In this respect, Muslim societies are no different. That is the nature of man and some individual inclinations cannot be tempered even by the pristine teachings of Islam. Corrupt state apparatus, corrupt politicians, oppression, economic deprivation and exploitation breed frustration and discontent. Despite these and the external influences which chart the course in Muslim societies, violence remains proportionately insignificant by any measure.[7] This is in itself a testimonial for the innate peace-loving nature of the Muslim whose first and foremost desire is to live in peace and harmony in accordance with the Qur'an and Sunnah.

Violence is committed by persons of all religious backgrounds but that does not make it religious in nature nor as being condoned by the faith of the perpetrators. Anyone committing or even contemplating

---

[6] This discussion does not cover domestic or interpersonal violence.

[7] Calculatèd as incidents per unit of population after excluding the work of foreign elements. In Muslim countries violence *appears* to be significant only because the media chooses to give it prime time.

any act of violence, other than in the course of legitimate self defense, while professing to follow Islam, must necessarily undertake a critical self-reevaluation because he/she is far off course as the actions betray their true convictions. Furthermore, many of the acts of violence being perpetrated in the name of Islam are against innocent Muslims. That is simply incompatible with Islam and the prescribed behavior for Muslims. A Hadith from Prophet Muhammad ﷺ states: *Whoever takes up arms against us, is not from us.*[8]

In Muslim countries, the reason for the spate of violence observed during the past decade or two appears to be twofold. The possession of vast natural resources has enticed the neocolonialists who seek to reoccupy or dominate those regions for control of the resources. Many of these Muslim countries also find themselves in strategic geographic locations. Secondly, there is an absence of a true central state authority, independent of foreign influence, which genuinely pursues the welfare of the society in accordance with Shari'ah with fair and equitable distribution of resources and national wealth. Social injustice and dissatisfaction with laws and practices that run contrary to Shari'ah serve as provocation. The majority of Muslims would welcome the establishment of the Shari'ah as the main source of law. It provides speedy and equitable rulings, unlike the protracted and complex Western system of justice.

For an additional discussion on this topic see Violence and Islam in Chapter 1, Islam and Violent Islam in Chapter 21, Creative Terminology for Islam and Muslims.

Definition of a Martyr (shaheed)

Think not of those who are killed in Allah's cause as dead. Nay, they are living, finding their sustenance in the presence of their Lord. Joyful because of what Allah has bestowed upon them of His grace, ...

(Surah 3, 'Al Imraan, ayaat 169-170)

To the non-Muslim mind, especially Westerners, the concept of

---

[8] The Translation of the Meanings of Sahih Al-Bukhari. MM Khan, Kazi Publications, Lahore, Pakistan, 1979. Volume IX, Hadith 191, page 153.

seeking martyrdom may appear peculiar or unnerving. For the Muslim, death is inevitable and the life span cannot be prolonged. The time, place and mode of death are predetermined. Miraculous recovery from a severe illness or surviving a serious accident is no more than a manifestation of the fact that the time of death had not come. While a person does not know how, when and where she/he is going to die, one that propels the individual to Paradise is the most desirable death. That is the reason behind the desire for martyrdom.

Broadly defined, a martyr is a person who is ready to sacrifice her/his life, the most precious possession, for a noble and legitimate cause. However, martyrdom does not come only through war. There are eight categories:[9,10] *one who dies fighting in the way of Allah,*[11] *those who die because of plague, abdominal disease, drowning or a falling building; those dying as a result of burns, pneumonia and delivery (childbirth); a person who dies fighting off attackers to protect his/her property.*

Martyrdom (*shahadah fe sabee lillah*) is desired as all sins are forgiven and the person is admitted to Paradise without any trial concerning worldly deeds. However, a true martyr can be identified only by God because the individual's intentions are known only to Him. Additionally, just before she/he dies, the person may commit an act which could be tantamount to disbelief or the reason(s) for desiring martyrdom maybe unacceptable. Such a person cannot be called a martyr, although outwardly it may appear as such.[12] Suicide does not bring martyrdom by any stretch of the imagination. Also see Suicide Bombers.

---

[9] The Translation of the Meanings of Sahih Al-Bukhari. MM Khan, Kazi Publications, Lahore, Pakistan, 1979. Volume IV, Hadith 82, pages 61-62.

[10] The Translation of the Meanings of Sahih Al-Bukhari. MM Khan, Kazi Publications, Lahore, Pakistan, 1979. Volume III, Hadith 660, page 397.

[11] This includes those dying in the defense of the homeland, from an unjust foreign attack.

[12] Prophet Muhammad ﷺ said: *A man may do what seem to the people as the deeds of the dwellers of Paradise but he is from the dwellers of the Hell-Fire and another may do what seem to the people as the deeds of the dwellers of the Hell-Fire, but he is from the dwellers of Paradise.* The Translation of the Meanings of Sahih Al-Bukhari. MM Khan, Kazi Publications, Lahore, Pakistan, 1979. Volume V, Hadith 514, pages 362-364.

Islamic View of Suicide and Killing

... so regard the life and property of every Muslim as a sacred trust.
... Hurt no one so that no one may hurt you.
... Remember, one day you will appear before Allah and answer for
your deeds. So beware, do not stray from the path of righteousness after
I am gone.[13]

Life is a sacred gift from God and must be cherished and protected. Therefore, taking a life without a just cause is strictly prohibited and subject to severe punishment in the Hereafter, unless forgiven by God. Justifications for taking a life include the death sentence for a justly convicted murderer, for high treason, serious crimes of morality that may endanger or destroy the fabric of society and during a legal and morally justified war.[14] The latter includes fighting external aggression and oppression, if the oppressed request help. Rules of warfare are very strict, they protect noncombatants and prohibit unnecessary destruction of crops and property, a moral high ground that has remained elusive for many in the West.

Suicide Bombers

A distinction must be made between suicide combat missions during war and suicide bombing in civilian areas. Suicide combat missions during a war for resisting aggression and for the protection of the lives and territories of the defenders are not uncommon war tactics and could be considered legitimate under the strict rules of warfare. Killing of innocent civilians through suicide bombings is murder. Suicide for any reason, including despair and terminal illness, is a major sin and is strictly prohibited.[15] A Hadith states: *A man was inflicted with wounds and he committed suicide, and so Allah said: My slave has caused death on*

---

[13] Excerpts from the Farewell Sermon: *Farewell Khutbah of the Prophet* ﷺ. Its Universal Values. Sakr AH. Foundation for Islamic Knowledge, Lombard, IL. 1993.

[14] A truly *legal and morally justified war*, not necessarily according to the definitions of the invader or aggressor.

[15] A person who commits suicide is punished in Hell-Fire perpetually reenacting the suicide. The Translation and Meanings of Sahih Al-Bukhari. MM Khan. Kazi Publications, Lahore Pakistan, 1979. Volume II, Hadith 446, page 252.

himself hurriedly, so I forbid Paradise for him.[16]

Suicide bombings in civilian areas may be the result of complex circumstances and it may not always be possible to identify the actual source(s) and intentions. For the most part, the perpetrators are not so-called religious fanatics or *religious extremists,* nor individuals overwhelmed by despair or seeking revenge. They are ordinary people persuaded by blinding systematic indoctrination and mind control, to serve the purposes of a few who mastermind such operations.[17]

Most of the present day suicide bombings have been occurring in Muslim lands, frequently in places of worship, in business areas or involve public transportation and deliberately target innocent civilians. If the suicide bomber really understood the consequences of his/her action, ie., the explosion shredding his/her body to pieces would be reenacted *ad infinitum* and that the killing of an innocent individual is equivalent to the killing all of mankind (Surah 5, Al Ma'idah, ayat 32), he/she would never even contemplate such an act. Unless mitigated or forgiven by God, such an act has the potential for the worst kind of eternal punishment, a far cry from the dream of Paradise.

The gravity of the offense of suicide attacks on innocent civilians is highlighted by two Hadith from Prophet Muhammad ﷺ. As the first Hadith indicates, it is forbidden to even point a weapon towards another Muslim.

None of you should point out towards his Muslim brother with a weapon, for he does not know, Satan may tempt him to hit him and thus he would fall into a pit of fire (Hell).[18]

Abusing a Muslim is fusuq (an evil deed) and killing him is kufr (disbelief).[19]

---

[16] The Translation and Meanings of Sahih Al-Bukhari. MM Khan. Kazi Publications, Lahore Pakistan, 1979. Volume II, Hadith 445, page 251.

[17] Increasingly, foreign spy/terror agencies are simulating suicide bombings using remote triggering.

[18] The Translation of the Meanings of Sahih Al-Bukhari. MM Khan, Kazi Publications, Lahore, Pakistan, 1979. Volume IX, Hadith 193, page 153.

[19] The Translation of the Meanings of Sahih Al-Bukhari. MM Khan, Kazi Publications, Lahore, Pakistan. 1979. Volume IX, Hadith 197, page 155.
Kufr (disbelief) is punishable by Hell.

Islamic View of Warfare

And do not take the life which Allah has forbidden, except for a just
cause ...   (Surah 17, Al Isra', ayat 33)

Fight in the way of Allah against those who fight against you, but do not
begin hostilities. Allah does not love aggressors.
                                                  (Surah 2, Al Baqarah, ayat 190)

For God is with those who restrain themselves, and those who do good.
                                                  (Surah 16, An Nahl, ayat 128)

The ultimate goal of Islam is the establishment of peace. Therefore, whenever possible, war is to be avoided and conflicts should be resolved through peaceful means. Although it is not desirable, war may become necessary as being the only means to stop injustices, unprovoked aggression, oppression and the killing of innocent people.[20,21]

War brings to surface the baseness and savagery in humans. Even today, such behavior persists in some segments of humanity and also fails to elicit serious condemnation. Keeping in perspective the damage caused by armed conflict, Islam introduced rules that attempt to modify human behavior and limit the death and destruction associated with war. These rules were established centuries before the rest of the world perceived such a need. Importantly, Muslims abided by the rules they established, unlike today, where even the founding nations blatantly disregard the rules they helped put in place.

Wars involving Muslims never resulted in indiscriminate blood-letting. Civilian populations were never targeted and "collateral damage" was unacceptable. Wars were either against aggressors or

---

[20] Surah 2, Al Baqarah, ayat 193: *And fight them until there is no more persecution, and Allah's way is established instead (and religion is for Allah). But if they desist, then let there be no hostility except against the evil-doers.*
...*Allah's way is established instead (and religion is for Allah)...*, ie., until God can be worshipped without fear of persecution, and none is compelled to bow down in awe before another human being. The Message of the Qur'an. Translated and Explained by Muhammad Asad. The Book Foundation, Bristol, England, 2003. Page 52.

[21] Surah 2, Al Baqarah, ayat 217: ...*persecution is worse than killing.*

were initiated by a call for help from oppressed populations. The liberated people were always free to practice the faith of their choice.

In 635 CE, when the Muslim armies were withdrawing from the Syrian cities which they had occupied for about a year, in order to make preparations for the final confrontation with the Byzantines at Yarmuk, the response of the population of Hims was as follows: *We like your rule and justice far better than the state of oppression and tyranny in which we were (under the Byzantines). The army of Heraclius we shall indeed, with your help, repulse from the city.*[22] This historical anecdote shows that the Muslims strictly adhered to the rules and did not harm or oppress the population, nor plunder and destroy their city. Had there been any injustices, the people would have been glad to see them depart.

Historians have also documented that after the first one hundred years of Muslim rule in greater Syria and Palestine, following the defeat and expulsion of the Byzantines, only about six percent of the population was Muslim.[23] Had there been any forced conversion to Islam, this figure would have been much higher.

War was disliked by Prophet Muhammad ﷺ. He called it deceit and urged Muslims to seek peace and security through prayer rather than engaging in military conflict.[24] He ﷺ said: *Do not wish to face the enemy (in a battle) and ask Allah to save you (from calamities) but if you should face the enemy, then be patient and let it be known to you that Paradise is under the shades of swords.*[25]

And those who defend themselves after a wrong is done to them, against such there is no cause of blame. The blame is only against those who

---

[22] Baladhuri, AA ibn Jabir, Kitab Futuh Al Buldan, The Origins of the Islamic State. Translated by Philip K Hitti, Columbia University, New York, 1916. Page 211. http://www.archive.org/stream/originsofislamic02albauoft#page/n3/mode/2up Last accessed August 2011.

[23] Courbage Y, Fargues P. Christian and Jews under Islam. Translated by Judy Mabro. IB Tauris Publishers, London, 1997. Page 11.

[24] The Translation of the Meanings of Sahih Al-Bukhari. MM Khan, Kazi Publications, Lahore, Pakistan, 1979. Volume IV, Hadith 268, page 167.

[25] *Paradise is under the shades of swords.* This refers to the promise of God that anyone who dies *fighting in the cause of God* will immediately be granted Paradise. The Translation of the Meanings of Sahih Al-Bukhari. MM Khan, Kazi Publications, Lahore, Pakistan, 1979. Volume IV, Hadith 210, pages 132-133.

oppress mankind, and wrongfully rebel in the earth. For such there will be a grievous penalty. (Surah 42, Ash Shura, ayaat 41-42)

Islamic Rules of Warfare

The Islamic rules of warfare incorporate rights for the enemy and others affected by the conflict. There is strict differentiation between combatants and civilian noncombatants and any form of injustice is prohibited. These rules come from three sources: The Qur'an, the Sunnah of the Prophet ﷺ, and the actions (sunnah) of the rightly guided Khalifahs and other virtuous companions of the Prophet ﷺ. The Shari'ah and all Islamic rules governing general conduct and behavior remain unchanged and in effect at all times.

Treaties

Existing treaties and agreements must be honoured. The moral duty to honour treaties and obligations is frequently absent or applied on a selective basis by aggressors. Islam requires that treaties be respected and prohibits dishonest and treacherous behavior.

Fulfill the covenant of God when you have entered into it, and do not break your oaths after you have confirmed them; Indeed you have made God your surety; for God knows all that you do.
(Surah 16, An Nahl, ayat 91)

If there is concern about violation of an existing treaty by the other party, it must first be annulled before going to war.

If you fear treachery from any people (with whom you have made a Covenant/treaty), then throw it back to them (so as to be) on equal terms, for God does not love the treacherous.
(Surah 8, Al Anfaal, ayat 58)

Hostilities

- These may not be initiated without just cause and not without a declaration of war

- Acts of vengeance are prohibited
- Noncombatants such as women, children, the old and sick may not to be purposely injured or killed
- Noncombatant clergy may not be killed and places of worship may not be damaged or destroyed
- Injured enemy soldiers who are unable to fight may not be attacked or killed
- Destruction, pillage, plunder of civilian property in the captured areas is prohibited. If anything is taken, the owner(s) must be compensated
- Medical assistance should be made available to the wounded and sick. The Crusader, King Richard of England, who suffered an illness during his Crusade campaign, was the recipient of such assistance which was provided by a Muslim physician sent by Salahuddin Ayyubi

The following is an excerpt from the instructions given by the first Khalifah, Abu Bakr ﷺ (632-634 CE), as he sent off the troops to confront the Byzantine aggression at Ajnadain (13 AH, 634 CE):

Do not commit misappropriation or fraud nor be guilty of disobedience to the Commander. Do not mutilate the dead and do not kill old men, women or children. Do not injure date palms and do not cut down fruit trees. Do not kill animals except for food. Do not harass monks.

Prisoners

- All human beings must be treated with respect and dignity
- Enemy prisoners must be treated kindly and may not be physically or sexually abused or kept in shackles
- Prisoners may not be tortured or executed
- They may be freed as a gesture of goodwill or ransomed as part of an exchange deal[26]
- Wounded or sick prisoners should be provided medical assistance
- Enemy corpses may not be mutilated and should be turned over to the enemy

---

[26] Surah 47, Muhammad, ayat 4.

Islam places the prisoner in the same social category as the indigent and orphan, ie., those needing sympathy and charity.

> ... And they feed, for the love of Allah, the indigent, the orphan and the captive. Saying: We feed you, for the sake of Allah alone. We wish for no reward nor thanks from you.   (Surah 76, Al Insan, ayaat 8-9)

Vengeance and Retaliation

> ... Establish worship and enjoin kindness and forbid iniquity, and persevere whatever may befall you ...   (Surah 31, Luqman, ayat 17)

The Qur'an, which is the Source of guidance from God, repeatedly commands to do good and avoid injustice. The Prophet ﷺ set the example for compassionate treatment of captives. He ﷺ said: *Allah will not be merciful to those who are not merciful to mankind.*[27] He ﷺ also warned: *Be afraid from the curse of the oppressed as there is no screen between his invocation and Allah.*[28]

Vengeance, collective punishment such as economic deprivation, sanctions, destruction of infrastructure and crops, and indiscriminate killing by any method including aerial bombardment, Haditha-Iraq type killings, etc., are strictly prohibited. Retaliation, if exercised, must be in a just and equitable fashion.[29] Although retaliation is permitted restraint, patience and forgiveness are encouraged.[30,31]

Honour Killings

The so-called *honour killing* may be defined as the killing of a person based on the belief that the victim brought dishonour to the

---

[27] The Translation of the Meanings of Sahih Al-Bukhari. MM Khan, Kazi Publications, Lahore, Pakistan, 1979. Volume IX, Hadith 473, page 351.

[28] The Translation of the Meanings of Sahih Al-Bukhari. MM Khan, Kazi Publications, Lahore, Pakistan, 1979. Volume III, Hadith 628, pages 376-377.

[29] Surah 16, An Nahl, ayat 126: *And if you punish your enemy, then punish them with the like of that wherewith you were afflicted.*

[30] Surah 2, Al Baqarah, ayat 194: *... there is the law of just retribution (qisas). Therefore, if anyone transgresses a prohibition by attacking you, you may do likewise. But always fear Allah, and know that Allah is with those who restrain themselves.*

[31] Surah 42, Ash Shura, ayat 43.

family/community or caused disgrace because of an act perceived as being unbecoming. The perpetrators are mostly males, usually but not always, they are also related to the victims. Factors that may trigger such killings include social issues, sexual acts (consensual or by assault), alleged dress code disputes, noncompliance with family directives, political matters, etc. It is estimated that annually between several hundred to a few thousand such killings occur world wide. The majority of victims are females. Importantly, such acts are not peculiar to any particular culture or religion.

The term *honour killing* seems to be used almost exclusively for the non-white population of the world, for immigrants to white majority countries, middle easterners and south Asians, many of whom are Muslim. The killing of a caucasian woman by her caucasian husband triggered by her affair with another man is still described as being a homicide and not honour killing, although the motive and results maybe identical.

Unjustified killing is unequivocally prohibited: *And do not take the life which Allah has forbidden, except for a just cause...* (Surah 17, Al Isra', ayat 33). A *just cause* means in the course of justice, such as after conviction for murder or high treason. The prescribed Shari'ah punishment for murder is death. However, the perpetrator's life may be spared by the victim's heirs. See Chapter 4, Islamic Law, Shari'ah and Fiqh.

The killing of one's own family member is considered an abomination. In pre-Islamic Arabia, infants (usually females) were buried alive because of the perceived shame of not begetting a male offspring or for financial reasons, ie., the fear of poverty. The practice of infanticide was stopped by Islam.

Islam requires that justice be served in every case of homicide. It also requires a fair and just trial, not one tainted by bias and emotion. The sentence for any individual fairly convicted for homicide or a so-called *honour killing* is the same. What is perhaps more important, and often forgotten by the perpetrators of homicide, is that sentencing and the execution of that sentence in this life does not absolve them of that guilt as he/she has also to answer for it on the Day of Judgement. In other words, additional punishment, which may potentially be eternal, awaits that person unless forgiven by God Almighty because of sincere repentance.

Concluding Summary

Every person's fate We have fastened on his own neck. On the Day of Judgement We shall bring out for him a book which he will see spread open. It will be said to him: Read your own record; Your soul is sufficient this day as witness against you. (Surah 17, Al Isra', ayaat 13-14)

While a world without wars remains elusive, the next best thing is to have a set of enforceable rules to regulate combatant activity. Islam provided such rules in the seventh century CE. These rules are fair and realistic and surpass any other codes of conduct established for armed conflict. Abiding by these rules is a moral obligation for all Muslims. History provides the evidence that Muslims abided by them. Examples are the conquest of Makkah by the Prophet ﷺ, the conquest of Syria and Palestine during the administration of Umar ibn al Khattab ؓ, the second Khalifah, and the capture of Jerusalem by Salahuddin Ayyubi. By contrast, there is the savagery displayed by those who do not subscribe to any rules of ethics and morality in conflict situations.

Even though it may be known that the enemy has committed atrocities, Muslims are advised restraint and patience. This is a twofold *Jihad*, ie., fighting in the cause of Allah to defend rights and freedom, and against oppression, and the exercise of restraint over the desire for revenge against a ruthless enemy.

Chapter Twenty-Five

Qiyamah

Introduction

Qiyamah is the event that is to occur when this present world comes to an end.[1,2] Every person that ever lived will be resurrected and assembled for the final accounting of deeds. Each person will be handed a record which will contain a minute by minute entry of his/her entire life, detailing everything and omitting nothing. This record of deeds will be the basis for judgement. Those whose good deeds are greater in number will be awarded Paradise. If the evil deeds outweigh the good, the fire of Hell will be the destination. No person will bear the burden of another's deeds nor share the consequences of another's sins. The single most important factor which will determine each individual's fate is God's decision to either punish or forgive.

While the final reckoning will be on the Day of Judgement, the actual process of accountability begins shortly after a person dies and is interred. For the good, the grave is made spacious and pleasant, but for the evil, punishment already begins.

In the Qur'an and Hadith, this event (*qiyamah*) is described by several different terms, each emphasizing a particular aspect. Some of these are: *Day of Judgement (youm ud deen), The Hour, The Final Day*

---

[1] *Qiyamah* refers to the Day of Resurrection (the rising of the dead), the Day of Final Judgement. The literal meaning of the Arabic word *qiyamah* is resurrection, turmoil, tumult, upheaval. The Hans Wehr Dictionary of Modern Written Arabic. Fourth Edition. McCowan JM, Editor. Spoken Language Services, Inc., Ithaca, NY, page 936.

[2] This subject is also discussed in Chapter 1, Islam, under Belief in the Day of Judgement.

(youm ul 'akhir), Day of Accountability (youm ul hisaab), Day of Mutual Disillusion (youm ut taghabun), Day of Gathering (youm ul jammah), Day of Decision, Day of Resurrection (youm ul qiyamah), Appointed Day (youm mim ma'loom). Though it is called a day (youm), in this particular context, it will not be a conventional day as its duration will be very long. No one except God has knowledge of the Day of Judgement.

Events Ushering the End of the World

Belief in the coming of Qiyamah and the final accounting is a part of the Muslim faith. Prophet Muhammad ﷺ described numerous signs and events that would occur leading up to that day, marking the end of this world. These include the prediction of periods of great hardships and trials (fitan), geopolitical and military conflicts, natural phenomena, and a gradual decay in the moral, social and ethical values of mankind, culminating in the appearance of the greater evil, ie., the impostor dajjal. An in-depth discussion of the predicted events can be found in Hadith books and in Ibn Katheer Dimashqi's Book of the End: Great Trials and Tribulations.[3]

Significant historical events are often preceded by lesser events. These latter signs are usually apparent long before the major event takes place. Unfamiliarity with these preceding lesser signs may result in failure to recognize the coming of the major events. In the following are a few of the signs of the approaching end of the world which were foretold by Prophet Muhammad ﷺ fourteen hundred years ago.[4,5,6,7] The sequence of occurrence of those events that have yet to transpire is not known.

---

[3] Ibn Katheer Dimashqi. Book of the End: Great Trials and Tribulations. Darussalam. Riyadh, S Arabia, 1996. ISBN 9960-9715-0-3

[4] The Translation of the Meanings of Sahih Al-Bukhari. MM Khan, Kazi Publications, Lahore, Pakistan, 1979. Volume IX, Hadith 235, 236 and 237, pages 179-182.

[5] Sahih Muslim. Kitab Al-Fitan wa Ashrat As-Sa'ah, Book Pertaining to the Turmoil and the Conditions of the Last Hour. M Matraji. Darul Isha'at, Karachi, Pakistan, 1998. Volume IV-B, pages 328-369.

[6] English Translation of Jami' At-Tirmidhi. Darussalam, Riyadh, S Arabia, 2007. Volume 4, pages 263-266, Hadith 2210, 2211, and 2212.

[7] Ibn Katheer Dimashqi. Book of the End. Great Trails and Tribulations. Darussalam, Riyadh, 2006. Pages 44-45.

- Time will pass quickly
- Good deeds will decrease
- Religious knowledge will be taken away
- General ignorance will spread
- About thirty liars/impostors will appear, each one claiming to be a messenger of God[8]
- Miserliness will enter into the hearts of people
- Afflictions will appear
- There will be famine
- Earthquakes will increase in number
- Killing and bloodshed will increase[9]
- The Euphrates river will uncover a mountain of gold[10]
- People will compete with one another in constructing high buildings
- A man when passing by a grave will say *Would that I were in his place*[11]
- Two big groups following the same religious doctrine will fight each other resulting in a great number of casualties
- The sun will rise from the west
- Appearance of the greater dajjal, the individual
- Coming of Mahdi ﷺ
- Isa ﷺ (Jesus, son of Mary ﷺ) will descend to earth
- Gog and Magog (Ya'juj and Ma'juj) will appear. These people will cause death and destruction across the world

---

[8] Sahih Muslim. M Matraji. Darul Isha'at, Karachi, Pakistan, 1998. Volume IV-B, Hadith 157R5, page 349.

[9] The relevance of this Hadith becomes apparent as the world witnesses senseless killing by governments, occupation forces, organizations, groups, and individuals alike. Prophet Muhammad ﷺ said: *... a time will come when the killer will not know why he killed and the victim would not know why he was killed.* Sahih Muslim. M Matraji. Darul Isha'at, Karachi, Pakistan, 1998, Volume IV-B, Hadith 2908, page 344.

[10] This Hadith also gains relevance in view of the events unfolding in that region. The Prophet ﷺ said: *The Hour will not begin until the Euphrates uncovers a mountain of gold, and the people fight for it. Out of every hundred, ninety-nine will be killed, and each man among them will say: Perhaps I will be the one who will be saved.* English Translation of Sahih Muslim. Darussalam, Riyadh, S Arabia, 2007. Volume 7, Hadith 7272, page 288. Reference may be to gold that is yet to be discovered or for the possession of the *black gold* for which that region has been reoccupied.

[11] The Translation of the Meanings of Sahih Al-Bukhari. MM Khan, Kazi Publications, Lahore, Pakistan, 1979. Volume IX, Hadith 231, pages 177-178.

Significant events that have yet to transpire include manifestation of the greater dajjal, coming of Mahdi ﷺ, descent of Isa ﷺ (Jesus) and the appearance of Gog and Magog (Ya'juj and Ma'juj).[12]

Two additional predictions warrant mention. In the context of the Day of Resurrection, Surah 81, Al Takwir, ayat 6 states: *And when the seas rise (or overflow)*. Scientists have predicted a rise in the level of the seas and oceans due to the melting of ice which threatens to submerge many port cities and low islands. The second prediction is from a Hadith which states: *The famine would not break out because of drought, but there would be famine despite heavy rainfall as nothing would grow from the earth.*[13] This prediction may be referring to events that have yet to take place. If understood figuratively, it may already be occurring in the form of increasing world hunger, switch to cash crops (tobacco in Malawi, poppy in Afghanistan, coca in South America, corn for ethanol production, coffee, etc), use of genetically modified seed with terminator genes that do not permit replanting, and destruction of crops and orchards by wars.

Events Preceding Afflictions

Of the numerous signs predicting the end of the world, changes in social and moral attitudes are assigned much significance. It is predicted in the Hadith, that certain social and moral practices would creep into society and that afflictions would occur as a consequence. Previously shunned or outlawed, many of those practices now find widespread acceptance. As the secular world continues to assert itself, those unfamiliar with these predictions may be carried by the waves they failed to recognize and thus remained unaware of the consequences they portend.

In the following are excerpts from a few Hadith. In the first Hadith, while the reference is to *my ummah*, ie., Muslims, the changes mentioned are also observed in people of other faiths. Thus far, Muslims who are the recipients of the final and most comprehensive Message from God, had for the most part, clung to the Islamic social

---

[12] Based upon analysis of the current geopolitical events, some contemporary scholars are of the opinion that the Ya'juj and Ma'juj are in the process of manifesting their presence.

[13] Sahih Muslim. M Matraji. Darul Isha'at, Karachi, Pakistan, 1998. Volume IV-B, Hadith 2904, page 341.

and moral values. However, as these Hadith predict, many of them will also fall prey to the secular world order and abandon those Islamic values. Prophet Muhammad ﷺ had said: *When my ummah does fifteen things, the afflictions will occur in it.*[14,15] These include the following:

- Trust is betrayed, things left with people are appropriated by them[16]
- Payment of Zakat is perceived as being burdensome[17]
- A man obeys his wife but disobeys his mother[18]
- A man treats his friend well but is harsh and distant to his father
- The leader of the people is the most base (despicable) individual among them[19]
- A man is honored because his evil is feared
- *Zina* (adultery and fornication) will become widespread
- *Khamr* (alcohol and other intoxicants) will be consumed[20]
- Silk will be worn by men[21]
- The use of female singers and music spreads

Some of the events predicted in the Hadith are unfolding today while others have occurred since the latter part of the past century,

---

[14] English Translation of Jami At-Tirmidhi. Darussalam, Riyadh, S Arabia, 2007. Volume 4, Hadith 2210, 2211, and 2212, pages 263-266.

[15] Ibn Katheer Dimashqi. Book of the End. Great Trails and Tribulations. Darussalam, Riyadh, 2006. Pages 44-45.

[16] In another Hadith he ﷺ said: *When honesty is lost, then wait for the Hour.* The Translation of the Meanings of Sahih Al-Bukhari. MM Khan. Kazi Publications, Lahore, Pakistan, 1979. Volume I, Hadith 56, pages 50-51.

[17] Payment of Zakat is an obligation. Also see Chapter 1, Islam.

[18] Parents are held in very high esteem and have been awarded certain privileges by God. Kindness, obedience and gratitude towards parents is obligatory for Muslims. For additional explanation of the meaning of this and the subsequent statement also see Chapter 8, Family and Social Issues.

[19] In another Hadith he ﷺ said: *...When the power or authority comes in the hands of unfit persons, then wait for the Hour.* The Translation of the Meanings of Sahih Al-Bukhari. MM Khan. Kazi Publications, Lahore, Pakistan, 1979. Volume I, Hadith 56, pages 50-51.

[20] English Translation of Sahih Muslim. Darussalam, Riyadh, S Arabia, 2007. Volume 7, Hadith 6786, page 45.

[21] Unless necessary for medical reasons, men are prohibited from wearing silk and gold.

including wars and senseless killing, increase in the number of natural catastrophes and famines. No one but an inspired Messenger of God could have made such predictions fourteen centuries ago and it would be difficult to dismiss them as coincidence.

Dajjal (antichrist)

The Arabic term, *ad dajjal,* means an impostor, deceiver, or liar.[22] *Dajjal* has been used to describe the phenomenon of the *antichrist.* The latter is interpreted as meaning *one resembling Christ in appearance and power.*[23] Prophet Muhammad ﷺ called this individual *al masih ad dajjal,* ie., someone who will attempt to impersonate the Messiah Jesus ﷺ, or even God.[24] Thus, *impostor* fits the description provided by him. The appearance of the dajjal is one of the greater signs closely related to the nearing of the end of this world. Although the dajjal will be active for a relatively short period of time, he is expected to cause widespread misery.[25] Prophet Muhammad ﷺ said: *There would be no creation (creating more trouble) than the dajjal from the creation of Adam to the Last Hour.*[26]

By executing extraordinary appearing feats such as making rain fall, making crops grow abundantly, causing drought and even simulating resurrection of a dead person, dajjal will be able to impress people and gain a significant following, proclaim prophethood and even divinity. His accomplishments may appear similar to the miracles performed by prophets and are listed in several Hadith.[27,28]

---

[22] It also means to deceive, cheat, smear with tar.

[23] *anti* has different meanings, depending upon it's usage. Antichrist (antichristos in Greek) does not necessarily mean *opposed to Christ.*

[24] Dajjal will attempt to impersonate Jesus ﷺ whose return to earth is anticipated.

[25] Sunan Abu Dawud, English Translation with Explanatory Notes. A. Hasan, Kitab Bhavan, New Delhi, India, 1997. Volume 3. Kitab al-Malahim, pages 1202-1203, Hadith 4307. When asked how long the Dajjal would remain on the earth, the Prophet ﷺ said: *Forty days, one like a year, one like a month, one like a week, and the rest of his days like yours.*

[26] Sahih Muslim. M. Matraji. Darul Isha'at, Karachi, Pakistan, 1998. Volume IV-B, Hadith 2946, pages 366-367.

[27] Ibn Katheer Dimashqi. Book of the End: Great Trials and Tribulations. Darussalam. Riyadh, S Arabia, 1996. Pages 99-105.

[28] English Translation of Sahih Muslim. Darussalam, Riyadh, S Arabia, 2007. Volume 7, The Book of Tribulations and the Portents of the Hour, pages 328-355.

Supernatural and extraordinary accomplishments have been attributed to a few of God's chosen people. Best known are prophetic miracles like the splitting of the moon by Prophet Muhammad ﷺ and those related to Moses ؊ and Jesus ؊.[29,30] These occurred *by God's permission (bi iznillah)*.[31] A few other individuals with extraordinary devotion to God, ie., saints, have also been known for extraordinary achievements. The latter are also possible only with God's permission. (Also see The Miracles of Prophets in Chapter 1, Islam)

Since dajjal fits into neither of these categories (prophet or saint), how will he accomplish his "miracles"? The truth is known only to God. The "miracles" may indeed be facilitated by God as a test for mankind and do not attest to his truthfulness.[32] However, some of them could also be the products of modern science or he may have help from amongst the Jinn. Under usual circumstances, Jinn are not visible to humans, although they can see us. They have the ability to transform themselves into human form, to the extent that they can assume the physical appearance of any person. They are also able to transform into animals or other living creatures such as snakes.

Since dajjal's objective will be to lead people away from true religion and the belief in One God, anyone accepting his claim to prophethood or divinity will be straying into shirk (associating partners with God) and to their own downfall, just like those who followed the mythical Pied Piper. Prophet Muhammad ﷺ described dajjal's anticipated misdeeds as the greatest *fitnah* (trial) of all times. He said:

Let him who hears of the dajjal go far from him, for I swear by Allah that a man will come to him thinking he is a believer and follow him (the dajjal) because of confused ideas roused in him by him (by the dajjal).[33]

---

[29] Surah 7, Al A'raaf, ayaat 107-122.

[30] See foot note 31.

[31] Surah 3, 'Al Imraan, ayat 49 states that Jesus ؊ said: *I come to you with a sign from your Lord, I fashion for you out of clay the likeness of a bird and I breathe into it and it is a bird, "by Allah's permission" (bi iznillah). I heal him who was born blind, and the leper, and I raise the dead, "by Allah's permission" (bi iznillah)...* (emphasis added).

[32] Some learned scholars consider him a magician and charlatan. Ibn Katheer Dimashqi. Book of the End: Great Trials and Tribulations. Darussalam. Riyadh, S Arabia, 1996. Pages 126-127.

[33] Sunan Abu Dawud, Translation by A. Hasan, Kitab Bhavan, New Delhi, 1997. Volume 3. Hadith 4305, page 1202.

The Return of Jesus ﷺ

Mahdi ﷺ, the rightly guided leader of Muslims, is expected to come about twenty-five years before Jesus ﷺ descends to earth in Damascus. Jesus ﷺ will eradicate all evil and kill the dajjal. He will marry and have children and all of mankind will follow Jesus ﷺ.

When Jesus ﷺ returns to earth, he will follow the faith prescribed by God for all of mankind, ie., the belief in One God who has neither partner nor son. Furthermore, Jesus ﷺ will affirm that Prophet Muhammad ﷺ is the final Messenger of God and he will follow the religion as taught and practiced by Prophet Muhammad ﷺ.

Manifestation of the Day of Judgement

They ask you of the destined Hour, when will it come to pass. Say: Knowledge thereof is with my Lord only. He alone will manifest it at its proper time. The heavens and the earth are heavy with it. It comes not to you save unawares ... (Surah Al A'raaf, ayat 187)

That Day will manifest without warning, catching people unprepared, casting terror into the hearts of those who disbelieved in God's Revelations[34] and those involved in evil acts. The implications of that Day will not be lost on any of the living or the resurrected. Each person will be concerned only about him/herself. Its awe will even cause a nursing mother to abandon her child. Those who believed in God and His Messengers and lived abiding by His rules will have nothing to fear. The disbelievers and perpetrators of evil will be most severely affected, bringing home the realization that they erred in their choice of disbelief and disobedience.[35]

Before your Lord (alone), is the recourse that Day. On that Day man will be informed of what he sent forward and what he left behind. Nay, man will be a witness against himself. (Surah 75, Al Qiyamah, ayaat 12-14)

---

[34] Including the Final Message (Islam) and the prophethood of Muhammad ﷺ.

[35] Prophet Muhammad ﷺ said: *It will be from among the most wicked people who will be living at the time when the Hour will be established.* The Translation of the Meanings of Sahih Al-Bukhari. MM Khan. Kazi Publications, Lahore, Pakistan, 1979. Volume IX, Hadith 187, page 151.

Some faces that Day will be shining and radiant. Looking towards their Lord. And some faces that Day will be dark and gloomy. In the thought that some great calamity was about to be inflicted on them.
(Surah 75, Al Qiyamah, ayaat 22-25)

Those who transgressed all bounds And had preferred the life of this world Will find themselves in Hell; But those who feared to stand before their Lord and curbed their souls' desires the Garden will be their dwelling place. (Surah 79, An Nazi'at, ayat 37-41)

Concluding Summary

... The Day that some of the Signs of your Lord do come, no good will it do to a person to believe then, if he believed not before, nor earned good through his Faith... (Surah 6, Al An'aam, ayat 158)

Then those whose scales are heavy, they are the successful. And those whose scales are light are those who lose their souls, they shall abide in Hell forever. (Surah 23, Al Mu'minoon, ayaat 102-103)

Belief in the resurrection after death in this world, accountability for all deeds and an eternal life, either in Paradise or Hell-Fire, is an essential part of a Muslim's faith. While determination of the ultimate abode is on the Day of Judgement, each individual's accountability begins soon after death. Therefore, the mindful attempt to conduct themselves in a manner that the record of deeds is always good, in anticipation of the unexpected.

There is no escape from the reality of the Day of Judgement also for those who do not believe in it or in the Hereafter and are content with the life of this world. Life on earth is transient and its allurements are a test.[36] Denial or disbelief does not erase the reality nor absolve one of the accountability and consequences of all deeds where each person is answerable only for him/herself.

The Day of Judgement will provide unmatched justice as there is no unfairness with God. The reckoning on that day will take into account

---

[36] Surah 21, Al Anbyia', ayat 111: *... it may be trial for you, and an enjoyment for a while.*

an individual's relationship with God (belief, compliance with His rules, etc) and also the relationships with others. Fairness and justice demand that each individual be held accountable for his/her own actions, and therefore, no one will bear the burden of another. The belief that someone else has or will be responsible for a person's actions/sins implies that there is unfairness in God's Court of Justice. That is simply not the case.

For those who wish to hasten the Day of Judgement because of their belief that it will place them in Paradise, the following verses may provide food for thought.

> And the lot of the wrongdoers is like the lot of their likes of earlier generations; so let them not ask Me to hasten it on.
>
> (Surah 51, Ad Dhariyat, ayat 59)

> Those who do not believe in it seek to hasten it, while those who believe are fearful of it, and know that it is the truth.[37]
>
> (Surah 42, Ash Shura, ayat 18)

No one knows when the Day of Judgement will come. That knowledge is with God alone.[38] In his capacity as a warner, Prophet Muhammad ﷺ described numerous portending events. Many of these signs have already appeared. One cannot help but notice the rapidity with which time passes. There is social and moral decay in society and competitive construction of high buildings is seen in many parts of the world. There is an increase in the number of wars, senseless violence and killing are widespread. Climate change, disease outbreaks, hunger and starvation, and natural disasters such as droughts, floods, earthquakes and tsunamis occur with seemingly increasing frequency. In addition, honesty and true religious knowledge are on the decline, and religion has been altered to suit and justify contemporary social needs and agendas instead of changing oneself to conform to the principles of religion.

---

[37] Not only the act of believing that it will occur but also in what it really means, ie., accountability for all deeds, the final Judgement and assignment of either Paradise or Hell-Fire.

[38] Surah 67, Al Mulk, ayat 26: *Say, The knowledge of its exact time is with Allah only, and I am only a plain warner.*

Additional Reading

Thomson A: Dajjal the AntiChrist. Ta-Ha Publishers Ltd. London, England, 1998. ISBN 1 897940 38 6

Ibn Katheer Dimashqi: Book of the End, Great Trials and Tribulations. Darussalam. Riyadh, S Arabia, 1996. ISBN 9960-9715-0-3

V. Glossary

GLOSSARY

Adhan / Azaan

The call to prayer (salat). It is pronounced loudly to indicate the time for obligatory prayer and also serves to summon the people to the mosque to pray in congregation.

'Adl

Justice.

Ahl al Kitaab

Ahl al Kitaab means *people of the book*. It refers to those who were recipients of earlier Divine Revelations, primarily the Jews and Christians.

Alhamdulillah

All Praise is due to God alone. This is an expression of the Glorification of God.

Allah سبحانه وتعالى (see Chapter 2, Allah)

This is the name God has given Himself. Allah and God have one and the same meaning.

Allahu Akbar

Allah (God) is greatest. This is also called the *takbir*.

'Aql

Intellect, ie., the ability to reason and understand. Also see Chapter 4, Islamic Law, Shari'ah and Fiqh.

Arafat

This is a plain, bordered by small hills, which lies about twenty kilometers southeast of Makkah. The pilgrims gather here during Haj on the ninth day of Dhul Hijjah. For its significance see Chapter 20, Common Islamic Terms and their Meanings.

Ashura

This is the tenth day of the month of Muharram, the first month of the Islamic calendar. For its historical significance see Chapter 20, Common Islamic Terms and their Meanings.

'Asr

Mid afternoon prayer. 'Asr is also the name of a surah of the Qur'an.

Ayat (ayah) (plural ayaat)

Literally, ayat means a sign or symbol. In the Qur'an, it is most frequently used as meaning *a (Divine) message*.[1] Each verse of the Qur'an is called an ayat.

Badr

This is a place about 150 kilometers south of Madinah, on the road (also the old caravan route) from Makkah to Syria. This was the site of the first and most decisive battles in Muslim history. This was fought on 16 Ramadan 2 AH (623 CE) between the attacking pagan Makkan tribes and the nascent Muslim community.

Bayt al Maqdis

The Arabic word *bayt* means house. *Al Bayt al Maqdis* means *The Sacred or Holy House* and *al Bayt al Muqaddas* means a *purified, sacred place*, free from polytheism. These names refer to Jerusalem and the surrounding country, namely the region that is Palestine. *Al Masjid al Aqsa (The Far Distant Place of Worship)* is located in Jerusalem and is the third most sacred Muslim sanctuary.

---

[1] The Message of the Qur'an. Translated and Explained by Muhammad Asad. The Book Foundation, Bristol, England, 2003. Page 513.

Believer

A believer or *mu'min* (plural *mu'minoon*) is a person whose submission to God is conscientious, willful, wholehearted and complete. A believer has complete trust in God, follows His Commandments unquestioningly and abides by the rules of the Shari'ah. Also see Chapter 1, Islam.

Dajjal

The literal meaning of dajjal is liar, deceiver, or impostor. Dajjal is the antichrist. Prophet Muhammad ﷺ called him an impostor who will attempt to impersonate the Messiah Jesus ﷺ (*al masih ad dajjal*). Also see Chapter 25, Qiyamah.

Deen

Religion. A comprehensive way of life. Also see Islam.

Dhimmi

Ahl al dhimmah or dhimmi means protected people. It refers to non-Muslims living under the protection of an Islamic State. Also see Islamic Definition of a Minority in Chapter 11, Minorities under Muslim Rule.

Dhul Hijjah

The twelfth month of the Islamic calendar.

Dhul Qa'dah

The eleventh month of the Islamic calendar.

Du'a

Supplication.

Eid ul Adha

Festival of the sacrifice. It occurs at the conclusion of the Haj, on the tenth day of the month of Dhul Hijjah, the twelfth month of the Islamic calendar. This commemorates the sacrifice of Prophet Abraham and his son Ismail (peace be upon them). Also see Chapter 20, Common Islamic Terms and their Meanings.

Eid ul Fitr

Festivity commemorating the conclusion of the month of fasting, ie., Ramadan. See Chapter 20, Common Islamic Terms and their Meanings.

Fajr

Early morning/dawn. This refers to the time of the first of the five daily obligatory prayers.

Fard

Obligatory. It refers to the obligatory devotional duties, such as prayers, fasting, Zakat, etc.

Fasting (Sawm)

See under Ramadan and also Chapter 20, Common Islamic Terms and their Meanings.

Fatwa

See Chapter 20, Common Islamic Terms and their Meanings.

Fiqh

Islamic jurisprudence. See Chapter 4, Islamic Law, Shari'ah and Fiqh.

Fitnah

Trial, conflicts.

Fitrah

The pristine nature in which man was created.

Hadd

See under Hudood.

Hadith (plural Ahadith)

The meanings of the Arabic word *hadith* are speech, talk, conversation, interview, narrative, account or report. In the context of Islam, it refers to all the actions, words, teachings and rulings of Prophet Muhammad ﷺ. A *Hadith Qudsi* is a narrative in which Prophet

Muhammad ﷺ reported what was said by God. Unlike the Qur'an, those are not God's Words. Also see under Sunnah.

Haj

This is the pilgrimage to Makkah and surrounding sacred places. It is one of the Five Pillars of Islam. The others are *Shahadah* (Testimony of Faith), *Salat* (obligatory prayers), *Fasting* during the month of Ramadan, and *Zakat*. Haj is an annual event occurring in the twelfth month of the Islamic calendar (Dhul Hijjah). Also see Chapter 1, Islam and Chapter 20, Common Islamic Terms and their Meanings.

Halal

Lawful, permitted.

Haram

Unlawful, prohibited.

Har'am

Sanctuary. Refers to the sacred sanctuaries in Makkah, Madinah and Al Quds (Jerusalem).

Hijrah

This refers to the emigration of Prophet Muhammad ﷺ from Makkah to Madinah which took place in July 622 CE and marks the beginning of the Islamic Calendar.

Hudaibiya'

A place about 16 kilometers from Makkah. This was the site of an important treaty between Muslims and the Makkan pagans. This treaty was signed in the month of Dhul Qa'dah, 6 AH (628 CE).

Hudood

Plural for *hadd*. This refers to the limits of the permissible and prohibited (*halal* and *haram*) which have been set by God. Violation of these limits is punishable by Divinely prescribed penalties.

Iddah

This is the prescribed period of waiting for women after divorce or death of the husband before remarriage is permitted. Also see Chapter 7, Marriage.

Ijma'

Consensus of knowledgeable people, ie., Muslim Scholars on matters of fiqh. It is one of the four sources for the Shari'ah. Also see Chapter 4, Islamic Law, Shari'ah and Fiqh.

Ijtihaad

Personal judgement of Muslim scholars on legal matters derived in conformity with the Qur'an and Sunnah. It is one of the four sources for the Shari'ah. Also see Chapter 4, Islamic Law, Shari'ah and Fiqh.

Imam

Imam means leader, spiritual and political. An imam is also the person who leads congregational prayers. Also see Chapter 20, Common Islamic Terms and their Meanings.

Iman

Faith, belief.

Isha

The late evening prayer. The time for this prayer begins about ninety minutes after sunset.

Islam

The word Islam is derived from *silm* which means peace, to be safe, secure, protected from harm, and to surrender. Islam is the complete submission/surrender to the Will of God. This is the term used by God to describe the religion He has chosen for the believers.

This day I have perfected your religion for you, and completed My favours upon you, and have chosen for you Islam as your religion (deen).

(Surah 5, Al Ma'idah, ayat 3)

Islam is a comprehensive *code of living (deen)*, guiding and providing answers and solutions to all problems, spiritual and secular, individual and communal. Also see Chapter 1, Islam.

Islamic Calendar and New Year

The Islamic calendar is based on the lunar cycle. There are twelve months in the year, beginning with the month of Muharram. Each month has either 29 or 30 days, depending upon the lunar cycle. The total number of days is 354. The *Hijrah* (emigration of Prophet Muhammad ﷺ from Makkah to Madinah) marks the beginning of the Islamic Calendar. Also see Chapter 20, Common Islamic Terms and their Meanings.

Islamic New Year's day

The Muslim new year starts on the first day of Muharram, the first month of the Islamic calendar. New year's day has no religious significance.

Isra' and Miraj

Isra' was the Night Journey of Prophet Muhammad ﷺ from Makkah to Jerusalem and Miraj was the Heavenly Visitation. This took place in the month of Rajab about eighteen months before the Hijrah to Madinah.

Jesus (Isa) ﷺ

See Chapter 20, Common Islamic Terms and their Meanings.

Jihad

The literal meaning of jihad is to *struggle* or *strive*. It is an all-round struggle against evil in every form.

Jinn

See Chapter 20, Common Islamic Terms and their Meanings.

Jizya

A tax payable by non-Muslims living under the protection of an Islamic State. It represents the equivalent of Zakat which is obligatory for all Muslims. Non-Muslims are exempted from paying Zakat. Some non-Muslims are also exempted from paying jizya. Also see Chapter 11, Minorities under Muslim Rule.

Jumada al Awwal (Jumada al Ula)
Fifth month of the Islamic calendar.

Jumada al Thani (Jumada al Akhira)
Sixth month of the Islamic calendar.

Jumma

This refers to Friday, the day for congregational prayer. The Friday congregational prayer is obligatory for men and boys who have attained puberty. Attendance is not compulsory for women. Women's participation varies with regional cultural traditions. The latter may have no Islamic basis. During the time of the Prophet ﷺ and the Khalifahs, women attended the Jumma Prayers.

Ka'ba

The Ka'ba was the first house built on earth for the worship of the One and Only God of the universe. It was rebuilt by Abraham and his first born son Ismail (peace be upon them). It is located in the Sacred Sanctuary in Makkah, Arabia (*al Masjid al Haram*). Also see Chapter 20, Common Islamic Terms and their Meanings.

Kafir (plural kuffar)

Disbeliever. One who does not believe in God or denies the existence of God, disbelieves in His messengers and Scriptures (books), and Al Qadar (destiny/fate). Also see Kufr.

Kalima

The literal meaning is *word*. In common usage it refers to the pronouncement of faith: *La ilaaha illallah Muhammadar rasool ullah*, ie., there is no deity worthy of worship besides Allah and Muhammad ﷺ is His messenger.

Khalifah (plural khulafah)

Caliph. The literal meaning is successor. Also see Chapter 20, Common Islamic Terms and their Meanings.

Khamr

Khamr is commonly understood as meaning wine. However, it's broader meaning includes all intoxicants. Islam prohibits the production, consumption, buying, selling and serving of all intoxicants.

Khutba

Sermon. A sermon precedes the Jumma (Friday) prayer. Other occasions for giving a sermon are the two Eid prayers and at the time of Nikah (marriage). The Eid sermon is given immediately after the Eid prayer on the first day of Eid. The Jumma sermon precedes the prayer.

Kufr

Disbelief in God and/or in any article of faith. This includes the five basic tenets (also known as The Five Pillars of Islam) and the six Pillars of Faith: belief in God, in the existence of angels, in all prophets and messengers sent by God, in the Revelations sent by God through all prophets, in the Day of Judgement (*youm ul Qiyamah*) and destiny/fate (*al Qadar*).

Lord

See Chapter 20, Common Islamic Terms and their Meanings.

Madrassah

See Chapter 20, Common Islamic Terms and their Meanings.

Maghrib

This means West. It also refers to the time of sunset and the early evening prayer (*maghrib salat*). The latter is due soon after sunset. The western extent of the Islamic Commonwealth, ie., Morocco is known as the Maghrib.

Mahr

A gift given by the husband to the bride at the time of marriage.

Mahram

This is a male relative of a woman to whom marriage is never permitted, eg., father, brother, uncle, son, nephew.

Makruh

Undesirable, unapproved. Although not prohibited or punishable under Shari'ah, anything assigned this category should be avoided.

Masjid

Literally, masjid means *a place of worship, a place for sajdah* (prostration during prayer). The term masjid is generic for a *place of worship*. It does not specify a particular structure but is commonly used for a mosque. Also see under Mosque.

Masjid al Aqsa

Far Distant Place of Worship. This refers to the Sacred Sanctuary in Jerusalem. Also see Chapter 5, Isra', Miraj and Jerusalem.

Masjid al Haram

The Sacred Place of Worship. This refers to the Mosque in Makkah, Arabia. That is where the Ka'ba is located.

Masjid al Nabwi

This refers to the Prophet's ﷺ mosque in Madinah, Arabia.

Mina

A place about six kilometers outside Makkah on the way to Arafat. During Haj, this is the first encampment site for the pilgrims after they leave Makkah.

Mosque (masjid)

A mosque is a place for prayer/worship. Typically, there is a prayer hall with a small niche (*mihrab*) indicating the direction of the *qibla*, ie., the Ka'ba in Makkah. The *qibla* is the direction in which Muslims face during prayer. The imam stands in this niche while leading congregational prayer. The minaret is a slender tower which is situated at a corner of the mosque structure. In times past, the minaret was used for calling the *adhan* (call to prayer). The person calling the adhan is a *mu'azzin*.

Mufti
A person who is qualified to give a legal opinion.

Muharram
First month of the Islamic calendar.

Mujahid (plural mujahidoon)
The mujahid is a person who is participating in Jihad. In the media, a frequent misrepresentation of mujahid is *holy warrior*. There is no such designation in Islam and jihad is also not a holy war. Also see Chapter 23, Crusades and Holy War.

Mu'min
See under Believer.

Mushrik
This refers to one who commits shirk. Muslim men and women are prohibited from marrying a mushrik. Also see under shirk.

Muslim Festivals
See Chapter 20, Common Islamic Terms and their Meanings.

Muslim Greeting
See Chapter 20, Common Islamic Terms and their Meanings.

Muzdalifah
A place between Mina and the plain of Arafat. During Haj, the pilgrims spend a night there (between the ninth and tenth of Dhul Hijjah) as they head back from Arafat to Mina.

Nafila (Nafal, plural Nawafil)

Optional or voluntary acts of worship. This may be in the form of prayers (salat) or other devotional activity. Obligatory practices are called Fard.

Nikah

Islamic wedding ceremony.

Prayer (salat)

See Chapter 20, Common Islamic Terms and their Meanings.

Qadar

Divine preordainment, destiny or measure.

Qibla

The direction in which Muslims face during prayer. This is the direction towards the Ka'ba in Makkah, Arabia.

Qur'an

The literal meaning is *reading*. It is the book which contains the literal Words of God that were transmitted through Prophet Muhammad ﷺ. Also see Chapter 1, Islam.

Quraish

A Makkan tribe that wielded significant political influence during the pre- and early Islamic periods. Prophet Muhammad ﷺ belonged to this tribe.

Rabi' al Awwal

Third month of the Islamic calendar.

Rabi' al Thani

Fourth month of the Islamic calendar.

Rajab

The seventh month of the Islamic calendar. It is one of the four sacred months. The other three are consecutive months: Dhul

Qa'dah, Dhul Hijjah, and Muharram. These months have been designated as such by Divine Injunction: *The number of months with Allah is twelve (in a year). So ordained by Him the day He created the heavens and the earth; and of these, four are sacred. That is the right religion. So do not wrong yourselves in them...* (Surah 9, At Taubah, ayat 36).

Ramadan and Fasting

Ramadan is the ninth month of the Islamic calendar. Fasting during this month is obligatory for all adult Muslims and children past puberty. Also Chapter 20, Common Islamic Terms and their Meanings.

Riba

Usury, interest. Islamic Shari'ah prohibits dealing in interest. Such *riba* maybe of two types: in monetary transactions such as monetary interest (*riba nasi'a*) and certain forms of barter dealings in which a superior quality item is taken in return for a larger quantity of lesser (inferior) quality items (*riba fadal*).

Sadaqa

Charity.

Safa and Marwa

These are the names of the two small hillocks adjacent to the Ka'ba. When Prophet Abraham ﷺ left his second wife Hajar (Hagar) and their infant son Ismail in the valley of Makkah, Hajar went from one hillock to the other, looking for help. In commemoration, the pilgrims walk this stretch seven times during the Umrah.

Safar

Second month of the Islamic calendar.

Salat (prayer)

See Chapter 20, Common Islamic Terms and their Meanings.

Sha'ban

Eighth month of the Islamic calendar.

Shahadah

To bear witness, legal testimony. It also means martyrdom. Shahadah also refers to the testimony of faith in Islam. A person who accepts Islam is required to take the shahadah:

Ashhaduan la ilaaha illallah wa ashhaduanna Muhammadar rasool ullah.

I bear witness that there is no god but Allah and I bear witness that Muhammad is His messenger.

Shari'ah

See Chapter 4, Islamic Law, Shari'ah and Fiqh.

Shawwal

The tenth month of the Islamic calendar.

Shirk

Polytheism. Worshipping someone or something other than God or in addition to God. Associating partners with God. Also see Chapter 20, Common Islamic Terms and their Meanings.

Subhan Allah

Glory be to Allah. To honor Allah above all unsuitable things that are ascribed to Him.

Sunnah

This refers to the practice of Prophet Muhammad ﷺ. Like Hadith, the word sunnah also means tradition and both terms (Hadith and Sunnah) mean and imply one and the same thing. The Sunnah carries the same authority as the Hadith since both the Prophet's ﷺ speech and actions were Divinely inspired. The Prophet's ﷺ life is an example to follow for all who accept Islam. Also see Chapter 1, Islam.

Nor does he speak of his own desire. This is no other than an inspired Revelation.   (Surah 53, An Najm, ayat 3-5)

... Say, I follow only that which is inspired in me from my Lord ...   (Surah 7, Al A'raaf, ayat 203)

Surah
This refers to a chapter of the Qur'an.

Tafseer
Explanation and commentary on the meaning of the Qur'an. Exegesis.

Taqwa
Taqwa is translated as meaning piety. A person who has taqwa is ever-conscious of God, strives to obeys His directives and fears His displeasure, ie., does what pleases God and avoids everything that that may incur His displeasure.

Tauheed
Belief in the Unity of God. Also see Chapter 1, Islam.

Tawaf
Circumambulation of the Ka'ba. This is required during performance of the Umrah.

Uhud
A mountain outside Madinah.

Ummah
Nation, community. It refers to Muslims collectively. All Muslims form one community, irrespective of race, color, language, ethnic origin and geographic location.

Umrah
Also called the *lesser pilgrimage*, in distinction to Haj. This is the pilgrimage to Makkah during any time other than that for Haj. The Umrah is also performed as a part of the Haj. Also see Chapter 20, Common Islamic Terms and their Meanings.

Wudu
Ablution. It refers to the ritual washing of the hands, face, arms and feet in preparation for prayer, before reading the Qur'an or any other

devotional activity.

Zakat
See Chapter 20, Common Islamic Terms and their Meanings.

Zamzam
This is the ancient water well in Makkah which was dug by the angel in response to the plea of Hajar (Hagar), Ismail's ﷺ mother. Even today this is a source of plentiful water for the pilgrims and others who visit the Har'am (Mosque surrounding the Ka'ba in Makkah).

Zuhr
This refers to the midday prayer.